Trading Blocs

Michigan Studies in International Political Economy

SERIES EDITORS: Edward Mansfield and Lisa Martin

Trading Blocs

States, Firms, and Regions in the World Economy

KERRY A. CHASE

The University of Michigan Press
Ann Arbor

Copyright © by the University of Michigan 2005
All rights reserved
Published in the United States of America by
The University of Michigan Press
Manufactured in the United States of America
ⓧ Printed on acid-free paper

2008   2007   2006   2005   4   3   2   1

A CIP catalog record for this book is available from the British Library.

Library of Congress Cataloging-in-Publication Data

Chase, Kerry A., 1969–
    Trading blocs : states, firms, and regions in the world economy /
Kerry A. Chase.
        p.   cm. — (Michigan studies in international political economy)
    Includes bibliographical references and index.
    ISBN-13: 978-0-472-09906-1 (cloth : alk. paper)
    ISBN-10: 0-472-09906-X (cloth : alk. paper)
    ISBN-13: 978-0-472-06906-4 (pbk. : alk. paper)
    ISBN-10: 0-472-06906-3 (pbk. : alk. paper)
    1. Trade blocs.   2. Trade blocs—History—20th century.
I. Title.   II. Series.

HF1418.7.C53   2006
382'.9'0904—dc22   2005016620

For Steph and Ella

Acknowledgments

I have many people to thank and debts to acknowledge in the writing of this book. Above all I must single out Jeff Frieden for being an exceptional scholar, generous adviser, and true friend. Jeff has served as an indispensable source of sage guidance and unwavering encouragement from the day he agreed to chair my Ph.D. dissertation committee. It has been my great fortune since I came to Tufts to have Jeff so close by, and I look forward to many future conversations with him about political economy, scholarship, and the New York Yankees.

I am grateful to all of my colleagues in the political science department at Tufts University for creating an environment of professionalism, community, and good humor. My department chairs, Jim Glaser and Vickie Sullivan, have been extremely supportive. Tony Smith read an early draft of the manuscript and offered excellent advice on how to present key points more effectively. Elizabeth Remick has been a terrific colleague and friend.

At UCLA, I learned much more from Ron Rogowski and Dick Rosecrance than I could ever communicate. Thanks also to Ben Bishin, Paul Frymer, Alan Kessler, and Chris Layne for giving me insights about political science (as well as diversions from it) over the years.

The German Marshall Fund of the United States provided funding for the project. This made it possible for me to write an initial draft of the manuscript as a visiting scholar at the Weatherhead Center for International Affairs at Harvard University. I would like to thank both organizations and the members of their staff who made this assistance possible.

Parts of chapters 2 and 6 draw from my article "Economic Interests and Regional Trading Arrangements: The Case of NAFTA," *International Organization* 57 (winter 2003): 137–74. I am grateful to *International Organization* and Cambridge University Press for their permission to use this article. Thanks also to Robert Feenstra and Deborah Swenson for sharing with me the offshore assembly trade data that I use in chapter 6.

Jim Reische guided the manuscript through the review process at the University of Michigan Press. I am grateful to him and to Lisa Martin and Edward Mansfield, the Michigan Studies in International Political Economy series editors, for having confidence in the manuscript and being diligent in securing external reviews. Two anonymous reviewers won my appreciation for taking the time and effort to read the manuscript carefully and present their suggestions constructively. I thank them for giving me valuable advice on how to improve the argument, evidence, and presentation.

My parents, Lori and Steve Chase, instilled in me an appreciation for scholarship, and they have encouraged and supported me in education, career, and life. My beautiful wife Stephanie has provided constant love and emotional support throughout. Since she's had to live with this manuscript for as long as we've been together, I'm sure she will be as happy as me to see it finally in print. And my adorable daughter Ella has spent many of her first days at my side, bouncing, swinging, kicking, and (on rare occasions) napping while waiting for daddy to finish working so he could play.

Contents

Tables

Figures

Acronyms

ACEA	Association of European Automobile Constructors
AFL-CIO	American Federation of Labor and Congress of Industrial Organizations
AFTA	ASEAN Free Trade Area
AICO	ASEAN Industrial Cooperation
AISI	American Iron and Steel Institute
AMA	Automobile Manufacturers Association
APTA	Automotive Products Trade Agreement
ASEAN	Association of Southeast Asian Nations
ATC	Agreement on Textiles and Clothing
ATMI	American Textile Manufacturers Institute
BBC	Brand-to-Brand Complementation
CCMC	Committee of Common Market Motor Vehicle Constructors
CECOM	Committee of European Copier Manufacturers
CEFIC	Conseil Européen des Fédérations de l'Industrie Chimique (European Chemical Industry Council)
CUSFTA	Canada–United States Free Trade Agreement
EACEM	European Association of Consumer Electronics Manufacturers
EC	European Community
EECA	European Electronic Component Manufacturers Association
EIA	Electronic Industries Association
ERT	European Roundtable
EU	European Union
EUROFER	European Confederation of Iron and Steel Industries
FBI	Federation of British Industries
FDI	Foreign direct investment
FIRA	Foreign Investment Review Agency

GATT	General Agreement on Tariffs and Trade
GDP	Gross domestic product
GSP	Generalized System of Preferences
HDTV	High-definition television
IDAC	Import Duties Advisory Committee
IT	Information technology
JAMA	Japanese Automobile Manufacturers Association
JETRO	Japan External Trade Organization
JSEPA	Japan-Singapore Economic Partnership Agreement
LDP	Liberal Democratic Party
MCA	Manufacturing Chemists Association
MES	Minimum efficient scale
METI	Ministry of Economy, Trade, and Industry
MFA	Multifiber Arrangement
MFN	Most favored nation
MVMA	Motor Vehicle Manufacturers Association
NACE	Nomenclature Générale des Activités Economiques (Statistical Classification of Economic Activities)
NAFTA	North American Free Trade Agreement
NFISM	National Federation of Iron and Steel Manufacturers
NIE	Newly industrialized economy
OAP	Offshore Assembly Program
OECD	Organization for Economic Cooperation and Development
OLS	Ordinary least squares
R&D	Research and development
RDI	Reichsverband der Deutschen Industrie (Federation of German Industry)
RTAA	Reciprocal Trade Agreements Act
SIC	Standard Industry Classification
SOCMA	Synthetic Organic Chemical Manufacturers Association
TRIM	Trade-related investment measure
UAW	United Automobile Workers
UNCTAD	United Nations Conference on Trade and Development
UNCTC	United Nations Center on Transnational Corporations
USITC	U.S. International Trade Commission
USTC	U.S. Tariff Commission
USTR	United States Trade Representative
VER	Voluntary Export Restraint
WTO	World Trade Organization

CHAPTER I

Introduction
A World of Trading Blocs

Trading blocs have been dramatically expanding throughout the world economy. In 1992, the European Union (EU) completed the single-market program and began a historic initiative for monetary union. The United States, Canada, and Mexico launched the North American Free Trade Agreement (NAFTA) in 1994. Even Japan, for years the only industrial country that was not a member of any regional arrangement, completed a trade agreement with Singapore in 2001. Overall, half of the regional trade agreements notified to the General Agreement on Tariffs and Trade (GATT) were negotiated in the last decade—133 in all since the creation of the World Trade Organization (WTO). At this writing, several post-Soviet states and past members of the Eastern bloc have lined up to enter the EU; thirty-four countries in the Americas envision free trade "from Alaska to Tierra del Fuego"; the Association of Southeast Asian Nations (ASEAN) is preparing to establish a free trade area; and Japan is exploring trade pacts with the Philippines, Thailand, Malaysia, and South Korea.

This book analyzes how domestic politics has driven the formation of trading blocs.[1] Its central claim is that states construct trading blocs in response to political pressures from organized interests in society. Understanding the formation of trading blocs and their external effects, I argue, requires an examination of the domestic system and the process of national policy-making. To accomplish this, the book develops an analytical framework that specifies the

---

1. The book uses the terms *trading blocs* and *regional trading arrangements* interchangeably. In general, there are three types of trading blocs. In *customs unions,* countries eliminate all restrictions on trade with one another and maintain common trade policies toward nonmembers. In *free trade areas,* members eliminate all restrictions on their mutual trade but retain separate, autonomous external trade policies. In *preferential trading arrangements,* members reduce barriers to trade within the group but do not practice free trade with one another or establish common policies toward nonmembers.

trade preferences of domestic actors and tests this framework in a comparative analysis of trading blocs from the 1920s through the 1990s.

The book's principal contribution is to demonstrate the significance of economies of scale in domestic pressure for trading blocs. Economic analyses, press accounts, and government reports routinely highlight larger-scale production as a benefit of regional integration, but its importance in motivating group lobbying has not been systematically examined. This study, however, finds the same actors repeatedly pushing for inclusion in a wider trading area: from Imperial Japan and the British Commonwealth to the EU and NAFTA, businesses in industries with large returns to scale have been key forces in the emergence of trading blocs. In addition, the book shows how the growth of multinational production sharing has spurred the creation of trading blocs. As businesses move discrete stages of manufacturing to different countries, they become interested in opening trade and harmonizing standards across the borders that link their investments. When groups that rely on scale economies or production-sharing networks have political clout, the book argues, trading blocs are likely to form.

Many previous studies of trading blocs treat states as unitary actors and examine the strategic incentives for participation in these arrangements. This work usually reaches pessimistic conclusions about the global effects of regional arrangements. Bhagwati (1998, 286) predicts that "divisions will be sharpened and the world economy fragmented" because trading blocs, once formed, "invite . . . defensive, if not retaliatory" reactions. Gilpin (2000, 8, 42) warns of a regressive spiral if "each regional movement attempts to enhance its own competitive position vis à vis other regions," and he concludes that the "unity and integration of the global economy are increasingly challenged by the spread of regional economic arrangements." Others (e.g., Thurow 1992; Garten 1993; Hatch and Yamamura 1996; Pomfret 1997) emphasize the perils of fortress Europe, a yen bloc, protectionism in NAFTA, and introverted, restrictive regional arrangements elsewhere. Some suggest that a three-bloc trading system is particularly volatile and dangerous (Krugman 1991; Froot and Yoffie 1993; Bergsten 2001).

The experience of the 1930s offers a vivid backdrop for anxiety about the recent drift toward regionalism. In this period, Britain and France established preferential trade with their colonial territories; Japan and Germany sought expanded empires of their own, first through trade, later through conquest. The growth of imperial blocs coincided with rising and sometimes prohibitive barriers against foreign goods: Japan increased import duties throughout the 1920s, the United States passed the Smoot-Hawley tariff in 1930, Britain's General Tariff reversed its longstanding free trade policy in 1931, France tightened import quotas that same year, and Germany imposed rigid exchange controls under its New Plan of 1934. The collapse of the trading system, the Great Depression, and World War II ensued, each in succession contributing to the destruction of the integrated world economy that flourished before 1914.

Lessons drawn from the interwar period and its aftermath are central to debates about how to interpret present trends. In the conventional wisdom, the rise of imperial blocs was a primary factor in the outbreak of beggar-thy-neighbor protectionism and mercantilist warfare. The belief that open, nondiscriminatory trading systems tend to be peaceful while closed, compartmentalized economic relations create conflict is implicit in most discussions about trading blocs, if not plainly stated in analogies to the 1930s. "Tariff discriminations," wrote Jacob Viner (1951, 355), a pioneer in the economics of regional integration, "poison international relations and . . . make more difficult the task of maintaining international harmony." Conversely, a world free of empires and exclusions is widely viewed as more cooperative and tranquil.

The U.S. diplomats who designed the blueprints for a new world order after World War II certainly thought so. Secretary of State Cordell Hull, who designated Britain's Imperial Preference "the greatest injury, in a commercial way, inflicted on this country since I have been in public life," regarded "trade discrimination . . . as the handmaiden of armed aggression" (Gardner 1969, 19). In applying this conviction, the State Department pushed foreign governments during the war to pledge to end unequal treatment and dissolve imperial trading links. The GATT codified these national commitments to nondiscrimination and multilateral liberalization, as the most favored nation (MFN) clause enabled members to share the benefits of significant tariff reductions achieved in a series of trade rounds after 1947.[2] Under the GATT, the European Community (EC) was the only trading bloc to realize lasting success; regional arrangements among developing nations in Latin America, Africa, and Asia amounted to mere acronyms that failed to open regional trade or collapsed amid acrimony—or both. As Hull and his cohorts had hoped, trade was liberalized, regionalism was infrequent, and a repeat of the interwar calamity was averted.

Recently, however, trading blocs have multiplied and flourished, as figure 1

2. GATT Article XXIV amended Article I to allow free trade agreements and customs unions to deny MFN treatment to other countries provided that these arrangements liberalized "substantially all" trade and did not "on the whole" increase "the general incidence of" trade barriers against nonmembers. An annex to Article I also permitted certain colonial and regional preferences to remain in force. On the origins of Article XXIV, see Chase 2005.

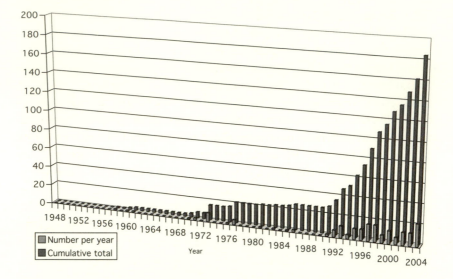

Fig. 1. The proliferation of regional trade agreements, 1948–2004. (Data from WTO, "Regional Trade Agreements Notified to the GATT/WTO and in Force," http://www.wto .org/english/tratop_e/region_e/eif_e.xls.)

demonstrates. While prior work tends to focus on particular regional arrangements—usually the EU or NAFTA—this book places them in the context of other integration efforts, including the more insidious imperial and regional schemes of the interwar era. In doing so, the book finds that the forces driving regionalism of late do not fully resemble those of the past. The case chapters show that while similar actors pushed for trading blocs in both periods, proponents of regionalism typically sought external protectionism in the 1930s but not in the 1990s. The argument and evidence suggest that businesses in contemporary regional arrangements have been more favorably inclined to external trade openness because these trading blocs have created opportunities to restructure production more efficiently. The book therefore rejects the 1930s analogy and concludes that today's regionalism is not a threat to the global trading system.

Analytical Puzzles and Proposed Solutions

The rise of trading blocs raises three fundamental questions for international economic relations. First, why do governments form or join regional arrangements? Second, what impact do trading blocs have on the multilateral integration of the world economy—do their members tend to raise trade barriers against the outside world or reduce them? Third, how does the creation of trading blocs affect economic, political, and military conflict and cooperation between regions?[3]

These questions are sequentially linked, yet many studies examine one in isolation from the others. In international relations theory, realists and liberals debate the third step, how regional arrangements affect outcomes at the systemic level. To realists, trading blocs signal a failure of international cooperation; to liberals, they are a method for successful collective action. The two approaches offer different conjectures about how trading blocs affect regional relations with the rest of the world, but they do not address how external policies are determined endogenously in the political systems of the countries involved. In economics and political economy, a large body of work examines step two, whether members of trading blocs are likely to raise or reduce foreign trade barriers. Yet much of this work presupposes a set of motives for regional integration that are not validated empirically: proponents of the regional arrangements as "building blocks" thesis often assume the dominance of pro-trade interests, while adherents to the "stumbling blocks" line of argument tend to emphasize incentives for protectionism.[4]

In short, we cannot understand step three without step two, or step two without step one. Instead of cutting into the problem from the middle and taking prior decisions as given, analytical work on trading blocs must start at the beginning. The book's theory proceeds from a set of analytical propositions about the motives for organized groups—principally firms and trade associations—to seek regional arrangements. The argument emphasizes two key factors in the political calculus of domestic actors that want to be part of a trading bloc. A primary consideration is the desire to gain scale economies. When small national markets inhibit the concentration of production in a country (or a region), firms that can capture unexploited scale economies in an enlarged market will push for trading blocs. A second important motive in pressure for regional arrangements is the ability to locate stages of production in different countries to take advantage of factor price differences.[5] If manufacturing can be divided and dispersed,

3. Economists are interested in a related set of questions but cast them differently. For example, Frankel (1997) examines the effect of regional blocs on trade patterns between the bloc and the outside world, on the welfare of the members of the bloc, and on world welfare. The first question is empirical; the latter two are normative. My objective in this book is to present explanations for the questions that I seek to answer and then to systematically evaluate these proposed explanations against the available evidence. While this exercise has important implications for the welfare issues that economists such as Frankel investigate, the purpose is positive and analytical, not normative. It is this difference that distinguishes modern *political economy* from *economics*, as chapter 2 explains.

4. The terms *building blocks* and *stumbling blocks* first appeared in Bhagwati 1991 (77).

5. Factor prices are the cost of inputs or resources used in the production process, usually labor, capital, and land.

then firms that can integrate production tasks across borders will seek regional arrangements. Thus, the formation of trading blocs reflects first and foremost the aggregate number and political strength of businesses that rely on scale economies or production-sharing networks to survive and prosper in the world market.

Building from this foundation, the book examines the conditions under which domestic actors are likely to seek to increase or reduce trade barriers against countries outside a regional arrangement. The key point is that regional integration is a dynamic process that affects—and potentially alters—the trade preferences of organized groups. If forming a trading bloc enables businesses to gain scale economies or deepen production sharing, then they will become more favorable to external liberalization. In this case, a protected regional market provides temporary shelter while firms restructure. But if firms cannot reorganize to expand product runs or outsource high-cost processes, domestic support for external trade protection is likely to persist. To the extent that regional trade liberalization increases import competition in activities with high comparative costs, protectionist pressures from these industries will intensify.

Because the approach offers predictions about the circumstances under which domestic groups are likely to support or oppose trading blocs, and the conditions that cause them to favor external protectionism or further trade liberalization, it provides insights into systemic outcomes such as the distribution of regional arrangements over time, the openness or closure of the global trade regime, or conflict and cooperation across trading blocs. However, the book does not attempt to explain systemic outcomes. Such a theory would have to include interstate bargaining and factors in the strategic environment that are outside the argument's scope. Rather, the approach confronts one aspect of these larger puzzles—how domestic distributional pressures affect the formation and evolution of trading blocs. In doing so, it lays a foundation for uniting theories of strategic interaction with domestic politics to develop more refined expectations about systemic outcomes.

Other Explanations

The book's explanatory framework draws from a large body of work in economics and political science, but it is distinct from both. Economic approaches provide useful first principles for understanding the distributional issues in regional integration at the domestic level (between industries or factors of production) and in interstate bargaining (between states). However, economic theory cannot explain the formation of trading blocs because these arrangements—like any policy other than total free trade—conflict with the national welfare assumptions at the core of all trade models. Economic studies therefore treat trading bloc formation as an exogenous decision and evaluate the static impact of this event on national and world welfare. Realist and liberal theories of international relations, in contrast, are sensitive to the political context in which trading blocs form and the dynamics of policy responses at the interstate level. Yet the exclusive focus on the geopolitical environment has led work in political science to disregard, until recently, the importance of political forces operating at the domestic level.

Customs Union Theory

Viner's *Customs Union Issue*, published in 1950, is the starting point for the economic analysis of trading blocs. In this seminal work, Viner did not offer a positive theory of the formation of customs unions. Instead, his purpose was to assess how shifts in the source of supply of goods after regional integration affected national and world welfare. He found that customs unions could have positive or negative welfare effects on members and nonmembers based on the net of "trade creation" and "trade diversion."[6] Since his analysis treated the decision to form a customs union and the level of the common external tariff as exogenously given, the welfare gain or loss in any particular case depended on factors outside the scope of his theory. Years later, Kemp and Wan showed that a customs union could, in principle, adopt a "compensating common tariff" that left nonmembers no worse off. Yet the decision to establish such an arrangement remains a puzzle for welfare-based trade models because the motives to stop partway along the road to free trade are unclear.[7] Eliminating all tariffs is always better for social welfare, so regional integration is a "second-best" policy. Thus, economists (e.g., Johnson 1965) concluded long ago that the motives must be "noneconomic."

An exception to the "second-best" finding is the case in which regional integration enables members to exploit market power over states outside the group. In this approach, a trading bloc can impose an optimal tariff that re-

6. Trade creation occurs when customs liberalization allows imports from one partner country (a more efficient source) to replace domestic production in another (a less efficient source); trade diversion occurs when imports from a partner country (a less efficient source) supplant imports from nonmembers (a more efficient source) due to the wedge between the intrabloc tariff and the external tariff (Viner 1950).

7. As Kemp and Wan (1976, 96) explain, countries have "an incentive to form and enlarge customs unions . . . until the world is one big customs union, that is, until world free trade prevails."

duces the demand for foreign imports and shifts the terms of trade to its benefit. Since the terms of trade improve with the height of the tariff and the number (or size) of countries in the bloc, trading blocs have incentives to raise tariffs and divert trade. This creates conflict in strategic interaction between regions, as each bloc's attempt to redistribute wealth reinforces a downward spiral of protection and retaliation (Krugman 1991; Saxonhouse 1993; Srinivasan, Whalley, and Wooton 1993). Yet even the authors of these models concede that they provide a "grossly unrealistic . . . description of trade politics" (Krugman 1993, 61). Thus, normative trade theory provides rigorous models but no compelling analytical scenario of the formation and evolution of trading blocs. More plausible explanations lie in the realm of politics.

Realist and Liberal Approaches

International relations theories examine the organization of trade in the geopolitical context of the international system. These approaches suggest that open trade is difficult to achieve because countries in an anarchic interstate system prefer to free ride by gaining access to others' markets without opening their own. Since states cannot credibly commit to liberalize without acting opportunistically and no central authority exists to monitor the fulfillment of national commitments, open trade requires costly contractual and enforcement mechanisms to overcome incentives to defect under anarchy (Keohane 1984).

In realist thought, global trade liberalization occurs only when there is a dominant or "hegemonic" power to supervise and enforce compliance with an open, multilateral trade regime (Krasner 1976; Kindleberger 1973). When the distribution of power is relatively equal, however, open trading systems break down. In these conditions, states increase protectionist barriers and form trading blocs.[8]

Though there are cases of declining hegemonic powers seeking refuge in trading blocs—a weakened Britain turned to Imperial Preference in 1931 and the United States embraced regional initiatives in the 1980s after its postwar preeminence had decayed—the proposition that open trade benefits the hegemonic power, while large, nonhegemonic states gain from closure, rests on shaky theoretical ground (Lake 1988; Stein 1984). Critics suggest that very large countries have incentives to exploit market leverage or to "limit price" to reap monopolistic advantages without encouraging potential challengers (Conybeare 1987; Gowa 1989). Following this reasoning, other realist argu-

---

8. Krasner (1976, 324) links trading blocs with hegemonic decline and "[p]eriods of closure." Also see Gilpin 1971, 407–9.

ments contend that powerful countries seek to gain private advantages rather than provide public goods. In one view, trading blocs are nested inside military alliances to limit trade-related "security externalities" and maximize the relative power of alliances (Gowa 1994; Gowa and Mansfield 1993; Mansfield 1993). Studies supporting this view suggest that trading blocs have malignant effects on global commerce because they are tied up with military disputes.[9] Another approach casts trading blocs as a means through which the strong exploit the weak, as large states can extract concessions from small neighbors by fostering close trade ties that would impose asymmetric costs if broken.[10]

Liberal approaches instead focus on how interdependence, market failures, and coordination problems affect trade relations. One set of arguments explains trading blocs as a response to conditions within a region. In these "functionalist" accounts, growing economic interactions have external consequences that are beyond the capacity of any state to manage individually, so countries that have reached a threshold level of market integration form regional arrangements to provide supranational regulation. Cooperation in one policy area in turn has "spillover" effects that motivate successively deeper levels of regional integration, as it is difficult to maintain different regulatory, customs, and administrative rules and procedures in the presence of intense intraindustry trade and large-scale capital flows.[11]

A second set of arguments emphasizes conditions in the global trade regime that promote regional cooperation.[12] Liberal institutional theories argue that transaction costs, incomplete contracts, and large numbers plague multilateral negotiations.[13] In this view, regionalism alleviates global collective action problems when international institutions are ineffective and hegemonic leadership is absent. In particular, regional arrangements speed initiatives to liberalize trade by reducing the number of participants and limiting monitoring and enforcement costs. Thus, small groups of countries with similar political, institutional, and cultural backgrounds can achieve "deeper integration" (Lawrence 1996) than is feasible multilaterally.

In contrast to the realist view that trading blocs are designed to enhance

9. At the same time, members of the same preferential arrangement are less likely to engage in military conflict with one another (Mansfield and Pevehouse 2000).

10. Hirschman (1945) outlines how Nazi Germany exploited the "influence effect" of trade to gain leverage in central Europe. Also see Gruber 2000.

11. Haas 1958 is the seminal functionalist work. Moravcsik (1998) and Mattli (1999) critique and modify elements of this approach.

12. Mansfield and Reinhardt (2003) empirically assess how conditions in the multilateral trading environment motivate the formation of regional arrangements.

13. See Yarbrough and Yarbrough 1992.

relative power or political influence, liberal theories regard regional arrangements as devices to exploit mutual gains from trade that are unrealized in global negotiations. These approaches suggest that regional blocs are not likely to raise new barriers to trade with outsiders; rather, they are useful halfway houses along the road to free trade to wean governments of their dependence on protection. For one, interregional interdependence constrains the development of self-contained trading blocs as long as threats to punish defection are credible and retaliation costly. Moreover, postwar regional arrangements have been embedded in the multilateral GATT-WTO structure. Finally, large countries remain committed to the multilateral process and nondiscrimination in international trade, even as they pursue regional initiatives (Haggard 1997; Lawrence 1996; Fishlow and Haggard 1992).

While these approaches illuminate conditions in the strategic environment that lead to alternative modes of organizing trade relations, both assume national preferences rather than explaining them. In realism, states prefer more relative power to less, and closed trading blocs are a strategy to enhance national power or the strength of alliances. In liberalism, states seek to maximize their gains from trade, and they pursue regional initiatives when transaction costs and free riding at the global level frustrate multilateral trade liberalization. These two strands of international relations theory yield opposing predictions: one is a theory of the 1930s calamity, when open trade and regional blocs proved mutually exclusive; the other is a theory of the last decade's apparent success, when the emergence of trading blocs coincided with progress (amid strain) at the multilateral level. Neither approach accounts for the range of possible outcomes within a common analytical framework.

Moreover, because structural theories focus on systemic outcomes, they miss important differences across countries in the same international structure and across industries in the same country. This variation is understandable only in the context of the policy process at the domestic level. Simply stated, realist and liberal theories are too abstract to fully explain the development and effects of trading blocs; systemic factors such as collective action, national power, and strategic interaction are insufficient. As a result, recent reviews of the study of regionalism (Haggard 1997; Mansfield and Milner 1999) call for scholars to examine national preference formation and domestic politics.

Domestic Perspectives

Domestic approaches illuminate the internal political factors that cause governments to pursue regional arrangements. A large body of work in economics and political science examines rent-seeking motives to form trading blocs. These approaches build from two premises: first, trade diversion provides rents for producers (who benefit from increased demand for their goods in a protected regional market) at the expense of consumers (who must pay higher prices); second, the costs of trade creation are concentrated on a small number of producers, while the costs of trade diversion are dispersed across a broad range of consumers (Johnson 1965; Cooper and Massell 1965). Trading blocs therefore tend to favor exporters that benefit from enhanced protection, because governments have incentives to exempt import-competing producers that would lose protection to ensure political support (Grossman and Helpman 2002, chap. 7; Hirschman 1981, chap. 12). Even when import-competing industries are liberalized, inefficient producers will seek to convert trade creation into trade diversion through higher barriers against third countries (Bhagwati 1993). Domestic groups also can abuse dispute settlement provisions and rules of origin against nonmembers to extend national protection to the regional level (Krueger 1997, 1999; Levy and Srinivasan 1996).[14] In this class of models, Levy (1997, 506) states, trading blocs "never increase political support for multilateral free trade."[15]

Other studies counter that regional arrangements facilitate trade liberalization by reducing rent-seeking pressure or strengthening protrade lobbies. If trading blocs establish a common external tariff or transfer authority to supranational institutions, protectionist national groups must reorganize at the regional level, where they will be larger, less homogenous, and more susceptible to free riding (Hanson 1998). Import-competing industries also lose political influence at the national level as their output contracts after regional trade liberalization (Richardson 1993). Third-country exporters injured by trade diversion will lobby to join trading blocs to regain lost markets (Oye 1992). In developing countries, regional trade agreements strengthen exporters and businesses with multinational ties and weaken import-competing firms and state-owned enterprises by ensuring that policy reforms are "locked in" (Tornell and Esquivel 1997; Maggi and Rodriguez-Clare 1998). Finally, regional arrangements help to overcome status quo bias when some groups are uncertain about the adjustment costs of multilateral trade liberalization (Wei and Frankel 1996).

However, these accounts generally fail to explain why states choose to liber-

14. Rules of origin are measures to block transshipment inside a free trade area. Their purpose is to prevent outsiders from exploiting tariff differentials among members by exporting to the least protected market.

15. Also see Krishna 1998.

alize regionally rather than multilaterally. Rather than treating trading bloc formation as an exogenous event that alters the preferences or lobbying capacity of protrade and antitrade interests, it is important to know why domestic groups prefer regionalism in the first place. Owners of locally abundant factors of production and producers of exported goods would gain more from multilateral or unilateral liberalization; they have few incentives to prefer a "second-best" policy unless superior alternatives are not feasible.[16] At the same time, regional trade liberalization erodes protection for locally scarce factors and import-competing producers, so these actors should prefer trade barriers at the national rather than the regional level. Because there are opportunity costs for competitive producers and adjustment costs for uncompetitive producers, explaining the creation of a domestic coalition supporting the formation of trading blocs is critically important.

To fill this gap, recent work incorporates imperfect competition and economies of scale into explanations for trading blocs. This research emphasizes incentives to ensure stable markets and capture excess profits in industries with large returns to scale (Chase 2003; Milner 1997; Busch and Milner 1994; Froot and Yoffie 1993). Regional integration offers especially large benefits to small-country firms, which can move down their cost curves once they gain access to a larger customer base (Casella 1996). But the implications for the multilateral trading system remain open to debate. On the one hand, entry barriers in industries with large returns to scale encourage protectionism (Froot and Yoffie 1993). On the other hand, multilateral liberalization benefits industries with large returns to scale because they tend to be export dependent.[17]

This body of work provides a promising approach to domestic support for trading blocs. Moreover, it represents an alternative way of thinking about the political economy of trade. Recent surveys underscore the growing recognition that factors omitted from standard trade models—scale economies, product differentiation, and intraindustry trade—are theoretically and empirically important in modern trade politics (see Frieden and Rogowski 1996, 28–30; Alt et al. 1996, 693–95). Yet unresolved analytical puzzles remain, and empirical work to date has not examined these variables in a systematic fashion on a large number of cases. This book helps to fill these gaps by offering an explanation

16. As a result, some accounts also assume that large numbers and high transaction costs in multilateral negotiations inhibit progress toward global free trade.

17. Busch and Milner (1994, 273) conclude, "the firms most likely to demand regionalism are also the least likely to favor external protectionism." Milner (1997), however, suggests that industries with large returns to scale tend to receive more trade liberalization in regional than in multilateral agreements.

for the formation and evolution of trading blocs that begins with scale-economy considerations in the political calculus of firms and business associations.

Plan of the Book

Chapter 2 presents a theoretical explanation of the motives for domestic groups to seek trading blocs. This section of the book emphasizes how opportunities to exploit scale economies and establish production-sharing networks influence the political behavior of businesses. The framework is then extended to evaluate the conditions under which domestic actors are likely to seek to increase or reduce trade barriers toward the rest of the world. Lastly, the chapter offers generalizations linking group preferences to national policy decisions, and it discusses how to measure the variables in the analysis.

The second part of the book presents case studies of the period between the world wars. The growing scale of manufacturing after the second industrial revolution caused firms with small national markets in Japan, Britain, and Germany to push to expand empires and form trading blocs. In these cases, chapter 3 shows, businesses that could not exhaust economies of scale inside imperial blocs sought protectionist barriers to blunt U.S. competition. The United States, by comparison, had a vast continental market to sustain mass production, and chapter 4 analyzes how large U.S. businesses pressed to dismantle foreign empires, dissolve trading blocs, and liberalize trade from the Smoot-Hawley tariff until the 1960s.

The third section of the book examines modern trading blocs. Chapter 5 shows that European business groups campaigned for the single market because small national markets and ongoing barriers to trade prevented the concentration of production. While some "national champions" sought external protection to deflect increased competition internally, the 1992 program helped to prepare European industries for more vigorous external liberalization as businesses expanded and regionalized production. In North America, chapter 6 explains, U.S. multinationals sought free trade with Mexico and Canada to allow them to reorganize factories, outsource labor-intensive tasks, and rescale production for a regional market. Though the NAFTA treaty included some exclusive provisions, this chapter finds that most supporters of regional free trade also backed multilateral liberalization. Chapter 7 demonstrates that the reluctance of Japanese businesses to establish Asian production networks has inhibited the creation of a yen bloc in Pacific Asia. Even with tentative recent moves toward regional arrangements, this chapter argues, Japanese firms have too great a stake in the multilateral system to seriously pursue an Asian trading bloc.

Chapter 8 concludes by examining how regional arrangements affect outsiders. Though many foreign exporters are harmed, foreign multinationals can reap large benefits when they gain a foothold inside a trading bloc. Today most multinational companies operate in each of the world's major trading areas, so they are neither helped nor harmed by an increase in trade protection across regions. This chapter further suggests that discrimination and exclusion in regional arrangements can help to promote restructuring, particularly when established businesses have large sunk costs. Because restructured firms typically grow more favorable to external liberalization, the book concludes that present trading blocs are not a threat to the WTO or the multilateral system.

CHAPTER 2

The Argument
Domestic Groups and
Regional Arrangements

The emergence of trading blocs has been an unmistakable development in recent years. Policy analysts, economists, and international relations theorists have widely examined the current drift toward regionalism, as well as past outbreaks of trade discrimination such as the interwar years. These studies generally focus on the economics or the geopolitics of trading blocs, but not the political economy of these arrangements.

This chapter presents a political economy framework to evaluate domestic factors in the design and evolution of trading blocs. Explaining how market interactions affect policy involves several steps. The first step is to characterize the trade preferences of domestic actors. Second, we need to understand why these domestic actors favor particular trade strategies to achieve their objectives. This requires insight into why some private interests prefer regional trade liberalization, a puzzle that is not resolved in existing studies. Third, we must analyze how domestic actors organize into groups to advance their policy goals and how the institutional process of policy-making influences which interests in society receive their desired policy response from the government.

Moving in sequence through each of these steps helps to unravel how market interactions affect domestic actors, how the preferences of domestic actors are aggregated into groups, and how organized groups influence national policy. The purpose is to answer two questions: Why do some domestic groups campaign for regional trade liberalization when there are unilateral and multilateral policy alternatives? Under what conditions will domestic groups seek to increase or decrease regional trade barriers toward the rest of the world after the formation of a trading bloc? This chapter lays out an analytical approach to these questions and the specific arguments that later chapters evaluate in a comparative analysis of trading blocs across regions and time.

The Dependent Variables

There are two dependent variables to be explained. The primary dependent variable is the trade preferences of domestic actors, expressed in terms of organized political behavior. These preferences vary along two dimensions. First, they can be liberalizing or protectionist: liberalizing policies reduce trade barriers to relatively low levels; protectionist policies raise trade restrictions to relatively high levels. Second, trade preferences can be discriminatory or nondiscriminatory. Nondiscriminatory trade policies adhere to MFN principles; discriminatory trade policies place some portion of trade outside MFN channels.

The secondary dependent variable is trade policy at the national level.[1] Policy outcomes are a function of the trade preferences of domestic actors, their capacity to organize collectively, and the intervening effects of political institutions in mediating group preferences. Policy outcomes also vary along the two dimensions outlined in the preceding.

For clarity, domestic actors' trade preferences (and national policies) can be situated in a two-by-two matrix, as in table 1. The level of liberalization or protection varies along one axis and the level of discrimination along the other. Moving clockwise, closed trading blocs, open trading blocs, free trade, and trade protection occupy the four cells. It is these gradations of policy preferences—and, by extension, policy outcomes—that the book seeks to explain.

The Method of Analysis: The Political Economy of Trade

The political economy of trade makes up a rich literature that has grown spectacularly over the last twenty-five years. Research in this area is divided among scholars who analyze state institutions and those who examine domestic groups in trade policy-making.[2] Disciples of both research traditions agree that the two approaches complement one another, as each focuses on a separate

---

1. This variable is secondary because the study does not account for all of the factors that affect trade policy. In addition to trade preferences and domestic actors' ability to organize, there are legislative and bureaucratic factors, strategic concerns, elite interests, and myriad other considerations in national policy. This book examines the *product* of national decisions and evaluates the extent to which it is understandable in terms of the variables under consideration, but it does not examine the decision-making *process* of public officials. As a result, it cannot provide an exhaustive description of the influences on trade policy. Instead, it seeks to account for as much variance as possible with a few simple explanatory factors.

2. There are too many contributions to this body of work to list here. Important work on interest groups includes Gourevitch 1986; Milner 1988; Rogowski 1989; Magee, Brock, and Young 1989; Frieden 1991; Alt and Gilligan 1994; Frieden and Rogowski 1996; and Hiscox 2002.

stage of the policy process. Thus, it is axiomatic that a full model of national policy must specify both the demands of policy coalitions and the institutional constraints that determine a government's inclination to satisfy domestic group needs.

The argument in this book begins with domestic actors and builds upward to derive expectations about national trade policy. The starting point is that "actors are regarded as having preferences for outcomes" (Frieden 1999, 40). Fundamentally, I assume that market actors—firms and workers—prefer more profits (or wages) to less. This material interest yields preferences over national policy: firms prefer policies that enable them to earn more profits to those that cause them to earn less; workers prefer policies that promote higher wages to those that restrain wages. While market actors' policy preferences normally cannot be observed, the lobbying strategies they employ to advance these interests are revealed in the political setting. Analysts can gain explanatory leverage over this behavior if "preferences can be deduced from prior theoretical principles" (Frieden 1999, 41). Explaining why market actors want the policies they seek and employ the political strategies they pursue to this end illuminates the pressures on governments to supply one set of policies rather than another. It is then possible to evaluate the direction and intensity of these pressures, and hence the policy decisions that are likely to result, by linking a deductive theory of preferences to a "complementary theory of the aggregation of preferences, from individuals and firms up to groups, sectors, classes, and nations" (Frieden 1999, 65).

The analytical framework focuses, first, on the trade preferences of domestic actors. In this exercise, I characterize domestic actors' trade preferences along the two dimensions in table 1: (1) the degree to which they advocate or oppose regional trade liberalization and (2) the level of their support for increased trade protection or further trade liberalization after regional integration. This is the most challenging task, and it receives the greatest attention in this chapter.

TABLE I. Typology of Dependent Variables

	Degree of Liberalization	
Degree of Discrimination	Low	High
High	(1) Closed trading blocs	(2) Open trading blocs
Low	(4) Trade protection	(3) Free trade

The second part of the explanation examines preference aggregation as domestic actors organize into groups. Here the key issue is whether businesses will act individually or lobby through industry associations. This section also addresses how organizational abilities and the design of state institutions affect the ability of domestic groups to obtain the trade policies they seek.

In the pursuit of a compelling political economy approach to trading blocs, I do not contend that group lobbying provides an exhaustive account of every regional arrangement formed over the years. States negotiate trade agreements for many reasons. Balassa (1961, 4) writes, "The considerations that have prompted . . . plans for the integration of independent national economies are by no means uniform; various factors must be given different weights in the movement toward economic integration in Europe and on other continents." No doubt political motives, not solely political economy ones, play an important role. Indeed, among the trade agreements negotiated of late are several purely political undertakings—peace, friendship, and cooperation pacts—with little economic substance or meaning.[3] After surveying this landscape, Gilpin (2001, 344) concludes: "The diversity of regional arrangements makes broad generalizations and overarching theories or explanations of regionalism impossible."

Even if generalization is difficult, it is not impossible; scholars can do more than merely provide limited evaluations of the effects of regional arrangements while taking their design as exogenously given. Clearly, free trade between the United States and Israel cannot be viewed in the same way as free trade between the United States and Mexico; the EC offered entry to Spain and Portugal for reasons different from those for it to extend an invitation to Malta. But even when close political relations or favorable strategic conditions permit regional initiatives to proceed, domestic pressures will come to the fore the more significant the arrangement economically. Outlining the private interests engaged in this process, and where they lead when domestic groups express them in the political arena, is indispensable to any explanation of the development, design, and evolution of trading blocs.

The Argument

The book's argument emphasizes how dynamic considerations motivate domestic groups to lobby for regional trade liberalization. The static effect of

3. One account characterizes several trade agreements recently under consideration as "soundbite economics" for "ministers . . . desperate to be seen to be active." See "Asian Ambition: Frustration with Deadlock at the WTO and a Fear of Becoming Isolated Have Prompted Pacific Rim Nations to Seek Security in Regional Free Trade," *Financial Times*, November 28, 2000, 24.

trade creation and trade diversion is not a strong motive for regional integration. Rather, the principal attraction of regional arrangements is the opportunity they create for businesses to reorganize operations. These restructuring gains are most significant when production technologies require a larger-than-national market to be profitable. Producers will exert pressure to eliminate barriers that restrict the range of the available market if subsequently they can employ these technologies more effectively. Producers that cannot make use of these technologies, however, will be less interested in regional integration; indeed, they might have reasons to oppose it.

Building from these basic propositions, the task is to specify the types of businesses that are technologically constrained by the geographic scope of the national market and those that are not. Attention to the dynamic effects of trading blocs helps to explain why some domestic groups lobby for regional trade liberalization while others fight it. The book makes two specific points.

First, producers seek trading blocs when access to a larger market enables them to take advantage of economies of scale in production. Firms with steep cost curves and a small domestic market will find it difficult to exploit scale economies. As a result, they will support regional arrangements to gain access to a wider market. If the domestic market is large or the potential economies of scale small, however, firms will be less constrained by national boundaries and less interested in an enlarged market.

Second, producers seek trading blocs when an integrated regional market enables them to move stages of production across borders. Because barriers to trade and investment restrict opportunities to take advantage of differences between countries in wages, skills, and capital costs, businesses that can redeploy intermediate production benefit from regional trade liberalization. Firms unable to move production abroad due to technological constraints are not affected by these barriers, so they have less incentive to push for their elimination.

Standard trade models ignore dynamic effects because they are derived from endowment-based theories of trade. Yet even casual observers recognize that the importance of this type of trade is declining. For one, trade less often follows the conventional pattern of countries with different factor endowments exchanging labor-intensive for capital-intensive goods. Instead, countries with similar endowments often exchange similar products: for example, the United States and Germany trade Ford and GM automobiles for BMWs and Volkswagens. Economies of scale and product differentiation are the factors most commonly adduced to explain this apparent anomaly.

In addition, production is not country specific: it is dispersed across borders, with different stages located where they can be performed most efficiently. Even

a Barbie doll travels through six countries before reaching its final sales destination.[4] A firm engaged in the process variously described as *foreign assembly,*
offshore manufacturing, outsourcing, or *production sharing* transfers intermediate goods between countries, often through intrafirm trade. In this case, two-
way trade occurs as part of an integrated production process within a firm. For
example, 34 percent of U.S. trade in 2000 involved affiliates of the same multinational firm rather than separate, independent firms (Zeile 2003, 22–23).

While theoretical accounts of these trends are growing, economics has not
yet produced a "new" trade model with the rigor to supplant established approaches.[5] Efforts to incorporate these factors into empirical work on the political economy of trade therefore rest on a less secure theoretical foundation.
Nevertheless, it is possible to draw analytical first principles from this literature
to illuminate how domestic actors evaluate their trade preferences when there
are opportunities to take advantage of scale economies or production sharing.
In advancing this argument, I seek to provide a persuasive account of the formation of trading blocs and to advance the case for including new variables in
the political economy of trade.

The next section draws from trade models in economics to develop the logic
underlying my expectations about producer support for trading blocs. The section that follows develops expectations about how regional trade liberalization
is likely to affect the preferences of domestic groups toward trade with countries outside the regional arrangement. After that, I address how the interests
of domestic actors aggregate at the associational level and work through the institutional process to affect policy outcomes.

Domestic Actors and Policy Preferences

The Standard Trade Model

In the standard political economy of trade, domestic actors demand liberalization or protection based on the income distribution effects of trade exposure. In
essence, trade preferences are a function of comparative costs; political cleavages
reflect the mobility of factors of production. If factors are mobile, the factor that
is abundant in an economy experiences an increase in its income, and the scarce
factor suffers a reduction in its income. In a two-factor model, trade divides capital and labor: the scarce factor will seek trade protection, while the abundant
factor will support trade liberalization. If factors are fixed, then trade increases

---

4. "Barbie and the World Economy," *Los Angeles Times,* September 22, 1996.
5. Helpman and Krugman (1985, 1989) attempt to integrate new approaches into standard
trade theory.

incomes for capital and labor producing export goods and decreases incomes for capital and labor producing importable goods. In this case, trade divides sectors: import-competing sectors will seek trade protection; export-oriented sectors will lobby for trade liberalization.[6]

Traditional trade models illuminate motives for trade liberalization or protection, but they do not explain why domestic actors would want free trade regionally but not globally. To be sure, preferential trade among a set of countries causes factor prices within the group to converge, which benefits export-oriented-specific factors and harms import-competing-specific factors. But if regional trade liberalization pushes relative prices and incomes in the same direction as global trade liberalization, then regional free trade is nobody's first choice. Exporters that gain from regional free trade would benefit more from worldwide free trade; regionalism is only a "second-best" alternative to multilateral liberalization. At the same time, generally regional free trade will injure import competitors, even if they may be harmed less than under global free trade; these groups therefore would want to block global and regional trade alike.

An exception is when all members of a trading bloc have high comparative costs in an industry. In this case, regional free trade creates rents: if there are barriers to divert external trade, the most productive import-competing industry (or the country in which regionally scarce factors are most abundant) can sell overpriced exports to its regional partners. Grossman and Helpman (2002, 208) summarize:

> Producers in the country that exports to its partner under [a free trade agreement] sometimes gain and never lose. These producers are one potential source of political support for an agreement. On the other hand, the producers in the country that imports from its partner under the agreement never gain and sometimes lose. Here we find potential resistance.

In short, standard trade models highlight three classes of preferences toward regional trade liberalization. First, producers with a comparative advantage at the regional but not the global level will favor regional trade liberalization to earn rents (cell 1 in table 2). External trade liberalization, however, would drive down regional prices and bid these rents away.[7] Second, low-cost exporters may support regional trade liberalization to advance toward global free trade

6. These two approaches build from the same endowment-based theory of trade; they simply make different assumptions about the ability of factors to move between industries in response to relative price changes. See Hiscox 2002.

7. This is the core of political economy models of protectionist trading blocs in chapter 1.

TABLE 2. Industry Preferences in the Standard Trade Model

Revealed Comparative Advantage (inside region)	Revealed Comparative Advantage (outside region)	
	Low	High
High	(1) Regional free trade External protection	(2) Regional free trade External free trade
Low	(4) Regional protection External protection	(3) Regional protection External free trade

piecemeal (cell 2). Since these producers can sell abroad without special privileges, a trading bloc serves as a "stepping stone" to more sweeping trade liberalization multilaterally.[8] Third, producers that compete with imports from countries in the region will oppose regional free trade (cells 3 and 4). The income effect is more negative, and opposition to regional trade liberalization more intense, the larger the share of national consumption that regional competitors can satisfy.

In these models, producers experience one-time income effects as prices adjust to the opening of regional trade. Endowments are fixed in the short run, comparative costs change slowly, and benefits from trade liberalization do not cumulate over time. The effects could be substantial for a small country that gains the opportunity to trade at the relative prices of a large neighbor. But static benefits are not likely to provide a powerful engine for regional integration among larger economies or between countries with competitive rather than complementary production structures. Clearly there must be other reasons why regional arrangements are so widespread and numerous.

In my argument, the critical motives are the restructuring effects of regional integration. When regional trade is liberalized, domestic actors adjust their market behavior to the new policy environment. This changes production patterns and yields new business arrangements. The effects are more significant than the interindustry adjustment that occurs when there are no scale economies and factors of production cannot move across borders, as in standard trade models. Some domestic actors benefit from this restructuring; others are harmed. The former group will campaign for regional trade liberalization; the latter will tend to fight it.

8. However, efficient exporters may be cautious if regional free trade were likely to provoke retaliation since trade protection or discrimination in other regions would hurt their products.

Studies of regional integration identify three kinds of dynamic processes.[9] First, there is increased competition, which breaks up monopolies; this reduces prices and enhances consumption efficiency. Second, there is increased market size; this promotes intraindustry specialization and cost reduction through economies of scale. Third, there is a reallocation of factors of production, as factor price differences stimulate capital and labor flows between countries. In keeping with my focus on producer incentives rather than consumer interests, my framework focuses on the second and third of these processes—scale economies and factor movements, principally capital flows.

Trade with Imperfect Competition

Students of economics have long recognized that certain methods of production exhibit increasing returns to scale. John Stuart Mill's classic *Principles of Political Economy* notes, "The larger the scale on which manufacturing operations are carried on, the more cheaply they can in general be performed."[10] Adam Smith's famous pin factory in *The Wealth of Nations* demonstrates how large-scale production can achieve lower costs per unit than an establishment with specialized labor tasks but short production runs. In general, scale economies reflect "indivisibilities," that is, fixed costs that are indivisible with respect to output. At the factory level, indivisible costs include capital requirements for plant and equipment, which can be amortized more rapidly when spread over large volumes to minimize costs per unit.[11] For a firm, indivisibil-

9. See Balassa 1961. Different regional arrangements trigger more or fewer of these dynamic effects depending on a number of considerations—incomes, production structures, market sizes, external trade policies, policies toward factor movements, the investment climate, and so on. Economic approaches take these variables as given and attempt to measure the size of the dynamic benefits in specific cases. In my framework, domestic actors base their trade preferences on expectations about the dynamic consequences of regional integration and the anticipated effects on their assets.

10. John Stuart Mill, *Principles of Political Economy, with Some of Their Applications to Social Philosophy* (book 4, chap. 2, 9), Library of Economics and Liberty, http://www.econlib.org/library/Mill/mlP57.html. Mill adds: "I cannot think, however, that even in manufactures, increased cheapness follows increased production by anything amounting to a law. It is a probable and usual, but not a necessary, consequence."

11. In steel and rubber, there are "economies of vertical integration" because the application of heat can be reduced when all stages of production are performed at one time and place. Chemicals, petroleum, and other refining activities exhibit "economies of increased dimensions" because tank construction costs are a function of surface area, while capacity is a function of volume. In automobiles, machinery, and many electronics, long production runs of standardized articles compensate for indivisibilities in fixed machinery by limiting downtime for recalibration. In each case, overhead costs (for energy, plant, or equipment) increase at less than a one-to-one relationship with output (see Pratten 1971, chap. 1).

ities arise from expenditures for research and development (R&D), product design, and advertising and marketing.[12]

The recognition that most international trade today does not follow patterns of factor scarcity and abundance prompted economists to introduce imperfect competition and scale economies into a series of "new" trade models developed since 1980. These models overturn many of the central tenets of standard trade theory: when markets are imperfect, free trade is not always optimal; comparative advantage, rather than being inherited from factor endowments as part of a country's immutable genetic code, can be shaped by government policy; and historical "accident," first-mover advantages, path dependence, and learning-by-doing upset otherwise predictable patterns of production and trade. Grossman (1992, 1) concludes: "imperfect competition enhances the potential gains from trade but also adds to the list of possible exceptions to the rule."

Three classes of strategic trade models exist in this body of work.[13] Under monopolistic competition, governments can capture economy-wide externalities by assisting activities that disseminate technology and knowledge to upstream or downstream industries. In profit-shifting models (Brander and Spencer 1992), subsidies can deter foreign market entry or limit the output of foreign firms, enabling domestic firms to expand and earn larger profits. In export promotion models (Krugman 1992), import protection encourages domestic firms to increase production of goods with scale economies, reducing their marginal costs until they can profitably export. While these models differ in their assumptions, each concludes that state intervention (under the right conditions) can improve national welfare.[14] Empirical tests are less certain, however: even if strategic policies create spillovers or shift profits, they also distort resource allocation and cause consumption inefficiencies (see Baldwin and Krugman 1988, 1992; Dixit 1992; Dick 1994). Most economists therefore conclude that state intervention under imperfect competition is no better for national welfare than when markets are perfect.

In my argument, producers have incentives to seek government support to

12. Once fixed costs have been paid, there is little marginal cost to deploy R&D embodied in a new invention or to expend advertising and marketing used to create a brand name.

13. According to Brander (1995, 1), "strategic trade policy . . . amounts to the study of trade policy in the presence of oligopoly." These models are "strategic" because producers take into account the behavior of foreign firms and foreign governments when they set prices and output.

14. In the monopolistic competition model, price equals average costs; perfect competition and zero profit conditions hold, but technological spillovers that are *external* to firms exist at the economy-wide level. In the profit-shifting and export promotion models, the excess of price over average cost creates pure profits or rents; competition is imperfect, and the scale economies are *internal* to firms.

help them earn "excess profits,"[15] even if this would attract resources from more productive activities or impose welfare costs on consumers and taxpayers. In particular, I generalize from export promotion models. The potential gains for producers are greatest when the conditions of these models apply. First, scale economies are internal to firms, so the benefits of export promotion policies accrue to incumbent producers in an industry and are not externalized to the economy as a whole. Second, internal economies of scale create entry barriers, so established producers can capture any increase in excess profits because it is costly for new entrants to begin production. Since the potential benefits are large and highly concentrated, the incentives for collective action to influence policy are high.[16]

Economies of Scale

Economies of scale are important to the political economy of trade for two reasons. On the one hand, trade enlarges the available market, which affects plant size. As a result, increased production due to trade reduces unit costs and in so doing yields excess profits. On the other hand, import competition makes it more difficult for domestic producers to price above marginal cost. Trade therefore can limit opportunities to expand production and reduce unit costs, which may force producers to sustain losses.

Theoretical first principles drawn from strategic trade models and studies of industrial organization help to explain domestic support for trading blocs. Figure 2 depicts a stylized cost curve relating average costs to the scale of production. The "minimum efficient scale," or MES (A, A*), is the level of output that minimizes average costs, or the point at which the potential economies of scale have been exhausted. For producers that remain on the downward-sloping portion of the cost curve (for example, at B, B*), some scale economies remain unexploited.

---

15. I use *excess profit* instead of the more conventional *rent* to avoid confusion between motives for protection in alternative trade models. Excess profits exist when price exceeds marginal cost, so producers earn more excess profits the greater their price-cost margin.

16. To extend this reasoning, I would not expect intense policy demands when scale economies are external to firms. In this case, gains from strategic trade policy accrue to producers in upstream industries (when there is technological spillover) or to new entrants (when returns increase with industry size). This limits the benefits of collective action because established firms cannot recoup their lobbying costs. As a result, my focus is the case of internal scale economies, imperfect competition, and pure profit. Within this class, the profit-shifting model is a highly stylized representation, and its results tend to be sensitive to assumptions. Outside of highly concentrated global industries such as aircraft, output and pricing are not so sensitive to government policy because strategic interdependence is less significant with many firms. Thus, I expect domestic interests to be channeled into export promotion.

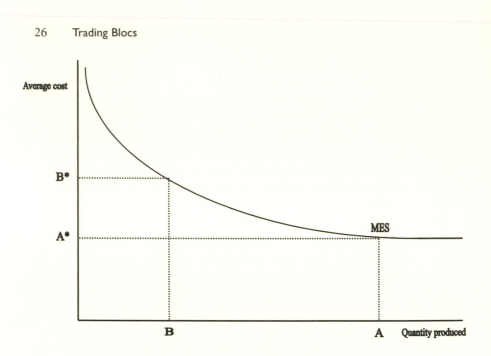

Fig. 2. Average cost with economies of scale

When scale economies have not been fully captured, producers have incentives to seek out a larger customer base to expand product runs. Regional arrangements can provide the larger markets necessary to gain these scale economies. On the one hand, regional trade liberalization opens up new export opportunities. This allows producers to reduce unit costs as output increases to serve regional partners.[17] On the other hand, trading blocs retain barriers against outside competition. External protection ensures that producers in the region fully internalize the scale effects of larger markets, making it possible to leapfrog foreign competitors through import protection as export promotion (cf. Krugman 1992). Regional trade liberalization therefore provides benefits that are not attainable through multilateral liberalization: under MFN rules, external trade barriers must be reduced equally for the imports of all countries; trading blocs, however, allow external protection to remain in place.

In short, producers are more likely to seek trading blocs the greater the cost

17. Corden (1972) identifies two effects when an enlargement of the market enables producers to exploit scale economies. First, there is "cost reduction" when increased output in one country replaces higher-priced, lower-scale production in the region. Second, there is "trade suppression" when increased production in the region replaces imports from outside the region. While these two effects have different implications for consumption, trade, and welfare, both involve unit cost reduction and excess profits for producers. As a result, I do not differentiate between them.

reduction effects they anticipate from regional trade liberalization. These gains are a function of two conditions. The first is the slope of the average cost curve, or simply the *returns to scale*. Second is the *size of the domestic market* available to them.

The *returns to scale* are important because producers gain more from increased scale the steeper the cost curve: each marginal increase in plant size yields more excess profits the larger the returns to scale. The difference in unit costs between producers of different sizes (for example, between A* and B* in fig. 2) denotes the "penalty," or the "cost in terms of reduced efficiency" (Bain 1959, 149), when scale economies are not fully exploited. When the cost curve is steep, this penalty is great, so producers reap large benefits from the opportunity to trade in a broader market. When the cost curve is flat, this penalty is small, so increased scale yields little cost reduction and little additional excess profits.

As a result, producers benefit more from an increase in plant size the steeper the cost curve. According to Silberston (1972, 377–78), "The more steeply the scale curve falls, the greater will be the opportunity for economies of scale, and the greater the impetus for firms to seek markets which transcend . . . national boundaries." If returns to scale are large, producers will support regional trade liberalization to increase output, reduce unit costs, and earn more excess profits. If returns to scale are small, producers will have little interest in a trading bloc because they can derive no benefit from longer production runs or increased capacity utilization. This reasoning leads to the first hypothesis:

HYPOTHESIS 1: *Support for trading blocs increases with the level of the returns to scale.*

Second, *domestic market size* influences support for trading blocs. "International economic competition," Gilpin (2000, 43) explains, "necessitates the availability of large domestic markets that enable domestic firms to achieve economies of scale." A market that is small compared to the potential scale economies "may not permit output at the minimum optimal scale at all, or may only permit output at this scale from a comparatively small number of firms" (Silberston 1972, 389). Producers are at a disadvantage when limited demand prevents them from concentrating production: if there is not enough room in the domestic market to exploit scale economies, they will have high unit costs; this makes it difficult to gain market share abroad to increase output and ride down the cost curve. Producers therefore will be hesitant to expand capacity, purchase new plant and equipment, and the like—even if such investments would maximize efficiency over the long run—because the potential is too great for short-run adjustment costs due to export competition and unused capacity. Instead, they are likely to produce at a suboptimal scale for the home market to minimize risk.

When technology creates opportunities for scale economies but the market is too limited, producers have strong motives to support trading blocs. Simply, an enlarged market allows producers to approach the MES more readily because "[s]teady economic expansion . . . tends to reduce the incidence of uneconomically small operations" (Bain 1959, 167). Opening the regional market while continuing to protect it from external competition makes it easier for businesses to expand production runs, increase capacity utilization, and rationalize production facilities. These in turn reduce unit costs and increase excess profits.

Producers in a geographically limited domestic market might still benefit from a trading bloc even if they already manufacture on a large scale. When small home demand requires producers to export to utilize existing capacity, any loss of foreign market share spreads overhead across a smaller volume of output, which raises unit costs. The risk of this sort of vicious cycle could cause producers to refuse foreign orders that require new plant and equipment or significant retooling. A trading bloc, however, guarantees stable access and insures against the threat that market closure abroad will create unused capacity. This allows large-scale producers in small national markets to make illiquid investments that rely on economies of scale.[18]

To sum up, small-scale producers in small home markets reap the largest benefits from trading blocs because they will have the greatest opportunity to expand capacity and concentrate production. But large-scale producers with small home markets will value the security of a regional arrangement as well, to the extent that they need to maintain foreign market share to capture scale economies. This leads to the second hypothesis:

HYPOTHESIS 2: *Support for trading blocs increases the smaller the domestic market relative to MES.*

Table 3 summarizes the main hypotheses about scale economies and producer support for trading blocs. For simplicity, the table shows continuous variables as binary outcomes. In terms of comparative static analysis, produc-

18. Hence the motives for small countries to reach "safe-haven" arrangements to guarantee secure access to a large market that might soon close (Hindley and Messerlin 1993).

ers with unexploited scale economies have greater incentives to seek regional arrangements the larger the returns to scale and the larger the MES relative to domestic market size. Stated as comparative dynamics, regional trade liberalization becomes more attractive as the MES increases as a share of the domestic market, as the gap between the MES and the scale of production attained widens, and as the returns to scale grow larger.

To provide real-world examples of these outcomes, each of the cells in table 3 includes examples drawn from NAFTA lobbying in chapter 6, since this case will be familiar to many readers. Industries in the United States with large returns to scale and large MES included pharmaceuticals, semiconductors and integrated circuits, computer equipment, farm and construction machinery, automobiles, and home appliances. As the hypotheses predict, representatives of these industries—trade groups such as the Pharmaceutical Manufacturers Association, the Semiconductor Industry Association, and the Automobile Manufacturers Association and companies such as IBM, Hewlett-Packard, Caterpillar, GM, Ford, GE, and Whirlpool—campaigned forcefully for NAFTA. Support for NAFTA was less intense when returns to scale were large but MES small relative to market size (for example, paper products and processed foods) and when MES was large but returns to scale small (plastic products, steel, and consumer electronics). When both MES and returns to scale were small (many

TABLE 3.   Economies of Scale and Preferences for Trading Blocs

Returns to Scale	MES Relative to Domestic Market Size	
	Small	Large
Large	(1) Weak support for trading blocs	(2) Strong support for trading blocs

	NAFTA examples:
	  Paper and paperboard
	  Grain mill products
	  Sugar and confectionery
	  Dairy products
	  Household chemicals
	  Beverages
		NAFTA examples:
		  Pharmaceuticals
		  Semiconductors
		  Computers
		  Construction machinery
		  Automobiles
		  Home appliances

Small	(4) Weak support for trading blocs	(3) Weak support for trading blocs

	NAFTA examples:
	  Cotton fabrics
	  Manmade fiber fabrics
	  Knitted goods
		NAFTA examples:
		  Steel
		  Consumer electronics
		  Plastic products

textile and apparel products), support was tepid, where it existed, and many groups opposed NAFTA.[19]

Cross-Border Capital Flows

Outsourcing and production sharing across borders have grown dramatically in recent years.[20] Standard trade models omit international flows of capital and labor so that trade is simply an exchange of factors of production embodied in finished goods. Neoclassical approaches that allow international factor movements predict capital flows from rich to poor nations in response to barriers to trade in capital-intensive goods.[21]

Clearly, barriers to trade in goods are not the main cause of trade in factors in production. Rather, production sharing occurs because cross-national differences—usually disparities in factor prices—allow certain tasks to be completed more efficiently abroad than at home. In developed countries, manufactured goods with labor-intensive aspects tend to face low-wage competition, especially when technology is standardized, production is difficult to automate, and sales are price-sensitive. Transferring labor-intensive tasks to labor-rich areas enables firms to reduce input prices and cut factor costs. When intermediate production moves to a location where it can be performed more efficiently, the capital- and skill-intensive processes left in the home country become more profitable.

Technological changes have caused production sharing to expand of late. Innovations in shipping, freight, and air travel have reduced the time and cost involved in moving products over long distances. With the advent of computers, satellites, and broadband connectivity, it is easier to coordinate the activities of far-flung affiliates. However, not all producers can relocate abroad to ex-

19. For more on the derivation of these expectations in the NAFTA case, see chapter 6 and especially table 27. The correlation is not perfect; after all, it is not reasonable to expect the theory to explain every case of industry lobbying. Moreover, some industries that the theory would expect to oppose NAFTA still supported it due to considerations not related to scale economies. For example, strict rules of origin and increased outsourcing opportunities (factors discussed in the ensuing sections) eventually won over some sectors of the textile and apparel industries.

20. Feenstra, Hanson, and Swenson (2000, 85) define *outsourcing* as "the practice in which firms divide production into stages and then locate each stage in the country where it can be performed at least cost." I use *production sharing* generally to refer to the participation of multiple countries in different stages of a manufacturing process.

21. This is the "Mundell equivalency," which states that either trade or factor flows can equalize factor prices (Mundell 1957). However, it does not explain why most capital flows occur between developed countries with similar factor endowments.

ploit these opportunities. Production sharing requires the physical separation of different stages of manufacturing, the capacity to specialize discrete processes between locations, and the ability to move intermediate components at acceptable cost. This is most feasible when production involves physically discrete steps, when different stages use different mixes of capital and labor, and when intermediate goods have high market value relative to weight (Grunwald and Flamm 1985).

Across industries, components-intensive electronics, semiconductors, and automobiles tend to be more conducive to production sharing than resource-intensive and energy-intensive metal, rubber, and paper.[22] Because opportunities to specialize across borders are unevenly distributed among industries and firms, production sharing has important effects on the trade preferences of domestic actors.

Production Sharing

Firms engaged in production sharing across borders transfer goods between a corporate parent and its foreign affiliates through intrafirm trade, or they import these inputs from unaffiliated suppliers. Intermediate components tend to be highly specialized and unique to a production process; indeed, many firms invest large sunk costs in products and processes for which no external market exists. Adjusting to any disruption in the flow of inputs across borders requires firms to externalize the market for intermediate goods—that is, share proprietary technology and information with local suppliers, which raises the risk of opportunism and market failure—or to interrupt the production process altogether. Both options are costly. As a result, firms involved in production sharing, especially those that own their suppliers, lack adaptability because their demand for intermediate goods is insensitive to market- or policy-induced changes in price.

Measures to reduce the costs and risks of cross-border trade therefore offer large benefits to firms engaged in production sharing. Helleiner (1977), Milner (1988), and Goodman, Spar, and Yoffie (1996) find that multinationals closely

---

22. Consider metal smelting and rolling versus semiconductor manufacturing. Metal ingots and sheets must be reheated if they cool prior to shaping. This makes it costly to separate production processes. In addition, metals are heavy and therefore expensive to transport, relative to their value. Semiconductor manufacturing, in contrast, involves several distinct steps, with capital-intensive stages (fabrication, testing) and labor-intensive stages (assembly, packaging) that can be easily performed at different places and times while weight-to-value ratios are low (see Caves 1996, 13–19).

integrated with their foreign affiliates tend to be forceful advocates for trade liberalization. When products move across borders between a corporate parent and its affiliates, multinationals "gain *at both ends* from tariff cuts, both as importer and exporter of the same product" (Lavergne 1983, 105). Indeed, multinational firms dependent on production sharing are not only importers or exporters—they are consumers.

Geographic proximity is a key factor in production sharing. Often there are diseconomies of scale in global production networks, so multinationals tend to focus on region-specific sourcing, manufacturing, and marketing (Wells 1992). Locations near the corporate parent offer several benefits: lower transport costs in the movement of goods between home and host countries, easier coordination with suppliers for firms that maintain low inventories and rely on just-in-time delivery systems, and shorter lead times when firms must adapt quickly to changes in demand or consumer tastes. As a result, production sharing primarily crosses borders between neighboring (or nearby) countries. Most large U.S. businesses have established regional production networks in North America during the past thirty years. Recently, Japanese and European firms have extended this practice to East Asia and the European periphery, respectively. In fact, foreign multinationals in North America conduct labor-intensive operations mostly in Mexico and Canada; U.S. multinationals outsource their European production to Italy, Ireland, and Spain.

The regional proximity of the different components of these networks helps to explain why production sharing promotes interest in trading blocs. The most important concern for firms engaged in production sharing is not to liberalize trade worldwide but to liberalize trade across the borders that link their separate investments. Moreover, free trade in goods is necessary but not sufficient to sustain regional production networks. Firms also need "deep integration" to harmonize national standards, establish dispute settlement procedures, eliminate trade-related investment measures (TRIMs), relax restrictions on equity ownership, and protect intellectual property rights (Lawrence 1996).

Multilateral negotiations on these sorts of behind-the-border trade barriers have yielded mixed results to date. In particular, the failure to integrate effective codes on foreign direct investment (FDI) into the WTO agreements has stimulated the pursuit of regional initiatives. If production sharing is internal to a region, regional arrangements will be an attractive institutional framework to liberalize this sort of trade. The potential benefits of liberalization are maximized and the negotiating costs minimized when it occurs regionally rather than through multilateral organizations.

In sum, firms involved in regional production sharing are more likely than those with wholly national operations to support trading blocs.[23] Just as multinationals benefit from internalizing the supply of specialized inputs to forestall disruptions in price or availability, so too do they benefit from policy commitments to forestall government actions that could elevate the costs of procuring these inputs. In this case the motive to lobby for trading blocs is to facilitate deeper integration, not to gain access to a larger protected market.[24] This reasoning leads to the third hypothesis:

HYPOTHESIS 3: *Support for trading blocs increases the more that firms are involved in regional production sharing.*

Domestic Actors and External Trade

In the analytical framework outlined in the last two sections, producers support or oppose trading blocs based on the anticipated distributional effects and the likely opportunities to reorganize production after regional trade liberalization. This framework provides an underpinning for hypotheses about domestic actors' preferences regarding external trade. As producers expand or contract economic operations and reallocate assets to adjust to the new trading environment, incentives for liberalization or protection toward countries outside the region may change. This in turn affects the trade policies domestic actors will seek—and so national decisions at one point in time shape policy into the future.

The task at hand is to specify how domestic actors evaluate their interests in the new trading environment. Most studies focus on the "immediate impact effect" (that is, the static outcome in terms of trade creation and trade diversion), but scholars are less certain about the "dynamic time path" that determines whether regional arrangements promote or retard multilateral integration (Bhagwati 1993, 31–35). Even if it is possible to distinguish which domestic actors support regional arrangements to satisfy protectionist motives and which desire further liberalization, there is the possibility of imperfect foresight. Because economic conditions are different once a trading bloc is formed,

23. To clarify, producers base their trade preferences on expectations about future economic opportunities as well as past investment decisions. If firms anticipate that a regional arrangement will promote the development of regional supply chains by opening up opportunities for intrafirm trade, then they are likely to support regional trade liberalization.

24. Cox (1996) suggests that external protectionism was a central motive in NAFTA lobbying by "regionalists" such as the U.S. automobile and electronics industries. This assessment, however, rests on their previous support for trade protection, not their involvement in production sharing per se.

domestic actors will have some uncertainty *ex ante* about how such an arrangement affects their interests.

Imperfect foresight is important because the previous section suggests that
the main supporters of regional trade liberalization are producers that anticipate opportunities to reorganize operations to gain scale economies or increase
production sharing (or both). This does not guarantee that they will be able to
do so, however. Any number of factors can intervene in the restructuring
process to produce results that were unexpected at an earlier point in time.
Thus, the effect of regional arrangements on policy toward external trade is an
empirical question—but one that first requires basic theoretical principles to
illuminate potential answers.

This section presents a series of hypotheses about protectionist pressures in
trading blocs. First, domestic actors with a weak competitive position will seek
protectionist measures against outside trade the more that regional trade liberalization increases import competition. Second, domestic actors that can reorganize to gain scale economies or establish production-sharing networks are
likely to become more favorable to multilateral liberalization. If these producers are not able to expand production runs or increase outsourcing, however,
then preexisting support for external protection will persist. Third, to the extent that regional integration attracts FDI from outside the region, domestic
actors are less likely to push for external tariffs and nontariff barriers. Instead,
they will tend to seek regulatory rules and TRIMs to limit foreign entry.

Import Competition and Trade Protection

In the perfectly competitive industries characterized in the standard trade
model, regional integration will not enhance productivity because cost curves
are flat and firms cannot engage in production sharing between labor-rich and
labor-scarce areas. In this case, domestic actors cannot capture any of the dynamic gains previously emphasized as an important motive for regional trade
liberalization. As a result, producers respond to one-time shifts in the source of
supply of goods (trade creation and trade diversion), and external trade preferences simply reflect factor cost considerations embodied in an industry's export orientation or its exposure to import penetration.

But even when forming a trading bloc does not trigger cost reduction, it can
intensify the pressure on domestic actors already disadvantaged in global competition. For this reason, import-competing producers that would enjoy reduced protection after regional trade liberalization are likely to resist it, or to at
least seek special exemptions to prevent or delay free trade in their products

(Grossman and Helpman 2002). If that fails, these firms have incentives to transform trade creation into trade diversion by lobbying to restrict third-country trade to compensate for intensified competition and lower prices after regional trade protection is lost (Bhagwati 1993, 36–37).[25]

HYPOTHESIS 4: *Industries that fail to secure exemptions for their products will lobby for more external trade protection the larger the increase in import competition after regional integration.*

If dynamic gains can be achieved through restructuring, however, domestic actors update their trade preferences as they adjust to the new trading environment after regional integration. When firms reorganize to exploit scale economies or increase production sharing, unit costs decline. Lowered unit costs alleviate the need for external trade protection because producers can compete more effectively in world markets. Under these conditions, domestic actors will become more favorable to external liberalization after the formation of a trading bloc.

Scale Economies and Trade Protection

Conventional wisdom holds that intraindustry trade produces no adjustment costs: as trade expands, producers differentiate their goods to compete on quality and variety rather than price. On this basis, work in political economy often suggests that the growth of intraindustry trade reduces domestic interests in trade protection.[26]

However, this is not a plausible description of the competitive effects of trading blocs. Regional trade liberalization places small-scale producers under stress from firms that can expand scale to the enlarged market; as competition increases and prices decline, these inefficient producers face pressure to accept a takeover or exit production (Müller and Owen 1989, 175–77). As this process unfolds, expanding firms absorb the manufacturing facilities of producers that are selling off their assets (unless these are converted to other activities or de-

25. Though it is possible that increased regional competition would weaken import-competing industries too much to successfully undertake a protectionist campaign (cf. Richardson 1993; Hathaway 1998), this is likely to be an unusual result that only occurs over the long run.

26. A justification for this is Krugman's (1981) theory of monopolistic competition, in which the gains from larger markets (greater product variety and larger-scale production) outweigh the income distribution effects. In this model, firms specialize in different products mixes; no producer loses market share or faces the prospect of elimination through import competition, so there is no pressure to reallocate assets into other activities.

molished and sold for scrap) and streamline these plants with their existing operations. Thus, trade liberalization with imperfect competition is not painless: some producers expand to gain scale economies in an integrated regional market; others become targets of mergers and acquisitions, or simply lose business and go bankrupt.

In the period when production is being rescaled for a regional market, firms are likely to favor the preservation of external trade barriers to block foreign competition while they restructure—indeed, this is a key incentive for regional arrangements over multilateral liberalization. Transitional protection is especially attractive when production in a region has been fragmented through FDI. In an integrated regional market, firms would centralize manufacturing for the entire region in a few locations to maximize scale economies. But preexisting trade barriers and TRIMs impede efforts to concentrate production because they encourage firms to operate plants in the market of final sale. Phasing out these measures leaves multinational firms with geographically dispersed factories that are functionally separated from one another and scaled for national rather than regional markets. Because manufacturing must be integrated regionally, functions specialized by location, and output concentrated, incumbent firms face heavy short-term restructuring expenses.[27] To compensate for this liability, producers that must reorganize across borders after regional trade liberalization are likely to favor protection against outside imports, at least while they adjust their operations.

When will protection provide a "helping hand along the learning curve" (Lipson 1982, 433) and when might it become a permanent dispensation for uncompetitive firms? In terms of comparative static analysis, producers need import barriers when unit costs exceed world prices so they can price above marginal cost; when unit costs are lower than world prices, producers tend to favor trade liberalization (at least on a reciprocal basis).[28] Unit costs in turn reflect the position on the cost curve relative to foreign competitors. If firms manufacture in short production runs, they will have high unit costs; foreigners will be able to sell in the region more cheaply, so domestic firms will have incentives to seek external trade protection. If over time firms are able to

27. In a standard model of FDI and trade as substitutes, liberalization allows multinationals to close inefficient plants and divest from host markets to centralize manufacturing in the home country. However, the fixed costs of establishing foreign affiliates are difficult to recover. As a result, multinational firms are more likely to specialize and integrate their operations than to end foreign production.

28. Trade protection provides rents, but it also interferes with foreign market access if it incites retaliation (Milner and Yoffie 1989).

achieve large-scale production compared to producers in other countries, then they will enjoy relatively low unit costs. At this point the need for trade protection diminishes.

Viewed dynamically, regional integration can be export promoting, as the opportunity to expand production lowers marginal costs until firms can profitably export beyond the region.[29] If this sort of restructuring takes place, protectionist pressure is likely to dissipate. Regional integration also can be export deterring, as it may promote oligopoly and inefficient entry rather than improved productivity (Horstmann and Markusen 1986; Dick 1994). If producers fail to gain significant scale economies, they will need continued trade protection to maintain domestic and regional market shares.

Thus, producers become more favorable to multilateral liberalization when conditions to exploit scale economies are present in regional arrangements. At the margin, producers will seek less external trade protection the more they experience cost reduction—that is, the greater the increase in the scale of output and the larger the returns to scale. The scale of output increases in greater increments the larger the regional market and the more integrated this market after regional trade liberalization. In short, regional market size and the level of internal liberalization generally determine the extent to which conditions to exploit scale economies are satisfied.

To summarize, the combined market after regional trade liberalization must be large enough and sufficiently integrated for firms to be able to expand production or specialize activities between parent plants and foreign affiliates. As this restructuring proceeds and firms gain scale economies, the need for trade protection declines. In this case, external barriers in trading blocs merely provide "breathing room" to prepare firms to compete more vigorously on a global scale. However, if the regional market is too small or internal liberalization is incomplete, then producers will not be able to achieve cost reduction. Under these conditions, firms will develop a vested interest in regional trade protection to reap monopoly rents that global trade liberalization would bid away.

HYPOTHESIS 5: *Producers with unexploited scale economies will seek to preserve external trade barriers. Over time, producers that gain scale economies inside a trading bloc will become more favorable to external liberalization.*

---

29. Krugman (1992, 80) explains, "the circular causation from output to marginal cost to output makes import protection an export promotion device."

Production Sharing and Trade Protection

Some analysts suggest that firms with regional supply networks have no interest in policies toward cross-regional trade. Since multinationals trade little
across continents, Wells (1992) argues, they regard the prospect of increased
protection between trading blocs with a "big yawn." However, if foreign competitors service regional markets through exports rather than local production,
firms already based in the region can earn rents from trade protection. Thus, it
is important to consider how regional production sharing affects preferences
toward external trade.

To the extent that increased offshore procurement reduces factor costs, the
effect on trade preferences should be the same as when producers gain scale
economies. If firms successfully integrate intermediate goods production between parent plants and foreign affiliates, they are likely to lose interest in trade
protection and become more favorable to multilateral liberalization. If economic and regulatory barriers to production sharing persist, however, firms
will continue to face competitive pressure from foreign producers with lower
comparative costs.[30] To the extent that regional arrangements fail to provide
deeper integration and policy harmonization, multinational firms will have
difficulty specializing operations between labor-rich and labor-scarce areas.
Under these conditions, their interest in external trade protection is not likely
to diminish.

HYPOTHESIS 6: *Firms that deepen production sharing after regional integration will become more favorable to external liberalization.*

Inward FDI and Trade Protection

The benefits of trading blocs for local producers—an enlarged, integrated market with barriers to outside imports—also serve as inducements to firms headquartered in other regions. Regional integration tends to stimulate inward FDI
when the unique advantages of foreign firms (proprietary technologies, managerial skills and practices, brand name recognition, advertising advantages,

---

30. A number of factors can undermine corporate restructuring after regional trade liberalization: an unstable investment climate, barriers to capital movements or profit repatriation, poor
transportation networks and customs delays (which interfere with just-in-time delivery systems
and continuous flow technologies), competing production structures among the countries in a region (which reduce factor cost differences), labor laws that prevent firms from adjusting skill ratios across plants through layoffs, and so on.

networks of suppliers and customers, and so on) can be easily deployed abroad. Global capital mobility therefore creates opportunities for multinationals outside an integrating region to relocate inside the trading bloc to benefit from regional trade liberalization.

This poses a problem for producers already established in the region. For one, inward FDI makes it difficult for incumbent firms to capture the gains from regional integration. When foreign firms substitute production in the region for imports from the outside, local producers reap less benefit from external trade protection: new entrants raise their prices to share in protectionist rents, while fewer imports arrive from outside the region to pay the tax.[31] Moreover, firms in industries with large returns to scale will have difficulty concentrating production if foreign competitors can gain market shares through FDI because entry pushes producers already established in the region up their cost curves. Finally, incumbents will be at a disadvantage if competitors can build state-of-the-art factories while they are trying to rationalize and streamline outmoded operations.

When production is internationally mobile, rules of origin and other TRIMs make it possible for incumbents to capture a larger share of the gains from regional integration. These measures protect local production because they deter FDI by foreign competitors that are not able to meet the requirements at acceptable cost. Rules of origin, for example, target companies that produce a certain share of value content or perform specific technical processes outside the region—usually (though not necessarily) foreign multinationals—by denying them free trade privileges. While rules of origin are generally designed to block transshipment when there are tariff differentials among the members of a trading bloc, their use as an entry restriction has received less attention.[32] Absent guarantees that new entrants will not be able to share in the benefits of regional integration, established firms are not likely to undertake costly investments to reorganize their operations. Forcing outsiders to pay an entry fee (that is, to source higher-cost local inputs) channels rents to incumbent firms that already have met these criteria. Excludability in turn limits free

31. As a result, studies suggest that protectionist lobbies are less effective when capital is mobile internationally. Grossman and Helpman (1996) suggest that FDI intensifies free riding in the domestic industry because entrants can share in the benefits of a lobbying campaign after the costs have been paid. Froot and Yoffie (1993) emphasize foreign entry, which they contend bids away the rents to local owners of capital.

32. Cadot, de Melo, and Olarreaga (2001) argue that restraining transshipment to preserve protectionist rents helps to neutralize opposition to a free trade agreement from import-competing industries. Krueger (1999) emphasizes incentives to export protection to regional partners through rules of origin.

riding, so the potential for entry barriers against outsiders makes it easier to mobilize lobbying efforts to liberalize trade and FDI regionally.

In sum, inward FDI—or the threat of it—is likely to defuse pressure for traditional forms of protection such as tariffs and nontariff barriers. But producers in industries with large returns to scale and internationally mobile capital will tend to seek origin rules to restrict foreign entry while they streamline operations, eliminate outmoded factories, and integrate production networks inside a trading bloc.

HYPOTHESIS 7: *If the formation of a trading bloc is likely to stimulate FDI from outside the region, industries will tend to seek TRIMs to limit foreign entry.*[33]

Moving from Trade Preferences to Policy Outcomes

The explanatory framework detailed in the preceding pages focuses on producers' trade preferences. To complete the argument, it is necessary to analyze how domestic actors organize into groups and work within policy-making processes to influence national policy choices. This requires attention to the collective action problems and political institutions that domestic actors face.

In the mobilization of domestic actors into groups, two relevant considerations are excludability and the cost of organizing a group (Alt and Gilligan 1994). Trade policy resembles a public good because its effects are not excludable—nobody can be prevented from sharing in the benefits after lobbying expenses have been paid. This creates collective action problems, notably free riding. In addition, it is costly to organize a group when many actors are involved and when production is dispersed geographically or economically (Olson 1965).

Excludability varies, at least in part, with factor specificity. As stated previously, domestic actors tend to organize as factors of production (capital, labor) when factors are mobile, and as sectors (textiles, automobiles) when factors are industry specific.[34] All else equal, it is more difficult for factors than for sectors to mobilize a lobbying campaign due to free riding (Alt and Gilligan 1994, 183–85).

---

33. This hypothesis is general to both free trade areas and customs unions. While rules of origin have attracted more attention in free trade areas like NAFTA, the EU case in chapter 5 shows that they are important to the workings of customs unions as well. Because there are incentives to limit foreign entry even when external trade practices have been fully harmonized, TRIMs will not necessarily be more prevalent in free trade areas than in customs unions.

34. The discussion in this chapter focuses on private firms (that is, owners of capital and land), but not labor. Chase (2003, 147–49) develops the analytical framework's implications for labor union preferences and whether groups will lobby as factors or sectors.

The framework presented here is consistent with the specific factors approach, though it is not derived from standard trade models. Work on industrial organization finds that scale economies and entry barriers tend to coexist (Stigler 1968; Caves and Porter 1976). Theories of FDI (e.g., Caves 1996) also emphasize specific assets, entry barriers, and imperfect competition. While to date these theories have not been formally integrated, they point in the same direction: high levels of factor specificity.

Factor specificity with imperfect competition has important implications for the organization of domestic actors into groups. On the one hand, it eases collective action because policy benefits are more excludable. Trade policy in imperfectly competitive industries "is virtually a private good" because the effects "are highly concentrated on single firms" (Gilligan 1997, 456, 464). Individual firms (or small groups of like firms) can more easily absorb the costs and internalize the benefits of their political activity. This alleviates free riding and increases the incentives to lobby.

On the other hand, factor specificity may lead to firm-based rather than sector-based lobbying. Sectors can be composed of firms with a range of unit costs if producers operate plants that vary in scale or the level of offshore procurement. Since these are characteristics of firms—and individual firms rather than sectors as a whole internalize the effects of policies that facilitate scale economies and outsourcing—industry solidarity could break down. It therefore is not clear that the sector is the relevant unit of analysis with imperfect competition.[35] The book's theory anticipates both industry-based and firm-based lobbying, but does not distinguish when one or the other will occur. In the end this is an empirical question, and disagreements between particular firms, and between firms and their trade association, are noted in the case studies when they arise.

Whether domestic actors lobby as sectors or firms matters only insofar as it affects their ability to influence policy. In practice, divisions between firms in the same sector may not be exposed in trade lobbying because producers have incentives to lobby as sectors even when policy effects are not felt at the associational level.[36] For example, trade associations tend to present a united front to maximize their weight in the policy process. To the extent that they do not, opposing interests will cancel out, undermining the political strength of the lobby group.

35. Even with interindustry trade, conflicts of interest between firms in the same industry are more common than standard trade models allow because markets can be segmented and products differentiated.

36. Milner (1988) studies characteristics of individual firms (export dependence and multinationality) and finds a high degree of coherence in business groups and industry associations.

Imperfect competition also affects the cost of organizing a group. If collective action costs are low, large, encompassing groups such as grassroots lobbies and political parties tend to be powerful. Small, concentrated pressure groups will have more political strength when collective action costs are high (Alt and Gilligan 1994). In these circumstances, industrial and geographic concentration will make it easier to influence policy.

In addition, however, collective action costs interact with political institutions. In democratic systems, politicians benefit (in terms of campaign contributions, for example) from the provision of sector-specific policies to organized groups, but they also face electoral constraints from voters and taxpayers who can penalize them for directing rents to special interests. Institutional analysis suggests that winner-take-all systems in particular reward concentrated interests, so long as these are dispersed across electoral districts (Rogowski 1987).[37] In undemocratic systems, well-connected interests benefit from the absence of established channels for exerting political pressure (due to voting restrictions, restraints on assembly, and the weakness of parties and intermediate associations) because these make collective action difficult for groups that face high organization costs.

This discussion suggests that imperfectly competitive industries are likely to enjoy organizational advantages, particularly in institutional environments that reward special interests over the median voter and concentrated rather than dispersed groups. In imperfect markets, a few large firms dominate. These types of industries ordinarily have small numbers of actors, concentrated interests, and firms with substantial resources at their disposal—all of which facilitate effective organization and political clout. In short, firms that are powerful in the market also are likely to be powerful in politics.

To summarize, the analysis proceeds from two sets of expectations about the organization of domestic actors into groups and their ability to influence policy. First, domestic actors in imperfectly competitive industries may have incentives to lobby as firms rather than as sectors. But even when firms in the same industry do not organize collectively, they will be able to mobilize political pressure to the extent that they are individually large and concentrated. Second, large employment size and concentration in production and physical space are likely to be associated with influence over government policy, particularly when collective action costs are high. Thus, "[t]he policy and political

37. Geographic dispersion is most influential in majoritarian systems with low party discipline (such as the United States) because geographically dispersed groups wield the greatest strength in the legislature (McGillivray 1997).

concerns of specific and concentrated economic sectors are expected to dominate in most instances" (Frieden 1991, 9).

Ultimately, however, moving from trade preferences to national policy outcomes is difficult. Coalition-building processes are notoriously difficult to predict, policy-making institutions tend to be unique to each country, and so
many other causal forces intervene. Because of these challenges, few scholars
systematically examine both the demand and supply side of domestic politics.[38] The approach in this book is not to attempt new theoretical claims but
rather to use the generalizations about collective action outlined in the preceding to provide descriptive insights into the politics underlying policy outcomes in the countries under examination. In some instances, such as the interwar German case in chapter 3 and U.S. policy before 1934 in chapter 4, gaps
between group preferences and policy outcomes are visible. Yet even where the
analysis cannot fully explain national policy choices, it is clear that the factors
on which the theory focuses played a key role.

Methods of Research

The book's analytical framework illuminates domestic actors' incentives to support or oppose regional trade liberalization and to seek an increase or a reduction in regional trade barriers. The case studies subject these hypotheses to
systematic scrutiny. This involves two research tasks. First, the framework's observable implications for the trade preferences of domestic actors in a given
country must be specified. Second, these expectations must be evaluated against
the actual behavior of organized groups.

The primary independent variables are technological features of production
that are distributed unevenly across industries: the size and extent of scale
economies and the capacity for production sharing. These variables can be
measured (though not always with precision) with data available in industrial
censuses and national trade statistics.

Measuring Economies of Scale

When there is the potential for scale economies, unit costs differ across plants
(or firms) manufacturing the same product in different volumes. Analysts cannot observe long-run average cost curves, however, so they have developed in-

---

38. Previous studies (e.g., Milner 1988; Rogowski 1989; Frieden 1991) evaluate domestic actors' raw preferences or assume that preferences alone determine policy.

direct methods of evaluation. This study draws primarily from engineering estimates, which estimate returns to scale and MES plant sizes from the unit cost data of engineers who design and construct factories. The MES is expressed in terms of annual output of an article by weight or number. The returns to scale are the elasticity of costs with respect to scale—usually the percentage increase in unit costs at one-half or one-third MES.

Because this method involves immense data burdens, information is available for a limited range of products.[39] Most of the available estimates were made between 1956 and 1975.[40] Because of changes in technology, these data probably reflect MES levels larger than those that prevailed before World War II. Developments in the last two decades also may call into question the validity of these measures. Recently, "flexible manufacturing systems" have emerged, particularly in capital goods industries using complex machinery to perform repetitive tasks (such as cutting, forming, welding, or assembling metal). Some analysts argue that flexible manufacturing has reduced the need for mass production. In this view, replacing large, specialized machinery with more adaptable equipment (numerically controlled machine tools, computer-aided design and manufacturing systems, industrial robotics, and the like) has enabled firms to shorten production runs or reduce batch sizes to differentiate products, minimize inventory and overhead, and limit the risk of excess capacity.

In many industries, however, technological changes have increased rather than reduced MES production levels. In synthetic fibers, the lowest-cost output per plant is at least 150 million pounds today, compared to 40 million pounds in the 1950s. In chemical intermediates such as ethylene and ammonia, MES levels increased from one hundred thousand tons to five hundred thousand tons. MES output for an integrated steelworks grew to six to nine million tons with the advent of basic oxygen furnaces and continuous casting. Radial technology for steel-belted tires also increased optimal plant sizes significantly. New consumer goods such as personal computers, videocassette recorders, and cellular telephones also have exhibited rising MES levels with standardization for mass markets.

Thus, there is little reason to believe that scale economies have diminished in importance. Unfortunately, MES statistics for a large number of industries

39. Observations must cover plants using the same technology and paying the same factor prices to control for external influences on production costs. As Bain (1959, 346) notes, "random differences in rates of utilization, techniques employed, wages or material prices paid" can introduce measurement error into these estimates.

40. Pratten (1988) compiles the results of numerous studies, including Bain 1959; Scherer 1970; Pratten 1971; and Scherer et al. 1975.

at several points in time simply do not exist. This makes empirical work challenging, but even estimates from a single point in time provide valuable insights.[41]

The appendix describes the method implemented in chapters 3 and 4 to measure an industry's scale position. In addition, chapter 6 employs a more direct method for estimating the returns to scale (a technique that requires large amounts of data, which are available only for the United States). Wherever possible, the cases also supplement engineering data with qualitative evidence from industry studies.

The framework's predictions are that producers will support regional trade liberalization when returns to scale are large and the MES is a significant proportion of the domestic market. Stated as comparative dynamics, producers are likely to become interested in trading blocs when returns to scale increase or MES levels grow. Pressure for external trade protection depends on the scale firms already have attained compared to foreign rivals. The greater the increase in scale after regional trade liberalization or the larger the regional market relative to the MES, the more it is likely that protectionism will diminish over time. But if the regional market is small and scale does not increase, then pressure for external trade barriers will persist or intensify.

Measuring Production Sharing

The technological features conducive to production sharing also are difficult to measure directly. For the most part, governments other than the United States do not collect data on outsourcing trade. Production sharing was generally uncommon before the 1960s, and so while chapter 3 presents qualitative details about FDI in specific industries where available, there is little evidence to suggest that this was a strong motive for interwar-era trading blocs.

For more recent periods, chapters 5 through 7 infer offshore manufacturing from trade flows and FDI stocks. A useful proxy is intrafirm trade as a percentage of domestic sales. Otherwise, foreign production in combination with trade patterns provides inferences about the level of production sharing. In industries with substantial foreign production and large trade shares in total output, offshore manufacturing is likely to be high. If there is significant foreign production with small amounts of two-way trade, or little foreign production

41. Another method is "survivor tests," which observe changes over time in the distribution of plants across size classes. But these produce crude and often indeterminate results, as usually there are multiple-size classes compatible with the definition of optimal plant size (see Stigler 1968, 71–73; Pratten 1971, 27–28).

at all, then offshore manufacturing is low. These measures at least should be correlated with unobservable production-sharing patterns.

The framework's observable implication is that firms in industries involved in outsourcing activity are likely to be the most favorable to regional trade liberalization to further develop regional production networks. Thus, support for trading blocs will tend to increase the greater the level of intrafirm trade in total output and the larger the share of foreign production in total sales. Over time, firms are likely to exert less pressure for external trade barriers the more that involvement in production sharing reduces labor costs. If outsourcing trade does not increase, firms will not curtail past protectionism.

Other Independent Variables

In perfectly competitive industries, proxies for comparative costs such as import penetration and export orientation provide the basis for expectations about domestic actors' trade preferences. Producers with a high export to output ratio are likely to be favorable to trading blocs the more these exports are regionally concentrated; if exports are destined for markets outside the region, producers will tend to oppose regional integration out of concern for foreign retaliation. In industries with a high import to consumption ratio, producers are more likely to oppose the formation of a trading bloc the larger the proportion of total imports from countries in the region. Over time, protectionist pressures are likely to intensify the more that regional trade liberalization enhances competition—that is, the greater the increase in imports to consumption.

Dependent Variables

The case chapters evaluate the strength of the association between the independent variables and the policy demands of domestic actors. The policy demands of domestic actors are then employed to explain national trade policy choices. The analysis has two objectives. First, it seeks to demonstrate a correlation between the hypothesized causal variables and organized group behavior. Second, the case studies illuminate how policy demands by domestic actors subsequently influence national policy choices

The book employs several techniques to evaluate the primary dependent variable, the policy demands of domestic groups. The case studies present material from public hearings, policy reviews, and other reports of political activity by organized groups, firms, and labor unions. Petitions to government agencies provide information about groups seeking special measures to gain access to markets abroad or restrict foreign imports into the domestic market (for example, through antidumping relief or a tariff increase). Where useful, the cases also employ archival records and secondary sources such as corporate histories and participant accounts of trade policy-making.

National policy choices can be more readily observed and measured. Treaties disclose the extent and pace of trade liberalization in regional arrangements, the origin rules and content requirements for each product, and relevant understandings regarding external trade protection. Changes in tariff rates and nontariff barriers (at the national level in free trade areas and regionally in customs unions) also are widely available.

Table 4 summarizes the variables in the study and the methods of measurement.

Omitted Variables

The explanatory variables in the analytical framework are not exhaustive, but they do help to explain the phenomena under examination—the formation and evolution of trading blocs. Clearly there are important geopolitical factors involved in this process as well. Regional trade agreements are international treaties. Interstate bargaining no doubt influences the pace and scope of internal liberalization and the level of external tariffs. In the course of negotiations, concentrated domestic groups might not dominate if there is a need to trade

TABLE 4.   Variables and Methods of Measurement

	Methods of Measurement
Dependent Variable	
Group lobbying	Qualitative determination based on government documents, company petitions, industry studies, and secondary sources
External trade barriers	Nominal tariff rates in national tariff code
	Duties collected divided by imports
	Counts of industry nontariff barrier petitions
	Nontariff barrier coverage ratios
Independent Variable	
Returns to scale	Engineering production function estimates
	Elasticity of value added per worker with respect to plant size
MES	Engineering production function estimates
Market size	Domestic sales plus imports minus exports
Production sharing	Intrafirm trade or outsourcing trade divided by total shipments
Import competition	Imports divided by consumption
Export dependence	Exports divided by total shipments
Inward FDI	Foreign firms' share of total shipments

off opposing interests to reach an agreement that satisfies each country's win-set. Evaluating the extent to which variations in policy reflect bargaining at the interstate level would require attention to factors in the strategic environment. However, strategic interaction between members of a trading bloc is left for others to address so that the main puzzle can be defined and analyzed in a manageable way.

Along with interstate bargaining, a range of factors such as cultural affinity, emulation, common development programs (import substitution in the 1960s, market-based reform in the 1990s), concerns about access to strategic materials, and political-military relations have influenced national decisions in trade policy. Unique features of regional arrangements are noted where relevant, but they are not integrated into the explanatory framework. This is problematic only if alternative explanations are less idiosyncratic than believed and if one or more outperforms mine. Even if interest group support is not always sufficient to explain national choices for regional integration, the book seeks to establish that it is necessary.

The Case Studies

The case chapters focus on large countries in the world's major trading regions. In the end, the emergence of trading blocs has reflected the efforts of key large states: without Britain, there would have been no commonwealth; without Japan, no East Asian Co-Prosperity Sphere; without the United States, no NAFTA.

The cases have been selected to illuminate differences across countries in the choice to form or not to form a trading bloc. Examples of countries with weak domestic pressure for regionalism permit counterfactual inferences about the conditions that cause states to deviate from a multilateral orientation. Since all domestic actors manufacturing tradable goods should have preferences over trade policy, country cases are free of bias as long as they include industries with the different economic characteristics outlined in the argument. Within countries, variation also exists across industries in the scope of regional trade liberalization and the level of external trade barriers.

The Interwar Period

After World War I, new manufacturing techniques required mass production to be profitably employed. During the 1920s, automakers and machinery producers introduced assembly lines; steelmakers built continuous strip mills; high-pressure chemical synthesis and larger tanks for refining liquids appeared in dyes, fibers, and fertilizers; and scale, R&D, and learning became critical in electrical and electronic equipment. Advances in rail transport and shipping made it easier for firms to concentrate production and market their goods on a wider scale. In response, factories increased dramatically in size.

The twenty years after World War I also witnessed an upsurge of protectionism, territorial expansion, and commercial discrimination. Japan imposed the world's highest tariffs in the 1920s and then sought to expand the boundaries of its empire through conquest. Britain abandoned free trade with the General Tariff and Imperial Preference. Germany used bilateral agreements to gain markets in central Europe and adopted strict exchange controls, culminating in the New Plan of 1934. These "1930s-model" blocs were "territorial in scope" and "tightly organized and politically circumscribed" (Frankel and Kahler 1993, 6). Imperial blocs typically raised tariffs against outsiders more than they reduced them internally, so trade destruction dominated trade creation (Eichengreen and Irwin 1995).

The United States instead pursued MFN-based trade liberalization in the years after the Smoot-Hawley tariff. Most U.S. producers had reached a high rate of output in an enormous national market, so they had no need for trade protection. Elsewhere, small-scale producers faced intense foreign competition, usually from the United States, and they struggled to gain market shares to sustain mass production. In Japan and Britain, firms with small plants sought to gain scale economies in trading blocs sheltered by high tariff walls; German heavy industry supported trade treaties in central Europe. The case studies trace how trade policy in these three countries responded to political pressure from industry groups that were disadvantaged in global competition due to small-scale production and geographically limited national markets.

The Postwar Period

In the last half century, reduced transport and communication costs with the advent of transoceanic air travel, the microchip, satellites, and the Internet have made it possible to specialize and coordinate production across borders and over long distances. These developments have extended the range of the available market and increased plant sizes in activities with large returns to scale. FDI also has grown as capital and technology have become more mobile internationally. Many multinationals have rationalized their operations to concentrate production and relocate labor-intensive tasks to labor-rich areas. These trends have unleashed intrafirm trade flows as intermediate inputs cross borders for assembly and final sale.

With the establishment of production-sharing networks, regional arrangements have provided a framework to ensure access to a regional market from one central location, free movement of intermediate goods within a company, and guarantees for FDI. Contemporary trading blocs have been oriented primarily toward eliminating "behind-the-border" distortions that inhibit multinational corporate expansion. The main purpose of the EC's single-market program was to harmonize product standards and eliminate the externalities of national control over nontariff barriers so that firms could rescale production for the regional market. In North America, multinationals sought free trade between the United States, Canada, and Mexico to liberalize FDI, strengthen intellectual property rights, and introduce dispute settlement procedures. Only in East Asia, where Japanese companies established regional supply networks only recently, has broad-based domestic pressure for regional integration failed to materialize.

These regional arrangements need not preclude further trade liberalization at the global level. Definitely there are exclusive elements in all regional arrangements. But domestic interests in trade liberalization regionally rather than globally are not necessarily protectionist in their motives. In fact, the book suggests that trading blocs can help to prepare companies—and countries—to compete more vigorously internationally. As producers gain scale economies and deepen production sharing, the need for protection against outsiders diminishes. When these adjustments occur, regional arrangements advance progress toward multilateral trade liberalization more than they undermine it.

The book's broader implication is that understanding the political consequences of globalization, both today and in the 1930s, requires that scholars evaluate the effects of market integration and technological change on microeconomic interests, as well as the impact of shifting preferences and domestic coalitions on policy responses at the national level. Studies that focus on the interests and actions of nation states fail to illuminate these internal political struggles. A few studies have noted the significance of scale economies and FDI in the political economy of trade, but none of this work integrates the dynamic benefits central to the formation of trading blocs into a single analytical framework. This book incorporates these factors into a domestic theory of trade preferences. The chapters that follow demonstrate that the analytical framework helps to explain political demands and national policies across a broad array of countries and time.

CHAPTER 3

Interwar Trading Blocs
Japan, Britain, and Germany, 1919–39

The collapse of the world economy into protectionism and trading blocs in the 1930s remains a mystery. An open, multilateral trading system built around a network of MFN trade treaties flourished from 1860 to 1913, but this commercial order never was restored after World War I. All but a few countries imposed higher tariffs in 1928 than they had in 1913 (Liepmann 1938). During the 1930s, states widely abrogated trade treaties and renounced MFN commitments. Tariffs, quotas, import licenses, exchange controls, and barter deals compartmentalized trade within formal and informal empires or blocked it altogether. On the eve of World War II, world trade flows were meager and heavily regionalized.

This chapter employs the theory developed in chapter 2 to explain trade policies in Japan, Britain, and Germany. The case studies highlight two important motives in domestic group lobbying in these countries. First, firms with low production volumes sought trade protection to compensate for high unit costs. Small size was most prevalent in products with the largest returns to scale, magnifying the need for trade barriers. Second, small home markets caused many firms to campaign to enlarge empires and form trading blocs. Thus, enthusiasm for imperial protection in domestic politics reflected small-scale production and limited national markets in industries facing competitive pressure to expand.

Industries with large returns to scale were not the only ones engaged in the policy process in these three countries. In each case, import-competing groups supported tariff increases but showed little enthusiasm for trading blocs; export-oriented groups opposed high tariffs and regarded trading blocs ambivalently. Several factors helped industries with large returns to scale build coalitions to influence policy, even though institutional structures in these countries differed. For one, industrial and geographic concentration facilitated collective action. In addition, supporters of imperial protection joined forces with other groups (usually farmers) whose policy interests could be reconciled with their own. Finally, control over dual-use technologies critical to military procurement elevated the political standing of heavy industry in Japan and Germany, where governments made rearmament a high priority.

Understanding why these three countries embraced imperial trading blocs helps to illuminate important factors in the multilateral system's collapse in this era. The causal sequence in the book's argument—from preferences to politics to policy—demonstrates how trade protection and imperial blocs responded to politically powerful domestic interests. Of the interwar trading blocs, Japan's was the first and the most exclusive, as tariffs increased steadily after 1923 and efforts to expand the empire through conquest followed in 1931. Britain maintained an open economy until 1931 but then abandoned nearly a century of free trade with the General Tariff and Imperial Preference. The Nazi regime in Germany used exchange controls to block imports and bilateral agreements to expand markets in central Europe after 1933. The chapter addresses these three cases in sequence, following a review of industrial and technological conditions in the wake of the Great War.

Technological Change and Economies of Scale

A series of developments in industry, technology, and markets around the turn of the century dramatically increased optimal scales in many manufacturing activities. The extension of electricity supply through the construction of new plants and the creation of large grids shifted energy away from steam power, making it easier for firms to employ continuous flow methods. The advent of the moving assembly line and other techniques enabled firms to expand production runs and minimize overhead costs per unit. And the growth of markets, especially for consumer goods, allowed firms to standardize general-purpose items to increase volume and throughput.

In several cases, new products requiring large scale to recover R&D costs or exploit learning-by-doing emerged from the laboratories of industrial chemistry and electrical engineering. The advent of rayon fiber (1913) promoted the growth of large chemical factories, which could maximize fuel economy and take advantage of indivisibilities in the use of chemical recovery devices (Markham 1952, 52–53). Synthetic fibers (starting with nylon), rubber, plastics, resins, and oil-based fuels—all produced in tens or hundreds of thousands of tons per year—soon followed. In the electrical industry, irons (1910), vacuum cleaners (1913), clothes washers (1916), dishwashers (1922), radios and electronic tubes (1923), and refrigerators (1925) joined the telephone as household items with a mass market.[1] Assembly lines churned out hundreds of thousands of these articles annually.

In other cases, the production of established goods expanded in response to a larger customer base or new manufacturing techniques. In automobiles, Ford Motor Company tripled its output after introducing the moving assembly line in 1913 (Wilkins and Hill 1964, 52–53). Producers of tractors, sewing machines, typewriters, lightbulbs, and the like applied the same techniques, with similar gains in efficiency. In steel, the first continuous strip mill was built in the United States in 1924 and in Europe in 1937. In chemicals, the Haber-Bosch process of nitrogen fixation made it possible to synthesize ammonia for fertilizers and explosives from air, rather than having to recover it from coke-oven byproducts. The hydrogenation of carbon led to synthetic methods for making heavy organic chemicals, while the manufacture of inorganic alkalies and sodas increased in scale with the shift from the Leblanc to the Solvay method (Svennilson 1954, 21–22, 132–33).

With these trends, products formerly made on a craft basis in small family shops were, by the 1920s, manufactured in large factories. In the United States from 1914 to 1929, output per plant jumped from 1,897 automobiles to nearly 25,000, from 210,000 tire casings to 1.6 million, from one hundred thousand pounds of rayon to four million pounds, from sixty thousand tons of steel to more than two hundred thousand tons (calculated from U.S. Bureau of the Census 1918, 1930). Growth in the scale of manufacturing coincided with the emergence of the modern, multiplant corporation and the application of scientific management principles (Chandler 1990). While producers in other countries generally lagged behind those in the United States, they were exposed to the same trends, gained access to many of the same technologies, and had to compete in the same markets. They therefore faced intense pressure to keep up. As technologies and goods requiring mass production were disseminated more widely after World War I, manufacturers in many countries experienced a systemwide shift in competitive conditions.

This shift was not uniform across industries. Many products remained handicraft items when fixed capital costs and overhead were low, basic components could not be standardized, and machines either could not effectively substitute for labor or required frequent recalibration. In cotton textiles, ring spindles and automatic power looms allowed higher throughput and lower labor content than mule spindles and manual looms, yet vertically integrated companies with

1. Bowden and Offer 1994, 729–30. The year represents when the product was introduced in the United States.

large factories still enjoyed few, if any, cost advantages over small shops. Industries such as apparel, footwear, ceramics, glass, and metal tools continued to supply customized goods using labor-intensive techniques and some simple machinery. The pressure to assimilate new technologies in response to shifts in market conditions therefore focused on specific industries.

When the potential for scale economies increases, as chapter 2 explains, the volume of output within the plant becomes a crucial determinant of a firm's competitive position and profitability. Firms producing on a small scale endure high production costs and wasted opportunities to earn excess profits; firms producing on a large scale enjoy lower costs and earn larger profits. The returns to scale, or the sensitivity of average costs to changes in scale, determine the penalty of small scale (in terms of higher unit costs) and the extent of the advantage of large-scale over small-scale producers. Finally, domestic consumption of products with large returns to scale affects the ease with which firms can introduce mass production technologies. Firms with large national markets can employ large-scale capacity producing for local consumers alone. If home demand is limited compared to the MES, however, firms need a wider market to gain scale economies that otherwise cannot be fully exploited.

These propositions inform the case studies that follow. Each country analysis begins with a review of trade policy in the interwar period. Next the primary explanatory variables are evaluated to generate predictions about domestic actors' trade preferences. These hypotheses are then compared to the political behavior of firms and organized groups. The case studies conclude by considering how collective action and institutional aspects of policy-making influenced the policy measures that governments implemented.

Imperial Protection in Japan

The Japanese Empire was the most protectionist of the interwar trading blocs. Though its colonial expansion predated World War I,[2] Japan pledged to allow "equal opportunity" for commerce in its occupied territories. Instead of reserving these markets for Japanese business, Japan for the most part observed the MFN rights of outside powers under the treaty ports until the 1920s.[3] The

---

2. Japan annexed Formosa (Taiwan) in 1895, took control of Manchuria and the Kwantung Leased Territory in 1906, and annexed Chosen (Korea) in 1910.

3. However, the Japanese military controlled the ports and the railways, the laying of telegraph lines, and other investments in transportation and communications infrastructures. Japan also granted colonial preference for certain primary commodity imports, but it abstained from establishing privileges for its own exports (Beasley 1987, 60–68, 91–100).

Japanese government then began to establish exclusive trade practices in its empire: it assimilated Korea into its tariff system in 1923; ten years later it severed Manchuria from Chinese customs and reduced duties on a number of products of interest to Japanese business.[4] As the Japanese army advanced into East Hopei, North China, and Shanghai in 1936–38, military-backed puppet governments dismantled the Chinese tariff regime and liberalized imports of Japanese goods. By 1940, Japan had set up special customs arrangements with Thailand, French Indochina, and the Dutch East Indies in its efforts to construct an East Asian Co-Prosperity Sphere.

The creation of an imperial bloc coincided with escalating trade barriers in Japan. After raising a number of duties in the first few years after World War I, the Diet passed a major tariff revision in 1926 to boost protection for manufactures. When the yen depreciated with the suspension of gold convertibility in 1931, specific duties were raised 35 percent to synchronize tariff rates and domestic prices. By this point, "Japan had the highest level of tariff protection in the world" (Yamazawa 1990, 146).

Myriad factors—too many to list here—played a role in the Japanese government's decision to impose high tariffs at home and exclusive trading rights in the empire. The theory developed in this book suggests that the technological changes of the postwar era created interest in an enlarged, protected market by pressuring many producers of capital goods and consumer durables to gain scale economies. Because firms could not reach optimal rates of output per plant while confined to the domestic market, they needed to sell in a wider economic area to manufacture in longer runs or larger batches. Thus, the small size of industry and the limited range of the Japanese market made tariff protection and an exclusive trading bloc attractive to producers struggling to adjust to the new competitive environment after the war.

The Scale of Japanese Industry

In Japanese manufacturing, factory-based production in large volumes began with the outbreak of World War I, as the decline in trade with the combatant powers elevated domestic prices and made import substitution profitable. An analysis of the stimulus to industry by the U.S. Consulate in Tokyo explained,

4. Jones (1949, 192) notes that Japanese firms could "secure rebates on customs duties and freight charges," which made it "practically impossible [for foreign firms] to trade directly with . . . firms located in Manchoukuo." Lockwood (1955, 50) refers to "open and disguised preferences, some of them official and others arising from the dominant position of Japanese nationals in the economic life of the colonies."

"The American principle of mass production and the application of scientific management were for the first time strongly advocated, and many factories were systematically planned on a larger scale."[5] After the war's end, heavy industry continued to expand. Contemporaries such as G. C. Allen (1940b, 43) noted, "in the trades in which there are substantial internal economies of large-scale production, Japan has lowered her costs by greatly enlarging the size of her plants." Studies record large factory expansions in steel, heavy machinery, electrical equipment, and synthetic and refined chemicals, where the doubling or tripling of output capacity per plant was common in the 1920s.

But even as the scale of manufacturing increased, Japanese firms remained far behind U.S. and European standards. According to Allen (1940b, 44), small plants and diverse product lines prevented firms from fully exploiting scale economies:

> plants in many of the large-scale industries are still either smaller or less highly specialized than are those of corresponding Western industries. In the iron and steel, motor tire and chemical trades, her producing units are small compared with those of the United States and Britain, and so she is unable to achieve all the technical economies open to her competitors. . . . In trades where she possesses some very large plants . . . these are far less highly specialized than are similar plants in competitor countries.

A survey by the Japanese government concluded: "though our productive industries are now in the early stages of transition to large scale production, they are still for the most part composed of small or medium undertakings which suffer from lack of capital resources and productive equipment" (quoted in Board of Trade, Department of Overseas Trade 1931, 31). Due to these handicaps, most producers faced high unit costs compared to foreign rivals.

Table 5 presents output per plant in Japan in a number of industries with large returns to scale, with comparisons to the scale of production in the United States. The data show that very short production runs were common. The exception is rayon, in which the leading firms (Teijin and Toray) kept pace with large increases in the MES to maintain the world's lowest unit costs (Allen 1940a, 672–73). Producers in other industries faced severe disadvantages. Steel tonnage per plant was one-fifth that of the United States, as the state-controlled Yawata Ironworks concentrated in specialty steel while a number of small producers fragmented the market for standardized articles (Yonekura

5. "Report on Private and Governmental Assistance to Export Trade in Japan," Tokyo, May 3, 1934, Consular Reports and Cablegrams, 1934–35, Box 9, RG 20.

1994, 55–56). Nissan's automobile capacity was less than one-twentieth the number of "knocked-down" cars assembled in local affiliates of Ford and GM; the other leading firm, Toyota, mainly subcontracted parts and made light trucks for the army (Mason 1992, 62–67). Yokohama and Bridgestone manufactured tires for a range of vehicles in plants one-eighth the size of U.S. factories. In a few industries, crowds of small concerns inhibited the concentration of production even when a single company (Tokyo Electric Light in lightbulbs, Chosen Nitrogen Fertilizer in chemical nitrogen) approached volumes typical of Western firms.

The main problem was that the small national market prevented mass production of goods with large returns to scale, as table 6 shows. Only rayon, due to strong demand from textiles, enjoyed a customer base comparable to that of

TABLE 5.   Scale of Production in Japan, 1931

Industry/Product	Units	Output per Plant	Percentage of U.S. Production
Chemicals and fibers			
Rayon	Thousand lb.	4,075	101.3
Dyestuffs	Thousand lb.	687	33.3
Synthetic ammonia[a]	Tons	5,891	30.3
Alkalies and sodas	Tons	8,868	24.4
Explosives	Thousand lb.	598	10.7
Basic materials			
Steel	Tons	36,953	18.8
Transportation equipment			
Aircraft	No.	23	36.9
Motorcycles[b]	No.	<1,200	<29.6
Trucks and buses	No.	<432	<15.6
Tires[c]	No.	112,500	13.1
Locomotives	No.	12	11.3
Automobiles[d]	No.	282	0.7
Machinery and electrical			
Typewriters[e]	No.	<6,012	<16.3
Lightbulbs	Thousand	1,696	13.5
Tractors[b]	No.	<552	<6.4

Source: Data for number of plants: Department of Commerce and Industry (various years); data for output: Supreme Commander for the Allied Powers (various years).

Note: No. = number of individual units.

[a]USTC 1937. Data are for 1929.

[b]Includes plants producing motor vehicles of different types.

[c]"Japanese Industrial Survey: Rubber—7/18/42," Reports on Japanese Industry, 1942, Box 1, RG 81.

[d]"Automobiles—8/18/42," Reports on Japanese Industry, 1942, Box 1, RG 81. Data are for 1933.

[e]Includes plants producing office machinery of different types.

TABLE 6. MES Production and the Japanese Market

Product	Lowest MES Estimate	MES Divided by National Consumption
Trucks[a]	250,000 units	473.5
Sewing machines[a]	500,000 units	161.3
Tractors[a]	90,000 units	114.2
Typewriters[a]	500,000 units	78.8
Motorcycles	200,000 units	63.1
Automobiles	500,000 units	18.4
Tires	5 million casings	11.1
Electric motors	360,000 units	6.6
Steel	6 million tons	2.3
Oil engines	100,000 units	2.3
Synthetic ammonia	200,000 tons	2.2
Radios	1 million sets	2.1
Rayon	40 million lb.	0.9
Dyestuffs	20 million lb.	0.8
Cotton fabrics	37.5 million sq. yd.	0.04

Source: Data from USTC 1945a, 1945b.
[a]Probably overestimated because no data on net imports.

the industrial nations. Otherwise, consumption was too low to support large additions to capacity even if the entire home market were reserved for Japanese goods. As Western factories returned to civilian production after the war, Japanese firms were pushed out of Asian markets they had entered when competition was absent. Thus, the resumption of trade imposed a painful retrenchment on companies that had expanded to serve excess demand. Firms were trapped in a vicious cycle: they needed to expand production runs, but they could not profitably sell abroad because unit costs were high. Lockwood (1955, 372, 378) notes, "those industries in which the economies of large-scale production are most pronounced were also those in which Japan remained at a disadvantage in foreign competition . . . [because of] the small size of the Japanese market to which they were largely confined."

Since low volume raised unit costs and undermined market shares in sectors with large returns to scale, Japanese firms had strong incentives to seek trade protection. Data from the U.S. Tariff Commission (USTC) indicate that the import share of consumption exceeded 15 percent in several areas of heavy industry, with rates over 45 percent in motor vehicles, most types of machinery, and chemicals other than rayon.[6] But closing the domestic market to external com-

6. Interwar Japanese trade data are compiled from USTC (1945a, 1945b), Oriental Economist (1935), and Mitsubishi Economic Research Bureau (1936).

petition would not by itself enable firms to transition to mass production: consumption was too low to permit even a handful of factories approaching the MES. Expanding trade would allow firms to produce for a larger market, but Japanese industry found it difficult to sell abroad because of short production runs and high unit costs. Only through access to an imperial market on privileged terms could producers overcome the scale advantages of foreign firms.

Export-Dependent and Import-Competing Industries

Industries with small returns to scale faced none of the disadvantages of the heavy and chemical industries. In the interwar period, Japan had a revealed comparative advantage in goods with simple technologies and small production units. Studies single out raw silk, knitted goods, pottery, toys, fans, parasols, matches, bicycles, enameled ironware, and canned foodstuffs as low-cost trades with production primarily in shops of less than five employees and few firms of more than one hundred workers (Lockwood 1955, 371–73; USTC 1936, 28). Though there were modern factories in cotton yarn, traditional spinners could compete with large mills employing the latest technologies because wages dominated production costs regardless of plant size. Textile weaving remained a family enterprise; 90 percent of all shops operated less than ten looms (Mitsubishi Economic Research Bureau 1936, 237–41). Thus, export-dependent industries were labor-intensive, small in scale, and highly competitive.

Two products, raw silk and cotton fabrics, accounted for one-third of Japan's exports. Thousands of rural households engaged in silk reeling, and three-quarters of this output was sold abroad. Cotton textile producers employed one out of every six industrial workers and exported two-thirds of their sales. More than 30 percent of output went to foreign markets in apparel and knitted goods, canned foodstuffs, pottery, footwear, glass and glassware, tea, and silk and rayon textiles.

Export-oriented producers had three reasons to oppose tariff increases in Japan and trade discrimination in the empire. First, they relied on imported inputs: textile materials (mostly raw cotton) accounted for two-fifths of all imports, while other craft-based industries used foreign rubber, leather, and wood. Second, while exporters enjoyed large shares of nearby markets, they sold most of their wares overseas: 80 percent of raw silk exports were shipped to the United States; 85 percent of cotton fabrics sold abroad went to China, India, the Dutch East Indies, Hong Kong, and Egypt (Mitsubishi Economic Research Bureau 1936, 245, 526). Because export industries could sell in competitive markets, they had little to gain from trade privileges in the region. Third, Japanese goods already faced substantial barriers abroad. Tariffs and quotas in the largest markets for cotton fabrics forced Japanese firms to find new outlets in South America, Africa, and the Middle East, while the Smoot-Hawley tariff in the United States blocked exports of footwear, pottery, porcelain, toys, canned foodstuffs, and carpets (Ishii 1981, 147–50, 194–221; Wright 1935, 219; Mitsubishi Economic Research Bureau 1936, 594). Foreign retaliation against tariff increases in Japan therefore was a serious threat to export industries.

Other than capital goods and consumer durables with economies of scale, food and raw materials were the main imports into Japan. Imports were especially large shares of consumption in sugar, soybeans, fats and oils, wheat, and rice; local producers of basic materials such as coal also faced competition. In every case except wheat, neighboring or nearby countries supplied the bulk of the imports: all soybeans came from Manchuria, Taiwan accounted for 80 percent of Japan's imported sugar, Korea and Taiwan supplied 85 percent of its imported rice, China and Manchuria provided 85 percent of imported coal.[7] In these industries, cheap imports pressured local producers to restrain prices. Opening trade with the region would drive down prices and further undermine the profits of Japanese farms and mines.[8] Import-competing producers therefore benefited from trade protection against all sources in East Asia.

Industries with Economies of Scale: Trade Preferences

Hypothesis 5 expects small-scale producers in industries with large returns to scale to support trade protection. In interwar Japan, organized groups in these industries campaigned vigorously for tariffs. Steel producers were among the first and most intense advocates of trade protection: facing renewed competition in the aftermath of the war, the Japan Industrial Club recommended higher tariffs, subsidies, and tax breaks in 1919–21; it then pushed to increase tariffs and subsidies in 1926 and 1932. To justify these demands, steel barons emphasized their need for government aid to rationalize production, expand

---

7. Ibid.

8. Japanese investors gained control over a substantial proportion of the farmland in Taiwan and Korea soon after they became colonies. For example, Japan's four leading sugar companies controlled 80 percent of the cane cultivated in Taiwan; four large trading firms managed 90 percent of the rice exported from Taiwan and Korea to Japan. Often colonial sugar was refined and colonial rice milled in Japan, then sold in the domestic market or reexported. This allowed Japanese firms vertically integrated with colonial suppliers to earn monopoly profits from tariffs on foreign sugar and rice, while small farmers faced price pressures from the colonies and foreign sources alike (Ho 1984, 369–75).

capacity, and reduce unit costs.[9] Nissan and Toyota worked through the Survey Council for the Establishment of the Automobile Industry to push for subsidies, tax exemptions, and higher duties on engines, chassis, and parts (Mason 1992, 73–79). Petitions to increase trade protection also were recorded for electric generators and motors, machine tools, dyestuffs, soda ash and caustic soda, and synthetic fertilizers (Uyeda 1933, 9–10; Board of Trade, Department of Overseas Trade 1928, 72; Molony 1989, 243–45; U.S. Bureau of Foreign and Domestic Commerce, various years).

Though it is difficult to link pressure for trade discrimination to specific sector groups, the available evidence is consistent with hypothesis 1 and hypothesis 2. Studies such as Tiedemann's (1971, 271–72) and Beasley's (1987, 38–39) find the strongest domestic support for an imperial trading bloc in heavy industry. "Because Japan's new large-scale industries still had high unit costs of production," Toshiyuki (1989, 24) explains, "those enterprises found it difficult to break into world markets. Therefore, they had to turn to the privileged markets in the formal Japanese empire to sell their products." Zaibatsu groups, in particular, "gave wholehearted support to the policy of militaristic expansion" (Jones 1949, 148). Once under Japan's political control, heavy industry pushed for trading privileges to favor Japanese exports in these areas. For example, the Japan Industrial Club, which represented capital goods producers, insisted: "Manchurian tariffs should be kept as low as possible to encourage the import of Japanese products. Industrial goods should be produced within Japan and exported to Manchuria" (Young 1998, 204).

Evidence of pressure for an imperial bloc is strongest in the steel industry. Steel firms generally emphasized that home market protection combined with exports to the empire would assist their efforts to reduce unit costs. Since capacity expansion also required secure supplies of iron ore and coal, steelmakers lobbied to suspend duties on imports from mines in Manchuria and Korea. In addition, integrated steel firms pushed to extend Japanese tariffs and subsidies to occupied areas to prevent imports from injuring their Manchurian operations or entering Japan at lower rates (Yonekura 1994, 113, 122, 142).

Vertical production arrangements and the need to dispose of surpluses also motivated support for imperial protection from chemical producers such as Chosen Nitrogen Fertilizer. According to Molony, "the most sophisticated Japanese companies were dependent on their manufacture in, and sales to, the

9. Steel firms with Zaibatsu ties pushed the government to subsidize only producers with capacity greater than thirty-five thousand tons. The head of the state-controlled Yawata works opposed tariff increases (Yonekura 1994, 110–21).

colonies." As a result, the advent of new methods of synthetic fertilizer production "increasingly required colonial expansion and was closely tied to economic imperialism. . . . Colonial expansion was integral to the growth of prewar technology-intensive companies like Nitchitsu" (Molony 1989, 243, 263).

On the whole, trade policy never was debated as publicly in Japan as in Britain or the United States—especially after the outbreak of war in China. The available evidence therefore does not permit a systematic, refined treatment of industry lobbying. But where business demands cannot be observed directly, tariff discrimination and its effect on trade flows can be examined. In a later section, the chapter returns to domestic support for imperial protection and provides further evidence (albeit circumstantial) that heavy industry sought closer imperial ties.

Export-Dependent and Import-Competing Industries: Trade Preferences

Export industries generally abstained from seeking higher tariff, and some actively opposed duties on other products. Producers of cotton fabrics were most favorable to open trade (Uyeda 1933, 15; Lockwood 1955, 540–44; Ishii 1981, 49–50). A British consular report, mindful of the "tendency in Japan . . . to establish industries and protect them with a high tariff wall," noted that "the cotton industry . . . has . . . never been in receipt of any direct aid from the Government and . . . do[es] not seem to be anxious for any direct help."[10] Exporters instead devoted their political efforts to blocking tariff increases for others. Cotton and silk textile firms campaigned against iron duties, out of concern that these would incite retaliation in India; weavers and hosiers pushed to limit protection for dyes and liberalize duties on yarn; and glassmakers objected to tariffs on alkalies and sodas (Yonekura 1994, 136; Uyeda 1933, 9–11; Board of Trade, Department of Overseas Trade 1930, 27). Among export-oriented industries, only producers of wool fabrics, bicycles, and wheat flour sought tariff increases on their products (Board of Trade, Department of Overseas Trade 1933, 33, 86).

Exporters also were circumspect about diverting trade to East Asia: they favored bargaining down tariffs outside the empire over discrimination within it. Thus, producers dependent on world markets generally opposed forming an imperial bloc (Fletcher 1989, 104–9). Notably, the cotton textile industry did not seek tariff privileges in Korea or in China once these areas came under Japan's

10. "Japan" 1927, 60.

control (Duus 1995, 245–48, 281–87).[11] Instead, textile trade associations pushed for trade treaties with the United States, the British Empire, and Latin American countries to preserve or expand access to these markets (Ishii 1981).

Import-competing groups lobbied to increase tariffs on their goods. The Imperial Agricultural Society campaigned for higher duties on rice, cereal farmers sought to raise tariffs on wheat, and cane growers lobbied to protect sugar (Uyeda 1933, 3–4, 11–14). Because the competition originated mostly within Japan's empire and dependent territories, these groups resisted plans to exempt imperial produce from import taxes, as hypothesis 4 expects. The Showa Coal Joint Sales Corporation, a cartel of the thirteen largest coal-mining firms, pushed for quotas on Manchurian coal.[12] Farmers lobbied to reinstate tariffs on rice from Korea and Taiwan after 1929 (Ho 1984, 363–64), and imports from the empire provoked growing protectionism among producers of sugar and soybeans (Young 1998, 211).

The Politics of Trade in Japan

Beneficiaries of imperial protection were not numerous, but they enjoyed political clout. Interwar Japan's political system systematically favored the interests of big firms and concentrated industries. The fourteen largest industrial combines controlled one-quarter of all invested capital. These "old" financial Zaibatsu owned a number of factories in engineering, electrical, and chemical industries, along with the largest steel works, coal mines, sugar refineries, and flour mills. During this period the "new" industrial Zaibatsu grew in size and influence, and this group began to dominate high-technology chemicals, motor vehicles, and machinery.[13] Industrial concentration complemented financial concentration: four or fewer firms manufactured more than two-thirds of output in dyestuffs,

11. Large cotton firms had another reason to oppose closer integration with Manchuria and China: many owned mills in North China, which ensured them access to these markets. These firms often used Chinese factories as export platforms to evade cartel restrictions in Japan. If Manchuria or China were assimilated into the Japanese empire, textile transplants would face the same export quotas and would have to compete with mills based in Japan. As a result, leading Japanese textile firms favored tariff autonomy for China and did not object to China's imposition of tariffs on cotton fabrics in the late 1920s (Chin 1937).

12. "Memorandum on Coal in Japan and Manchuria" 1933.

13. The old Zaibatsu included Mitsui Mining, Mitsubishi Mining, Sumitomo Mining, Asano Steel Works, Sumitomo Metal Industries, Mitsubishi Heavy Industries, Mitsubishi Electric Company, Asano Shipbuilding, Sumitomo Chemical, and Sumitomo Cable Manufacturing. Among the new Zaibatsu were Chosen Nitrogen Fertilizer, Hitachi, Nissan Motor Corporation, and Toyota Motor Corporation.

passenger cars, alkalies and sodas, steel, coal, sugar, and wheat flour—and each of these industries backed the protectionist cause.

Large industrial combines entered many of these activities to receive government incentives targeted to private groups with sufficient capital and managerial expertise to begin large-scale production. The mutual dependence of public and private interests enabled the "money cliques" to influence policy through informal connections with powerful bureaucrats and political sway in the Imperial Diet. Allen (1940a, 731) explains:

> while the development of the Zaibatsu has been dependent in a large degree upon privileges bestowed on them by the State, they cannot be regarded merely as the passive instrument of a policy determined independently of them. If the State uses the Zaibatsu to carry out its designs, those designs themselves can be in some measure molded by pressure from the Zaibatsu.

One-third of all members in the Diet were closely identified with business interests; 28 percent of the upper house and 12 percent of the lower house were connected to a Zaibatsu group directly or through family ties (Tiedemann 1971, 280–81). Weakly developed political parties heavily depended on financial contributions from big business.[14] While the Diet often rubber-stamped the policy initiatives of the bureaucracy, large industrial enterprises also wielded disproportionate influence with civil servants in the cabinet ministries (Johnson 1982, 47–50). Finally, protectionist businesses were overrepresented in official committees such as the Council on Tariffs, which was formed to bypass the Diet's cumbersome procedures (Fletcher 1989, 99–101).

Export industries did not enjoy the same advantages of financial and industrial concentration or affiliation with Zaibatsu groups. Only the Japan Cotton Spinners Association was highly concentrated, as six firms owned half of the industry's capital equipment. However, yarn producers lacked close ties to the Zaibatsu (Ishii 1981, 31–32). Other export industries were crowded with small, financially strapped family firms. Though some of these activities concentrated in industrial centers (cotton fabrics and ironware in Osaka, pottery in Nagoya), others such as raw silk and weaving were geographically dispersed. Small firms also relied on Zaibatsu trading networks to procure imported inputs and market their goods abroad. This made collective action against Zai-

14. According to Ishida (1968, 299), "Since the Japanese political parties lack mass organizations, economically strong interest groups that desire to influence the political parties provide them with financial support which more than compensates for the absence of membership fees or contributions from party members."

batsu interests difficult. Moreover, state organs subjected these industries to rigorous control and regulation in the 1930s, which both reflected and aggravated their overall weakness in Japanese politics (Allen 1940a, 643; Lockwood 1955, 234).

The collapse of Japan's quasi democracy and the military's ascendance after 1931 extended the political influence of the large industrial combines at the expense of small firms. Though the military, particularly the Kwantung army's officer corps, propagated an anti-Zaibatsu hostility popular with peasants and small businesses, its need for armaments, munitions, vehicles, and communications obliged it to compromise with, and rely upon, the Zaibatsu. Thus, the army courted newer firms such as Nissan and Chosen Nitrogen Fertilizer to develop colonial resources for the war in China (Udagawa 1990b; Molony 1989). In turn, "close contact with Japanese Army leaders" and "heavy Army support," in the words of the U.S. consul in Yokohama, allowed Nissan to secure policies that handicapped foreign rivals (Mason 1992, 94). Since the old Zaibatsu could mobilize large amounts of capital, the military offered them special privileges, contracts, concessions, and leases to invest in occupied territories as well (Allen 1940a, 626–45; Hadley 1970, 40–42). Thus, the large industrial combines were able to resist military control and retain substantial influence even in wartime Japan.

Tariff Changes, 1920–36

Most industries with large returns to scale, through their protectionist preferences and political influence, secured higher tariffs after 1920. Steel duties increased from 7.5 percent to more than 20 percent. The 25 percent tariff on automobile parts was raised in 1932 to 35 percent for engines and 40 percent for other components to block U.S. affiliates from assembling "knocked down" vehicle kits into complete cars. The 1936 Motor Manufacturing Enterprise Act imposed import licensing and additional taxes on foreign automobiles; another tariff increase in 1937 brought duties to 70 percent for complete vehicles and 60 percent for parts. Tariffs on synthetic dyes jumped from 20 percent to 35 percent in 1926, and imports also were subject to import licenses. Duties on electrical machinery, communications equipment, machine tools, and industrial engines more than doubled in the 1926 tariff.[15]

Along with heavy industry, primary producers also received large tariff

---

15. Information on tariff changes appears in *Commerce Reports* (U.S. Bureau of Foreign and Domestic Commerce) and *Board of Trade Journal,* various issues.

increases. Farmers secured higher duties on products from outside the empire to ensure that colonial imports came at the expense of foreign countries, not domestic producers. The rice tariff doubled in 1930, pushing domestic prices 40 percent above world prices. Higher duties for sugar nearly extinguished imports from outside the empire, as protection surged from 10 percent before the war to 60 percent by 1932. These measures helped to reconcile protectionist pressure from farmers and miners with free access for colonial primary produce, as barriers against imports from outside the empire caused trade diversion and created rents for landowners in Japan and the colonies.

Ordinary least squares (OLS) regression allows a more systematic test of the relationship between key variables and Japanese tariffs. In this analysis, the dependent variable *tariff* is either the tariff rate or specific duties divided by average import prices (depending on whether duties were assessed ad valorem or in fixed amounts per unit) in 1935.[16] The primary independent variable is *scale*, which is described in the appendix. *Imports* as a share of consumption and *exports* as a share of sales are proxies for comparative costs. *Concentration*, which captures an industry's capacity to organize politically, is the share of production in plants with more than one thousand workers.

The results appear in table 7. *Scale* has the correct positive sign and is statistically significant. To interpret the coefficient, consider the difference between Japan's strongest industry, rayon, and its weakest, automobiles: all else equal, the automobile industry's predicted tariff is 21.6 percentage points higher than the rayon industry's. *Imports* and *concentration* are positively signed and statistically significant. Tariff rates favor concentrated industries in particular, as each one standard deviation increase in *concentration* increases tariffs by 12 percentage points, compared to 6.8 percentage points for *scale* and 4.3 percentage points for *imports*. *Exports* is incorrectly signed and not significant.

While the number of cases is small, and the results must be qualified accordingly, table 7 illustrates three important points. First, small-scale industries were more likely to receive high tariffs, particularly when returns to scale were large. This shows that the Japanese government tended to satisfy protectionist demands from producers that could not take full advantage of scale economies. Second, import-competing industries also were effective at gaining high tariffs. Third, more-concentrated industries received significantly greater protection, which suggests that concentration facilitated collective action.

16. Tariff rates are from Department of Finance 1935.

TABLE 7.   OLS Regression Results for Japanese Tariffs in 1935

Tariff $= -0.49 + 0.35$ (Scale) $+ 0.17$ (Imports) $+ 0.02$ (Exports) $+ 0.78$ (Concentration)
          (0.13) $(0.08)^{***}$ $(0.07)^{**}$ (0.15) $(0.11)^{***}$

$F = 16.58^{***}$
Adjusted R-squared $= 0.75$
$N = 22$

Note: Standard errors are in parentheses below the parameter estimates.
$^{***}p < .01$ $^{**}p < .05$ $^{*}p < .10$

The Imperial Trading Bloc

The tariff changes just described applied to Japan's colonies, Taiwan and Korea, as well as the home islands. Industries with large returns to scale and import-competing primary producers thereby gained wider margins of preference over foreign rivals in the empire. Policy in Japanese-occupied territories (Kwantung, Manchuria, and North China) favored these same interests. In Manchuria, "the import tariff was devised to encourage the inflow of capital equipment for the mining, metallic, and heavy manufacturing industries" (Jones 1949, 192). In addition to lower duties on industrial and building materials from Japan, exchange controls and government licensing prohibited foreign imports of rice, sugar, wheat, flour, and other primary goods.

Heavy industry received additional assistance through the aggressive application of TRIMs against foreign multinationals. Udagawa (1990a, 27) states, "Japan's effort to exclude foreign capital in the 1930s was the most decisive of any nation's to pursue obstructing and protective policies for the sake of its own domestic industries." Japanese telephone companies won exclusive procurement rights from the Ministry of Commerce and Information, producers of lightbulbs and sewing machines lobbied to force GE and Singer to share technology, and Nissan and Toyota secured production quotas and import restrictions against Ford and GM. After 1930, state officials pressed U.S. multinationals to sell their assets to local investors. The army even blocked Ford from buying land for a new factory at Yokohama (Mason 1992, 47–52, 79–97). Mason (1992, 72–73) concludes: "business interests wielded influence over official actions even during this extraordinary ascendancy of the military."

Military and civilian officials forced Western firms to liquidate investments in Manchurian heavy industry as well.[17] In one case, Japanese administrators

17. The Japanese administration in Manchuria sought to avoid blatant discrimination to promote international acceptance of the new regime. Thus, many trading privileges for Japanese firms were not in observable aspects of the tariff structure but in opaque regulations such as exchange allocations, import licenses, public procurement, and government-sanctioned monopolies.

raised duties on foreign motor vehicles and blocked the creation of a U.S. assembly plant in Dairen. The U.S. Consulate in Manchuria explained: "The Army's interference . . . is simply a refusal to allow these American motor cars a price advantage in the Manchurian market." The Manchurian tariff revision, this report concluded, "amounts mainly to manipulation designed to encourage construction in Manchuria and to favor Japanese export commodities."[18]

These sorts of regulations allowed Japanese firms to dominate private investment in the empire. In practice, Zaibatsu groups providing the capital and technology necessary to begin production in occupied areas were granted a monopoly position. While many Japanese firms in this "enclave economy" secured financing from public sources and final authority over certain management decisions rested with the military, nonetheless they enjoyed substantial leeway to "function like private enterprises in a free market" (Myers 1996, 138–39). These activities concentrated in armaments, explosives, munitions, primary metals, building materials, motor vehicles, communications gear, and machinery, not the light industries in which Japan enjoyed a comparative advantage. Large-scale capital inflows not only promoted industrial development and military mobilization, they also helped to finance increased imports of Japanese capital goods into occupied areas.

Trade data demonstrate that Japanese policy encouraged production and exports in industries with large returns to scale. From 1931 to 1935, steel exports jumped 900 percent, machinery 600 percent, and motor vehicles 540 percent. Sales to Manchuria, North China, and the colonies accounted for 90 percent of this increase. During this period, exports of textiles, apparel, pottery, and glassware remained stable or fell (calculated from data in Mitsubishi Economic Research Bureau 1936, 515–17). Concentration ratios for heavy and chemical industry exports to Manchuria and North China jumped dramatically after the occupation of these areas. By comparison, the regional concentration of exports was much lower for textiles, pottery, and glassware, and these ratios declined between 1929 and 1936. Yet in Hong Kong and South China—markets temporarily beyond the reach of Japan's army—exports were not skewed toward the heavy and chemical industries, and light industry enjoyed more of an advantage (Schran 1994, 214–20).

Japanese market shares for motor vehicles, machinery, and iron and steel in Korea, Taiwan, and Manchuria in the 1920s show a similar empire effect. In Korea and Taiwan, market shares declined after the war, before rebounding once measures favoring colonial goods were instituted after 1923. In Manchuria, market shares bottomed out in 1930 and then bounced back after Japan seized control and revised the province's tariff.[19]

These trends demonstrate that the trading bloc served as "a protected Empire-wide market for Japanese-made producer goods, which were not yet competitive in free markets" (Schran 1994, 207). Imperial protection enhanced domestic market shares and provided an export outlet for firms that needed to gain scale economies to match producers outside Asia. According to Yamazawa (1975, 59), "Japan's tariff protection reached its highest level in the late 1920s and early 1930s, during which the most rapid cost reduction was realized in many production areas." Since the rapidly expanding heavy and chemical industries quickly saturated additional markets in the colonies and Manchuria, these areas provided only a temporary palliative—making further expansion into densely populated markets in North China and elsewhere in East Asia increasingly attractive.

The point is not that business interests *caused* Japan's aggressive bid for territorial conquest but rather that economic conditions *predisposed* Japan to seek out markets in the region. Nor does this imply that friction never existed between military officials who wanted more territory and business leaders who wanted larger markets. Indeed, military plans after 1937 increasingly conflicted with the interests of the heavy and chemical industries, which objected to controls on private enterprise and feared war in Asia would undermine industrial development. More than industry's need for a wider protected market, military concerns about access to oil, rubber, and iron ore dictated expansion into Southeast Asia to form the Co-Prosperity Sphere (Fletcher 1989, 144–50). Even so, a symbiotic relationship existed between firms that viewed nearby territories as an economic lifeline and military leaders who sought self-sufficiency in manufacturing, food, and raw materials. Autarky inside an imperial bloc therefore catered to varied interests: heavy industry's need for exclusive markets, the military's desire to build up armaments and control vital strategic materials, and racist-nationalist nostalgia for a united Asia under Japanese control.

Britain and Imperial Preference

Economic unity in the empire was long debated in British politics with the founding of the Fair Trade League in 1881, Joseph Chamberlain's Tariff Reform movement after 1903, and the formation of groups such as the Empire Industries

---

19. Market shares were compiled from data in Oriental Economist 1935 and Wright 1935, 352–58.

Association in the early 1920s. But while the dominions introduced lower tariffs for empire goods in 1894, Imperial Preference failed to gain widespread popularity in England before 1930. Finally, at the Ottawa Conference in 1932, Britain established a formal trading bloc in its empire.

Imperial Preference took a half century to materialize because Britain had to abandon the free trade policy in effect since the abolition of the Corn Laws before it could offer preferential treatment to the commonwealth. Cracks in free trade's facade first appeared with the wartime McKenna tariff, which applied duties on automobiles, clocks, watches, and musical instruments, and the Dyestuffs Importation Act, which established import licensing for dyes. After the war, the Safeguarding of Industries Act instituted protection for "key industries." The Conservative government subsequently levied tariffs on silk and rayon, reinstated McKenna duties on automobiles, and extended these tariffs to tires. Protection became the norm in 1931, when the Import Duties Act imposed across-the-board tariffs ranging from 10 to 33 percent.

When Britain abandoned free trade, it also instituted Imperial Preference. Before 1931, most imports remained free from all sources (though McKenna goods, silk, and rayon from the commonwealth were taxed at less than the general rate). In the Ottawa Agreements, however, Britain guaranteed access for dominion agriculture and imposed tariffs and quotas on foreign meat, dairy products, cereals, fruits, and vegetables, thereby establishing preferences for food. In return, the dominions expanded preferences for Britain—often by imposing new or higher duties on foreign products.[20] With these tariff changes, margins of preference for British goods reached 22.5 percent in New Zealand, 20.2 percent in Canada, 19.3 percent in Australia, 5.6 percent in India, and 2.6 percent in South Africa (MacDougall and Hutt 1954, 246–47). Though the British Empire never evolved into a self-contained unit like Japan's trading bloc in East Asia, these policy changes nonetheless represented a dramatic shift to protectionism.

As public support for free trade weakened, industries with unexploited scale economies moved to the forefront of the movement for tariff protection at home and privileged access to the commonwealth. These producers began to face competition from rivals in the United States and Germany in the years before World War I. After the war, it became clear that British firms had inefficient factories with short production runs and outmoded equipment. With too many producers vying for limited domestic demand, firms needed protection at home and markets abroad to sell more goods, expand in size, and reorganize operations. Their response was to seek shelter inside the empire.

20. "The Ottawa Conference" 1932.

The Scale of British Industry

In the nineteenth century, England's proficiency in textiles, shipbuilding, railways, and basic materials such as coal, iron, and steel earned it the title "workshop of the world." Many technological advances during the second industrial revolution also originated in England. The transition to mass production in the electrical, mechanical, and chemical industries began around World War I and continued after the war. This led to rapid increases in the size of manufacturing establishments, as the Board of Trade's Committee on Industry and Trade (1929, 176) noted "a strong tendency . . . for enterprises engaged in production to increase in average size, a tendency which shows no sign of reaching its limit."

But Britain's head start was more a liability than an advantage. The Board of Trade's Committee on Commercial and Industrial Policy (1918a) diagnosed the key problems after the war. Early industrialization made steam power so accessible that producers were slow to convert to electricity. Older factories lacked modern layouts and the latest machinery, yet firms were reluctant to demolish inefficient plant and replace outmoded equipment. Because large capital investments could not be quickly amortized, firms often expanded by enlarging and remodeling existing plants rather than constructing new ones. In the United States and Germany, on the other hand, a late start encouraged producers to build large, modern plants and close old factories.

Britain's liabilities in the new, large-scale industries were apparent even before World War I. In 1914, the biggest companies in metallurgy, in mechanical and electrical engineering, and in chemicals produced on a smaller scale and captured lower home market shares than foreign rivals. In contrast to the United States and Germany, Britain's largest enterprises clustered in light industry, not heavy industry (Chandler 1990, 275–78). As a result, its position was strongest in textiles, coal, and shipbuilding—products of the first industrial revolution—and consumer goods such as food, beverages, and tobacco. As Broadberry (1997, 157–58) explains, British industry achieved high productivity and performed well in global competition when it could rely on "craft-based flexible production" (as in textiles) or when mass production was difficult to implement (as in shipbuilding).[21] But firms were weakest in the industries with the greatest scale economies, where intensive use of skilled labor could not compensate for low volume.

21. Broadberry (1997, 158) finds that "poor British performers tended to be industries where high throughput techniques had been successfully developed in the United States, but where demand conditions or resources and factor endowments simply prevented the adoption of such techniques in Britain."

Table 8 shows the scale of production in British industry. In industries with large returns to scale, volume was lowest in automobiles, tractors, electrical goods, steel, and dyestuffs. Britain's automobile factories employed as many workers as U.S. plants but produced one-tenth as many vehicles; even the largest plants had considerably shorter production runs than in the United States. Similar disadvantages existed in machinery, as the total British production of tractors and typewriters trailed output per factory in the United States. In the electrical industry, the Board of Trade's Committee on Commercial and Industrial Policy (1918a, 14) noted, large "numbers of small concerns have arisen, each struggling against the other, with resultant high costs of production." Short production runs prevailed in household items such as refrigerators, lightbulbs, vacuum cleaners, and small electric motors (Jackson 1954). Britain's twenty largest steel firms produced just one-third the output of U.S. Steel and barely equaled Germany's Vereinigte Stahlwerke (Hannah 1976, 121).[22] In dyes, "even the largest British firms . . . were pygmies in comparison . . . [to] the large-scale operations of [German] coal tar firms" (Richardson 1968, 286–87).

In most other chemicals and products such as tires and aircraft, British industry was less far behind but still trailed foreign rivals. Only producers of motorcycles reached world-class standards. Nobel's explosives plant was the largest of its kind, and firms had a strong position in alkalies (Broadberry 1997, 159–63). ICI owned the world's second-largest synthetic nitrogen plant, but its capacity was just one-quarter that of IG Farben's giant facility at Merseburg (Reader 1975, 39). Courtaulds was among the leading rayon producers, though it could not match the output per plant of its U.S. subsidiary, AVC (Coleman 1969, 322–29). As the aircraft industry expanded production for military procurement, several medium-sized firms competed for market shares (Fearon 1978).

The limited range of the British market was a handicap for small-scale producers. The Board of Trade's Committee on Industry and Trade (1928a, 162) observes, "the Americans' huge home market gives them a great advantage in the prosecution of [mass production] methods . . . [but] attempts in the same direction in this country ha[ve] been discouraging." Table 9 shows local consumption compared to the MES for several products. Only in motorcycles, dyes, and rayon was British consumption at least one-third the U.S. level. Moreover, the British market could support more than one MES plant in just a handful of cases. As a result, firms attempting to increase volume often created a glut of goods and triggered painful adjustments.[23] With so little domestic steel con-

22. Only three steel mills could produce four hundred thousand tons annually (Burn 1961, 432–33).

23. Cases in point include Ford's auto plant at Dagenham and ICI's synthetic nitrogen facility at Billingham (Hannah 1976, 133).

TABLE 8.   Scale of Production in Britain, 1930

Industry/Product	Units	Output per Plant	Percentage of U.S. Production
Chemicals and fibers			
Synthetic ammonia[a]	Tons	58,975	303.8
Alkalies and sodas	Tons	31,852	87.7
Dyestuffs	Thousand lb.	1,374	66.6
Explosives	Thousand lb.	2,862	51.3
Rayon	Thousand lb.	2,034	50.6
Transportation equipment			
Motorcycles	No.	3,206	79.0
Aircraft	No.	31	49.1
Tires	No.	347,514	40.4
Locomotives	No.	37	34.5
Trucks and buses	No.	316	11.4
Automobiles	No.	3,909	9.9
Basic materials			
Steel	Tons	55,458	28.2
Pig iron	Tons	89,745	22.2
Electrical and machinery			
Electronic tubes	Thousand	625	33.0
Lightbulbs	Thousand	3,272	26.0
Sewing machines	No.	8,116	23.5
Tractors	No.	1,682	19.4
Vacuum cleaners	No.	37,534	11.6
Typewriters	No.	2,010	5.4

Source: Data from Board of Trade 1934.
Note: No. = number of individual units.
[a]USTC 1937. Data are for 1929.

sumption, Chandler (1990, 284) observes, "Only a courageous and somewhat irrational set of British steelmakers . . . would have made the investment required to build and integrate works in Britain large enough to compete in price with those of Pittsburgh and the Ruhr." The steel industry was not alone in this challenge: the six leading automakers controlled 90 percent of a market one-twentieth the size of the United States, where four firms dominated.

Since firms could not achieve large volumes producing for domestic demand, many sought to export. But manufacturing for a number of markets made it difficult to capture unexploited scale economies. In automobiles, machinery, electric motors, and basic steel, the diverse needs of foreign consumers prevented firms from mass producing standardized articles. Many firms specialized in craft-based, skill-intensive goods where low volume was less of a liability, such as custom-built textile machinery and boat engines; simple farm implements such as plows, harrows, and drills; and larger projects such as railway electrification,

TABLE 9.   MES Production and the British Market

Product	Lowest MES Estimate	MES Divided by National Consumption
Tractors	90,000 units	26.94
Typewriters	500,000 units	8.24
Synthetic ammonia	200,000 tons	3.85
Trucks	250,000 units	3.74
Electric motors	360,000 units	3.35
Automobiles	500,000 units	3.15
Sewing machines	500,000 units	3.12
Motorcycles	200,000 units	2.42
Oil engines	100,000 units	0.93
Rayon	40 million lb.	0.89
Radios	1 million sets	0.61
Dyestuffs	20 million lb.	0.57
Tires	5 million casings	0.50
Steel	6 million tons	0.24
Footwear	300,000 pairs	0.003

Source: Data from Board of Trade 1934.

power plant construction, and wire and cable installation (Saul 1977, 35–36). British firms therefore fared best in export markets when they could differentiate their products and compete on quality and craftsmanship.

Variety could not substitute for low costs and inexpensive prices in generic, mass-produced goods, however. As U.S. factories expanded to serve foreign consumers, British firms were pushed back first in neutral markets and then inside the empire (Marrison 1996, 12–13). Of the industries producing on a small scale, none captured even 30 percent of the imperial market in 1929. Only producers of motorcycles managed large increases in market share after the war.[24] With the burden of high unit costs, "British firms found it difficult to secure the requisite market outlets to justify mass production" (Elbaum and Lazonick 1986, 15–16).[25] As a result, even as their market position in the empire deteriorated, they became increasingly dependent on it.

In sum, industries with large returns to scale manufactured in short production runs compared to the same industries in the United States. The small

24. Data are available in Board of Trade, Customs and Excise Department 1930.
25. Elbaum and Lazonick (1986, 7) add:

Britain's rivals were better able to rationalize the structure of orders and ensure themselves market outlets required for mass production. . . . [With] more secure and expansive domestic markets, foreign rivals, with more modern, capital-intensive technology attained longer production runs and higher speeds of throughput than the British.

British market forced producers to export, but these firms could not undersell rivals abroad. To compensate for insufficient home demand, they needed access to a wider trading area. This made Imperial Preference an attractive means to divert imports and gain market shares in the commonwealth. Firms with size disadvantages also needed tariffs in the domestic market because of high unit costs. Most industries with large returns to scale therefore had incentives to seek both trade protection at home and a trading bloc in the empire.

Exporting and Import-Competing Industries

Two-fifths of industrial labor in interwar Britain worked in three export trades: textiles, shipbuilding, and coal. Mass production techniques were difficult to apply in these areas, so few scale economies existed. Textile manufacturers were beginning to use capital-intensive methods with mechanical innovations in spinning and weaving, but the need to tailor fabrics to shifting consumer tastes inhibited volume and throughput (Lazonick 1986, 19–23). In shipbuilding, basic components were not standardized, and the largest yards could accommodate the construction of only four to six ships at a time (Lorenz and Wilkinson 1986, 110–19). In coal, productivity declined with total output as workers had to dig deeper and thinner seams. In these cases, firms relied on the high productivity-to-wage ratio of Britain's skilled workforce and a reputation for quality (and in coal, the proximity of British collieries to the sea).

When local factor endowments rather than scale determined production costs, industries using skilled workers tended to be export oriented, while those intensively using low-skill labor, natural resources, and land faced import competition. The textile industry was the most export-dependent branch of the economy: more than 80 percent of cotton fabrics and 40 percent of wool fabrics were sold abroad. Producers of pottery and china, cutlery, and metal tools exported more than one-third of their output. One out of every five tons of coal excavated from British mines was sent overseas.

However, a number of factors conspired to create falling export volumes and growing unemployment after the war: overvalued sterling, rising real wages, declining productivity, higher foreign tariffs, and import substitution abroad. In coal, output per man-shift fell behind continental European mines, undermining Britain's position in nearby markets (Svennilson 1954, 109–10). Cotton textile sales to Japan, China, Hong Kong, and India—markets that absorbed more than half of exports in 1913—failed to rebound after the war and declined further in the 1920s. Exports of wool textiles also fell, and imports doubled; unemployment reached 25 percent in 1930. Other consumer goods such as apparel, footwear, hosiery, and carpets faced intense import competition and negative trade balances as foreign labor surpassed British productivity at lower wages.

In the three major export trades (cotton textiles, shipbuilding, and coal), imports were less than 1 percent of consumption; the problem was falling export volumes, not competition at home. These industries had nothing to gain from abandoning free trade: tariffs could only provoke retaliation and a further loss of markets abroad.

Incentives for Imperial Preference also were mixed. On one hand, most foreign sales of export-oriented industries were outside the empire. For example, 80 percent of coal exports went to Europe, Scandinavia, and the Mediterranean due to high transport costs; even with tariff advantages over foreign competitors, the empire was too far away to take more British coal (Allen 1933, 37–41). In cotton fabrics, the dominions other than India absorbed only 15 percent of exports. Moreover, when labor-intensive industries sold large amounts in the empire, they enjoyed dominant market shares even without tariff discrimination. British wool producers, for instance, accounted for 90 percent of the yarn, flannel, and fabric imports in the dominions (Board of Trade, Committee on Industry and Trade 1928b, 226). There simply was not much trade from other countries to divert.

On the other hand, Australia, New Zealand, and Canada had become increasingly protectionist to promote import substitution. When British firms faced difficulty selling in the commonwealth, competition from foreign exporters was less of a problem than tariffs that often surpassed 30 percent. Indian duties on British cotton fabrics increased from 3.5 percent during the war to 25 percent by 1931. Even higher barriers existed in Australia, New Zealand, and Canada.[26] Cotton mill owners therefore had an interest in tariff concessions to defend access to India's market. Exporters of footwear, cutlery, metal manufactures, pottery, and china also could benefit from Imperial Preference if this induced trade creation (by reducing tariffs on British goods) more than trade diversion (by raising margins of preference over foreign goods).

In contrast to export-oriented producers, industries facing import competition could benefit from trade barriers in the domestic market. Import pressures were most intense in silk textiles and fabric gloves, and foreign currency depreciation created import competition in paper, glass and glassware, apparel,

---

26. In India, British textiles enjoyed a 5 percent margin of preference over foreign goods, which increased to 6.25 percent in 1931. This, however, was not enough to allow them to maintain their position in competition with local cotton mills and cheap Japanese exports (Redford 1956, 231–32, 281–84).

hosiery, and rubber footwear as well. Each of these industries had strong incentives to demand trade protection. Moreover, the commonwealth presented no competition: imports from the empire exceeded 2 percent of consumption only in paper manufactures. Since Imperial Preference required first abandoning free trade and imposing tariffs on products from outside the empire, it would be just as attractive to these industries as tariffs alone.

Producers of foodstuffs and other agricultural goods, however, faced competition from the dominions' vast ranches and croplands. Initially, displacement was most severe in grains and dairy products. But with the development of new refrigeration methods, foreign beef, pork, and livestock began to appear in the United Kingdom. Even if there were no imports from outside the empire, British farmers would have to contend with cheap produce from the dominions. Stabilizing domestic food prices therefore required restrictions on imports from all sources. The dominions, however, sought to promote food exports, and they would not grant increased margins of preference unless they received corresponding benefits in food. Thus, protection for British farmers conflicted with Imperial Preference for industry. Still, tariffs on foreign food to establish Imperial Preference were a necessary first step to defeating the free trade system. And for British farmers, some protection was better than none at all.

Industries with Economies of Scale: Trade Preferences

A major political cleavage in interwar Britain was the division between industries with large returns to scale and the traditional export trades. Members of these two factions belonged to the same trade associations—the Federation of British Industries (FBI), the National Union of Manufacturers, the Empire Industries Association, and the like.[27] Yet the differing market interests of large, capital-intensive heavy industries and the skilled labor-intensive light industries created antagonism after World War I. The electrical, chemical, and motor industries, which needed to maintain high volume, were more likely to petition for McKenna or Safeguarding of Industries duties. In contrast, textiles, coal, shipbuilding, engineering, and other export industries were anxious about losing markets overseas and less inclined to seek trade protection at home. These

---

27. The FBI was Britain's largest industrial association: by 1920 it counted twenty thousand firms as members, as it brought together Manchester's free traders and Birmingham's protectionists. The National Union of Manufacturers was smaller and more homogenous, with about three thousand firms in the steel, engineering, and motor industries. With more freedom to engage in political activity, it faithfully represented the protectionist cause. The Empire Industries Association also was important in the push for tariff protection and Imperial Preference (Boyce 1987, 9–11).

divisions immobilized the large manufacturing associations, which generally took a neutral position on trade matters, leaving industry-based pressure groups and local chambers of commerce to fill the political vacuum (Marrison 1996, 328–29, 339–40, 348–51).

Trade groups in activities with large returns to scale formed the backbone of the movement to end free trade. Industries with small-scale production relative to foreign rivals issued the earliest and most persistent appeals for trade protection, as hypothesis 5 anticipates. The automobile industry "actively supported the protectionist cause" (Snyder 1944, 152). Austin, Morris, Leyland, and Joseph Lucas lobbied through the British Motor and Allied Manufacturers Association to continue wartime tariffs as the McKenna duties were set to expire in 1919 and 1923. These firms also sought to extend the tariff on cars to commercial vehicles and tractors (Marrison 1996, 318, 375–76; Snyder 1944, 31–32). In the dye industry, British Dyestuffs and ICI pushed to extend tariffs and licensing in the Dyestuffs Importation Act to block German competition (Reader 1970, 271). As for steel, the Board of Trade's Departmental Committee on the Iron and Steel Trades (1918d, 29) noted the "practically united feeling of the British iron and steel producers" in favor of tariffs. The National Federation of Iron and Steel Manufacturers (NFISM) petitioned for Safeguarding duties on a number of iron, steel, and wire products in 1925 (Carr and Taplin 1962, 350–53, 375–80).[28] Steel firms insisted they could not begin to reorganize "unless assured of the home market" because "the small orders . . . are not nearly enough. . . . it is the orders for imported steel that can alone give the big plants what they need" (Tolliday 1984, 52, 56). While the NFISM recommended 25 percent duties on steel products, large steelmakers pushed for 33 percent; producers of wrought iron sought tariffs as high as 50 percent (Carr and Taplin 1962, 477).

Other industries with unexploited scale economies sought trade protection as well. Producers of electrical goods advocated tariffs "sufficiently high to protect effectively the electrical industry" (Board of Trade, Departmental Committee on the Electrical Trades 1918a, 11–12). The Electrical and Allied Manufacturers Association later told the government that it wanted "to get a

---

28. The Steel Rerollers Association initially opposed tariffs on basic steel, which firms imported from northern Europe and then rolled into finished steel products. Integrated steel firms (United Steel, Richard Thomas, Stewarts and Lloyds, South Durham) sought tariff protection to secure these orders for themselves and drive the rerollers out of business. The largest importer of unfinished steel (Guest, Keen, and Nettlefolds) dropped its opposition to steel duties in 1926, and the rerollers then pushed for tariffs on finished steel (Tolliday 1984, 53–54; "Iron and Steel Reorganization 1932" 107–9).

protectionist tariff" (Rooth 1992, 39).[29] This group sought duties on radio components, lightbulbs, and spark plugs (Marrison 1996, 272–73). Producers of sewing machines, farm machinery, and locomotives also were inclined toward protection (Marrison 1996, 247–48).[30] The leading tire producer, Dunlop, began to push for restrictions on U.S. imports in 1916, and after the war the Rubber Tire Manufacturers Association petitioned to extend McKenna duties to tires (Dunlop 1949, 139–42; Snyder 1944, 154). Courtaulds supported rayon tariffs, while small firms in the Cellulose and Chemical Manufacturers Association were even more emphatic about the need for protection.[31]

In a few cases, firms remained favorable to open trade or made a halfhearted conversion to protectionism. Lower ammonium sulfate prices due to foreign dumping eventually led ICI and other agrochemical manufacturers to ask the Board of Trade for duties on artificial fertilizers in 1932 (Reader 1975, 149). Other sectors of the chemical industry, such as alkalies and explosives, declined to seek protection (Marrison 1996, 71–72, 307). Rooth's (1992, 39) study of protectionist pressures in Britain finds that only two capital-intensive industries backed free trade: motorcycles and electric wire and cable.

Heavy industry also was a vocal supporter of Imperial Preference. Boyce (1987, 114) notes that leaders in heavy industry widely believed "that the world was being transformed by the advent of large-scale, mass production industry with its demand for large and stable markets." These executives argued that the United States would flood world markets with low-cost manufactures and drive down prices as its production outpaced national consumption. Many concluded that tighter economic links with the empire were needed to ensure a secure mass market for high-volume goods (Rooth 1992, 71–73). In response, corporate leaders formed the Empire Industries Association, the Empire Economic Union, and the Empire Producers Organization to advance their interest in imperial protection (Garside 1998, 50–51). In addition, sixteen prominent figures in the heavy and chemical industries united to

29. The chairman of General Electric (not affiliated with GE in the United States) explained, "if the sluices of importation are not closed only one of two things can happen—we shall be ruined, or in self-defense we must make an agreement with our foreign competitors asking them to please let us live . . . in England and they may have the rest of the world" (Davenport-Hines 1984, 200).

30. The Board of Trade's Committee on Commercial and Industrial Policy (1918a, 13) noted that "a majority [of firms] consider that import duties are necessary," but it declined to recommend tariffs. The protrade views of skill-intensive producers (textile machinery, marine engines, boilers, wagons, and structural engineering products) apparently outweighed the interests of high-volume sectors such as sewing machines, office and farm machinery, and locomotives.

31. "The Silk Duties" 1932, 1066. Coleman (1969, 260–63, 328) implies that Courtaulds did not lobby for tariffs, but his discussion and other sources suggest otherwise.

sponsor a proclamation favoring Imperial Preference in the *London Times* in November 1929.

The steel industry was an early convert to Imperial Preference. As far back as 1886, steel barons told a Royal Commission they needed preferential trade to reserve imperial markets for surplus produce. Steel firms also backed Chamberlain's Tariff Commission in 1903. When that failed, many pushed the dominions for preferences to divert trade from the United States and Germany (Carr and Taplin 1962, 119–24, 254, 374, 509–11). After the war, the Board of Trade's Departmental Committee on the Iron and Steel Trades (1918d, 29–30) recommended a commonwealth exemption from tariffs. In the 1920s, the NFISM pushed for duties on food and raw materials from outside the empire and criticized the government's refusal to abrogate MFN, and steel representatives sought a generous scale of tariff preferences at Ottawa (Wurm 1993, 38, 81, 176).

In the chemical industry, ICI sought to retain the empire "as an exclusively British trading area" through a system of tariffs and cartel arrangements in alkalies, explosives, and agrochemicals (Reader 1970, 170). According to Reader (1975, 229), "ICI's foreign policy . . . was the policy of establishing the British Empire as ICI's 'natural market,' which foreigners did not invade, and of leaving foreigners alone in theirs." Alfred Mond, the chairman of ICI and a founder of its predecessor, Brunner-Mond, advocated trade protection in Britain with a common imperial tariff.[32] As a leading figure in the Empire Industries Association and the Empire Producers Organization, Mond hoped to join Britain and the commonwealth in "a self-sufficient economic system" (Reader 1975, 9).

Newer industries joined the movement for an imperial bloc later, but with the same enthusiasm. Automakers were particularly favorable to Imperial Preference. The Society of Motor Traders and Manufacturers emphasized the need for tariff advantages in the empire to combat U.S. "dumping" (Lowe 1942, 93). In addition, automakers favored tariffs on foreign food with free entry for imperial produce to encourage the dominions to widen preferences for British goods.[33] Producers of tires and aircraft sought Imperial Preference to close em-

---

32. Booth and Pack (1985, 81–82) write:

> The imperial vision derived from [Mond's] identification of trends toward the formation of trading blocs, both in North America and in Europe. The options for Britain were either to join one of these units or to form its own bloc based on the empire. . . . Within this protected unit, British capital could provide the major stimulus to development and growth with the promise that guaranteed markets would promote continuing efficiency and productivity improvements.

33. Other industries were less enthusiastic about food duties but generally supported them in the interest of Imperial Preference (Marrison 1996, 415–17).

pire markets to U.S. goods.[34] The machinery industry widely agreed on the need for preferences in the empire; producers of agricultural and office machinery were most supportive (Board of Trade, Departmental Committee on the Engineering Trades 1918c, 24, 38; Board of Trade, Committee on Industry and Trade 1928a, 166). Electrical firms also sought a preferential imperial market in which to expand sales (Davenport-Hines 1984, 56–59).

In sum, though it is difficult in some cases to connect demands for Imperial Preference with narrow sector-based interests, the available evidence suggests that producers with large returns to scale and a small home market were strong and consistent advocates of a trading bloc with the empire, as hypotheses 1 and 2 expect. In addition, while several firms and trade associations openly opposed Imperial Preference, none produced in industries with significant scale effects.

Exporting and Import-Competing Industries: Trade Preferences

In evaluating the trade preferences of British industries, it must be noted that no import barriers existed in the domestic market (except for a few products subject to Safeguarding duties). With free trade and an overvalued currency, even some low-cost industries had incentives to seek trade protection. Even so, export industries generally supported the continuation of free trade, and they lacked enthusiasm for proposals to establish Imperial Preference. The coal, shipbuilding, and cotton textile industries all opposed tariffs and preferences because they needed foreign markets and cheap sources of imports (Board of Trade, Committee on Commercial and Industrial Policy 1918a, 67).[35] The Manchester Chamber of Commerce favored the repeal of the Safeguarding of Industries and Dyestuffs Importation acts by more than four to one, as textile producers complained these measures were "injurious to trade."[36] In coal, the Hull Chamber of Commerce condemned the new tariff policy and urged the government to adhere to free trade.[37] Shipbuilders lobbied against tariffs on iron and steel.[38]

34. Dunlop statement in *Economist* 114:1101; Fearon 1978, 76.
35. Marrison (1996, 251) calls this "the most tangible evidence . . . of any industrial commitment to Free Trade."
36. "Manchester and 'Safeguarding of Industries'" 1921, 333; "Manchester and Protection" 1923, 11.
37. "Coal and Tariffs" 1923, 953–54; Marrison 1996, 91–93.
38. Constructional engineers and tinplate producers joined shipbuilders in their efforts to block steel tariffs. Other steel consumers favored steel tariffs to advance their own protectionist agenda. The Society of Motor Manufacturers and the Electrical Industries Council were sympathetic to steel tariffs, while the British Engineers Association dropped its opposition to duties in 1928 (Carr and Taplin 1962, 477–78; Marrison 1996, 278–81).

Even as economic conditions worsened after 1930, shipbuilders and coal mine owners held out hope that devaluation would stifle pressure for a General Tariff (Marrison 1996, 421–22). In cotton textiles, however, antiprotectionism began to weaken. A 1930 poll found three-quarters of Manchester merchants favoring some form of protection, with only one-quarter for free trade. Some also began to favor tariff preferences for the empire. In the crown colonies, Lancashire sought measures to exclude "competition from certain industrial countries with lower standards of life," namely Japan (Redford 1956, 239–40, 251–52). But its principal concern was the Indian market: though cotton merchants did not seek trade preferences against all competitors, they did advocate the abrogation of MFN rules to allow special restrictions on Japanese goods in India and elsewhere in the empire (Marrison 1996, 184–91; Redford 1956, 252–59).

Even so, the cotton textile industry denounced proposals for a self-contained imperial system as an obstacle to the revival of foreign trade; it objected to increased tariffs against foreign countries and trade diversion on the grounds that greater access to imperial markets should not come at the expense of foreign exports. Instead, firms pushed to reduce commonwealth tariffs to ensure trade creation. The Manchester Chamber of Commerce grumbled that the Ottawa Agreements would not result in "any substantially increased volume of trade" (Redford 1956, 270–71). Textile producers later urged the government to extend Imperial Preference to any country outside the empire that would reduce its tariffs on British goods.[39]

While cotton fabric producers became more open to Imperial Preference, the wool textile industry was more favorably inclined to tariff protection than other exporters. After the war some branches of the wool trade, such as long-staple yarns and fabric for women's apparel, sought modest tariffs (Board of Trade, Departmental Committee on the Textile Trades 1918e, 68–70). A 1923 vote in the Bradford Chamber of Commerce, the seat of the wool industry, found a slim majority in favor of tariffs against countries with depreciated exchange rates.[40] Safeguarding petitions soon followed in 1924 and 1929. Bradford, however, was not as interested in Imperial Preference as Manchester, as wool textiles producers pushed the dominions to reduce tariff protection in their domestic markets but did not seek special restrictions on foreign goods.[41]

Import-competing industries were more emphatic about the need to end

39. "The Cotton Trade and Ottawa" 1932, 1070; "Lancashire and Ottawa" 1932, 1401; Redford 1956, 244–47.
40. "Bradford's Cry for Protection" 1923, 394; "Bradford and Protection" 1923, 787.
41. Porter 1979, 43–44; "Canadian Tariff Problems" 1933, 1165.

free trade. After the war, the Silk Manufacturers Association lobbied for 25 percent duties on silk yarn and fabrics, with an exemption for the empire. Other
branches of the textile industry, such as embroidery and lace, hosiery, knitted
goods, underwear, and fabric gloves, also supported trade protection. Between
1921 and 1923, industry groups petitioned for Safeguarding duties on glass
and glassware, cutlery, silk fabrics, and gloves, while rubber manufacturers
sought tariffs on footwear from the Far East and Canada (Board of Trade, Departmental Committee on the Textile Trades 1918e, 82, 99, 103–6; Coleman
1969, 262; Lowe 1942, 53–56).

The most intense demands for trade protection came from agriculture, particularly grain growers in southern England and producers of meat and dairy
products in the north. After the war, farmers lobbied for duties on wheat and
meat, and they complained that measures like the Safeguarding of Industries Act
favored the needs of industry.[42] As prices for cereals and other primary products
dropped after 1926, the National Farmers Union intensified its agitation for tariffs (Rooth 1992, 43). Though some farmers supported Imperial Preference
(which conflicted with their interest in tariffs on all imports) "for the sake of a
common front against free trade" (Brown 1943, 19), the National Farmers Union
sent no representatives to the Ottawa Conference to protest agriculture's use as a
"bargaining chip" to secure tariff advantages for British industry. Its calls to exclude foreign produce became more passionate as Argentine, Scandinavian, and
U.S. meat flooded the British market in anticipation of wider margins of preference on food from inside the empire (Cooper 1989, 154–56, 184–85).

The Politics of Trade in Britain

In the fifteen years after World War I, the free trade system so firmly en-
trenched since 1846 gave way to protectionist pressures from a number of domestic groups. By 1932, the political influence of industries seeking tariffs and
Imperial Preference reached critical mass. Several factors helped these industries realize their policy objectives.

First, there was little organized domestic opposition to either trade protection
or Imperial Preference by 1930. Producers seeking tariffs rarely lobbied against
duties on their inputs because every breach in Britain's commitment to free
trade enhanced their chances of securing protection themselves.[43] Historically

---

42. "Agriculture and Protection" 1923, 827.
43. Shipbuilders' opposition to steel duties was an exception. Also, the National Farmers Union
protested duties on agrochemicals but apparently accepted tariffs on steel and agricultural machinery as long as Britain instituted taxes on food (Marrison 1996, 281–84; Hutchinson 1965, 16–17).

the bulwark of free trade was trade union defense of the "cheap loaf" and agitation against "stomach taxes," as workers refused to accept that wage gains from tariffs would not be lost in higher prices for food. But workers in automobiles and the safeguarded industries increasingly backed trade protection in the 1920s. In 1930, the Trade Union Congress abandoned its free trade position and advocated a General Tariff with Imperial Preference in a joint manifesto with the FBI. That same year, London's financial community endorsed tariffs on goods from outside the empire so the dominions could earn sterling on exports to Britain to repay their loans (Boyce 1987, 251–56).

Second, the war and the technological developments of the postwar era shifted political power from exporters and financial interests to capital-intensive industries. Though coal, shipbuilding, and cotton textiles remained the largest branches of the British economy, "new industries dependent on the domestic and imperial market" had become "the dominant sectors in terms of industrial output and employment" (Garside 1998, 51). The heavy and chemical industries had several large companies, concentrated market structures, and substantial financial resources, which enhanced their capacity for collective action. While there were large corporations in coal, shipbuilding, and cotton textiles, industrial structures were more competitive.[44]

Finally, the institutions of British government weighed concentrated interests more heavily after the war. Historically, direct elections reduced collective action costs for the working classes and export-oriented groups. This diluted the organizational and financial advantages of protariff interests, resulting in a more open trade policy than would have been likely if legislators or bureaucrats had set rates of protection (Irwin 1994). With the introduction of wartime tariffs, however, the government established the Import Duties Advisory Committee (IDAC) to hear industry claims. The purpose of the IDAC was to limit the scope for logrolling and vote trading—its mandate was to consider economic efficiency, not political expediency. But in practice the committee was sensitive to the needs of industries seeking help (Wurm 1993, 65–70). Moreover, the private deliberations of the IDAC, which heard testimony only from groups with a direct interest in the product under consideration, were more favorable to protectionist interests than a public hearing or a debate on

44. Export industries were not concentrated industrially, but they were concentrated regionally—cotton textiles in Lancashire and wool textiles in Yorkshire. As a result, the economic distress of lost markets was geographically localized. Capie (1983, 93–94) concludes that British institutions were more sensitive to regional problems than industry lobbying. However, his data are broadly aggregated at the industry level, and others have criticized his measures of effective protection.

the floor of Parliament (Tolliday 1987, 310–11). Once the IDAC decided in favor of tariffs, the government typically accepted its recommendation.

Of course broader political currents were important as well. The Conservative Party's victory in 1924 quickly resulted in protection for automobiles, tires, rayon, and silk. As the Labour government of 1929 to 1931 held the line against pressures for more tariffs, protectionist industry groups gravitated toward the Conservative Party and "did everything possible to influence . . . workers to vote Conservative" (Snyder 1944, 152). The Conservatives' return to power in the midst of financial crisis in 1931 finally completed the overthrow of the free trade system.

Instituting Tariffs, 1915–36

Table 10 presents regression results for British tariffs in 1936.[45] The variables are the same as for Japan in table 7, and all variables have the same signs as before. *Scale* and *concentration* are strongly significant, while *imports* is weakly significant. Due to lower overall tariffs in Britain than in Japan, a one standard deviation increase in *concentration* increases tariffs by 4.9 percentage points, while comparable figures for *scale* and *imports* are 4.8 percentage points and 2.8 percentage points, respectively. As with Japan, *exports* were not statistically significant after controlling for *scale*. Industries with large returns to scale often had high export to sales ratios because national markets were small, yet this did not diminish their enthusiasm for trade protection.

As the results imply, industries with large returns to scale usually received tariffs higher than the 10 percent benchmark rate in the Import Duties Act. The most heavily protected industries included dyestuffs (50 percent tariffs plus import licensing), rayon (tariffs ranging from 43 to 87 percent), and steel, automobiles, tires, motorcycles, and tractors (33 percent). Import-competing industries also received higher-than-average tariffs, though not as high as in industries with large returns to scale. Industries that were export oriented but that did not have large returns to scale (for example, textiles, coal, and shipbuilding) received little trade protection by comparison.

Imperial Preference

Britain's objectives at the Ottawa Conference were to open commonwealth markets and also secure larger margins of preference over third-country

---

45. British tariff rates are from the National Institute of Economic and Social Research (1943).

TABLE 10.   OLS Regression Results for British Tariffs in 1936

Tariff $= -0.32 + 0.32$ (Scale) $+ 0.18$ (Imports) $+ 0.05$ (Exports) $+ 0.39$ (Concentration)
          (0.13) (0.10)***   (0.10)*   (0.09)   (0.11)***

$F = 10.92$***
Adjusted R-squared $= 0.59$
$N = 28$

Note: Standard errors are in parentheses below the parameter estimates.
***$p < .01$ **$p < .05$ *$p < .10$

imports.[46] The dominions, however, were committed to industrial development—for its own sake and to allocate the sterling earned on exports to debt
repayment instead of imports—and industrial interests were powerful
enough to resist deep tariff cuts on British goods. Generally the best offer dominion negotiators would issue was tariffs fashioned to equalize British and
colonial costs of production. Instead of lower duties on British goods, the dominions raised tariffs against foreign countries to reconcile preferences for
Britain with protection for domestic industry (Rooth 1992, 80–100). At Ottawa and after, external tariffs in the dominions increased on 95 percent of the
goods for which Britain received preferences, but tariffs against Britain increased on 60 percent of these goods. Imperial Preference was, therefore, a
more protectionist arrangement than Britain desired, as its exports to the empire still faced severe barriers (MacDougall and Hutt 1954, 250–51).

A second source of trade diversion was Britain's desire to protect its farmers
in the face of dominion pressures to expand primary exports. The dominions'
supply of agricultural exports exceeded Britain's import demand for most
goods; thus, even with prohibitive tariffs against countries outside the empire,
higher prices for British farmers were incompatible with unrestricted entry for
colonial food. Moreover, Britain wished to limit price increases for consumers,
so its tariffs on wheat, dairy products, and fruit fell short of what the dominions wanted, and in meat products they had to accept quantitative controls instead of large preferential margins that would have allowed empire producers
to raise prices and earn rents. Finally, price supports for British farmers main-

---

46. The political influence of industry groups over British diplomats at the Ottawa Conference
is difficult to evaluate. Before the conference, the Board of Trade, with the assistance of the FBI and
chambers of commerce, created lists of concessions for negotiators to request from the dominions.
At Ottawa, representatives of the NFISM, the British Engineers Association, the Association of
British Chemical Manufacturers, and the Society of Motor Manufacturers consulted with British
and Canadian officials on a daily basis.

tained or increased domestic output, which reduced the demand for imports from the dominions (Drummond 1974, 185–86, 270–73).[47]

Corporate executives in automobiles, chemicals, steel, and other industries with large returns to scale cheered the Ottawa Agreements, even when Imperial Preference fell short of their goals. There is evidence that tariffs and preferences stimulated production in these industries. Steel output increased 70 percent between 1931 and 1934, while imports were cut in half. Colonial market shares in automobiles increased from 21 percent to 41 percent, as exports more than doubled. The tariff wall also helped firms reap economies of mass production in dyestuffs, rayon, and tires (Richardson 1967, 83–85, 238–39).

Yet the program of tariffs and preferences had unintended—and undesirable—consequences for British industry. Preferential trade induced foreign firms to set up factories in Britain or the empire to share in the benefits. After the McKenna tariff, U.S. automakers established Canadian assembly plants to reduce duties on exports to Britain. Tariffs also stimulated U.S. and German FDI in the United Kingdom in automobiles, tires, and electrical items such as lamps, vacuum cleaners, and generating machinery. At the opening of a Firestone plant in 1928, a British official commented, "by imposing a 33 percent tariff on tires the Government had extended an invitation to Mr. Firestone to manufacture tires in England rather than pay $1,000 per day in import duties" (Dunning 1956, 259). Soon after Ottawa, Ford and GM established affiliates in Australia, New Zealand, and South Africa to assemble imported bodies and chassis into complete vehicles.

Production in the commonwealth by U.S. multinationals limited the potential market for British firms. Even with Imperial Preference, British firms occasionally paid *higher* tariffs than U.S. firms because the dominions taxed unassembled parts at lower rates than finished products. Though British firms pushed for strict rules of origin to block tariff preferences for foreign products,[48] the dominions would not curtail inward FDI, nor did British officials consider emulating the restrictions that existed in Japan and Germany. Thus, the commonwealth maintained a tolerant attitude toward foreign multinationals, even though allowing outsiders to share in the benefits of Imperial Preference reduced the profits that British firms could earn.

In some cases, British firms could scale dominion tariff walls only by

47. Agricultural imports into Britain increased 12 percent between 1931 and 1935, with imports from the dominions up 42 percent and imports from foreign countries down 32 percent (Rooth 1985, 189–90).

48. For example, the British Society of Motor Manufacturers sought a 75 percent empire content rule. "Products Affected by Change," *New York Times,* February 1, 1933, 29.

beginning production in the empire themselves. A few large steel firms, disgruntled with the rapid pace of import substitution, opened mills in the dominions (Wurm 1993, 100–102). ICI moved a portion of its fertilizer, alkali, and explosives capacity to the empire (Reader 1975, 198–211). But local production subtracted from exports from the United Kingdom, which made it more difficult to employ unused capacity and exploit additional scale economies.

In short, once Imperial Preference was established British firms still were not able to move down their cost curves far enough to effectively compete with their foreign rivals. Faced with these problems, many firms that applauded the Ottawa Agreements grew dissatisfied with their market position in the empire. A 1936 FBI memo grumbled that commonwealth tariffs were too high and wages and currency values too low for British producers to reap the benefits they desired.[49] Even so, industries that had sought Imperial Preference saw no alternative to dependence on the empire, however inadequate, and they resisted the use of these hard-earned privileges as concessions in MFN treaties with other countries (Rooth 1992, 101–9, 157–58). Enduring political support in turn made the Ottawa system a difficult sinecure for the British government to discard before World War II and after.

Autarky and Grossraumwirtschaft in Germany

Germany's interwar political position was unique in two respects. First, Germany did not regain customs autonomy under the Versailles Treaty until 1925. From that year to 1933, tariff policy was in a constant state of flux. Significant increases in industrial protection nevertheless were rare during the Weimar period. Though tariffs on manufactures were slightly higher in 1929 than in 1913, most duties were less than 20 percent of import prices. Agricultural protection moved steadily upward, however, as transitional duties gave way to major tariff hikes between 1929 and 1933.

Second, Germany enjoyed neither a geographically contiguous empire like Japan nor a commonwealth of former colonies like Britain. When the Weimar government launched efforts to expand markets for German goods, it had to deal with neighboring states with de facto political and economic independence. In 1931, the Foreign Ministry negotiated a customs union with Austria and preferential agreements with Hungary and Romania. But French and British objections led to the customs union's abandonment, while farmers

---

49. "Looking Askance at Ottawa" 1936, 355.

scuttled the reciprocity treaties after the Brüning regime's fall (Spaulding 1989, 317–19).

Nazi finance minister Hjalmar Schacht perfected the scheme for preferential trade treaties launched under Brüning. Agricultural protectionism limited the scope for trade treaties in the Weimar period, since Germany had to accept more food from abroad to receive greater market access for its manufactures. But exchange controls in the New Plan allowed the Finance Ministry to redirect trade toward the agrarian nations of central Europe without undermining domestic agricultural prices. These measures also provided a means to discriminate against hard currency nations without openly violating MFN.

Between 1933 and 1936, Germany reached trade treaties with Hungary, Romania, Yugoslavia, and Bulgaria. Under a complex system of controls and barter arrangements, countries exporting to Germany had to buy German goods to liquidate clearing surpluses. Preferential exchange allocations and purchasing agreements allowed foreign producers to sell at domestic German prices while bypassing the trade barriers that supported such high returns. At the same time, the system required central European governments to manipulate tariffs, quotas, and exchange policies to make German goods attractive in their markets. As a result, these commercial treaties caused trade diversion from hard currency countries to balance the trade of clearing nations (League of Nations 1938, 33–35).

Foreign exchange regulations also provided generous protection for German producers, at the expense of high prices for consumers. The New Plan squashed hard currency imports to one-twentieth of their 1930 levels. Moreover, German authorities discharged foreign exchange and permitted barter imports only for items that did not compete with domestically produced goods. The USTC (1943, 10) observed:

> Under the New Plan . . . the official control of foreign trade transactions was practically complete and was applied in a highly discriminatory manner—the term discriminatory being used both in the sense that meticulous judgment was exercised with respect to every detail and in the sense that actions taken often involved discrimination against individual commodities, concerns, industries, or countries in favor of others.

These measures coincided with an extensive domestic program of public works and military procurement. Thus, the Nazi economic system blocked hard currency imports; pushed industrial exports to agrarian countries; and accelerated rearmament to stimulate manufacturing, substitute for lost markets abroad, and prepare for territorial conquest.

The Scale of German Industry

In 1914, Germany dominated the world chemical industry and challenged the United States for leadership in steel and electrical equipment. But defeat in World War I severely weakened these industries. Territory lost in the Versailles Treaty contained 72 percent of Germany's iron ore deposits, 43 percent of pig iron output, 36 percent of crude steel, 30 percent of rolling mill capacity, and mines producing fifty million tons of coal per year (Chandler 1990, 550). Chemical and electrical companies had overseas affiliates expropriated and patent protection nullified. In areas of German superiority, such as dyestuffs and synthetic nitrogen, the Allied countries promoted import substitution. And grave financial problems made it difficult for firms to acquire the capital they needed to rebuild demolished factories after the war.

The chemical, electrical, and metal industries nevertheless retained their technical expertise, and German firms enjoyed a bigger domestic market than those in Britain or Japan. "The dominance of large establishments," the National Industrial Conference Board (1931, 29) noted, "is particularly marked in the important exporting industries . . . [the] heavy metallurgy, electro-technical, and chemical industries." The leading chemical firms joined in 1924 to form IG Farben, the world's largest chemical combine. Because of its modern factories, high outlays for R&D, and technology and expertise in high-pressure chemical processes, the company excelled in organic chemicals, artificial fertilizers, and pharmaceuticals (Schröter 1996, 38–39). IG Farben sold more dyes than the United States, Britain, and Japan combined, and it also produced the majority of the world's synthetic nitrogen in an enormous factory at Merseburg. In metals, the Vereinigte Stahlwerke was the world's second-largest steel conglomerate. In electrical engineering, Siemens and AEG were major producers of industrial machinery, Osram was Europe's largest manufacturer of lightbulbs, and Bosch was a leader in ignition equipment.

However, German firms were weak in mass-produced consumer durables. The United States dominated this area due to its highly developed consumer market—workers earned high wages, so they could afford the latest amenities. In Germany, wages were too low for long product runs for automobiles, home appliances, electric lamps, telephones, radios, and the like. German companies making consumer goods used more labor than U.S. firms, yet they were less productive due to low volume. "American enterprises assumed technological leadership," Dornseifer (1995, 204) argues, "as soon as their volume of production surpassed German output."

German output per plant in industries with large returns to scale, shown in table 11, is consistent with these observations. Producers of dyestuffs and chemicals (other than rayon) were the largest of their kind. German steel mills averaged 70 percent of U.S. output per plant, even though some of the largest steelworks had been lost to France. Volume also approached U.S. standards in locomotives, tires, and lightbulbs. However, automakers manufactured only one-seventh as many cars as the typical plant in the United States. Daimler-Benz and BMW produced high-cost specialty vehicles (and aircraft engines) in small volumes, and they relied on public contracts plus periodic injections of capital from Deutsche Bank to remain solvent (Heuss 1994, 403–4). Small-scale production also prevailed in office machinery, farm equipment, sewing machines, and rayon.

While Germany's market generally was larger than Britain's, table 12 suggests that it was much smaller than the U.S. market (except for motorcycles and most chemicals). This was a major constraint for producers of mass-marketed

TABLE 11.   Scale of Production in Germany, 1929

Industry/Product	Units	Output per Plant	Percentage of U.S. Production
Chemicals and fibers			
Dyestuffs[a]	Thousand lb.	13,167	638.3
Synthetic ammonia[b]	Tons	94,757	488.1
Alkalies and sodas	Tons	41,188	113.4
Rayon	Thousand lb.	1,888	46.9
Transportation equipment			
Motorcycles	No.	3,336	82.2
Locomotives	No.	86	80.9
Tires	No.	560,404	65.1
Aircraft	No.	33	52.6
Automobiles	No.	6,008	15.2
Basic materials			
Pig iron[c]	Tons	294,222	72.7
Steel[c]	Tons	135,013	68.7
Machinery and electrical			
Lightbulbs	Thousand	7,513	59.8
Radios	No.	9,761	33.9
Tractors	No.	1,774	20.5
Typewriters	No.	7,439	20.2

Source: Data for number of plants: Statistisches Reichsamt 1929; data for output: League of Nations (various years); Board of Trade, Department of Overseas Trade (1928–33).

Note: No. = number of individual units.

[a]U.S. Bureau of Foreign and Domestic Commerce 1924. Data are for 1923.
[b]USTC 1937.
[c]National Industrial Conference Board 1931, 174. Data are for 1927.

consumer goods. In 1929, Americans bought 4 million automobiles, Germans only 120,000; 12 million U.S. households owned radios, compared to 3.2 million in Germany; the U.S. market absorbed nearly fifty million electronic tubes, Germany less than six million (Dornseifer 1995, 203–4). When firms enjoyed a strong competitive position, they usually depended on foreign markets. For example, just sixty thousand ignition systems were sold in Germany each year compared to two million in the United States, so Bosch and other auto parts producers exported widely within Europe (Heuss 1994, 363–64). In the late 1920s, IG Farben exported 55 percent of its output and two-thirds of its dyes; Siemens and AEG exported 42 percent and 38 percent of their production, respectively; half of German steel was sold abroad, 30 percent directly, and 20 percent through finished goods industries (James 1986, 122–23; National Industrial Conference Board 1931, 101–2). As industries began to face difficulty mass producing standardized articles for the domestic market, they specialized in "low-volume, high-value-added market segments and niches of the capital goods sector" to take advantage of low wages for skilled labor (Dornseifer 1995, 206).

This discussion suggests that German heavy industry was bifurcated. Small-scale firms, particularly those manufacturing for consumers or acting as suppliers to consumer industries, could gain from trade protection and exclusive markets abroad. However, the chemicals, electrical capital goods, and steel industries were dominant (in the case of chemicals) or at least competitive with the United States on world markets. Thus, the theory predicts that these industries should favor multilateral free trade because large-scale firms would be expected to seek as wide a market as possible.

TABLE 12. MES Production and the German Market

Product	Lowest MES Estimate	MES Divided by National Consumption
Trucks	250,000 units	6.61
Tractors	90,000 units	5.20
Automobiles	500,000 units	4.12
Typewriters	500,000 units	3.10
Motorcycles	200,000 units	0.99
Rayon	40 million lb.	0.79
Radios	1 million sets	0.59
Synthetic ammonia	200,000 tons	0.44
Tires	5 million casings	0.37
Dyestuffs	20 million lb.	0.25
Steel	6 million tons	0.20

Source: Data for number of plants: Statistisches Reichsamt 1929; data for output: League of Nations (various years); Board of Trade, Department of Overseas Trade (1928–33).

But for large-scale, competitive German industries, reliance on foreign markets was a severe liability once worldwide depression and protectionism surfaced. Steel mills operated at 25 percent of capacity in 1931, as domestic demand fell to 22 percent of 1929 levels; capacity use in the electrical industry dropped from 78 percent in 1929 to 42 percent in 1932 (Abraham 1981, 155; Feldenkirchen 1999, 97). The shriveling domestic market forced German producers to shift to activities less exposed to global trends because they could not find new export outlets. Companies moved away from core products lines and entered areas in which low volume was less of a handicap or where first-mover advantages could be gained. As IG Farben lost its technological edge in dyes, pharmaceuticals, and photographic chemicals, the firm diversified into synthetic rubber, plastics, and fibers, and it even embarked on a costly effort to synthesize fuel from coal. This made the syndicate dependent on domestic sales and government procurement to maintain throughput for these new products (Hayes 1996, 55–58). Siemens and AEG began to rely on government contracts for electrification, power plants, and railways (Schröter 1996, 39–40). Steelmakers tightened cartel restrictions to maintain prices and intensified their dumping of surplus steel abroad.

In this environment, neighboring markets in central Europe offered attractive prospects for expanded sales to employ idle factories. The successor states of the Austro-Hungarian Empire were IG Farben's third-largest market (after the United States, which was becoming impenetrable, and the Netherlands), and though incomes were low, sales growth had been rapid (Schröter 1983, 148–54). Central Europe also became a greater focus of business for Siemens and AEG (Schröter 1996, 45–47). As steel producers sought to increase sales in the region, they faced growing competition from Czechoslovakia. In each of these industries, firms suffered from substantial unused capacity, and they needed new markets in the east to compensate for closing markets in the west and lost sales at home.

Exporting and Import-Competing Industries

Germany's leading exporters in the interwar period were the chemical, electrical, and primary metal industries. Other producers dependent on sales abroad specialized in craft-based, skill-intensive activities: ships and sailing vessels; railway equipment; musical and photographic instruments; machines for working textiles, footwear, and paper; and metal goods such as instruments, tools, and cutlery. In these industries, products were manufactured to detailed specifications, and factories were smaller than for mass-produced items (Brady

1933, 142–43). In addition, Germany exported basic materials such as coal, cement, and glass, and its textile industry also was oriented toward foreign markets, though its productivity was not as high as in Britain.

Import penetration was almost nonexistent in manufacturing. As in Japan and Britain, agriculture faced the most severe foreign competition. The large grain plantations to the east had been under intense price pressure from American wheat, rye, and corn since the advent of the railroad in the late nineteenth century. Imports of Scandinavian and South American meat and dairy products also harmed small peasants in central and western Germany. Thus, German farms depended on long distances, poor transportation, and trade protection to compensate for very high costs.

Before the war, the countries of central Europe specialized in primary goods not produced in large quantities in Germany: soybeans, sunflowers, rapeseeds, tobacco, and cotton. But after the war, farmers in the region competed more and more with German production, particularly in cereals, meat, and dairy products. These countries found it difficult to sell abroad as prices declined in the 1920s because, though their land was more productive than Germany's, they too were high-cost producers by world standards (Basch 1943, 187–91). As a result, mutual trade involved German sales of manufactured goods in return for the primary products of developing Europe. Preferential tariff reductions therefore would increase price competition for German farmers and would be likely to arouse intense rural opposition.

Industries with Economies of Scale: Trade Preferences

Trade divided German heavy industry from the end of the war to the return of tariff autonomy in 1925, as firms in iron and steel, electrical equipment, and machinery held "widely divergent views" (Spaulding 1989, 197). The auto industry, which was "obsessed by a great fear of foreign competition . . . [from] the cheap American car" mobilized intense pressure for trade protection (Board of Trade, Department of Overseas Trade 1925, 119). The steel barons of the Ruhr valley also advocated tariffs to sustain cartel prices. But other industries with large returns to scale favored open trade. Siemens, AEG, and Bosch wanted low tariffs to promote exports. IG Farben sought gasoline duties to assist its synthetic fuel program, but otherwise it too supported low tariffs (Ropke 1934, 33–37; Schröter 1996, 42–44).

Abraham (1981, 23–24, 195–202) suggests that cleavages in German manufacturing during the Weimar period split domestic-market-oriented, antilabor basic industries (coal, iron, and steel) and export-oriented, labor-neutral finishing industries (chemicals, electrical equipment, and machinery). The former group wanted macroeconomic expansion, tariffs, and cartel restrictions to push up domestic prices, while the latter sought low input prices and MFN trade treaties to promote exports. Domestic-market industries also were more tolerant of high agricultural tariffs than finishing industries: to the basic industries, rural prosperity would stimulate demand for manufactures; to the finishing industries, tariffs would incite retaliation and block access to markets abroad.

Adverse international conditions—the loss of export markets and the evaporation of foreign loans—broke the stalemate over agricultural tariffs and trade treaties. After 1930, large firms in the Reichsverband der Deutschen Industrie (RDI) aggressively pushed for regional trade agreements, as "[i]ndustrial circles began to plan a trade strategy that abandoned the pacific market of northern and western Europe and overseas in favor of the 'imperial' market of eastern and southern Europe" (Abraham 1981, 24). At first big business continued to support MFN to safeguard trade with industrial countries (Grenzebach 1988, 15–16). But more radical measures to expand exports gained popularity as declining foreign sales pushed heavy industry into a contracting domestic market.[50] By 1931, the Mitteleuropäische Wirtschaftstag, an association of heavy industries and exporters, advocated a customs union with Austria and economic expansion to the east (Abraham 1981, 227–28). The chemical, electrical, and metal industries were among the first converts in the push for markets in the region (Strandmann 1986, 91–92, 108–11).

While few large businesses questioned the need for Grossraumwirtschaft (literally, "large-area economy") in the economic environment of the depression, there were competing visions of this regional unit (open or closed, formal or informal) and Germany's role in it. In one vision, central European satellites would be agricultural appendages to supply food and raw materials, while rearmament and public works would stimulate domestic demand for manufactures (Berghahn 1996, 15–18). Steelmakers backed this option to sustain cartel prices and ensure direct control over raw material supplies. For example, Thyssen and other large steel firms embraced programs for economic self-sufficiency and supported the Nazi Party politically and financially (Hallgarten 1952). Automakers and aircraft manufacturers also supported autarky and

---

50. Large businesses were slow to back Grossraumwirtschaft because "[t]heir traditional export orientation was too deeply rooted to be dropped on a whim." As the Great Depression deepened, however, firms no longer able to sell profitably abroad "became increasingly attracted to . . . an alternative to a world market-oriented export policy [which] would be implemented through an enlargement of the market, to be forcibly achieved by political and, if necessary, military means" (Volkmann 1990, 185–89).

rearmament due to their dependence on government contracts and their inability to compete with imports (Reich 1996, 81–87; Homze 1976, 63).

Other sectors of heavy industry "favored a more open arrangement that would allow at least some trade with other countries in the West" (Berghahn 1996, 18). Export-dependent firms were not prepared to retreat within the regional market, and they initially regarded Nazi plans for autarky with suspicion. Siemens and AEG, for example, sought to increase exports to the east to relieve overcapacity, but neither was "prepared to abandon external markets" because industrial Europe provided the greatest demand for their products (Schröter 1996, 47–48). Bosch also wanted to preserve global trade ties because developing countries consumed few automobile components (Heuss 1994, 405–14). Krupp, a diversified producer of basic metals and finished goods such as machinery and railway equipment, supported bilateral trade treaties as a temporary expedient until "the return of normal trading conditions," but the firm criticized proposals to establish "an isolated, autarkist state" (quoted in Overy 1994, 136).

IG Farben eventually moved away from the liberal trade preferences of the electrical and machinery industries and backed the isolationist, autarkic views of the automakers and steel barons. At first corporate leaders regarded autarky in a German-led bloc as undesirable, but they gradually accommodated their policy interests to the Nazi program (Hayes 1987, 43–45, 268–70; Turner 1985, 246–49). As early as 1933, the firm expanded its coal-based fuel and synthetic rubber programs in return for state subsidies (Borkin 1978, 60–63). In external policy, "IG Farben tried to uphold free trade," but it also "somewhat incongruously" advocated forming a trading bloc through a customs union with Austria and bilateral trade agreements in central Europe (Schröter 1996, 50).[51] The firm also initiated barter exchanges with central European countries and established long-term contracts to stimulate exports and promote raw materials production abroad (Kaiser 1980, 70–72).

IG Farben's conversion to imperial protection was complete by the end of the first New Plan. A 237-page memo to the Nazi Ministry of Economics, titled "IG Farben's Neu-Ordnung" (New Order), presented the firm's vision of dominance in the German Grossraumwirtschaft. The memo included proposals for administering the chemical industries of conquered territories to IG Farben's benefit through trade preferences favoring German goods; detailed tables laid out the

51. Company chairman Karl Duisberg asserted in 1931: "Out of the small national economic space, the strong industrial states . . . looking for markets push toward greater international economic spaces. . . . This tendency was started by the United States . . . [and] also in Europe this aim of the regional economic space seems to be gradually taking shape" (Berghahn 1996, 17).

firm's desired tariffs on external trade in each market. "Imports from North America," the memo concluded, "shall be eliminated or controlled" so that the U.S. chemical industry could never expand beyond its national market.[52]

In sum, in the early postwar years the heavy and chemical industries (other than automakers and steel) pushed for open trade. But once other states closed their markets and established imperial blocs, this alternative was no longer available to Germany. As foreign trade disintegrated and the Great Depression deepened, firms began to advocate a trading bloc in central Europe. Out of necessity more than choice, Germany's chemical and electrical industries adapted their interest in markets abroad to the Nazi Party's goal of a self-sufficient regional economic zone—not because this served the interests that the book's theory adduces but as a second-best outcome brought about by the intervening effects of worldwide depression and protectionism abroad.

Exporting and Import-Competing Industries: Trade Preferences

Finished goods manufacturers in Germany tended to be export oriented, and unlike iron and steel, they were not ruled by cartel arrangements. These industries generally opposed tariffs at home and supported trade agreements to both the east and west. In particular, the Association of German Machine-Building Firms and small producers of ironware such as cutlery and hand tools opposed tariffs on iron and steel, which raised their input costs and made the negotiation of trade treaties more difficult.[53]

Farmers, on the other hand, consistently sought greater trade protection. Once Germany regained tariff autonomy, they insisted on the reinstitution of the 1902 tariff rates. Thereafter, farmers continued to push for tariff hikes, import licenses, and price controls to inflate domestic food prices. This pressure peaked in 1930, as Agriculture Minister Walter Schiele acknowledged that agricultural pressure groups wished that "the price level for all agricultural products be uncoupled from the world market" through "a closed system of tariffs" (Spaulding 1989, 203–4, 321–26).

Agricultural protectionism limited the potential scope for trade treaties, since Germany could not grant preferential access in food and raw materials without inciting protests from plantation owners and peasants. Expanded trade with central Europe particularly threatened peasants who produced

52. "IG Farben's Neu-Ordnung," Correspondence and Reports relating to German Cartels, Monopolies, and Industrial Firms, 1943–46, Box 10, RG 151.

53. To mute this opposition, steelmakers offered rebates to finished goods producers for metal incorporated in exports (Ropke 1934, 33–35).

meat, dairy products, vegetables, and fruits. Moreover, the Junkers would not accept duty concessions, even though most competition in grains and cereals came from the Americas. As the German market grew increasingly impenetrable, agrarian states sought commercial agreements to secure customs preferences, or at least place a ceiling on German tariffs. The Reichslandbund (German Agrarian League), however, lobbied against trade treaties with Romania and Hungary in 1931. This group also protested the proposed customs union with Austria, even though Austria's more-industrialized economy posed less competition for German farmers (Ránki 1983, 54–56; Kaiser 1980, 21–30).

With Hitler's accession to power, farmers pushed for even higher tariffs. Soon the German market was so tightly sealed that the Nazi regime could grant preferential treatment without disrupting domestic agriculture: import controls and monopoly marketing arrangements allocated quotas to favor specific countries; the government could purchase large quantities at negotiated prices, with little effect on domestic producers (Ránki 1983, 125–26). As one memo explained, "controlled foreign imports" produced "fewer disadvantageous consequences for German agriculture." This made it easier to preserve "the secure organization of domestic production and market relations" (Grenzebach 1988, 36). Schacht was then free to pursue bilateral trade agreements in the region with little dissent from large farmers or peasants.

The Politics of Trade in Germany

Industrial politics in interwar Germany favored two groups: large agriculture and heavy industry. The ascendance of these two blocs dates to the historic iron-rye alliance in the 1879 tariff. For the Junkers, political power flowed from control over the Ministry of Agriculture and influence in the Reichstag. For steel barons, large size, concentration, and close ties to the Finance Ministry translated into political clout. A postwar alliance between the Reichslandbund and the Union of German Iron and Steel Industrialists reconstituted the iron-rye coalition in the most protectionist political party, the German Nationalist Party. By the late 1920s, however, the Junkers' political importance had declined, while exporters in the chemical, electrical, and machinery industries had grown in stature. These branches of heavy industry backed more liberal, protrade parties, and they wielded influence in the Economics Ministry and the Foreign Office (Spaulding 1989, 188–95). Within the RDI, IG Farben chairman Karl Duisberg served to bridge the basic industries and consumer goods producers, and an uneasy balance prevailed between steel interests and the other manufacturers (Abraham 1981, 125–34). Divisions over trade were thus institutionalized in the major industrial association and the Weimar cabinet, which stalemated policy-making.

The interests of these competing groups converged as the depression deepened. This convergence coincided with the advent of Hitler's regime in 1933. Under the Nazi government, foreign trade measures did not require the Reichstag's approval; instead, they were implemented by executive order. Yet pressure groups in heavy industry enjoyed several sources of influence in the cabinet and the Economics Ministry.

For one, heavy industry was highly concentrated: a few companies controlled large shares of output in most sectors, and the leading firms dwarfed their rivals. IG Farben was two-thirds of the chemical industry; the number two firm, Wintershall, had less than one-tenth as much invested capital, and the next fifteen largest companies added to one-third of IG Farben's book value (Hayes 1987, 17). In electrical equipment, Siemens and AEG were responsible for two-thirds of all production. Seven steel firms produced 80 percent of output. Even the auto industry, though small by U.S. standards, was composed of a few companies. In each case, large conglomerates had integrated backward into raw materials and diversified into related product lines. As the leaders of industrial cartels and near monopolists in a range of products, these firms enjoyed economic and financial clout.

Moreover, the priority the Nazi regime placed on public works and rearmament provided a means through which economic power was translated into political sway. Hitler's designs required large supplies of basic materials; expanded use of electrical power; increased production of vehicles, munitions, and explosives; and self-sufficiency in raw materials, particularly oil and rubber. As a result, public works and rearmament benefited not only the traditional war industries but also companies that could use state contracts to compensate for lost foreign markets for consumer goods. Though leading private firms later would have to compete with state-run enterprises—particularly after 1936—their influence was less contested in the early years of the Nazi government, when the new course in trade policy was charted. Active participation in rearmament and the rise in public procurement therefore provided a source of political influence for members of heavy industry.

In short, while National Socialist ideology glorified the peasantry and small shopkeepers at the expense of big business, once in power the Nazis were favorable to large firms in heavy industry. Mason (1968, 176) writes:

From 1933 to 1936 economic policy . . . was left to the propertied classes. . . . This division of labor and the approval given in economic circles to the aggressive moves in foreign policy in these years was based on the belief that industry and the [Nazi Party] shared a common imperialist program. This apparent consensus of opinion is . . . evident in the cooperation between heavy industry, the military, the party and the civil service in the question of rearmament.

In particular, the Four-Year Plan of 1936 reflected the political dominance of IG Farben, as Germany's armaments program focused on developing chemical substitutes for raw materials. The industries favored in this plan—chemicals, steel, engineering, and building materials—received preferential treatment in the allocation of foreign exchange and raw materials. "The Four-Year Plan," an Economics Ministry official noted, "was, in fact, an I.G. plan" (Borkin 1978, 71). Even if heavy industry did not bring the Nazi Party to power or finance it to any large degree, it nevertheless grew close to the state and the military in the course of the rearmament program, and through these ties the leading firms enjoyed considerable power in economic policy.

Trade Policy, 1925–36

Trade protection from the return of tariff autonomy to the advent of the Nazi government focused almost exclusively on agriculture. The 1925 tariff included per ton duties of 3.5 RM on wheat and 3 RM on rye. After several tariff revisions, duties reached 18.5 RM for wheat and 20 RM for rye by 1930 (Spaulding 1989, 215–18, 323–27). These rates were nearly three times world prices, while barley tariffs were almost twice as great as world prices. High rates of protection also prevailed for wheat flour (326 percent of import prices), raw sugar (280 percent), hogs (160 percent), fresh and chilled meat (120 percent), butter (93 percent), and tobacco (63 percent) (League of Nations 1935, 18–20; USTC 1943, 40–41).

Due to the farm lobby's strength, a relaxation of food tariffs in return for market access for manufactured exports was infeasible. Trade talks with Poland and Czechoslovakia from 1925 to 1927 went nowhere (Spaulding 1989, 240–71). The Foreign Ministry reached commercial treaties with Romania and Hungary in 1931, but pressure from agrarian groups and the objections of the agriculture and interior ministries scuttled the treaties. A customs union with Austria also was aborted due to complaints from farmers and pressure from foreign governments opposed to Germany's deviation from MFN.

After 1933, however, the Nazi government limited foreign exchange allocations and imposed agricultural quotas to squeeze imports. Under these conditions, imports could be shifted toward neighboring countries without undermining high food prices in Germany (Spaulding 1989, 329–38). The Economics Ministry reached its first bilateral agreement with Bulgaria in 1933; farm lobbies issued few objections, as Bulgaria provided little competition in the German agricultural market. Thereafter, Germany signed commercial arrangements with Hungary, Romania, and Yugoslavia in 1934 and revised its treaties with Bulgaria and Yugoslavia in 1936. In these agreements, Germany contracted to purchase specified amounts of primary goods—grains such as wheat, corn, and barley; meat products such as beef cattle, pork, bacon, and lard; and other items, including flax and hemp, hides and skins, and fruits and vegetables—at fixed prices considerably higher than world markets would bear. The Nazi government also demanded greater supplies of strategic materials—oil from Romania, copper and bauxite from Yugoslavia—as a quid pro quo for paying high prices for cereals and meat.[54]

In return, Germany received tariff preferences of 20–30 percent for a number of industrial goods: steel, machinery, electrical goods, glass and glassware, plastic and rubber products, textiles, apparel, and footwear. Initially, central European governments were reluctant to openly favor German exports; preferences were kept secret or granted in the form of trade credits, quota or exchange allocations, transportation subsidies, and state contracts to disguise violations of MFN (Basch 1943, 161–69). Bulgaria, for instance, imposed 35 percent surtaxes on hard currency imports, which encouraged purchases of industrial goods from Germany instead of its competitors. Hungary granted special licenses for products previously prohibited from entering customs. Yuogoslavia allocated government contracts to German firms such as Krupp, which was selected to build rolling mills and an iron foundry at the Zenica steelworks.

As central European countries accumulated growing clearing balances on their German exports, they adopted more direct measures to favor Germany. Officials routinely manipulated tariffs, import quotas, and exchange allocations to make German exports more attractive and discriminate against competing goods because clearing balances could not be liquidated through the operation of private markets if these goods were too expensive to sell domestically. After 1936, economic expansion in Germany and the reorientation toward armaments production created a shortage of goods at home and made it difficult for industry to fill orders abroad at reasonable prices. Germany's

---

54. Strategic materials could be sold for hard currency, so countries were reluctant to part with such commodities in purchasing arrangements and barter deals (Ránki 1983, 136–50; Kaiser 1980, 75–79).

short-term solution was to increase arms deliveries to the region. In addition, however, clearing partners were forced to purchase lower-quality items at inflated prices to prevent their standing balances with Germany from ballooning. The USTC (1943, 25) asserts that because Germany paid "premium" prices for food and raw materials, countries in return had to accept deliveries of superfluous goods "such as aspirin, toys, harmonicas, and so forth" to reduce clearing credits.

This impression that Germany flooded central Europe with useless surpluses is exaggerated (Andersen 1946, 58–59). Basch (1943, 181) points out that the share of machinery and capital equipment purchased from Germany totaled 80 percent for Bulgaria, 70 percent for Hungary, 50 percent for Yugoslavia, and 35 percent for Romania; Ellis (1941, 264) adds that the export drive in central Europe was most successful in electrical goods, machinery, and transportation equipment such as motorcycles. The Economics Ministry sought to stimulate exports of capital goods and armaments and limit sales of raw-materials-intensive consumer goods, so bilateral arrangements strongly favored heavy industry at the expense of light industry. Tariff structures and exchange policies in central Europe reflected this bias, resulting in a sharp decline in the export of consumer goods such as textiles. In addition, large firms in heavy industry received preferential exchange allocations from German authorities to serve their import needs.

Overall, bilateral trade agreements contributed to the economic recovery. In the depths of the depression, heavy industry faced insolvency in spring 1934. Subsidies and tax breaks from the Reichswehr Ministry could not keep these companies afloat. Export promotion also was critical to the armaments program because firms refused to enlarge plants or build new ones without guaranteed outlets for surplus production (James 1986, 380–87). With preferential access to Danube markets, heavy industry could dispose of capital goods no longer saleable in western Europe. The 1934 trade agreement with Romania, for instance, amounted to 22 million RM worth of investment goods—40 percent of Germany's yearly exports to that country in a single deal. The 1936 treaty with Yugoslavia doubled German exports from 20 million RM to 40 million RM. "Such barter arrangements," Grenzebach (1988, 176, 231) concludes, "provided German big business with guaranteed orders on a scale unthinkable during the doldrums of the Depression. . . . Without these new markets for German industry . . . the scope of the German economic recovery is scarcely conceivable."

In sum, heavy industry pushed for trade treaties in the region after the decline in foreign sales in 1929. Initially, industry groups showed no favoritism for markets to the east as opposed to the west, and they supported the MFN clause in German trade. As the situation worsened after 1931, however, large companies in the heavy and chemical industries advocated open discrimination as they sought to expand markets in central Europe. In response, Germany negotiated a series of trade treaties between 1933 and 1936. The trade agreements plan was directed toward countries in which German capital goods would not face direct competition; thus, Czechoslovakia was not included in this economic sphere because the Nazi government could not "count on a domination of the market by German businessmen" (Spaulding 1989, 389). Preferential trade was designed to exclude the exports of other countries: as a Yugoslav official noted, "there could be no question of Yugoslavia granting industrial preferences to another country" (Grenzebach 1988, 143).

Beginning in 1937, securing the requisite raw materials for war became more of a focus of Nazi economic policy than export promotion. With diminished export capacity due to rearmament, Germany could not sell enough abroad to satisfy its need for food and raw materials. Unable to acquire these resources through peaceful trade and unwilling to slow its armaments program to free production for foreign consumers, the Nazi regime instead prepared for conquest to permit "the significant expansion of the living space, that is, the raw material and food product base of our people," as one memo put it (Ránki 1983, 154–56; Grenzebach 1988, 238–40). Whether German heavy industry encouraged or supported this policy shift is debatable. But even if these firms did not favor the "Ludendorffian solution" (Berghahn 1996, 17) of autarky, brutal annexation, and Lebensraum ("living space"), they nonetheless cooperated with the Nazi economic program in its early years to profit from the formation of a protected trading bloc.

Conclusion: Trading Blocs in the Interwar Period

The formation of protectionist trading blocs in the interwar period was a response to the emergence of technologies that demanded larger markets. By the 1920s, many products of the second industrial revolution were most efficiently manufactured in large factories. Difficulties assimilating these new technologies caused firms to advocate two sorts of policy responses. First, firms with short production runs encountered stiff competition from larger rivals—usually more efficient U.S. firms. These producers reacted by lobbying for trade protection to regain the domestic market and catch up to competitors abroad. Second, firms with geographically limited home markets pushed for preferential trade because they could not mass produce for national consumption alone. Customs integration with colonies, dependencies, or neighboring countries provided opportunities to exploit scale economies by expanding output and gaining market shares through trade diversion.

Imperial protection produced few reasons for producers to push trade policy in a more liberal direction. These trading blocs were not large enough to release firms from the constraints of small national markets, particularly with the breakdown of normal trade across regions and the depressed economic climate of the period. In some cases firms could ride partway down their cost curves, but rarely could they match the volume characteristic of U.S. factories. Moreover, there was little prospect of production sharing to exploit intrabloc differences in factor prices. Production processes were technically difficult to break up, so firms sought to concentrate all stages of manufacturing at one location; with the exception of Japan, which transferred some heavy industry to occupied territories, FDI inside interwar trading blocs was minuscule. Incentives to continue to expand high tariff walls outward therefore persisted up to World War II.

The collapse of the interwar trading system does not validate the conventional view that equates regionalism with protection. Rather, two distinct historical conditions motivated protectionism.[55] First, 1930s protectionism was, in large measure, a reaction to U.S. industrial supremacy. The United States monopolized the industrial progress of the prewar era due to its large consumer market and innovation in mass production methods. For other countries, catching up in international competition was a matter of diverting enough trade in imperial and regional markets for producers to capture scale economies. Second, the power of exclusion was very high in the interwar economy: because of technological limitations and policy restraints, it was difficult for foreign firms to invest inside trading blocs to share in their benefits. Countries therefore could reserve imperial markets for national producers, provided that tariffs were high enough to deny outsiders a price advantage. Thus, protectionism and trading blocs reflected the need to expand the scale of production and the ease of excluding outsiders in an era when capital was not mobile across borders.

55. This is not to dismiss the role of forces such as the absence of hegemonic leadership, shifts in the international balance of power, the global macroeconomic crisis, or changes in the political composition of governments. Clearly the interaction of many factors made the interwar collapse more complete (and more tragic) than it might have been otherwise.

CHAPTER 4

The United States and Multilateral Trade Liberalization, 1922–67

As Japan, Britain, and Germany withdrew from the world trading system in the 1930s, the United States redoubled its commitment to MFN principles and embarked on a crusade to end discrimination in international commerce. In the process, the U.S. government reversed its historic protectionism. Soon after the Smoot-Hawley tariff, the Reciprocal Trade Agreements Act (RTAA) of 1934 launched a program of bilateral negotiations to liberalize tariffs and dissolve preferential arrangements. This policy culminated in the creation of the GATT, which achieved significant multilateral tariff reductions in six negotiating rounds from 1947 to 1967.

This chapter examines why the United States campaigned to reduce tariffs and restore the principle of nondiscrimination against the tide of protectionism and trading blocs. The book's analytical approach relates this policy shift to the economic interests of industries with large returns to scale. In contrast to industries abroad, which were slow to introduce techniques to increase throughput and lengthen production runs, U.S. industries achieved very large output volumes. Producers could effectively exploit scale economies in the enormous domestic market, usually without relying on foreign sales.

Because the leading firms in mass production industries were the largest in the world, they had little reason to support trade protection. This chapter shows that large-scale producers favored cuts in U.S. tariffs and reciprocal agreements to open markets abroad. These firms wanted liberalization worldwide, and they did not push for the creation of a trading bloc. In fact, firms with subsidiaries abroad consistently resisted bilateral arrangements with Canada. For industries with large returns to scale, liberalization and MFN were inseparable components of trade strategy.

However, postwar reconstruction in Europe and Japan narrowed international differences in scales of production, undercutting the dominant position of U.S. firms. Discontent with unreciprocated tariff cuts festered in the 1950s, and more and more mass production industries expressed misgivings about further trade liberalization. In the Trade Expansion Act of 1962, several formerly protrade industries sought safeguards against foreign competition; a few others were openly protectionist. Regional initiatives also gained ground as firms moved manufacturing offshore and developed production-sharing networks. In 1964, the United States sought its first waiver under GATT Article XXIV to implement free trade in automotive products with Canada. In the twilight of the Kennedy Round, the liberal era in U.S. trade policy ended, and a new strategy—first protectionist, then regional in its approach—began to take shape.

From Smoot-Hawley to the GATT

The U.S. government's quest for a global market free of trading blocs dates to the years after World War I. Until then, the United States had employed a conditional version of MFN, under which tariff reductions in bilateral agreements were not freely extended; instead, countries maintaining trade treaties with the United States had to "pay" for improved preferential rates with additional concessions. But conditional MFN, the USTC concluded in a series of postwar studies, encouraged foreign governments to discriminate against U.S. trade to allow bargaining room to obtain future tariff benefits. Unconditional MFN, the USTC argued, would promote an "open door" abroad through the enticement of a minimum tariff schedule for all countries practicing nondiscrimination. The Tariff Act of 1922 therefore approved the use of an unconditional MFN clause in commercial treaties, and equal tariff treatment became a central tenet of foreign economic policy (Parrini 1969, 19–22, 227–37).

But even as the United States shifted to unconditional MFN, it also raised duties on a range of agricultural goods and manufactures, established protection for "war baby" industries deemed critical to national security, and introduced measures to combat dumping, exchange depreciation, and price deflation in the war's aftermath. In 1930, Congress passed the Smoot-Hawley tariff, commonly described as the highest tariff in U.S. history. Initially conceived as relief for farmers, this bill hiked duties on thousands of items and extended generous rates of protection to many sectors of manufacturing (Taussig 1931, chaps. 10–11).

After Smoot-Hawley, however, the United States reversed its longstanding policy of trade protection. During President Franklin Roosevelt's first term, Secretary of State Cordell Hull advanced a trade agreements program built on tariff reciprocity and unconditional MFN. Hull wanted to scale back U.S. tariffs, but he recognized that this could not be done unilaterally. In the wake of the failed 1933 World Economic Conference, Hull also doubted the prospects for "a worthwhile multilateral undertaking." Bilateral negotiations, he concluded, offered the best means for the United States to reduce its tariffs, engage other countries in the process of liberalizing trade, and promote the open door abroad (Gardner 1964, 40–46; Evans 1971, 5–7).

Congress approved Hull's initiative in the RTAA, which permitted the Roosevelt administration to reduce tariffs by up to 50 percent. In contrast to the 1922 Tariff Act, which failed to stimulate trade negotiations and thus left no breaches in the tariff wall (Parrini 1969, 237–46), the State Department used RTAA authority to conclude twenty-three treaties by 1940 and nine more during World War II. Diplomats from the United States focused their efforts on Hull's great nemesis, Imperial Preference in the British Commonwealth. In trade negotiations with Canada in 1935 and with Britain and Canada in 1938, the United States pushed for concessions on items with the greatest discrimination against U.S. goods to reduce trade preferences. Yet the State Department rarely insisted on equivalent tariff reciprocity, as it accepted a number of tariff bindings, rather than tariff cuts, in return for real reductions in U.S. duties. Thus, the primary achievement of the RTAA was substantial, enduring trade liberalization in the United States, rather than the opening of foreign markets. By 1945, U.S. tariffs had been reduced 44 percent to their lowest level since 1913 (Eckes 1995, 141–51).

During and after World War II, the State Department intensified its campaign to break up empires and dissolve trading blocs. In the 1941 Atlantic Charter, U.S. officials pushed Britain to accept trade "without discrimination and on equal terms" as a crucial postwar objective. The Lend-Lease Agreements reinforced this commitment: in return for wartime assistance, Article VII required U.S. allies to pledge support for "the elimination of all forms of discriminatory treatment in international commerce, and . . . the reduction of tariffs and other trade barriers." Britain again promised to end tariff preferences as a condition for postwar loans in the Anglo-American Financial Agreement of 1945 (Gardner 1969, 41–67, 107–8, 152–57).

The State Department laid out the procedure to fulfill these obligations in its *Proposals for an International Conference on Trade and Employment,* which stated: "members should enter into arrangements for the substantial reduction of tariffs and for the elimination of tariff preferences, action for the elimination of tariff preferences being taken in conjunction with adequate measures for the substantial reduction of barriers to world trade" (Notter 1949, 629).

Under this formula, allied nations would reach an agreement to liberalize tariffs and empire preferences. In the meantime, Britain and the other colonial powers could not raise existing margins of preference or introduce new ones. Moreover, while the *Proposals* envisioned "mutually advantageous" results through reciprocal bargaining (that is, the United States would ease trade barriers to compensate empires for lower margins of preference), nondiscrimination took primacy over trade liberalization, as preferences would have to be "eliminated" while tariffs only needed to be "reduced."

The United States pursued these objectives at parallel conferences in Geneva and Havana in 1947–48. The main obstacle in these negotiations was Britain's insistence on preserving Imperial Preference and currency controls. Ultimately the State Department conceded these points: both the GATT treaty of October 1947 and the Havana Charter of March 1948 exempted existing preferential systems from MFN rules; other provisions authorized governments to employ trade and currency controls, even if discriminatory, to alleviate balance of payments problems. In addition, Article XXIV of the GATT permitted further departures from MFN for customs unions and free trade agreements. Finally, the tariff schedules in the GATT treaty committed the United States to cuts of up to 50 percent on a wide range of goods, in return for small reductions or mere bindings of foreign tariffs and margins of preference (Zeiler 1999, 108–26).

The State Department's efforts to promote free trade multilateralism faced a second obstacle as well: protectionist sentiment among segments of U.S. society and Republicans in Congress. Protectionists denounced the Havana Charter as too much liberalization too quickly, while perfectionists objected to the treaty's myriad loopholes and exceptions to free trade principles and MFN rules. When President Harry Truman withdrew the Havana Charter from consideration in the Senate in 1950, the provisional GATT treaty became the de facto international trade regime. Moreover, the sweeping power to liberalize tariffs conferred in early versions of the RTAA was curtailed. After 1947, RTAA bills restricted negotiating authority to one or two years and limited tariff cuts to 10–20 percent. Congress also added an escape clause to revoke tariff concessions that confronted domestic producers with surges of import competition, and it introduced peril point provisions to prohibit tariff cuts the USTC deemed harmful to domestic industry.[1] Weighed down by these constraints, the next four GATT rounds to 1960 yielded less significant tariff reductions than those negotiated at Geneva in 1947 (Pastor 1980, 99–103; Evans 1971, 11–20).

---

1. The peril point soon lapsed but was reinstated in 1951.

The Trade Expansion Act of 1962 temporarily boosted the slowing pace of multilateral liberalization, as President John F. Kennedy won congressional authority to cut tariffs up to 50 percent across the board. The Kennedy Round of the GATT reduced tariffs by 35 percent. But to win the right to launch a new trade round, Kennedy first had to appease protectionist pressures from labor-intensive industries and low-skill workers by tightening quantitative restrictions on textiles, raising tariffs on glassware and carpets, and introducing Trade Adjustment Assistance for workers and firms uprooted by trade (Zeiler 1992, 87–129).

The Kennedy Round's completion in 1967 marked the apex of the GATT. Discontent in the United States with what many regarded as unreciprocated tariff cuts festered throughout the 1950s and into the 1960s. The U.S. government had not pushed Britain to immediately end Imperial Preference; it had tolerated discrimination against U.S. goods by encouraging Europe to liberalize internally and form the EC; it had not aggressively pushed Japan to dismantle protectionist barriers. As reconstruction in these countries advanced, U.S. industry faced growing competition. With the trade surpluses of the early postwar period eroding, arguments that the United States could no longer accept uneven tariff bargains gained ground. Calls for reciprocity to open markets abroad and retaliation to punish unfair foreign trade barriers intensified.

Three important conclusions emerge from this overview of U.S. trade policy between 1922 and 1967. First, the United States steadfastly supported non-discrimination and multilateralism after its adoption of unconditional MFN. The RTAA automatically extended negotiated tariff concessions to all countries that had a trade treaty with the United States. In the years before World War II, the State Department sought to break down tariff margins in the British Empire; during the war it extracted pledges to eliminate these preferences altogether. Though provisions in the GATT treaty, the Havana Charter, and the Marshall Plan compromised these multilateral principles to facilitate European reconstruction and cold war unity, the U.S. government sought a waiver under GATT Article XXIV only once—the Automotive Products Trade Agreement (APTA) with Canada in 1964. For nearly half a century, the United States adhered to nondiscrimination even as others expanded empires and formed trading blocs.

Second, the United States reversed its historic protectionism soon after the Smoot-Hawley tariff. Duties paid as a percentage of manufactured imports declined from 40 percent in 1930 to less than 7 percent in 1967. In most of the treaties negotiated between 1934 and 1945, the United States accepted steep tariff cuts in return for concessions of little value. The first six rounds of the

GATT likewise exchanged significant reductions in U.S. tariffs for limited market-opening measures abroad. Though foreign governments emphasized, correctly, that the United States entered negotiations as a high-tariff country until 1948, tariff reductions were unequal both before and after this date. Legislation in the United States mandated *reciprocal* trade liberalization, but in practice trade liberalization was almost unilateral.

Third, enthusiasm for further tariff cuts waned after 1950. The U.S. government made limited tariff reductions in the four rounds that followed the inaugural GATT conference in 1947. Though the Kennedy Round produced comprehensive liberalization across the board, protectionist lobbying was building in the United States. Nontariff barriers spread to substitute for the tariffs previously bargained away. Pressure began to surface for retaliation to punish trade partners for unfair trade barriers and unreciprocated tariff cuts. All of this was a prelude to the changes that would overtake U.S. trade policy in the next decade.

Industry Groups and Trade Preferences

The first part of the chapter generates expectations about trade preferences in industries with large returns to scale in two time periods, 1922–45 and 1945–67. In most of these industries, large-scale production created incentives for firms and business groups to support trade liberalization. Expectations about trade preferences are then compared to lobbying activity in the two periods. The analysis finds that throughout the eras under examination, most firms and business associations in industries with large returns to scale advocated tariff cuts and nondiscrimination. However, small-scale producers, principally in the chemical industry, sought to block trade liberalization in the years before the war, while industries whose scale position was declining after the war began to push for trade protection in the 1950s.

The second part of the chapter examines industry coalitions, party politics, and policy-making processes. While large-scale firms in heavy industry campaigned for trade liberalization, light industries pushed for the Smoot-Hawley tariff and sought to block trade liberalization in subsequent years. Institutional changes that shifted authority over tariffs from the legislative to the executive branch—factors outside the scope of the book's theory—are critical to understanding the shift in U.S. policy during this period. Though some protectionist industries had the political clout to resist deep tariff cuts, no longer could they engage in the sort of tariff pork barreling that was typical before 1930. A statistical analysis of U.S. tariffs demonstrates that after three decades of liberalization, industries with large scales of production had low tariffs in 1964, while labor-intensive and geographically concentrated industries remained more heavily protected.

The chapter's final section evaluates why the United States never formed its own trading bloc when empires and preferential arrangements were expanding in the 1930s or when Europe and developing countries launched regional initiatives after 1950. Notably, growing cross-border trade and extensive FDI in Canada never stimulated discussions for a regional arrangement until 1964; in fact, U.S. firms with Canadian affiliates fought measures to liberalize regional trade throughout the period. This section argues that the enormous mass market in the United States made a trading bloc unnecessary. Instead, U.S. multinationals were content to invest behind Canada's high tariff walls, as long as the Canadian government did not modify the regulatory bargain for their branch plants.

The Scale of U.S. Industry after World War I

Writing in 1931, F. W. Taussig (1931, 473) noted: "the successful American industries are those turning out great quantities of a single product by large-scale methods." Almost all of the mass production industries in the United States enjoyed extraordinary advantages of large scale. The most prominent example is the automobile industry: between 1910 and 1914, Ford's production of passenger cars increased from 18,664 to 248,307. By 1929, both Ford and GM produced 1.5 million autos, while no European or Asian producer made as many as 80,000 (Wilkins and Hill 1964, 52–53). Companies in the United States also dominated global markets for most types of high-volume machinery: Singer, for example, produced 2.5 million sewing machines in 1913, two-thirds of world production (Davies 1976, 162); NCR sold 150,000 cash registers, a 75 percent market share (Cortada 1993, 70–73). On average, assembly lines in the United States turned out five times as many tractors, four times as many typewriters, and twice as many sewing machines as the largest plants overseas—in fact, the output of tractors, typewriters, and refrigerators *per plant* surpassed the total production of these items in Britain and Japan. Overall, the world's twelve largest automobile firms, nine farm machinery firms, and five office machinery firms were American.

Table 13 displays the scale of U.S. output for twenty-one products in 1929. In seventeen of these products, U.S. firms achieved the world's largest scales. Firms were most dominant in assembly-line consumer goods: average factory output was more than four times greater than in any country for automobiles, typewriters, tractors, and sewing machines. In many producer goods as well, size advantages compensated for expensive labor due to steep cost curves, as U.S. plants generally maintained higher productivity while employing fewer workers than foreign factories. Steel mills in the United States, for instance, produced 1.5 times more than German plants and four times more than British factories, which helped to offset wages twice as high as Britain's and four times the German level (Berglund and Wright 1929, 56–62).

Only in chemicals was the United States at a disadvantage. Dye makers operated "little more than assembly plants . . . entirely dependent on intermediates imported from Germany" (Haynes 1945, 313). The combined output of the largest synthetic nitrogen producers, Allied Chemical and Dupont, was

TABLE 13.   Scale of Production in the United States, 1929

Industry/Product	Output per Plant	Largest Competitor	Percentage of Largest Competitor's Output
Transportation equipment			
Automobiles	39,534	Germany	658.0
Trucks and buses	2,777	Germany[a]	
Aircraft	63	Germany	190.2
Tires	860,858	Germany	153.6
Locomotives	106	Germany	123.7
Motorcycles	4,058	Germany	121.7
Electrical and machinery			
Typewriters	36,909	Germany	496.2
Tractors	8,658	Germany	488.0
Sewing machines	34,511	Britain	425.2
Vacuum cleaners	54,124	Germany[a]	
Electric refrigerators	22,946	Germany[a]	
Electronic tubes	1,894,725	Britain	303.2
Radios	28,802	Germany	295.1
Lightbulbs	12,561,538	Germany	167.2
Basic materials			
Steel	196,421 tons	Germany	145.5
Pig iron	404,638 tons	Germany	137.5
Chemicals and fibers			
Explosives	5,578 thousand lb.	Germany[a]	
Rayon	4,021 thousand lb.	Japan	98.7
Alkalies and sodas	36,309 tons	Germany	88.2
Synthetic ammonia[b]	19,414 tons	Germany	20.5
Dyestuffs	2,063 thousand lb.	Germany	15.7

Sources: Data from U.S. Bureau of the Census 1930.

[a]Exact figure for Germany cannot be calculated due to industry definitions.

[b]USTC 1937.

one-fifth of IG Farben's capacity (Markham 1958, 102–3). European multinationals dominated the rayon market, as U.S. firms failed to keep pace with technological changes that increased MES production to seventy million pounds per plant (Markham 1952, 49–50).[2] In inorganic chemicals, efforts to implement mass production resulted in excess capacity and damaging price wars (Haber 1971, 176–77). Industrial chemistry in the United States simply lacked the economies of scale in production and R&D to compete with Germany and Britain. Moreover, the higher wage burden made the failure to achieve mass production very costly. In rayon, for instance, production costs exceeded Japan's by 177 percent, Italy's by 93 percent, Germany's by 40 percent, and Britain's by 20 percent, even though U.S. firms nearly matched European and Japanese producers in scale (Markham 1952, 171).

Where U.S. firms achieved a larger scale than foreign rivals, the large internal market was an enormous advantage. Automobiles are the prototypical case: Americans bought twenty-five times more cars in 1929 than consumers in any other country. Firms producing electrical appliances also achieved "unequaled levels of output" due to the "huge domestic market" (Backman 1962, 283). Domestic steel consumption supported forty-four steelworks with more than half a million tons of capacity and eighteen others over a million tons, whereas Germany had only eight with more than a million tons of capacity and Britain just three of more than half a million tons. In addition to the large population, high wages increased the demand for labor-saving industrial machinery and home appliances, long distances created a market for transportation and communications equipment, and abundant arable land enhanced the need for tractors and other farm machinery.

Table 14 shows that in most cases, the market in the United States allowed room for many plants with long production runs. For example, U.S. consumers purchased 4 million cars; with an MES of 500,000 autos per model, the market could support eight plants. By comparison, Britain, Germany, and Japan together consumed 307,000 autos, less than two-thirds of one MES plant. The domestic market was smaller than MES levels in only one product, motorcycles, as the popularity of the cheap automobile restricted sales. Consumption in the United States was more than twice as great as consumption in the next largest foreign market in every case except motorcycles, synthetic ammonia (because organic nitrates were abundant), and dyestuffs (where high prices choked off domestic sales).

---

2. Markham (1952, 7) notes: "The technology of rayon production is one of the few mass-production techniques wherein European scientists and industrialists have set the pace."

These figures explain why U.S. firms exported less than British, German, and Japanese firms, despite their larger scale. Chandler (1990, 52–53) notes:

> Th[e] rapid, continuing rate of growth of consumer demand, like the geographical extent of the market, provided American entrepreneurs with more opportunities—in more industries—to exploit the economies of scale and scope than existed anywhere else in the world. . . . Because they had the world's largest and fastest growing domestic market, American manufacturers were much less dependent on foreign trade than were those of Britain and Germany.

In most of the heavy and chemical industries, U.S. firms exported no more than 15 percent of sales, much less than firms in the same industries in other countries—not because of any disability in international competition but because domestic demand absorbed most of their production. Farm machinery producers, for instance, regarded exports as "sideline or incidental sales, to be welcomed. . . only if they did not interfere with domestic sales" (Broehl 1984, 597). With a mass market in which to exploit economies of scale, U.S. firms faced none of the handicaps that motivated industry groups in Japan, Britain, and Germany to push to expand protected markets in imperial trading blocs.

In sum, U.S. firms gained first-mover advantages in most industries with large returns to scale, as the enormous home market aided the development

TABLE 14.   Relative Size of the U.S. Market

Product	MES Divided by U.S. Consumption	Largest Foreign Market	U.S. Consumption Divided by Foreign Consumption
Motorcycles	8.10	Germany	0.1
Sewing machines	0.93	Britain[a]	3.4
Synthetic ammonia	0.92	Germany	0.8
Typewriters	0.91	Germany	3.4
Tractors	0.54	Germany	9.7
Electric motors	0.52	Britain[a]	14.4
Trucks and buses	0.40	Britain[a]	9.3
Rayon	0.30	Germany	2.6
Dyestuffs	0.24	Germany	1.1
Radios	0.21	Germany	2.8
Oil engines	0.14	Britain[a]	6.7
Automobiles	0.12	Britain	25.4
Tires	0.08	Germany	4.9
Steel	0.05	Germany	4.1

Source: Data from U.S. Bureau of the Census 1930; U.S. Bureau of Foreign and Domestic Commerce 1930.
[a]Data for Germany are not available.

and use of mass production techniques in the years around World War I. With these advantages, U.S. industries had little reason to seek trade protection. They also had no need for a trading bloc: they controlled a market of continental proportions, which facilitated cost reduction to levels low enough to allow sales abroad when local demand could not absorb surplus output. Preferential arrangements would only encourage more of the discrimination that already limited U.S. goods in colonial empires and continental Europe by the 1920s. Trade liberalization to open these foreign markets therefore was best achieved on a nondiscriminatory basis.

Mass Production Industries: Trade Preferences, 1922–45

Producers of automobiles, farm implements, and office and sewing machinery emerged as forceful advocates of trade liberalization well before the RTAA in 1934. Because firms in these industries had exploited the potential economies of scale, they declined to seek tariff increases on their goods and opposed trade protection for others during the 1920s, as hypothesis 5 anticipates.

Automakers were the most actively involved in trade lobbying. In 1929, the National Automobile Chamber of Commerce asked Congress to reduce automobile tariffs from 25 percent to 10 percent (U.S. Senate 1929 3:821–47). Ford sought to eliminate these duties, and it "vigorously opposed" Smoot-Hawley, which executives believed would incite retaliation abroad (Wilkins and Hill 1964, 205–6). In 1932, the auto industry launched a media campaign on the virtues of tariff reductions and reciprocal trade treaties.[3] The Automobile Manufacturers Association (AMA) pushed for "compensatory liberalization from those countries which offered potential outlets" (Gardner 1964, 39), and the group later supported Hull's trade program enthusiastically.[4]

Firms and trade associations in other assembly-line industries echoed these views. Singer pushed to move sewing machines to the free list and expressed fears of foreign retaliation against U.S. tariffs.[5] Office machinery firms publicly deplored Smoot-Hawley because tariffs prevented foreigners from earning dollars to buy U.S. goods. NCR sought liberalization to alleviate "tariff barriers,

3. "Reciprocal Tariffs Urged," *New York Times*, January 13, 1932, 21; "Auto Group Seeks Reforms on Tariff," *New York Times*, July 31, 1932, sec. 4, 1.
4. "Auto Makers Back Hull on Exports," *New York Times*, November 9, 1934, 38.
5. Singer communicated with policy makers privately and declined to testify at tariff hearings. Small firms in the Independent Family Sewing Machine Manufacturers raised the specter of import competition from Singer's foreign affiliates, which were "everywhere behind the tariff wall and secure," to defend the tariff as necessary protection against foreign competition *and* Singer (Davies 1976, 159–62).

trade restrictions and money complications," which injured "productivity [at] the Dayton factory" (Cortada 1993, 179). Typewriter companies supported reciprocal trade negotiations "earnestly and unanimously" (U.S. House of Representatives 1943, 1075). Farm equipment producers such as International Harvester and Caterpillar also pushed for trade agreements (U.S. House of Representatives 1945 2:2878). Other industries favoring the RTAA included producers of tires, aircraft, radios, telephones, and electrical appliances.[6]

Among the industries producing on a large scale, as shown in table 15, the steel industry's failure to seek trade liberalization is the principal inconsistency with hypothesis 5. Historically, steelmakers sought tariffs so imports would not undermine cartel prices—hence the nineteenth-century aphorism, popularized by steel-using industries, that the tariff was the "mother of trusts." After the turn of the century, however, the steel industry limited its protectionist demands (Berglund and Wright 1929, 224). Testifying to Congress in 1929, the American Iron and Steel Institute (AISI) recommended tariff increases only for pig iron and certain classes of bar iron. The group added: "we have complacently accepted the reduction in duty on the finished product [since 1909]" (U.S. Senate 1929 3:6).[7] But in the depths of the depression in 1932, the AISI campaigned against foreign subsidies, dumping, and exchange depreciation.[8] Though it never testified to Congress on any of the five RTAA bills up to 1945, the AISI protested lower steel duties in treaties with Belgium and Britain in hearings of the Committee for Reciprocity Information.[9]

Small-scale producers, table 16 demonstrates, mostly pushed for tariff increases and actively opposed trade agreements (the exception being the motorcycle industry). Dye manufacturers were the leading protectionists. The American Dye Institute lobbied for a restrictive system of tariffs and import licenses during World War I, with levies based on domestic prices rather than import prices to safeguard against dumping and exchange depreciation. In 1922, the group pushed to increase these barriers to block German firms from reentering the U.S. market. In 1929, the Synthetic Organic Chemical Manufacturers Association (SOCMA) defended its high tariffs of 55–60 percent with

6. "Divide on Treaty for French Trade," *New York Times*, June 26, 1935, 6. GE and Westinghouse supported lower tariffs for all of their products except lightbulbs (U.S. House of Representatives 1940 2:1202–3).

7. One producer pushed for duties higher than those requested by AISI but conceded that, unlike U.S. Steel and Bethlehem, "my plant is a small one and, consequently, I have not that volume of business" (U.S. House of Representatives 1929 3:1875).

8. "Steel Imports Cited in Drive on Dumping," *New York Times*, May 8, 1932, sec. 2, 7.

9. "Steel Men Decry New Tariff Cuts," *New York Times*, April 7, 1935, sec. 5, 1, 6; "Jobs Lost to 3,900 by Steel Imports," *New York Times*, July 15, 1935, 15.

additional specific duties per pound (U.S. House of Representatives 1929 1:68–76; Bidwell 1956, 188–90).

The rayon industry also was active in the protectionist cause. Producers sought higher tariffs in 1922 and pushed, without success, for a valuation system like the one for dyestuffs (USTC 1922, 420–21). In 1929, the Rayon Institute asked Congress to raise duties—which averaged 45 percent plus specific levies by weight—to save small plants from bankruptcy (U.S. Senate 1929 13:55–72). Firms producing ammonium sulfate and explosives sought greater trade protection as well (USTC 1922, 47, 543–45; U.S. House of Representatives 1929 1:309–13). Only companies making alkalies such as soda ash and caustic soda declined to seek higher tariffs, as they found existing rates "adequate" even

TABLE 15.   Trade Lobbying in Large-Scale U.S. Industries, 1922–45

Industry/Lobby Group	Position on the RTAA and Tariff Cuts: Support (+) or Oppose (−)
Automobiles	
National Automobile Chamber of Commerce; Ford; GM (1929)	+
AMA (1934–45)	+
Office machinery	
American, Michigan, and St. Louis Cash Register (1922)	−
Office Equipment Manufacturers Institute; Typewriter Manufacturers Export Association (1940–45)	+
Sewing machines	
Independent Family Sewing Machine Manufacturers (1922)	−
Farm machinery	
Caterpillar (1935)	+
International Harvester (1945)	+
Trucks and buses	
Ford; GM; Mack; International Harvester; White Motor (1929)	+
Electrical appliances	
National Electrical Manufacturers Association (1929)	+/−
Aircraft	
Aeronautical Chamber of Commerce (1940)	+
Tires	
Rubber Association of America (1922)	+
Goodyear (1940)	+
Steel	
AISI (1929–35)	−

TABLE 16.   Trade Lobbying in Small-Scale U.S. Industries, 1922–45

Industry/Lobby Group	Position on the RTAA and Tariff Cuts: Support (+) or Oppose (−)
Motorcycles	
Harley-Davidson; Motorcycle Manufacturers of America (1922)	+
Explosives	
Trojan Powder (1922)	−
Sporting Arms and Ammunition Manufacturers Institute (1945)	−
Rayon	
Tubize Rayon (1922)	−
Rayon Institute; Delaware Rayon (1929)	−
Rayon and Synthetic Yarn Producing Industries (1935)	−
Dupont; five other rayon firms (1945)	−
Alkalies and sodas	
Monsanto; Hooker Electrochemical; ten other firms (1922)	−
MCA (1934–45)	−
Synthetic ammonia	
Committee of Byproduct Coke Producers (1922–29)	−
Shell Chemical; Koppers (1933)	−
Dyestuffs	
SOCMA (1929–45)	−

though "foreign chemical trusts" paid lower wages (U.S. House of Representatives 1929 1:841–44).

After 1934, the chemical industry fought trade treaties and repeatedly challenged the constitutionality of the RTAA. The leading firms, such as Dupont, Allied Chemical, American Cyanamid, Monsanto, Dow, and Hooker Electrochemical, were openly hostile to tariff cuts, and SOCMA and the Manufacturing Chemists Association (MCA) testified against all five RTAA bills up to 1945. The dye industry vigorously defended American valuation and objected when the USTC recommended a cut in dye tariffs in negotiations with Switzerland (Bidwell 1956, 159–61; Haynes 1954, 60–61). Rayon producers complained that they could not survive a reduction in trade protection in treaties with European countries.[10] These firms argued for tariff hikes because even with the "rise in mass production of rayon" they still could not compete effec-

10. "Testimony of the Rayon and Synthetic Yarn Producing Industries," March 8, 1935, Trade Agreements Program File, 1934–35, Box 7, RG 20.

tively due to wages four to ten times higher than in Japan and Germany (U.S. House of Representatives 1945 2:2540–43).

To summarize, only producers of chemicals, which were small in scale compared to European rivals, opposed trade liberalization. Most of heavy industry had no need for trade protection because of its high rate of output. Instead, these industries sought tariff reductions in the RTAA. Moreover, they supported liberalization on a nondiscriminatory basis to open foreign markets and dissolve imperial arrangements.

The Scale of U.S. Industry after World War II

International differences in the scale of production were substantial immediately after the war but narrowed soon thereafter. In the 1950s, Britain, Western Europe, and Japan rebuilt their devastated industries and introduced new plant and equipment to replace assets destroyed in the war. This trend reduced—and occasionally eliminated—the cost advantages of U.S. firms. Nonetheless, most assembly-line industries in the United States remained world leaders, even when their relative scale of production was not as great as in 1929. Table 17, based on data from 1958, demonstrates that most U.S. factories still employed mass production techniques more effectively than those in other countries.

Still, there were prominent reversals of fortune. One such shift occurred in steel, as Hogan (1971 4:2092) noted:

> companies in Europe and Japan . . . have grown in size . . . so that they can install large, modern facilities and take advantage of economies of scale in a manner which was not possible heretofore. . . . Before World War II, there were very few large strip mills in operation outside the United States. . . . With the growth of the industry abroad, this has changed radically, for now in place of companies with one-half million tons or at most two million tons of steelmaking capacity, there are companies capable of producing many millions of tons.

The problem for the steel industry was not only that production runs were comparable in the United States and abroad; firms with large sunk investments in open-hearth methods also were slow to adopt new blast oxygen furnace technologies. As a result, Japanese (and later Korean) companies with lower labor costs and more efficient manufacturing processes achieved higher productivity, even in slightly smaller plants.

Major changes also occurred in electrical machinery, office machinery, sewing machines, and motorcycles. By 1958, European and Asian firms manufactured these goods on a comparable scale with cheaper labor. In electrical machinery, the United States maintained low costs for mass-produced motors and generators, but European firms moved ahead in heavy power-generating equipment, which could not be produced on an assembly line because custom craftsmanship to detailed specifications often was required (Bidwell 1956, 218, 233). In office machinery, U.S. firms gained leadership in electronic computers but lost their dominance in established products such as typewriters and calculators. Scale and cost advantages in sewing machines also declined rapidly.

In the chemical industry, however, U.S. firms improved their position. Strength in new petroleum-based chemicals helped to offset competitive weak-

TABLE 17.   Scale of Production in the United States, 1958

Industry/Product	Output per Plant	Largest Competitor	Percentage of Largest Competitor's Output
Transportation equipment			
Aircraft	54	Britain	287.9
Trucks and buses	23,861	Britain[a]	261.7
Automobiles	77,856	Britain[a]	219.1
Tires	1,275,886	Britain	177.8
Motorcycles	3,343	Germany	79.9
Electrical and Machinery			
Electric refrigerators	116,838	Britain[a]	330.5
Lightbulbs	35,167,621	Britain[a]	311.6
Electronic tubes	4,960,635	Britain[a]	310.0
Computing machines	2,977	Britain[a]	296.6
Tractors	14,848	Britain[a]	125.9
Typewriters	68,397	Germany[b]	
Sewing machines[c]	16,347	Germany[b]	
Basic materials			
Steel	309,509 tons	Japan	91.6
Chemicals and fibers			
Explosives	9,083 thousand lb.	Britain[a]	148.9
Rayon	39,883 thousand lb.	Japan	124.5
Alkalies and sodas	122,316 tons	Germany[b]	
Synthetic ammonia	106,208 tons	Britain[a]	102.1
Dyestuffs[d]	1,211 thousand lb.	Britain[a]	81.4

Source: Data from U.S. Bureau of the Census 1961; Board of Trade 1963; Prime Minister's Office 1962; Statistisches Bundesamt 1965.

[a]Comparable data for Germany and Japan are not available due to industry definitions.

[b]Comparable data for Britain, Germany, and Japan are not available due to industry definitions.

[c]Data are for 1954.

[d]Data are for all coal tar chemicals.

ness in dyes, inorganic chemicals, and synthetic fibers. Mergers in the dye industry led to "lower costs through larger-scale production and economies in
management" (Bidwell 1956, 182), but the German firms created out of the IG
Farben trust remained world leaders. Synthetic nitrogen capacity per plant
doubled between 1937 and 1955, despite the entry of several firms into the industry (Markham 1958, 106–7). Producers also increased output per plant in
rayon and synthetic fibers such as nylon and polyester.

The book's analytical framework predicts that changes in relative scale will
alter industry trade preferences. While successful mass production industries
should continue to favor tariff reductions and reciprocal trade agreements,
protrade preferences should weaken in industries with declining relative scale.
Specifically, producers of steel, office machinery, sewing machines, and motorcycles had incentives to drop out of the trade-liberalizing coalition. In contrast,
lobbying for protection is expected to diminish in synthetic fibers, industrial
chemicals, and agrochemicals. In dyestuffs, opposition to trade liberalization is
likely to remain strong.

Mass Production Industries: Trade Preferences, 1945–67

Producers in large-scale industries generally continued to favor trade liberalization after 1945, as shown in table 18. As European and Japanese reconstruction proceeded, however, many began to concede that their competitive
position was eroding. A Ford executive stated this succinctly: "the United
States may not inherently retain any industrial advantage it now has by virtue
of the size of our home market," he explained to Congress in 1958, because
European firms "have shown their ability to match and on occasion exceed us
in deriving the benefits, technological and economic, from such large-scale
production" (U.S. House of Representatives 1958b, 240). Even so, the AMA
and the Big Four (GM, Ford, Chrysler, and American Motors) consistently
backed trade liberalization (U.S. House of Representatives 1956b, 894–904;
1962 6:4080–91). Producers of mining and construction machinery advocated
tariff reciprocity vigorously (U.S. Senate 1955 3:1824–34; U.S. House of Representatives 1956b, 1031–37). Caterpillar argued that there should be "no
form of protection from competitive foreign machinery" because of "the great
importance of exports as a means of accentuating the benefits of mass production" (U.S. House of Representatives 1958b, 253, 266). Firms making
home appliances and electric lamps remained favorable to trade liberalization, as GE insisted the electrical industry would willingly "bear its fair share

TABLE 18.   Trade Lobbying in Large-Scale U.S. Industries, 1947–62

Industry/Lobby Group	Position on the RTAA: Support (+) or Oppose (−)
Automobiles	
AMA; Ford; Chrysler; Studebaker (1947–62)	+
Aerospace equipment	
Aerospace Industries Association; United Aircraft; Champion Aircraft (1953–62)	+
Electrical appliances	
GE; Institute of Cooking and Heating Appliance Manufacturers (1947)	+
Borg-Warner (1962)	+
Consumer electronics	
Radio-Television Manufacturers Association (1953–55)	+
Semiconductors	
EIA; Fairchild (1958–62)	+
Telecommunications equipment	
National Electrical Manufacturers Association (1955)	−
ITT (1958–62)	+
Tires	
U.S. Rubber (1951)	−
Century Tire and Rubber (1958)	+
Farm and construction machinery	
International Harvester; Caterpillar; Black and Decker; several small firms (1947–62)	+
Locomotives and railway equipment	
Baldwin Locomotive Works (1947)	+
Union Tank Car (1962)	+
Electrical machinery	
GE; Westinghouse; Allis-Chalmers; other firms (1955–58)	−

in terms of tariff reduction [and] the consequent increased imports" (U.S. House of Representatives 1947, 713).[11]

In other industries, dissenting voices were heard. Some producers complained that multilateral tariff reduction increased import competition without improving market access abroad, while others sought stronger escape clause and peril point provisions in trade legislation. For example, the Elec-

11. Though GE's household appliances and lamps divisions supported freer trade, its power-generating equipment section testified on behalf of the Buy American Act, as noted later in the chapter (Bauer, Pool, and Dexter 1963, 206–7).

tronic Industries Association (EIA) and the Radio-Television Manufacturers Association backed RTAA bills in the 1950s but grumbled about the absence of "true reciprocity" in GATT agreements. In hearings on the 1962 Trade Act, the EIA protested the use of nontariff barriers abroad to offset negotiated tariff cuts. In response, the group urged Congress to revise escape clause and peril point procedures (U.S. House of Representatives 1953 2:1449–55; 1958b 2:2846–47; U.S. Senate 1962 1:498–505). ITT continued to support the RTAA (U.S. Senate 1958 1:507–8), but the telephone equipment section of the National Electrical Manufacturers Association protested that reciprocal tariff concessions provided "no real reciprocity" due to regulatory barriers to entry in foreign telephone systems (U.S. House of Representatives 1955, 2582–83). Producers of tires for motor vehicles remained favorable to trade liberalization, but U.S. Rubber turned against the RTAA because of alleged German dumping of bicycle tires (U.S. Senate 1951 1:827).

Complaints from industries that had lost a once-dominant scale position, shown in table 19, were more intense. Though steelmakers did not oppose the RTAA in the 1950s, they criticized the State Department's failure to secure equivalent tariff concessions from foreign countries. As competitive pressures increased, the AISI pushed for procedures to ensure that tariffs could be reinstated if conditions in the industry worsened (U.S. House of Representatives 1958b 2:1828–37; 1962 6:3983–87). Firms manufacturing heavy power-generating equipment protested preferential procurement by foreign governments. Westinghouse in particular launched a sweeping attack on the policy of reciprocal tariff reductions:

> These rates are completely inadequate to protect us and our workers against foreign competition. . . . [T]here has been no trade liberalization abroad for the substantial tariff concessions we have made. . . . It is harder today to sell American-made electrical equipment in foreign countries . . . than it was either in the 1930s or just after the war. (U.S. House of Representatives 1955 1:1063)

Westinghouse organized a pressure group of producers of custom-made generators and transformers to lobby to exclude foreign rivals from public procurement in the United States (U.S. House of Representatives 1955 2:2030–38, 2052–57; 1958b 1:471–544). GE, on the other hand, carefully sought more favorable procurement practices without compromising its larger interest in trade liberalization, as executives emphasized that the firm's support for "Buy American" provisions did not change its desire for "the gradual and selective revision of our tariffs" (U.S. House of Representatives 1955 1:885).

TABLE 19.   Trade Lobbying in Small-Scale U.S. Industries, 1947–62

Industry/Lobby Group	Position on the RTAA: Support (+) or Oppose (−)
Rayon	
Rayon Yard Producers Group (1949)	−
American Viscose (1955)	−
Manmade Fiber Producers Association; Rayon Staple Fiber Producers Association (1962)	−
Petrochemicals and plastic materials	
Dupont; Monsanto; Dow (1955–62)	−
Texaco; other petroleum firms (1962)	+
Alkalies and inorganic chemicals	
MCA (1947–62)	−
Dupont; Monsanto; Dow (1955–62)	−
Office machinery	
Typewriter Manufacturers Export Association (1953)	+
Typewriter Manufacturers Export Association (1956)	−
Smith-Corona; Royal McBee (1959)	−
Sewing machines	
White Sewing Machine; Terry Sewing Machine (1955)	−
Dyestuffs	
SOCMA (1947–62)	−
American Cyanamid; Allied Chemical and Dye (1955)	−
Dupont; Koppers (1962)	−
Steel	
AISI (1958–62)	−
Motorcycles	
Harley-Davidson; Mustang; Indian Motorcyle (1951–55)	−

In motorcycles, typewriters, and sewing machines, firms turned against trade liberalization and lobbied to reinstate high tariffs on their products. Harley-Davidson, Mustang, and Indian petitioned for escape clause relief in 1951 to withdraw negotiated concessions on motorcycles (USTC 1953). Harley-Davidson argued that it could not survive without tariff protection because motorcycles, unlike automobiles, could not be mass-produced to compensate for low wages abroad.[12] The Typewriter Manufacturers Export Association, one of the

12. Harley-Davidson complained that foreign governments negated their tariff concessions through import licensing, exchange depreciation, and nontariff measures. The firm concluded, "reciprocity has hurt our motorcycle business . . . to the point where our home market is just about the only market we have left" (U.S. House of Representatives 1953 1:52–59).

groups most favorable to trade in the prewar era, also turned protectionist. The leading firms supported the RTAA until 1953, but then in 1956 they urged Congress to remove typewriters from the free list unless European countries offered steep tariff concessions (U.S. House of Representatives 1956a 3:1635–38). In 1959, Smith-Corona and Royal McBee sought escape clause relief (USTC 1960). Sewing machine producers "strongly opposed any further reduction in the duties on the importation of sewing machines," especially from "cheap-labor countries" such as Japan. They too wanted escape clause relief, firms told Congress, but they doubted their application would be accepted (U.S. Senate 1951 2:1395–97; U.S. House of Representatives 1955 2:2097–2102).[13]

The chemical industry remained fiercely protectionist, despite the improvements made in industrial and agricultural chemicals after the war. The industry's largest firm (Dupont), third-largest (Allied Chemical), fifth (Dow), sixth (American Cyanamid), eighth (Monsanto), and tenth (Koppers) all appeared before Congress at least once between 1947 and 1962 to oppose the RTAA, while SOCMA and the MCA lobbied against all six trade bills in this period. To limit the scope for further tariff cuts, these groups demanded that trade legislation stipulate escape clauses, peril points, and product-by-product negotiations involving "qualified industry advisors" (U.S. Senate 1962 2:718–23).

With the European chemical industry devastated after the war, U.S. chemical companies nonetheless maintained that they were disadvantaged by high wages and poor technological skill; high-volume production, they asserted, could be applied to standard bulk chemicals but not more advanced compounds (U.S. House of Representatives 1953 1:152–58, 226–34). By the late 1950s, firms further emphasized that the scale advantages of the early postwar period were quickly disappearing as Europe rebuilt:

> [Foreign plants are now] comparable in size to those existing in the United States. . . . The economies of large-scale and modern technology, added to the advantages of lower wage and salary scales, result in substantially lower costs to European and Japanese chemical industries. . . . We are losing our past advantage due to larger volume output, as our competitors in Western Europe expand their operations. . . . Opening the U.S. market . . . will spur them to even further expansion. (U.S. House of Representatives 1962 5:3297–98)

13. Italian and Swiss affiliates importing components for final assembly in the United States urged Congress to dismiss these claims because "[t]he scale of production in the United States is larger, bringing about mass production economies not possible abroad" (U.S. House of Representatives 1955 2:2565).

Moreover, chemical industries in a reconstructed, integrated European market could appropriate scale economies more easily, according to Dupont executives:

> [European integration] has provided market opportunities for foreign manufacturers comparable in size to those in the United States, and consequently big enough to support the construction of plants equal in size and operating efficiency to ours. . . . we are in the process of losing the advantages of size and advanced technology which have contributed so importantly to the chemical industry's favorable trade balance of recent years. (U.S. Senate 1962 3:1274)

As a result, the chemical industry argued, tariff cuts would allow foreign producers to increase market share in the United States, with no offsetting benefit for U.S. companies. "We are not concerned with exporting," a Monsanto executive explained: "We believe we will lose most of our chemical exports in time, when these foreign plants are finished. We are concerned with preserving our domestic market" (U.S. House of Representatives 1955 1:1090).

In short, even in the favorable market environment of the early postwar years, the chemical industry's ingrained protectionism was unshakable. Chemical companies not only opposed further trade liberalization for coal tar derivatives, dyes, synthetic fibers, and explosives, they also fought to defend American valuation and to extend it to other products. In opposing further liberalization, dye makers complained that tariff cuts "over our protest" in the 1951 GATT agreement would cause growing import penetration (U.S. House of Representatives 1953, 152). The Rayon Yarn Producers Group insisted that the 50 percent tariff cut imposed against the "pleading of the industry" in 1949 "exceeded . . . the peril limit" (U.S. House of Representatives 1949, 223–26). In 1960, producers filed, unsuccessfully, for escape clause relief for staple fibers (USTC 1961).

Domestic Coalitions, Institutions, and Party Politics

The preceding analysis demonstrates that most U.S. industries with large returns to scale, with the exception of chemicals, dominated world markets after World War I. As expected, these producers generally opposed tariff increases in the 1920s, and after 1934 they advocated concessions to foreign countries in return for tariff reductions abroad.

The antitariff coalition of heavy industries competed with protectionist light industries for influence over policy. Businesses in textiles, clothing, footwear, pottery, glassware, and the like lacked global trade ties and feared foreign competition. Firms in these industries manufactured in family shops or small factories because returns to scale were small. If left unprotected, these producers would suffer import competition from labor-rich countries. Labor-intensive industries therefore formed the backbone of the protariff movement, and they rallied the strongest resistance to reciprocal trade liberalization.

The puzzle in U.S. trade policy is why mass production industries failed to block tariff increases in 1922 and 1930 and why labor-intensive industries were unsuccessful in their efforts to defeat the RTAA between 1934 and 1962. To illuminate how group pressure and political influence shaped policy outcomes, the analysis considers the intervening effects of coalition formation, party politics, and political institutions.

Smoot-Hawley

Cleavages between large-scale mass producers and labor-intensive industries first emerged in the debate over the 1922 tariff. Labor-intensive businesses coalesced in pressure groups such as the American Tariff League to push for higher duties to block imports and prevent deflationary gold outflows. Large companies in assembly-line industries lobbied through the National Foreign Trade Council and similar organizations to expand markets and promote nondiscrimination abroad. The "bargaining tariff" compromised these opposing interests, as large firms accepted higher duties designed to equalize domestic and foreign production costs in return for provisions to reduce these tariffs in reciprocal trade treaties through the operation of unconditional MFN.[14]

But the State Department negotiated no significant commercial treaties under the legislation, so bargaining tariffs failed to open markets or promote equal tariff treatment. By 1930, Wilson (1971, 94) writes:

> business internationalists . . . were no longer willing, as they had been in 1922, to accept high duties in return for promises of downward revision through flexibility. . . . Consequently internationalists were much more outspoken in their criticism of the 1930 tariff than they had been of the Fordney-McCumber legislation.

Capital-intensive heavy industries joined export-oriented Midwest agriculture and Wall Street banks with overseas loans to form an antitariff coalition. A few

14. Big business regarded this as an "open door tariff," as the double-column schedule could be used to reward countries practicing nondiscrimination with concessions and punish those using discrimination with high duties (Parrini 1969, 214–20, 234–35; Wilson 1971, 65–70).

big businesses (such as Ford) even lobbied Congress to lower duties on their products or to block tariff increases for others. On the opposite side, labor-intensive manufacturing, border farming, and small banks pushed for tariff hikes. This latter group dominated the congressional debate and successfully persuaded legislators to raise duties to unprecedented heights in the Smoot-Hawley tariff (Eichengreen 1989).

Two factors exogenous to the book's theory prevented mass production industries from realizing their trade preferences in policy. The first was party politics: the tariff hikes of 1922 and 1930 occurred in party-line votes during Republican control of the legislative and executive branches. Second, institutional procedures for setting tariff levels encouraged protectionist logrolling. As Schattschneider (1935) demonstrated, Smoot-Hawley exposed a basic defect in trade politics: protariff groups declined to oppose duties for one another in a game of "reciprocal noninterference," while free riding limited countervailing pressure from antitariff groups. This asymmetry in organizational skill made legislators prone to protectionist pork barreling to satisfy the constituents that mobilized on trade issues. Committee structures, legislative processes, and the final bill reflected this bias—members of Congress were assigned responsibility for the tariff schedules of interest to industry in their districts; committee hearings produced twenty thousand pages of testimony, mostly from protariff interests; and the Senate bill included 1,200 amendments. The implication was clear: for trade liberalization to occur, control over tariff making had to be transferred from congressional committees beholden to special interests to an executive capable of acting in the general interest.

The RTAA

After 1930, mass production industries pushed more vigorously for trade liberalization, especially once the Great Depression's effects were felt (Wilson 1971, 97–98). Group pressure was necessary—though not sufficient—to trigger the shift to the RTAA. In addition, partisan change provided a permissive condition: the Democrats swept the 1932 national elections, as Roosevelt won the presidency and his party gained both houses of Congress. Though Roosevelt's cabinet included such protectionist figures as Secretary of Agriculture George Peek, Cordell Hull and other top officials hailed from the Democratic Party's antitariff wing. In fact, the most substantial liberalization under the RTAA coincided with the five terms served by Roosevelt and his successor, Harry Truman—a twenty-year stretch during which Democratic control of Congress was almost uninterrupted.

Partisan change made possible a second key shift: institutional innovation in trade policy-making. The RTAA, Haggard argues, defeated protectionist logrolling through two specific channels. First, Congress no longer set tariffs on specific goods; it merely voted on whether or not to continue delegation to the executive. Because the presidency served a broad national constituency, it could internalize the policy effects of pressures to satisfy narrow district interests. Second, reciprocal trade concessions linked tariff reduction at home to liberalization abroad. This motivated protrade groups to lobby for the RTAA to gain access to foreign markets. Over time, trade agreements expanded the size of the export sector, which led to more protrade lobbying (Haggard 1988).

Pastor (1980, 91) suggests that "there are few interest group political analyses of the 1934 Trade Act" because the influence of private interests "was not discernable either in hearings or in the final bill." Instead, various accounts have emphasized the liberal philosophy of Hull's State Department (Haggard 1988); the ideational connection between the Smoot-Hawley tariff and the Great Depression, which motivated officials to reform trade institutions (Goldstein 1993); and the Democratic Party's desire to enact more permanent liberalization than it had accomplished previously (Bailey, Goldstein, and Weingast 1997). Still, these arguments lack a cogent theory of institutional change: the new policy-making structure seems to materialize spontaneously, while the politics that produced it remains opaque.

The brevity of the RTAA hearings in 1934 does not mean that private actors exerted no influence. Quite the contrary, Hiscox (1999) demonstrates that constituency interests—particularly, the growth of export interests in manufacturing—were the source of party positions and extant institutional structures. In fact, lobbying by firms and trade associations in mass production industries was a critical factor in the changes in the trade policy process. Advocates of tariff reduction argued that only the executive, not the Congress, could properly conduct foreign trade relations. This group recognized that trade liberalization required the insulation of tariff-making authority from protectionist interests. Protectionists countered that the RTAA was an unconstitutional delegation of authority to the president; they knew that the Smoot-Hawley system could survive only if Congress retained control over trade.

The political influence of these competing coalitions is not apparent in hearings in Congress or in the Committee for Reciprocity Information because of selection bias. In most hearings, roughly three-quarters of the witnesses testified against RTAA bills and tariff negotiations; representatives of mass production industries appeared infrequently. Opponents of trade liberalization had more incentives to speak publicly in an effort to amend (if not defeat) unfavorable trade bills in Congress and spare themselves tariff cuts once their products had been placed on the table for negotiation. Supporters of trade liberalization had other channels of influence, for example through trade negotiators in the State Department, and they did not need special exceptions to suit their interests.

Thus, the RTAA by itself was no "magic bullet" (Hiscox 1999). Institutional changes "created the opportunity for free traders to implement their particular vision of economic policy," but they "did not mandate the lowering of tariff levels" (Goldstein 1993, 140). Protariff groups could have persuaded the State Department to offer foreign countries only token concessions in 1934, but they didn't; after 1937, delegation could have been ended at any time, but it wasn't. In each extension of the RTAA legislation, policy questions (the length of trade-negotiating authority, the maximum level of tariff cuts, the principal supplier rule, the inclusion of escape clauses and peril points) masqueraded as institutional questions. The outcome of these debates hinged critically on the balance of political influence between protariff and antitariff groups. Representatives of labor-intensive industry testified to Congress in numbers disproportionate to their size and sway because they already had been defeated on the larger question of whether or not the United States would set tariffs through international negotiation. They could not defeat the legislation altogether; they could only hope to modify and dilute it to provide some refuge from harmful tariff cuts.

Institutional and partisan influences in trade policy lie outside the book's theory, and it must be acknowledged that they have been introduced into the preceding discussion in a descriptively ad hoc fashion. This does not mean that the theory is wrong; rather, it suggests that while the preferences of domestic political actors play a significant role, they cannot fully explain policy outcomes. To systematically examine how economic interests affected trade policy at the industry level, the next section turns to statistical methods.

Statistical Analysis of U.S. Tariffs

The analysis examines U.S. tariffs in 1964, after several rounds of RTAA and GATT tariff reductions (though before the Kennedy Round agreements had been phased in). The dependent variable, *tariffs,* is the value of duties collected divided by total imports.[15] The units of analysis are three-digit Standard Industry Classification (SIC) industries, with independent variables measured for 1958.

To estimate the effects of scale economies, the analysis uses *scale,* which is

---

15. Tariff rates are an appropriate measure of trade protection for this period because anti-dumping duties and other nontariff barriers were rare outside of agriculture.

described in the appendix and employed in chapter 3.[16] *Import competition* and *export dependence* capture comparative cost considerations reflected in trade patterns. Because these two trade variables perform poorly, the models include an alternative measure of comparative costs, *labor intensity*, which is wages divided by value added. There are two proxies for collective action costs: *industry concentration* is the share of output in plants with more than one thousand workers; *geographic concentration* is the percentage of all workers located in the five states with the largest production.

The first column of table 20 includes all of the independent variables except *scale.* The best predictors of tariffs are *labor intensity* and *geographic concentration.* The strength of *labor intensity* suggests that elements of comparative costs not reflected in trade patterns were important in tariff setting. This makes sense since the U.S. economy was not heavily exposed to trade, and low import penetration in part reflected past industry success in securing tariff protection (hence the incorrect negative sign for *import competition*). The strong positive effect of *geographic concentration* also is predictable, since geographically localized protectionist industries such as textiles, apparel, and footwear should have been less vulnerable to free-rider problems (though some protrade industries, such as automobiles, were geographically concentrated too). *Export dependence* is weakly significant, and *industry concentration* has no effect on tariffs.

The second column adds *scale* to the model, and this variable is statistically significant with the correct positive sign. A likelihood ratio test rejects the null hypothesis that *scale* has no effect on *tariffs* at $p < .05$ ($\chi^2 = 4.19$). Table 21 shows how predicted tariffs change as relative scale and the returns to scale vary. The figures illustrate that tariff rates were sensitive to the scale position of industries and the size of the returns to scale. Holding returns to scale constant, tariffs fall as relative scale rises: moving from relative scales of 0.5 at the low end to 3 at the high end, tariffs decline by 7.6 percentage points at modest returns to scale, 14.6 percentage points at large returns to scale, and 21.2 percentage points at very large returns to scale. Variation in returns to scale magnifies the effect of relative scale, with a 6.1 percentage point tariff increase at very small scales and a 7.5 percentage point tariff decrease at very large scales.

This analysis confirms that even though party politics, institutional structures,

16. Again, note that when scale is small, this measure is greater than 1; when scale is large, it is less than 1. To preserve cases, industries with very small returns to scale were entered as 1 to represent a neutral effect of scale economies on unit costs. While this coding decision affects the coefficient estimates, and the results accordingly should be treated with caution, it is not likely to systematically bias the results because the true value will be underestimated in some cases and overestimated in others.

and foreign policy priorities were important factors in the pace and scope of liberalization in U.S. trade, factors operating at the industry level played a critical role in tariff setting.

U.S. Trade and Canada

At the same time that the United States sought multilateral trade liberalization to pry open foreign empires and trading blocs, it abstained from forming pref-

TABLE 20.   OLS Regression Results for U.S. Tariffs

		Tariffs in 1964
Variable		
Scale		0.61**
		(0.30)
Import competition	−0.06	−0.09
	(0.13)	(0.13)
Export dependence	−0.29*	−0.25
	(0.16)	(0.16)
Labor intensity	0.21***	0.22***
	(0.07)	(0.07)
Industry concentration	−0.02	0.00
	(0.03)	(0.03)
Geographic concentration	0.17***	0.16***
	(0.05)	(0.05)
Constant	−0.00	−0.61**
	(0.03)	(0.30)
F-ratio	5.88***	5.69***
Adjusted *R*-squared	0.15	0.17

Note: Cell entries are OLS regression coefficients, with standard errors in parentheses. $N = 137$.
***$p < .01$ **$p < .05$ *$p < .10$

TABLE 21.   Marginal Effects of Scale and Returns to Scale on U.S. Tariffs

	Change in Unit Costs at One-Half MES			*Marginal Effect of Returns to Scale*
Relative Scale	5%	10%	15%	
0.50	16.5	19.5	22.5	6.1
0.75	14.7	15.9	17.0	2.4
1.00	13.4	13.4	13.4	0.0
1.50	11.7	10.1	8.6	−3.1
2.00	10.5	7.9	5.5	−5.0
3.00	8.9	4.9	1.3	−7.5
Marginal effect of relative scale	−7.6	−14.6	−21.2	

erential arrangements of its own. "Free trade multilateralism," Gardner (1969, 17) writes, reflected

> the transformation of the United States into a major exporter of mass-pro-
> duced industrial products. These products were particularly vulnerable to
> the impact of tariff preferences and other forms of discrimination.... [The
> country's] growing industrial efficiency might be progressively offset if
> American products were not guaranteed equal access to foreign markets.

Controlling a market of continental proportions allowed mass production industries to look to the world market rather than a regional sphere. Firms therefore wanted a general reduction in world trade barriers more than exclusive
benefits in selected countries. Only in chemicals did competitors exploit scale
economies better than U.S. companies. Yet there is no evidence that chemical
producers desired exclusive privileges abroad, as these firms instead devoted
their energies and political resources to defend the tariff at home. On the
whole, industry showed no interest in a trading bloc.

Devotion to the principle of nondiscrimination is particularly evident in
U.S. relations with neighboring Canada. In 1911, these two countries negotiated a reciprocity treaty that failed to pass the Canadian parliament. After
1911, preferential trade with Canada was a recurrent political issue. However,
large U.S. companies consistently opposed such initiatives. Most had invested
in Canadian manufacturing, and regional integration between the United
States and Canada would harm these small-scale affiliates. As a result, U.S.
heavy industry called for a rather incongruous policy of eliminating barriers to
American goods everywhere except in Canada.

The Branch Plant Movement

Investment by U.S. companies in foreign manufacturing dates to the late nineteenth century. Machinery firms such as Singer and International Harvester set
up overseas outlets to perform product demonstrations and after-sales servic-
ing; then suppliers of public utilities, such as ITT, moved abroad to secure foreign contracts that required local capacity; automakers began to manufacture
abroad, followed by tire producers, before World War I; and after the war the
electrical and electronic industries established foreign affiliates. The U.S. Bureau of Foreign and Domestic Commerce (1931, 11) noted that U.S. branch
plants produced mostly in "large-scale industry, which gives scope for the
application of American production methods, with the emphasis on the scale
of production and high productivity per man." The motives were to circumvent

tariffs, nontariff barriers, and exchange controls; minimize transport costs; challenge foreign rivals on their home turf; and exploit monopolistic advantages in the control of proprietary assets.

The incentives to invest in Canada were simple: high tariffs made exporting difficult and local production attractive. Under Canada's National Policy, automobiles and farm machinery, two important U.S. exports, paid 35 percent duties, and engines and parts were taxed at 30 percent (Marshall, Southard, and Taylor 1936, 199–203). In response, U.S. automakers set up assembly plants in Windsor, just across Lake Ontario from Dearborn, Michigan, the hub of automobile production in the United States. By 1929, U.S. firms produced five and a half vehicles in Canada for each one imported from the United States. Producers of tires, tractors, farm implements, machinery, and electrical equipment soon followed in kind.

While the branch plants enjoyed generous trade protection, they also faced pressure to increase local content. For example, Canada increased tariffs on automobile parts in 1926 to force U.S. affiliates to produce components locally or develop linkages with domestic suppliers. When foreign investors complained that taxing parts at higher rates than finished vehicles encouraged imports at the expense of domestic production, the Canadian government introduced tariff rebates on imported parts for branch plants with 50 percent local content; foreign components used in exported vehicles received a full duty drawback. Firms equipped to meet this target (such as Ford) lobbied for and embraced the new rules, which raised entry barriers for competitors (Traves 1984, 137–47). In fact, several branch plants supported strict rules of origin for Imperial Preference on exports to the British Commonwealth. In contrast, those with "primitive assembly operations" sought to delay or block local content mandates (Marshall, Southard, and Taylor 1936, 275; Williams 1986, 85–88).

Inside the small Canadian market, branch plants generally manufactured broad product lines in low volumes. Under pressure from tariffs and local content rules, two-thirds of U.S. affiliates surpassed 75 percent Canadian content in 1932. Due to "the loss from reduced scale of operations, the lower efficiency of labor, and the duplication of plant and management" (U.S. Bureau of Foreign and Domestic Commerce 1931, 11), productivity was low: two out of every three U.S. affiliates in Canada reported higher unit costs than their corporate parents (Marshall, Southard, and Taylor 1936, 232–33). Even in the most efficient plants, an electrical industry executive stated,

> [foreign] costs are approximately the same in spite of the fact that the
> foreign factories use American designed tooling, American production

methods, American "know-how," and have wage costs about one-third to one-fourth of the United States wage costs. . . . The reason can be partly found in volume. . . . Specialized operations are so many times more expensive that the advantage of lower wage rates is more than offset. (Backman 1962, 297)

But FDI nevertheless was profitable because tariff walls and entry restrictions allowed branch plants to pass off elevated costs to Canadian customers by marking up prices 30–40 percent (Marshall, Southard, and Taylor 1936, 237–39).

This arrangement was stable as long as Canada did not cut tariffs after branch plants were locked in to increased production and local content. Several U.S. firms attained leading positions in the Canadian Manufacturers Association and joined together to defend trade protection before the Canadian Tariff Board (Marshall, Southard, and Taylor 1936, 275–76; Scheinberg 1973, 229–32). For example, Ford opposed proposals to reduce automobile tariffs, arguing that "the present margin of protection should be continued" since the industry was "still in the formative stage" (Wilkins and Hill 1964, 131–32). International Harvester and Deere, the leading producers of farm machinery, also turned protectionist once they had factories inside Canada's tariff wall (Radosh 1967, 48–50; Wolman 1992, 91–92).

In the United States, these firms fought plans to liberalize bilateral trade—even as they pushed for reciprocal trade treaties with European countries and the British Empire (other than Canada). The USTC (1920, 76) reported, "American manufacturers with branch establishments in Canada were opposed to reciprocity because it promised to open the Canadian market to other American products in competing lines." The Commerce Department advised against trade talks with Canada because "American capital invested in Canadian industries is due to the Canadian protective tariff policy" and "free trade . . . would naturally detract from the value of the investment" (Scheinberg 1973, 233). When President Roosevelt considered trade negotiations with Canada, advisers again warned that the "branch plants have tended to support the maintenance of a high tariff wall by Canada."[17]

Trade agreements between the United States and Canada in 1935 and 1938 were carefully crafted to avoid upsetting this status quo. The State Department's objective was not to liberalize Canada's general tariff but to attack Imperial Preference. While Canadian duties against the United States helped the branch plants and harmed U.S.-based exporters, Imperial Preference exposed

17. "American Branch Plants in Canada," August 1934, Country Files, 1933–35, Box 1, RG 20.

both to greater competition from Britain. Multinationals from the United States therefore pushed to reduce the preferences British goods enjoyed under the Ottawa Agreement. Some also sought to reduce Canadian duties on parts exported from the United States—but none wanted Canada opened to imports of finished goods.[18] Indeed, too much trade liberalization aroused protests from companies invested in the branch plant system: for instance, U.S. firms in the Canadian Automobile Chamber of Commerce petitioned the Tariff Board to reverse tariff cuts in the 1935 treaty and restore the old duties because, they argued, "reduced protection will undermine the stability of the industry."[19]

The Rise of Canadian Industrial Policy

The collapse of the multilateral payments network and the restructuring of the world economy during and after World War II disrupted Canada's economy and the branch plant system. During the war, Canada accumulated sterling balances on exports to the British Commonwealth while payments for imports from the United States drained its foreign exchange. This problem worsened after the war, as European countries facing a dollar shortage continued wartime restrictions on the use of hard currency for imports. Without a system to transfer balances on exports to the British Empire to pay for imports from the United States, Canada needed either to export more to or import less from the United States to stem the loss of dollar reserves and prevent a balance of payments crisis.

The loss of imperial markets was troublesome for the branch plants. Before the war, firms used Canadian affiliates as export platforms and granted exclusive rights in commonwealth trade to gain scale economies.[20] After the war, U.S. multinationals opened new factories or enlarged existing ones in Britain

18. "Report of the Committee for Reciprocity Information in Connection with the Negotiation of a Reciprocal Trade Agreement with Canada," Trade Agreements Program File, 1934–35, Box 7, RG 20.

19. "Auto Makers Ask Canada to Kill Treaty Auto Rates," *New York Times,* December 17, 1935, 11. The petitioners were GM, Chrysler, Hudson-Essex, Studebaker, and International Harvester. Nash Motors and Willys-Overland, neither of which operated branch plants, complained that without tariff cuts they were "prevented from shipping . . . products into Canada on a fair and equitable basis" ("Report of the Committee for Reciprocity Information in Connection with the Negotiation of a Reciprocal Trade Agreement with Canada," Trade Agreements Program File, 1934–35, Box 7, RG 20).

20. In the interwar period, Ford, GM, and Chrysler factories in Canada exported 25–50 percent of their production because sales to Australia, New Zealand, and South Africa boosted output during winter down periods. In fact, Ford-Canada exported three times more than Ford-U.S., even though it produced one-tenth as many cars (Wilkins and Hill 1964, 44, 120).

and Western Europe because they had to produce inside the sterling area and the European Payments Union to sell there. Export opportunities for Canadian branch plants evaporated (Safarian 1966, 116). In automobiles, the effect was dramatic: in 1948–49, Ford's exports from Windsor declined from 41,141 to 17,415.[21]

As U.S. affiliates confined their sales to the Canadian market while continuing to rely on imported parts, Canada's trade deficit soared. Some Canadian officials believed that this persistent strain on the balance of payments could be relieved if the branch plants could serve a wider market by specializing for export. Barriers to trade with the United States, the Department of Trade and Industry argued, perpetuated an inefficient industrial structure; removing these barriers would encourage branch plants to "develop specialized production in Canada for export to the U.S. domestic or export markets as an offset to Canadian industry's imports from the U.S." (Williams 1986, 110). Soon after the 1947 GATT conference, Canadian officials asked the U.S. government to negotiate "further tariff cuts, particularly in the manufacturing goods field, which would make possible a better balance in the enormous one-way trade associated with our branch plants" (quoted in Granatstein 1985, 39). Canadian nationalists and U.S. firms in the Canadian Manufacturers Association countered that without tariffs the branch plants lost their raison d'être and would simply migrate back home. Fearing a repeat of the 1911 Reciprocity Treaty debacle, Canada's prime minister Mackenzie King abruptly broke off these negotiations in the spring of 1948.

With trade policy unchanged, the "miniature replica" branch plant structure endured. The limited range of the Canadian market allowed room for only a few plants large enough to take advantage of scale economies. In many sectors, however, the leading U.S. firms all owned Canadian affiliates; once one entered the market, competitors followed so the first mover could not capture the benefits of producing behind the tariff while others had to export over it.[22] As a result, branch plants produced well short of U.S. output levels (Eastman and Stykolt 1967, 7–10; Task Force on the Structure of Canadian Industry 1968, 79–80, 136–37). Those with high unit costs reported that "production runs

21. In the same period, exports from Dearborn dropped from 88,559 to 53,700. Ford's United Kingdom factory received top priority in commonwealth markets previously serviced from the United States or Canada because mass production required exports of nearly 100,000 vehicles (Wilkins and Hill 1964, 374, 407–8).

22. For example, the Canadian market could not support a single MES plant for electric ranges and refrigerators, yet ten and twenty-three factories, respectively, produced these goods (Eastman and Stykolt 1967, 253–55).

were shorter, or volume was lower, or that these, in turn, led to relatively less tooling and mechanization" (Safarian 1966, 204–5).[23] As Ford-Canada's chairman told the House of Commons in 1953: "Without the tariff, we could not possibly compete with the United States manufacturers, and the reason is solely one of volume. . . . Because the volume in the U.S. is thirteen times that in Canada, unit costs of production are substantially lower" (quoted in Dykes 1982, 26).

In an attempt to fix its balance of payments problems and reform its antiquated industrial structure, the Canadian government began to aggressively apply industrial policy after 1960. These moves upset the regulatory bargain that attracted FDI and, with growing frequency, caught the branch plants in the middle of disputes with the United States. As these conflicts threatened to provoke a trade war, efforts to reorganize the branch plant system and discipline Canada's use of TRIMs gradually produced a formal governance structure to manage bilateral trade and investment. The automotive industry provides an early example of this dynamic at work.

The Automotive Products Trade Agreement

In 1962, the Canadian government established a duty remission program that offered automakers a dollar in tariff rebates for each dollar increase in exports over their monthly average for the previous year. The main purpose was to reduce Canada's $500 million deficit in automotive products, which accounted for one-third of its overall trade deficit. Subsequently the U.S. Treasury Department opened a countervailing duty inquiry when a radiator producer, Modine Manufacturing, complained that the duty remissions were unfair export subsidies. Treasury's preliminary inquiry indicated that the refunds constituted illegal "bounties" or "grants" under U.S. law.

Eager to avoid a trade war, U.S. automakers urged the two governments to negotiate a bilateral agreement on automotive trade and investment.[24] In testi-

---

23. Eastman and Stykolt (1967, 13) explain:

[The] scale of output is below the modern best-practice scale. Runs of single products in Canadian factories are short, with the result that excessive time is used in changeover for each unit of output. The machinery used is often inefficient because indivisibilities in the use of the most modern methods of production can be overcome only at higher scales of production for individual plants than exist in Canada.

24. Officials in the United States emphasized that the law required them to impose countervailing duties if the duty remissions were found to be an export subsidy. In response, Canadian officials hinted they would increase local content requirements on automobiles if the United States

mony to a Canadian Royal Commission in 1961, Ford, GM, and American Motors advocated mutual tariff elimination so "the full cost benefits of U.S. mass production . . . would then be passed on to Canadian consumers" (Royal Commission on the Automotive Industry 1961, 40–41).[25] These firms also appealed to U.S. officials to negotiate a free trade agreement.[26] In contrast to 1935 and 1948, when automakers were satisfied with high Canadian tariffs, now they had strong motives to support free trade. Because of consolidation, only the Big Four remained in business (Studebaker had just closed its last U.S. factory), so high-cost Canadian affiliates no longer faced competition from automobiles exported from the United States. As a result, outsiders could be excluded from sharing in the benefits of free trade—provided that it was not extended to third countries through the MFN clause.

Initially the State Department was cool to the idea of a bilateral arrangement that would exclude third countries. One memo discerned a "progressive movement across national borders toward the integration of a particular industry" but concluded that a common market with Canada was not "in the cards" because "our economic interests are too broad geographically to make such an arrangement feasible."[27] Another briefing paper amplified this concern: "getting around our most favored nation commitment could have some erosive impact on this basic element in our international trade policy. What is more important, perhaps, we could excite Congress to think of other and more far-reaching departures from MFN. We do not take this risk lightly." But if the United States adhered to MFN, "the Europeans would get a free ride on $300 million of finished

---

retaliated. According to U.S. firms, "such a decision by Canada would require them to make additional investments in Canada of several hundred million dollars, in order to protect the $600 million investment they already have there. For this reason, Ford, GM and Chrysler have stated that they would be placed in serious difficulty by the imposition of countervailing duties" (Memorandum from Secretary of State Rusk to President Johnson, Washington, DC, September 18, 1964, U.S. Department of State 2001, 690).

25. These firms argued that tariffs perpetuated the assembly-plant structure because low volume forced branch plants to import components with large economies of scale, such as engine blocks and automatic transmissions. Without trade barriers, branch plants could specialize in a limited range of models for both markets and could import models not produced in Canada from the United States. (Canada's tariffs were 17.5 percent on finished vehicles and up to 25 percent on parts; U.S. tariffs were 6.5 percent on complete vehicles and 8.5 percent on most parts.) The Royal Commission (1961, 50) agreed that bilateral free trade offered an "escape from low-volume production in Canada," but the Canadian government instead chose the duty remission scheme.

26. Chrysler pushed for more tariff protection for its affiliates in its Royal Commission testimony, but it subsequently joined the majority and supported free trade.

27. "Memorandum of Conversation with R.A. Winter," Regional Executive for Canada, Ford International Group, July 14, 1961, Lot File 65D493, Records relating to Economic Matters, 1956–66, Box 1, RG 59.

vehicle exports." The State Department therefore decided that the United States should seek a waiver under GATT rules for automotive trade with Canada to ensure "that there would be no free riders, e.g. Volkswagen."[28]

The sticking point in the negotiations was Canada's longstanding concern that free trade would cause the branch plants to close. Without tariffs and industrial policy to guide investment, Canadian officials argued, production would concentrate in the larger market. To prevent automotive production from migrating back to the United States, they insisted on limiting free trade to original equipment manufacturers already in Canada. Canada also demanded production commitments from U.S. firms.[29] In separate letters of undertaking with the Canadian government, the Big Four agreed to maintain 60 percent Canadian value added in their domestic sales and to assemble one vehicle in Canada for every vehicle sold there.

Firms in the United States accepted production safeguards in return for free trade because in an uncertain trading environment they might face more restrictive measures. Thus, National Security Adviser McGeorge Bundy reported to President Lyndon Johnson: "The big companies are all in line, Ford and Chrysler with gusto."[30] Ford executives told Congress that "the limited free-trade approach" was "entirely reasonable" given the risk of new regulations to shift production to Canada and increase exports to the United States. GM officials agreed that the APTA, while "not free of difficulties," was a "workable plan" (U.S. House of Representatives 1965, 127–96). With restraints on entry and tariffs still in place on imports from outside North America, U.S. automakers could internalize the full benefits of free trade to compensate for the costs of reorganizing the division of labor between affiliates and the corporate parent.[31]

28. "Negotiations with Canada on Automobile Trade," September 29, 1964, Lot File 65D493, Records relating to Economic Matters, 1956–66, Box 2, RG 59.

29. A Commerce Department official explained:

Because of the small size of their industry, the Canadians believed that unlimited free trade would result in their industry being swallowed up by the much larger and efficient industry south of the border. They therefore sought . . . assurances. . . . We on our side saw no such need because of the size of our industry, its very great efficiency, its lower cost, and its great ability to compete. (U.S. House of Representatives 1965, 104)

30. Memorandum from the president's special assistant for National Security Affairs (Bundy) to President Johnson, Washington, DC, November 27, 1964, U.S. Department of State 2001, 692.

31. Auto parts producers protested that content rules and duty remissions for Canadian branch plants favored non-U.S. subcontractors. The United Automobile Workers (UAW) complained that Trade Adjustment Assistance for uprooted workers was inadequate, but it nonetheless expressed hope that free trade in automobiles would be extended to other sectors (U.S. House of Representatives 1965, 255–82).

The State Department accepted the production undertakings because, one memo stated, "Once we get to a free trade regime, it will have its own momentum—and we will all benefit from it."[32] Multinationals such as Dupont, Procter and Gamble, U.S. Steel, and IBM already had issued calls for bilateral free trade,[33] and a few industry groups sought special tariff arrangements after the APTA was negotiated.[34] But for the most part, the *New York Times* observed, "U.S. subsidiaries have been organized as branch offices behind Canadian tariff walls and are little interested in, or equipped for, free trade."[35] A comprehensive free trade agreement would have to wait another twenty years, as chapter 6 details.

Conclusion: Toward North American Free Trade

The period marked by the conclusion of the Kennedy Round represented the end of an era in U.S. trade policy. From World War I to the 1950s, mass production industries enjoyed extraordinary cost advantages from large-scale manufacturing. As a result, firms in industries such as automobiles, farm machinery, sewing machines, office machinery, and electrical and electronic equipment opposed tariff increases in the 1920s and pushed for trade liberalization after 1930. These industries also supported unconditional MFN and pushed to eliminate trade discrimination, even as the world moved toward a closed system of regional blocs. Their political strength sustained the RTAA through successive rounds of the GATT after World War II, even though the tariff concessions of foreign countries were not as substantial as those made by the United States.

As large firms in mass production industries pushed for trade liberalization worldwide, they opposed regional integration between Canada and the United States. Most had chosen local production for the small, tariff-protected market in Canada, despite the high cost of manufacturing products with large returns to scale in small factories. Once these investments were sunk, U.S. firms had a

32. "Negotiations with Canada on Automobile Trade," September 29, 1964, Lot File 65D493, Records relating to Economic Matters, 1956–66, Box 2, RG 59.

33. "Free Trade Envisioned," *New York Times*, October 5, 1955, 54; "Market Tie Seen for U.S., Canada," *New York Times*, February 14, 1961, 51; "More Ties Urged for U.S., Canada," *New York Times*, January 24, 1965, 1; Williams 1986, 146.

34. The U.S. Embassy in Ottawa reported: "the greatest interest has been shown by the chemical and machinery industries" ("Functioning of U.S.-Canadian Automobile Arrangement and Possibility of Other Special Trade Arrangements," U.S. Embassy Ottawa to Department of State, February 26, 1965, Subject Numeric Files, 1964–66, Box 991, RG 59).

35. "More Ties Urged for U.S., Canada," *New York Times*, January 24, 1965, 7.

vested interest in preserving the trade barriers that separated Canada from the United States.

After 1950, the coalitional base of the RTAA began to fragment. Reconstruction in Europe and Japan enabled foreign producers to combine mass production techniques with low wages. More and more U.S. firms favored escape clauses and peril points in trade legislation to slow or reverse the pace of liberalization. At the same time, U.S. multinationals began to rethink their strategies toward Canadian manufacturing. As the branch plants became more exposed to foreign competition and Canada increasingly asserted its right to regulate FDI during the 1970s, the need for a more comprehensive trade agreement covering other sectors grew accordingly.

Two trends accelerated the transition to regionalism. First, U.S. companies began to move production offshore to alleviate high labor costs. Initiatives such as Mexico's Border Industrialization Program encouraged intrafirm trade and signaled a shift in production relationships within multinational companies in North America. Second, as tariffs dropped to insignificant levels by the end of the Kennedy Round, miniature replica production in separate national markets no longer made sense. Inefficient branch plants became a severe liability, but investments in fragmented manufacturing facilities already had been sunk. Rather than closing down foreign affiliates once the conditions that produced them disappeared, U.S. multinationals integrated them into regional supply networks. This created a constituency for the sorts of regionally oriented trade policies the United States previously had spurned and, in turn, planted the seeds for the NAFTA treaty, the subject of chapter 6.

CHAPTER 5

The EU
Fortress or Beachhead?

In 1957, six European countries joined together to form the EC. But even as membership grew to nine in 1973 and twelve by 1985, the common market remained unfinished because nontariff barriers expanded across Europe once tariffs on intra-EC trade had been eliminated. The spread of these protectionist measures stimulated political pressure to complete the common market, which culminated in the Single European Act in 1986.

This chapter shows that industry groups that could not fully exploit economies of scale pushed for the 1992 program to establish the single market. For these industries, European integration offered an escape from small domestic markets: it would allow companies to expand in size and standardize production, stimulating efficiencies that could not be attained while operating on a national basis.

The Single European Act in turn affected Europe's trade policy toward the rest of the world. Completing the single market unleashed adjustment processes across borders, particularly in activities with large returns to scale, as national industries and individual firms expanded and contracted in different locations. Competitive burdens on small-scale firms provoked protectionist pressures leading up to 1992. Inward FDI by foreign multinationals also caused European producers to seek TRIMs to prevent outsiders from capturing the benefits of the common market.

To date, however, popular concerns about a fortress Europe have proven to be unfounded. In the first decade after the single market was completed, only quotas on Japanese automobiles and a few classes of steel were extended Europe-wide. Though antidumping measures and state aids occasionally substituted for trade protection lost since 1992, protectionist pressures in industries such as textiles, apparel, and footwear did not produce higher trade barriers. Moreover, industries with large returns to scale grew more favorable to open trade as larger companies moved down their cost curves and small-scale producers disappeared. As a result, European import policy did not take a protectionist turn after the Single European Act.

An Incomplete Common Market

The postwar Marshall Plan planted the seeds of European integration, as the United States stipulated economic and political collaboration as a condition for financial aid. In Article 5 of the Convention for European Economic Cooperation, signed soon after the U.S. Congress passed the European Recovery Program in 1948, the future EC countries agreed to discuss the prospects for a regional arrangement. Already Belgium, Holland, and Luxembourg had launched a customs union, and France had informed the GATT that it intended to negotiate free trade with Italy (Milward 1984, chap. 2).

The 1951 Treaty of Paris, which created the European Coal and Steel Community, marked the formal start of European integration. Under this arrangement, outlined in the Schuman Plan, European countries established common policies and market-sharing arrangements in coal and steel to alleviate shortages, facilitate industrial planning, and integrate Germany into a transnational arrangement to control its future war-making capacity. The Treaty of Rome, in which Germany, France, Italy, Belgium, Holland, and Luxembourg agreed to form a customs union, followed in 1957. The plan envisioned the creation of a common market with free movement for goods, services, capital, and labor.

The first phase of integration from 1958 to 1973 eliminated tariffs and quotas on European goods. The six EC members negotiated as one for the first time in the Kennedy Round of the GATT. By 1968, the common external tariff was in place, and customs duties and quantitative restrictions on intra-EC trade had been eliminated. In 1973, the EC grew from six to nine with the addition of Britain, Ireland, and Denmark.

But despite the elimination of tariffs and quotas, product markets were not fully integrated. Distortions persisted due to differences in tax laws, technical barriers, varying national standards, domestic subsidies, closed procurement markets, border inspections, and myriad other restrictions. Moreover, these sorts of nontariff measures proliferated in place of the barriers that had been liberalized.

Import restraints were especially common in industries dominated by "national champions," that is, companies with a legacy of state support and in some cases state ownership.[1] As formal trade barriers disappeared, national

---

1. Examples include Renault, Usinor-Sacilor, Thomson, and Machines Bull in France; British Steel, Rover, and ICL in Britain; and Fiat, Alfa-Romeo, Italsider, and Olivetti in Italy.

champions for the first time faced competition in their home markets. In response, governments employed special protective measures to insulate these companies from external pressures. Nontariff measures enabled national champions to preserve domestic sales and market shares; without state intervention, some of them would have gone out of business or been absorbed by other firms.

With national markets segmented, firms seeking to expand European sales could not standardize products and rescale manufacturing to serve the entire region. Many established factories outside their home countries because import limits made it easier to produce in the market of final sale (Franko 1976, 103–4, 148–53). The Dutch electronics company Philips, for instance, operated plants in every EC country—about 250 in all. The firm and its affiliates manufactured "seven types of TV sets equipped with different tuners, semiconductors, and plugs to meet differing national standards" (Hufbauer 1990, 6); each model required a separate production process.[2] In an effort to grow within the constraints of fragmented markets, many companies diversified into multiple product lines, which spread manufacturing and R&D more thinly. Throughout the EC, European multinationals were nationally oriented and less closely integrated across borders than non-European affiliates in the region (United Nations Center on Transnational Corporations [UNCTC] 1990, 23–26).

The spread of national-level restrictions thus threatened the common market's viability. Firms seeking larger than national markets could not reap the full benefits of regional integration: as long as restraints on trade existed and technical standards and regulatory rules varied so widely, they could not penetrate the domestic markets of high-cost competitors, they could not specialize production across borders to take advantage of factor price differentials, and they could not rationalize duplicate activities and organize manufacturing, marketing, and distribution on a continental basis. Indeed, the European Commission's Cecchini (1988, 31) Report found "innumerable cases of Europe-wide business rationalization which are not even attempted because of the costs involved." Moreover, market segmentation in the EC coincided with a loss of market shares abroad for European firms, which heightened concerns about declining competitiveness.

These problems provoked calls to lift the surviving restrictions on the movement of goods, services, capital, and labor. In 1985, a European Commission White Paper, "Completing the Internal Market," detailed the benefits of

---

2. Philips also made almost two thousand kinds of lightbulbs due to differences in national standards (Dai 1996, 167–68).

eliminating these remaining barriers and identified 289 measures for member countries to implement. The proposal targeted four types of barriers: fiscal barriers (such as taxation), national-level quotas against nonmembers, market access restrictions (for example, public procurement and regulations on banking, insurance, and transportation), and border barriers (such as technical standards, administrative rules, and border inspections). Subsequently, the white paper became the foundation for the 1992 program to complete the single market.

European Industry and Economies of Scale

The first step in identifying producer preferences is to evaluate the importance of scale economies. In the book's analytical approach, support for the single-market program is likely to be strong where national markets were too small to exploit scale economies and trade barriers hampered firms' efforts to expand. Industries with large returns to scale would have opportunities to exploit cost reduction in a unified market, with positive and negative adjustment effects as national industries (and individual firms) expanded and contracted across borders. Particularly where barriers to intra-EC trade sustained price differentials across markets, low-cost producers would be able to streamline operations and drive out or acquire small, high-cost producers. In these industries, a more efficient cost structure would benefit the surviving firms in global competition.

National Market Sizes

In a number of EC industries, incomplete market integration kept production fragmented. The European Commission, noting that "minimum efficient size has increased since the 1960s," identified several branches of manufacturing in which "technological change has exerted pressure to create ever-larger production units" (Emerson et al. 1988, 127). This study found that the entire EC market could support fewer than ten MES plants in 11 percent of all manufacturing sectors, and 10–20 MES plants in another 16 percent of sectors. In these cases, the largest national markets had room for only four or five MES plants at most. Eliminating the remaining barriers to trade would lift the constraints of national market size and allow producers to operate on an EC-wide basis—which would encourage firms to expand throughput, lengthen production runs, and pursue mergers and acquisitions.

Table 22 shows market sizes in Europe compared to the MES for thirty-seven products. Markets were small or returns to scale large in motor vehicles, transportation equipment, and tires; branches of industrial machinery, such as trac-

TABLE 22. MES Production and the EC Market, 1984

Product	MES as a Percentage of EC Market	Largest National Producer	MES as a Percentage of Largest Producer
Large returns to scale			
Aircraft	90.1	France	
Trucks	22.3	Germany	94.1
Typewriters	21.1	Germany	69.2
Tractors	20.3	Belgium	78.6
Videocassette recorders	18.5	Germany	500.0
Motorcycles	11.9	Italy	27.8
Semiconductors	10.1	Germany	41.1
Automobiles	9.9	Germany	26.4
Steel	8.3	Germany	25.5
Washing machines	8.2	Italy	23.6
Televisions	7.9	Germany	30.6
Primary aluminum	7.6	Germany	25.7
Refrigerators	7.3	Italy	22.4
Industrial engines	7.0	Germany	7.6
Electric motors	6.5	Germany	10.8
Tires	6.1	France	17.4
Petrochemicals (ethylene)	6.0	Germany	15.5
Manmade fibers	5.1	Germany	11.4
Synthetic ammonia	3.8	Netherlands	15.1
Synthetic rubber	3.4	France	10.8
Beer	2.2	Germany	6.1
Glass bottles	2.0	France	5.5
Refined petroleum	1.7	Germany	12.9
Cement	1.3	Italy	5.2
Paper	1.2	Germany	4.4
Iron castings	0.9	Germany	2.3
Paperboard	0.7	Germany	2.8
Carpets	0.5	Belgium	1.3
Building bricks	0.3	Germany	0.9
Small returns to scale			
Cigarettes	11.6	Germany	43.6
Storage batteries	3.5	Germany	8.4
Soap	2.7	France	8.8
Detergents	1.4	Germany	4.3
Bicycles	0.9	Germany	3.3
Cotton fabrics	0.6	Italy	2.1
Synthetic fabrics	0.5	Belgium	1.3
Footwear	0.1	Italy	0.3

Source: Data for number of plants: Eurostat, *Structure and Activity of Industry* (various years); data for output: United Nations 1993.

tors and engines; office and computing equipment, electrical machinery, electronic equipment and components, and household appliances; steel and nonferrous metals; and industrial, synthetic, agricultural, and petroleum-based chemicals. Scale economies were less significant in food processing, beverages, and tobacco; nonmetallic minerals; metal manufactures; textiles, apparel, and footwear; paper products; instruments and precision machinery; and basic chemicals such as paint and soap. These findings are consistent with other studies of European manufacturing such as Emerson et al. 1988; Buigues, Ilzkovitz, and Lebrun 1990; and Smith and Venables 1988.

In the industries with important scale economies, an integrated European market left room for thirty or fewer MES plants—more than any national market could support, but many less than the number of factories then in operation. Removing barriers to intra-EC trade therefore would enhance competition and break up oligopolies, allowing large, low-cost producers to expand, sometimes at the expense of small, high-cost producers. Of the firms already competing in the market, a few "European champions" would emerge in each industry, along with a handful of smaller, differentiated producers. This meant that some national champions could go out of business once they lost the trade protection that enabled them to survive.

The scale of production in the EC at the time the single-market initiative was launched provides further insights into how integration would affect national industries. Large-scale producers in industries with large returns to scale would be likely to benefit from the completion of the single market; small-scale producers, however, would be exposed to competitive pressures as trade liberalization and policy harmonization moved forward. Industries with inefficient-scale manufacturing at the national level therefore had incentives to oppose European integration unless measures could be developed to compensate them for the loss of trade protection in their domestic markets.

The Scale of European Industry

In the early years of the EC, many analysts believed that European firms were too small to effectively compete with industrial giants from the United States. To meet "le défi Americain" (Servan-Schreiber 1968), it was argued, European firms constrained by their national boundaries needed a larger internal market within which to gain scale economies. In the first phase of EC integration, firms in industries such as automobiles, trucks, and home appliances did expand product runs (Owen 1983). But European companies made fewer gains than their U.S. rivals:

The competitive advantages of U.S. [companies] ... were not matched by European firms, many of which were still recovering from the Second World War and confined to their relatively small home markets. This imbalance in competitive strength in international markets meant that U.S. firms reaped many of the benefits of European integration in the early days of the Common Market by becoming leaders in several key markets in the Community. (UNCTC 1990, 5–6)

In the years preceding the 1992 program, "many firms in the Community ... lost ground to their United States and Japanese competitors, not only in extra-regional markets, but in the Community itself" (UNCTC 1990, 18). Particularly in industries with large returns to scale, intra-EC trade barriers enabled high-cost producers to survive and prevented low-cost producers from expanding to challenge the leading firms from the United States and Japan. The European Commission concluded: "it is in these sectors that the Community's competitive position is currently most under threat" (Emerson et al. 1988, 128).

Differences in industry definitions make extensive comparison across countries difficult. As a first cut, table 23 displays the scale of European manufacturing for five products. The data confirm that U.S. industries achieved longer product runs or larger batches. German producers generally attained scales comparable to non-European firms, with France not far behind. But size dis-

TABLE 23.   Scale of Production in the EC, 1980–89

Product/Units	Year	EC-4	Percentage of U.S. Production	Germany	France	Britain	Italy
1980–82							
Motor vehicles (no.)	1980	134,223	88.4	176,775	199,654	86,261	69,990
Steel (tons)	1980	425,668	71.9	1,640,440	1,183,415	193,080	263,846
Manmade fibers (thousand lb.)	1980	33,674	68.4	54,931	32,775	21,419	28,950
Televisions[a]	1982	251,200	45.0	415,000	287,500	180,000	128,889
1988–89							
Tires (thousand)	1989	3,763	81.3	3,536	3,612	3,110	6,220
Manmade fibers (thousand lb.)	1988	37,314	76.4	62,382	59,686	13,143	34,423
Steel (tons)	1988	817,393	73.1	1,742,455	1,300,781	860,373	385,074
Motor vehicles (no.)	1988	108,765	55.1	148,583	94,458	71,586	117,424

Source: Data for number of plants: Eurostat, *Structure and Activity of Industry* (various years); data for output: United Nations 1993.

Note: No. = number of individual units.

[a]Data for the EC: Commission of the European Communities 1985, 72–81; data for the United States: U.S. Congress 1983, 113–14. Since ten of the sixteen U.S. factories were Asian, a relative scale of 45.0 is a reasonable baseline estimate for the EC compared to producers in Asia.

advantages in British and Italian industry were considerable. Due to the restricted range of these data, the following discussion draws extensively from qualitative information.

The chemical industry was Europe's traditional area of dominance. German firms were world leaders in specialty chemicals, while French and British producers maintained strong positions in volume-intensive basic chemicals. In pharmaceuticals, German and British companies amassed large R&D budgets and secured many new patents, but French and Italian drugmakers were smaller, with fewer financial resources. In synthetic fibers, average output per plant was four-fifths of the U.S. level and 20 percent greater than Japan's. European firms in these sectors already were large in size and international in scope. Though nontariff barriers, such as price controls for pharmaceuticals, left some room to exploit scale economies at the plant level, further liberalization generally was not going to place significant cost pressures on firms or provoke industry-wide adjustment (Commission of the European Communities 1988d, 48–50, 74–76, 130–38). The main exceptions were ammonia and especially petrochemicals: ethylene crackers and chemical refineries in Europe achieved only two-thirds of the average scale in the United States, even though capacity per plant doubled after 1970 (Molle 1993, 56–59).

Primary metal was another industry with areas of strength. Nonferrous refineries and smelters achieved large output scales, particularly for aluminum and copper. Steel mills increased in size with the development of blast oxygen furnaces and corporate mergers at the national level. German steelmakers and a few French firms approached world-class levels of output. However, Britain's steel industry faced severe overcapacity, and Italy had more steelmaking facilities (135) than the five other original EC members combined (127). As a result, European volume as a whole was barely half of the Japanese level, and national champions dominated in France (Sacilor), Italy (Finsider), Britain (British Steel), Belgium (Cockerill Sambre), Holland (Hoogovens), and Luxembourg (Arbed). State aids to inefficient companies, along with production quotas and minimum prices, forced low-cost German and Dutch steelmakers to sell surpluses outside the EC because they could not easily export within it (Howell et al. 1988, 177–89).[3]

In the automobile industry, smaller mass producers such as PSA Group, Renault, Fiat, and Leyland (until its sale) had a weak competitive position due to

3. This provoked antidumping and countervailing duties in the United States. The U.S. Commerce Department found subsidization rates of 15–20 percent for Usinor, Sacilor, Italsider, A.F.L. Falck, and British Steel. Krupp, Klöckner, and Hoesch in Germany and Hoogovens in Holland received some subsidies in 1980, but these were small by comparison (Tarr 1988, 190–91).

volumes of barely two hundred thousand vehicles per platform. Though the home market shares of these national champions declined continuously after 1960, the EC market was "single only in name" due to differences in equipment standards, inspection requirements, and local taxation. Incompatible national standards forced firms to engage in costly duplication (Cecchini 1988, 55–56).[4] Market segmentation existed in both automobiles and trucks, as prices were much higher in countries with local manufacturing than in those dependent on imports. Without import barriers and state aids, automakers SEAT, Leyland, Renault, and Volvo and truck makers DAF and ENASA might have gone bankrupt in the 1980s (Sleuwaegen 1991, 111–15; Commission of the European Communities 1990, 76). The larger mass producers—Volkswagen, Ford, and GM—and specialist automakers such as BMW, Daimler-Benz, and Alfa Romeo had more to gain from completing the single market and less to fear from foreign competition.

In information technology (IT), "the smallness of European firms, insufficient levels of R&D spending ... [and] national markets of insufficient size and sophistication" placed EC industry at a severe disadvantage (Sandholtz 1992, 74).[5] In response, governments encouraged consolidation and employed subsidies, procurement preferences, and technical barriers to nurture national champions. But these practices prevented manufacturing from being regionally concentrated. "Protected and fragmented national markets have served to foster smaller, less efficient plant sizes, and to increase design and distribution costs," Bowen (1991b, 252) concludes of the semiconductor industry. As MES production grew—firms needed a 6 percent world market share to recoup construction costs for modern facilities in 1990, compared to 3 percent in 1970—EC producers fell hopelessly behind (Bowen 1991b, 230–34), and Europe's share of the world semiconductor market declined from 25 percent in 1970 to 12 percent in 1985 (U.S. Congress 1991, 203).

Weakness in electronic components filtered downstream, as "the higher price-cost margins made possible by protected national markets, together with import restrictions, dissuaded consumers from purchases that could have permitted the achievement of greater production levels" (Bowen 1991b, 252). Computer consumption in Europe was one-quarter that of the United States,

4. For example, France blocked common standards for windshields, tires, and weights and dimensions during the 1970s.

5. Mackintosh (1986, 75) explains the weakness of European IT firms more dramatically: "their 'national' sales were too small to yield them the benefit of competitive economies of scale; neighboring European national markets had the appearance of bloody battlegrounds, with wounded 'National Champions' trying to fight off the invading transoceanic hordes."

and IBM held market shares of at least 60 percent in all EC countries except France. The top EC firms were smaller than IBM's "second-rank U.S. competitors" (Mackintosh 1986, 85), and the six largest companies held only 10 percent of the world market.[6] In telecommunications gear, national markets were too small to amortize the fixed costs of R&D and manufacturing.[7] The procurement practices of the national service providers, along with incompatible standards and restrictive certification procedures, preserved equipment makers' home market sales and blocked low-cost suppliers from operating on a regional basis (Cecchini 1988, 50–54). With the European market segmented into nine different switching systems (compared to four in the United States and three in Japan), CGE-Alcatel "was manufacturing three distinct but overlapping lines of public switch" (Commission of the European Communities 1997, 64), and the average factory produced one million lines—a fraction of the U.S. level of seven million (Emerson et al. 1988, 86; Sandholtz 1992, 229).

The consumer electronics industry was in the worst shape of all. Companies often had to expend considerable development expenses and reset assembly lines to meet differing national standards (Cecchini 1988, 33–34). In televisions, France used the Séquence à Mémoire standard, a Thomson patent, while Germany required Phase Alternation by Line, which AEG-Telefunken held. As a result, "European industry was fragmented into a large number of plants with relatively small production volumes serving segmented markets" (Cawson et al. 1990, 224), and producers maintained scales that were "suboptimal compared to plants in Japan" (Bowen 1991a, 264). The gap was even wider in videocassette recorders, and Japanese firms used their large cost advantages to cut prices and undersell EC producers. Bowen (1991a, 266) concludes: "market fragmentation explains the low rate of exploitation of economies of scale by European manufacturers and correspondingly why their production costs are often 20–35 percent higher than those of their Japanese competitors."

In each of these industries, the creation of a single market would allow larger European companies to expand in size and gain scale economies. A consolidation trend already had started in the 1980s.[8] Further concentration would be

6. IBM spent $2 billion on R&D in 1983, while the largest EC companies (Siemens, Machines Bull, and Electronic Data Processing) each recorded sales less than $1.4 billion (Mackintosh 1986, 136–39).

7. According to Cecchini (1988, 51), "Even the larger EC member states have small markets—compared to Japan, let alone the United States—and these are segmented, there being little intra-EC trade."

8. Consumer electronics merged into three main groups led by Philips, Thomson, and Nokia. In computers, Nixdorf and ICL were acquired, and Philips ended production, leaving Siemens, Olivetti, and Bull. In automobiles, Peugeot and Citroën merged to form PSA Group.

possible if the barriers that protected national champions came down. Small-scale firms, however, would lose market shares. In automobiles, the European Commission expected the number of platforms to decline from 30 in 1985 to 21 in a single market. This meant that PSA, Renault, Fiat, or Rover (Leyland's successor) might not survive the transition to the single market (Commission of the European Communities 1988a, 23–24). Likewise, ending steel subsidies would help large-scale German firms employ additional capacity at the expense of state-run enterprises such as Finsider and British Steel seeking to elude bankruptcy. In petrochemicals, industry-wide concentration would pressure inefficient firms to close their refineries. Twelve telecommunications suppliers survived in a market that could support three or four once nationalistic links with service providers were ended (Sandholtz 1992, 84–89). Small electronics firms, particularly in France and Italy, faced possible extinction due to their "limited scale of operations" (Commission of the European Communities 1985, 11). And so it was for the industries with substantial unexploited scale economies.

These circumstances left small-scale companies with three options. First, they could seek to defeat the single-market program to preserve their national champion status. Second, they could lobby to delay or block the implementation of directives that would erode national protection and domestic-market shares. Third, they could seek external trade protection to compensate for increased competitive pressures in Europe. Higher barriers to outside trade would allow EC firms with unexploited scale economies to stay in business if non-European producers could be pushed out. Indeed, without enhanced protection against external trade, many groups would be likely to try to delay and dilute single-market directives or defeat them altogether. Thus, the single market and external trade were closely linked: imports from outside the EC provided an outlet for groups facing tougher competition as internal barriers to trade were liberalized and national standards harmonized.

However, external trade barriers would not help if foreign multinationals could freely invest inside the single market. In several industries with large returns to scale, U.S. firms had a significant and longstanding EC presence. Multinationals were firmly established and produced with high local content in industries such as automobiles (where Ford and GM accounted for one-quarter of production) and computers (where IBM held 58 percent of the market). In these cases, trade policies and regulatory rules could not effectively discriminate between European and U.S.-owned firms.

The threat was that new entrants would transfer productive capacity to Europe to share in the single market's benefits; this would enhance competition and erode the market shares of EC firms, pushing them up their cost curves. In electronic components, Intel, Motorola, and Texas Instruments were opening or expanding semiconductor-manufacturing facilities. Moreover, Japanese companies had started to manufacture automobiles and consumer electronics in Europe: Toyota, Nissan, and Honda had established automobile factories in Britain, while several firms began production of TVs and VCRs in Britain and Germany. Japanese FDI in consumer electronics had worsened the "fragmented industrial structure which resulted in the establishment of too many plants of suboptimum scale and considerable excess capacity" (Young, Hood, and Hamill 1988, 183). Foreign entry raised similar concerns about overcapacity and price wars in automobiles and semiconductors.

In this environment, EC producers, especially those with small-scale operations, had incentives to push for TRIMs and other regulatory rules to hinder or block foreign multinationals. Content requirements and trade restrictions on imported components and subassemblies would ensure that the benefits of 1992 accrued to European firms rather than those headquartered outside the EC.

Industries with Constant Returns to Scale

In industries with small returns to scale, completing the single market would be less disruptive. Large national markets and small returns to scale limited the potential benefits of completing the single market, since producers would not experience opportunities for cost reduction. Instead, producers would gain or lose based on local factor endowments. Thus, national industries with small MES production and large domestic markets would be expected to resist the single-market program or, as an alternative, seek to enhance protection against external trade, only to the extent that they anticipated greater import competition within the EC.

But most adjustments based on national comparative advantage already had occurred in the EC's earlier phase. Markets were highly integrated in all but a few industries such as food and tobacco, nonmetallic minerals, metal products, and leather (Cecchini 1988, 27). Production and trade patterns in the EC therefore reflected specialization and different consumer tastes rather than market segmentation. While Europe was falling further behind in industries with large returns to scale, its competitive position was stable in activities with limited scale economies, such as textiles, apparel, leather, paper, and processed foods (Emerson et al. 1988, 11–19).

In textiles and apparel, the single market offered few opportunities to further specialize according to comparative advantage. Textile and clothing markets in the EC were highly integrated despite differences across countries in value-added taxes and labeling requirements; indeed, some firms in northern Italy found it easier to sell in Germany and France than in southern Italy. Europe already had lost much of its low-end production, except for labor-rich areas in Spain, Portugal, and Greece, and the surviving firms specialized for niche markets in high-value-added segments and outsourced labor-intensive tasks due to high wages at home (Commission of the European Communities 1988c, 41–56, 102–5).

The key issue for these industries was not internal liberalization, which would have little effect, but rather harmonization in external trade policy. Under the Multifiber Arrangement (MFA), national quotas varied widely because discord in the EC thwarted a common external policy. Differences in quotas in turn diverted MFA imports from high-quota to low-quota countries. In response, France, Italy, Belgium, and Ireland imposed Article 115 measures to block transshipment and shelter protected textile and apparel producers from gaps in Europe's external trade policy. Disruption in sheltered national markets would occur if these restrictions were phased out and quotas harmonized at the EC level. Moreover, producers in Mediterranean Europe gained from trade diversion because they competed with developing nations in standardized, price-sensitive goods.

The food-processing and tobacco industries also were likely to experience significant competitive effects from the completion of the single market. Because of content regulations (such as restrictions in France on the use of aspartame in soft drinks, pasta purity laws in Italy, and beer laws in Germany), packaging and labeling requirements (for biscuits, cakes, chocolate and confectionery, soup, baby food, and ice cream), tax differences (on beer, for instance), and health standards, barriers to intra-EC trade were substantial (Commission of the European Communities 1988b, 94–173). Though scale economies were small in primary processing (transforming crops into edible food products) and secondary processing (processing and packaging refined food products), large firms could benefit from opportunities to expand marketing and distribution networks for brand-name products. The food and tobacco industries were highly multinational already, but European food processors (other than Unilever and BSN) lacked the distribution and marketing strength of foreign multinationals such as Nestlé, Heinz, Philip Morris, Kelloggs, Coca-Cola, and PepsiCo because they focused on national markets and lacked EC-wide strategies (McGee and Segal-Horn 1992, 28–32, 43–44). Breaking down the barriers that fragmented consumer markets would make it easier for companies to distribute and sell pan-European brands to compete more effectively with foreign rivals.

TABLE 24. Import Competition in the EC

Industry	Import Share of Consumption		
	1984	1992	Percentage Change
Import share >10%			
Lumber	41.2	36.2	−12.0
Paper and pulp	32.0	32.3	0.8
Textiles	13.6	17.7	30.4
Clothing	13.3	23.2	74.6
Footwear	11.0	22.8	107.1
Import share <10%			
Processed foods	8.2	7.6	−25.2
Wood products	6.4	10.7	67.4
Glass and glassware	5.9	7.7	30.4
Plastic products	5.4	7.3	36.1
Converted paper products	4.6	5.8	25.6
Furniture	4.1	6.7	63.9
Metal products	3.1	4.8	53.9
Beverages and tobacco	2.2	2.1	−2.7
Soaps and detergents	1.1	2.4	116.2

Source: Data from Eurostat, *Panorama of EU Industry* (various years).

Table 24 displays Europe's external trade patterns in industries with small returns to scale. The data show heavy import penetration in industries with high labor costs or natural resource dependence: labor intensity fueled external competition in textiles, clothing, and footwear, while poor forest reserves and reliance on imported pulp hurt the paper and lumber industries.[9] In glass and glassware, plastic products, metal products, furniture, processed foods, and beverages and tobacco, external competition was not significant.

The preceding discussion anticipates that the elimination of the remaining trade barriers and harmonization in the EC were likely to have the largest distributional effects in textiles, apparel, and food processing. In textiles and apparel, abolishing Article 115 and harmonizing external trade would create incentives for nationally oriented, high-cost producers to seek protection against external trade. Adjustment also would occur in the food and tobacco industries through competitive pressures on small national producers and high input costs for primary processors of fruits, vegetables, meats, grains, and dairy products. In this case, however, the presence of foreign multinationals in Europe suggests that it would have been futile for high-cost producers to seek

9. European paper mills averaged less than one-quarter the capacity of more efficient Scandinavian mills, but national markets were large compared to the MES (Zavatta 1993, 91–92).

higher barriers to external trade if integration produced heavy internal adjustment costs.

The other endowment-based industries were not likely to experience significant competitive effects from further market integration. EC producers already had strong motives to support high barriers against outside trade in lumber, paper, and footwear. The completion of the single market would not increase competition enough to make these protectionist preferences any more intense.

Industry Preferences on Completing the Single Market

Lobbying activity in the EC prior to the completion of the single market is not easy to evaluate. The European Parliament rarely held hearings, so organized groups had few opportunities and little incentive to publicly communicate their preferences in Strasbourg. The Directorates-General for trade, competition, and economic and financial affairs in the European Commission, the administrative arm of the EC, lacked an institutional mandate to solicit the opinions of private groups, as cabinet departments and executive agencies do in the United States. Though the European Commission encouraged lobbying to learn the views of European and national interest groups—and it often sought business and trade union input when directives were in the drafting stage—most contacts with private actors were informal and confidential (Calingaert 1994, 34–39).

Moreover, much lobbying remained national, despite the growing centralization of authority in Brussels, because the positions of the member states in the Council of Ministers were the key factors in the policy-making process. In national capitals, political pressure was not as open as in Washington, D.C., nor was it exerted through formal civic channels. Calingaert (1994, 34) explains: "Chief executives of large European companies do not normally seek to influence governments through public pressure. Rather, they concentrate on private, informal means." Large firms in particular could exert influence outside public view because, a European Commission official noted, "when necessary they can ring up their own prime ministers and make their case" (Sandholtz and Zysman 1989, 117).

In short, policy-making involved "informal relationships and negotiations" that "because of their informal character, are not clearly reflected in documents," Fielder (2000, 76) notes. The official hearings and reports that are publicly available therefore provide little insight into lobbying behavior in the EC. The analysis that follows draws from secondary texts, newspaper reports, and, where useful, public documents to examine lobbying on the completion of the single market and the evolution of external trade policy in Europe. Though the information in these sources is not as thorough or as conclusive as material drawn from public cases of lobbying, still it illuminates the general direction of industry trade preferences in Europe.

The politics of the single-market program is especially obscure. Moravcsik (1998, 318) finds "broad-based business support in all countries for the [Single European Act] as a tool to increase the global competitiveness of firms." At the industry level, the single market was most popular among capital goods producers such as "automotive, machine tool, chemical, and electronics firms," and "multinational firms in capital-intensive sectors." Opposition centered in food processing, while national champions with few exports "viewed liberalization of regulatory standards and public procurement most unfavorably" (Moravcsik 1998, 328). However, "business did not take a proactive role," Moravcsik (1998, 344) argues, because "the great majority of businessmen believed that the effects of 1992 on corporate costs would be small. . . . Though industrial restructuring was viewed as inevitable, removal of trade barriers was an unimportant factor, for most European [multinational companies] were already organizing on a continental scale."

Moravcsik accordingly doubts the influence of the European Roundtable (ERT), an alliance of European multinationals. Though the group closely monitored progress in the implementation of the European Commission White Paper directives, "the ERT did not originate single market proposals." Rather, he argues, the ERT was cool to the white paper initially, as its members desired aggressive industrial policies more than the removal of border barriers and harmonized standards. The group also did not meet with the Monnet Committee until late 1984. "On balance," Moravcsik (1998, 355–56) concludes, "the most that can be said for European multinationals is that they offered vocal support in 1985–86 once others had developed proposals for internal market liberalization."

Others assign higher importance to the ERT lobby's support for completing the single market (see Messerlin 2001, 74, 133). There is substantial evidence that large companies began to push for liberalization in the early 1980s—before the European Commission developed the proposals issued in the white paper. According to Calingaert (1994, 37):

> The initial thrust . . . came from business community sectors that were concerned with Europe's long-term ability to compete in an increasingly global market. Led by firms such as Philips, they developed a plan for re-

moving the remaining obstacles to the free movement of goods, services, capital and people, an idea embraced by the new commission.[10]

Businesses articulated these demands through ad hoc groups of large firms organized specifically to push for the completion of the single market, such as the ERT. Formed in 1982 after discussions between Volvo chief executive Pehr Gyllenhammar and Etienne Davignon, vice president of the European Commission, the ERT held its first meeting in early 1983. In a memo to Davignon, the group asserted that it needed liberalization because "[t]he European market must serve as the 'home' base necessary to allow European firms to develop as powerful competitors in world markets" (Fielder 2000, 89). Pamphlets such as *Changing Scales* explained how firms could gain scale economies through further integration. In 1984, sixteen corporate heads again petitioned the European Commission to create a pan-European market in which "the barriers of customs, tariffs and national preferment on public procurement are removed . . . [and] health, safety, and other standards are standardized."[11] An ERT report later that year complained, "progress toward the creation of a European Common Market continues to be frustratingly slow" (Fielder 2000, 89).

Thus, "when Jacques Delors, prior to assuming the presidency of the Commission in 1985, began campaigning for the unified internal market," Sandholtz and Zysman (1989, 116) note, "European industrialists were ahead of him." Fiat chairman Giovanni Agnelli (1989, 62), echoes this view:

> the politicians . . . in 1957 first conceived the idea of a common market—often over objections from the business community. Now the situation is reversed; it is the entrepreneurs and corporations who are keeping the pressure on politicians to transcend considerations of local and national interest.

In advertisements in the *Financial Times,* several companies threatened to move overseas if the single-market initiative stalled. French firms in the ERT mobilized pressure on the Mitterand government, which assisted the push for the single market (Cowles 1995, 509–516). On the eve of the vote on the Single European Act, twenty-seven large companies called on the Council of Ministers to commit to the creation of a unified market: "it is vital for the conti-

---

10. Gaster (1994, 262) adds: "Much of the original impetus behind EC-92 came from those who believed that what Europe needed above all was larger companies to compete with the American and Japanese giants, and who argued that larger companies could only come from a larger domestic market."

11. "Bosses Want the Common Market Brussels Never Built" 1984, 75.

nent's economic well-being," the group asserted, "that the Common Market leaders give a clear signal that the organization will achieve its goal of complete economic integration by 1992."[12] Subsequently, the ERT established the Internal Market Support Committee to maintain pressure on national governments to follow through on European Commission directives (Cowles 1995, 518–19).

Within the integration movement, Philips was prominent. Chief Executive Wisse Dekker believed a common market was critical to industry's global standing (Dai 1996, 92–95). A 1983 company memo asserted that only with the single market completed could "industry compete globally, by exploiting economies of scale, for what will then be the biggest home market in the world today: the European Community home market" (Sandholtz and Zysman 1989, 117). Dekker's report to the European Commission, *Europe 1990: An Action Plan,* anticipated the recommendations in the white paper issued later that year (Fielder 2000, 82).

Along with Philips, IT companies pushing to liberalize trade and harmonize standards included consumer electronics firms Thomson and Thorn-EMI; data-processing equipment makers Olivetti, Machines Bull, Nixdorf, and STC-ICL; and telecom gear producers Siemens, CGE-Alcatel, and Plessey (Cawson et al. 1990, 183–84; Sally 1995, 188–89). These companies were "an important and vocal constituency . . . pressing for the completion of the internal market" (Sharp 1991, 73). IT firms also lobbied for Brussels to institute R&D programs for computers, semiconductors, telecommunications, and microelectronics. Through collaboration on an EC-wide basis and closer integration in a genuine common market, these firms argued, they could pursue the mergers, strategic alliances, and technology-sharing necessary to compete effectively in global markets (Sandholtz 1992, 173–75, 237–41).

Other industries with large returns to scale supported the single market as well, though divisions between firms surfaced. In the automotive industry, specialist producers of luxury vehicles, which faced little competition in their market niche, advocated radical integration. Mass producers, however, split over elements of the single-market program because heavy adjustment costs would fall on the weaker companies. Thus, Volkswagen, Ford, and GM "largely welcomed an open internal market," while PSA, Renault, and Fiat expressed "reservations" (Stephen 2000, 179).

The single market also divided the steel industry. German steelmakers and Hoogovens wanted to eliminate production quotas and end state aids. But national champions Usinor and Sacilor in France, Finsider in Italy, and British Steel in Britain supported protection against low-cost German and Dutch

12. "West European Leaders Meet Today," *New York Times,* December 2, 1985, A3.

competitors; these firms also sought continued financial assistance from their national governments.[13] The head of EUROFER, an executive at Hoogovens, pushed to restore free markets in steel as rapidly as possible, yet the *Financial Times* reported that most "EUROFER members are of the opinion that it is still too early to liberalize the quota system."[14] Specialized steel firms feared competition on equal terms with national champions receiving generous state aids, while the leading companies outside Germany and the Netherlands opposed liberalization with or without subsidies.[15]

To summarize, the available information on lobbying for the single market generally supports hypothesis 1 and hypothesis 2, though the evidence is sketchy to be sure. Of the twenty products with large returns to scale and small national markets in table 22, firms in six of these activities (typewriters, videocassette recorders, semiconductors, automobiles, steel, and televisions) openly pushed for the completion of the single market. An earlier section of this chapter noted that smaller national champions in industries with large returns to scale would have incentives to oppose the 1992 program to keep their home markets protected, and in the automobile and steel industries this appears to have been the case. It is not clear, however, why the same sorts of political divisions did not surface in the IT industries, where support for the single market was uniformly strong.

European Protectionism before 1992

The preceding section suggests that firms in industries with large returns to scale, especially larger companies, pushed for the single market so they could reorganize to match foreign rivals. Supporters of the 1992 program generally believed that more open, integrated markets would provide a stimulus for companies to restructure.

As barriers to intra-EC trade were being liberalized, however, firms previously protected in their home market would face price pressures, and national oligopolies would be broken up. Moreover, in many industries the largest Eu-

13. Germany even threatened countervailing duties against subsidized imports from EC countries. In a compromise, the European Commission raised German production quotas and extended the phaseout of subsidies to the end of 1985. The commission's ban on subsidies drove most public support underground but did not end it (Howell et al. 1988, 63–81).

14. Cynics regarded Director-General Hans-Gunther Vorwerk's promarket views as a response to Hoogovens's opening of a new mill "that would be able to operate at a higher rate if output controls were removed" ("How Roles Have Been Reversed," *Financial Times*, October 16, 1985, 18).

15. "Small Steelmakers Fear Easing of EEC Controls," *Financial Times*, June 14, 1985, 1; "EEC Steel Control Plan Meets Heavy Opposition," *Financial Times*, October 2, 1985, 20.

ropean companies could not compete effectively in the global economy. Finally, there was a risk that inward FDI would dissipate the benefits of the single market for European-owned firms. Each of these concerns created incentives for protectionism against external trade.

As a result, industries that united to campaign for the 1992 program did not share the same external trade preferences. Pearce and Sutton (1985, 5) note: "Lowering internal barriers is an objective common to both 'Euro-protectionists' and 'liberals.' What divides them is whether this should be accompanied by industrial policy and greater external protection." For companies vulnerable to competitive pressure during the transition to the single market, there was concern that without higher barriers to outside trade, "the benefits of this large domestic market, notably economies of scale, might be lost to their U.S. and Japanese competitors" (Pearce and Sutton 1985, 5). In such cases, protectionist pressures were intense leading up to 1992.

Industries with Economies of Scale

Among the industries with large returns to scale, only producers of chemicals and pharmaceuticals declined to seek higher trade barriers. In particular, Germany's Verband der Chemischen Industrie viewed "itself as a guardian . . . of free trade" (Grant, Paterson, and Whitston 1988, 184). Consistent with the EC chemical industry's large-scale operations and multinational ties, leading firms in other countries also did not seek protection against imports from outside Europe (Sally 1995, 193–194). In petrochemicals, the industry's weakest branch, Belgian, French, and Italian firms formed a cartel to coordinate capacity cuts (firms in Germany, Britain, and the Netherlands opposed cartelization), but the Conseil Européen des Fédérations de l'Industrie Chimique (CEFIC) did not ask the European Commission to allocate quotas or implement price controls (Grant, Paterson, and Whitston 1988, 228–31). Producers of inorganic chemicals and fertilizers petitioned for antidumping duties against Asian and Eastern bloc countries, but the products covered were small as a percentage of imports. National industries also had no voluntary export restraints (VERs) or quotas on chemicals and pharmaceuticals as of 1992.

Outside of the chemical industry, European companies actively lobbied for import barriers. Small-scale producers likely to lose business with the completion of the single market issued the most intense calls for protection. For the steel, automobile, and consumer electronics industries, whose comperatively small scale of production is shown in table 23, this external protectionism is consistent with hypothesis 5.

In steel, the EC-wide system of production quotas and minimum prices, and state aids at the national level, already blocked imports from efficient steelmakers inside the EC and low-cost mills outside Europe. In 1985, the VER against fifteen foreign suppliers was relaxed, as quotas for target countries increased 3 percent (though this was less than the rise in market demand over the period). The EC eliminated quotas for the European Free Trade Area in 1988 and converted the remaining import restraints to surveillance measures (Howell et al. 1988, 97–98). Steelmakers responded by filing fourteen antidumping cases, mostly against Eastern bloc countries.

In automobiles, quantitative controls limited Japan's market share to 1 percent in Spain, 2 percent in Italy, 3 percent in France, 11 percent in Britain, and 15 percent in Germany.[16] Technical barriers to trade also blocked Japanese trucks in EC markets (Sleuwaegen 1991, 122–23). In the run-up to 1992, PSA, Renault, and Fiat lobbied through the Committee of Common Market Motor Vehicle Constructors (CCMC) for Europe-wide quotas to replace the national restrictions that would soon disappear under the single-market program. Only Rover (which had a strategic alliance with Honda) and German automakers Volkswagen, Mercedes, BMW, and Porsche declined to support tough import restraints.[17]

Two events caused automakers to converge around a proposal to limit Japan to 15 percent of the EC market. First, Volkswagen tilted toward more stringent measures and joined Renault and Fiat in a formal request to the European Commission for transitional quotas. Second, the CCMC was disbanded, and its members formed the Association of European Automobile Constructors (ACEA), a group that included Ford and GM but excluded PSA to isolate its hard-line chairman Jacques Calvet (Mason 1994, 442–44; McLaughlin and Jordan 1993, 149–50). Subsequently, the European Commission negotiated an arrangement to limit Japanese exports to 1.23 million vehicles, roughly equal to 1989 levels, until 1999.[18] As table 25 demonstrates, lobbying by the six mass producers for the VER on Japanese automobiles was strongly correlated with vehicle output per platform.

In consumer electronics, the expiration of patent licenses for televisions and

16. In the European countries without domestic automobile production, Japanese market shares averaged 25–30 percent.

17. The protectionists sought to limit Japan's market share to less than 10 percent for ten years. Daimler-Benz and the other German specialists advocated less severe restrictions lasting no more than five years. GM, Rover, and initially Volkswagen leaned toward this less protectionist approach (Stephen 2000, 115–29; Mason 1994, 435–37).

18. Calvet denounced this "hateful agreement" and urged France to withdraw from the EC if the commission refused to impose French quotas Europe-wide (Mason 1994, 445–48).

TABLE 25.   Scale of EC Automobile Production and Trade Lobbying

Firm	Output per Platform	Protectionist Pressure
Volkswagen	278,773	1
Ford	260,496	3
GM	218,169	2
Fiat	215,584	4
PSA	195,154	6
Renault	189,189	5

Source: Production data from Commission of the European Communities 1988a, vol. 11, 86–90.

Note: Protectionist pressure is ordered from 1 (least protectionist) to 6 (most protectionist) based on each firm's position on the Japanese VER. The Pearson correlation of output per platform and protectionist pressure is -0.818, which is significant at $p < .05$ (two-tailed test; $N = 6$).

the arrival of videocassette recorders in consumer markets triggered protectionist lobbying in the run-up to 1992.[19] As in automobiles, companies organized across borders to persuade the European Commission to grant trade protection while they restructured and pursued mergers and joint ventures. Philips and Thomson endorsed a seven-year VER against Japanese televisions to allow time to reorganize. "There is no way we can survive ... in the medium term with our volumes of production," executives at Grundig and AEG-Telefunken lamented (English 1984, 245). Firms complained even more loudly about foreign competition in items such as VCRs, CD players, and camcorders, where national standards provided no protection. Philips and Grundig launched an antidumping suit against Japanese VCRs in 1982.[20] The next year, the European Association of Consumer Electronics Manufacturers (EACEM), led by Philips and Thomson, petitioned to increase audiovisual equipment tariffs to 19 percent.[21] The EACEM later filed antidumping claims against South Korean and Japanese VCRs and CD players, while Philips and Grundig demanded 25–30 percent tariffs on audio products. Without higher duties, they asserted, factories would have to be closed and moved offshore (Cawson et al. 1990, 313–14).

Producers of semiconductors and electronic components, data-processing

19. The patent system limited market penetration by denying Japanese firms transmission licenses, particularly for large-screen TVs, or requiring them to pay large fees (Cawson et al. 1990, 224–25).

20. Siemens and eight other producers of VCR components joined the claim. Philips and Grundig dropped their petition when the European Commission negotiated an EC-wide VER to limit Japanese shipments to 4.5 million units (Cawson et al. 1990, 254–58).

21. The European Commission approved the 19 percent tariff (an increase from 8 percent for VCRs and 9.5 percent on CD players) for a period of three years, after which the tariff reverted to 14 percent.

equipment, and telecommunications gear also wanted higher trade barriers, though they did not seek protection as actively as consumer electronics companies. The European Commission even reduced semiconductor tariffs from 17 percent to 14 percent in 1985, but it refused to reciprocate the move to zero tariffs by the United States and Japan due to lobbying pressure from firms. In 1986, EC companies formed the European Electronic Component Manufacturers Association (EECA) to pursue antidumping actions against memory chips from Japan.[22] In computers, the European Commission imposed import surveillance measures against Japanese computers, though there were no formal import restraints. However, preferential procurement practices and prodigious R&D subsidies reduced the need for higher tariffs or antidumping duties (Flamm 1987, 160–68). In telecommunications as well, firms successfully blocked measures to open EC procurement markets to foreign competition, so they had less reason to seek additional protectionist measures.[23]

Industries with Constant Returns to Scale

Protectionist pressures before 1992 in industries with small returns to scale concentrated in textiles, apparel, and footwear—exactly those industries that experienced the largest increase in import penetration in the preceding years, consistent with hypothesis 4. In glassware, rubber, ceramics, and metal products, trade associations did not actively seek import barriers in the EC or at the national level.

Producers of textiles and apparel generally favored tough restrictions against developing countries. Though German and Dutch firms, which were highly specialized and less exposed to external competition, sought only soft quotas, producers in France, Italy, and Britain faced heavy adjustment pressures from external imports, and they lobbied for stringent controls in MFA III (1982–86) and MFA IV (1986–91) (Pearce and Sutton 1985, 107–12). However, MFA III "was the peak of EC protection in these sectors" (Messerlin 2001, 289). MFA IV allowed a higher rate of import growth and reduced the number of

22. Siemens, SGS Microelettronica, Thomson, and Motorola joined in a 1988 petition against dynamic random-access memories from Japan, but IBM and Philips declined to participate. This suit resulted in antidumping duties and a system of floor prices (Flamm 1990, 245–49).

23. "How Europe's Phone Monopolies Are Warding off the U.S. Giants" 1984, 110. In contrast to consumer electronics and semiconductors, telecommunications equipment producers, due to their cozy relationship with national service providers, faced little competition from foreign giants AT&T and NEC. Siemens also held back from seeking new protectionist measures to avoid retaliation against its U.S. affiliates—which was not a concern for national champions CGE-Alcatel, Plessey, and Italtel (Cawson et al. 1990, 365; Sally 1995, 194–96).

countries and products covered—though the textile industry responded to this modest opening with antidumping suits on cotton fabrics and bed linens.

The run-up to the single market coincided with the expiration of MFA IV. Low-margin producers in Spain, Portugal, and Greece worried that exporters (particularly China, which had passed Turkey as Europe's top supplier) would target their markets after liberalization. Moreover, the trade association Comitextil argued that the transition to a single EC quota would radically increase imports from Asia. These concerns slowed the opening of textile and clothing markets in Europe (Grilli 1992, 185, 190; Costello and Pelkmans 1991, 83).

The footwear industry experienced similar problems, but it was more divided. The European Commission concluded that some transitional protection—VERs with certain exporters and transitional subsidies—was necessary to compensate firms hurt by internal liberalization. But as trade associations in Italy, Spain, France, and Britain pushed for quotas, multinationals such as Nike, Reebok, and L.A. Gear mobilized against stricter trade barriers (Costello and Pelkmans 1991, 81).

Regression Analysis of EC Nontariff Barriers

If the book's theory is correct, then scale economies, multinational production, and factor cost differences reflected in trade patterns should affect policy, not just lobbying. In the run-up to 1992, the relevant issue in the EC's external trade policy was nontariff barriers. Because the Uruguay Round was still under negotiation, external tariffs in the EC had changed little in the previous decade. Moreover, as the previous discussion implies, new protectionist measures generally took the form of VERs and antidumping duties.

Alas, nontariff barriers are difficult to quantify. Most empirical studies use binary dependent variables to denote the presence or absence of a nontariff barrier, but this method sacrifices too much valuable information. The following analysis employs coverage ratios, which measure the percentage of imports in an industry covered by a nontariff barrier. (Since these barriers vary in severity, the level of precision is not the same as for other measures, such as tariff rates.) The dependent variable is imports of products covered by VERs and antidumping duties as a share of all imports in 1992 at the three-digit Nomenclature Générale des Activités Economiques (NACE, Statistical Classification of Economic Activities) level.[24]

---

24. A VER list appears in GATT (1993, 73–75). Antidumping measures are from Stanbrook and Bentley 1996. Imports are from Eurostat, *Panorama of EU Industry* (various years).

The analysis includes eight independent variables. *Market size* is MES divided by EC consumption. *Scale economies* is an index of the size of scale economies, a proxy for the returns to scale. *Multinational production* is the proportion of industry sales produced outside firms' home markets. *Import competition* and *export dependence* are imports-to-consumption and exports-to-sales ratios for trade with non-EC countries. *Intra-EC trade* is trade inside the EC divided by production. *EC concentration* is an index of sales concentration at the EC level. *National concentration* is a weighted average of industry concentration across the EC member states.[25]

Table 26 presents Tobit regression results.[26] In the two models, one includes *EC concentration* and the other *national concentration.* In both models, external trade patterns have no effect on nontariff barriers; *import competition* even has an incorrect negative sign. Instead, *intra-EC trade* has a statistically significant positive effect on the level of trade protection, which suggests that industries facing competition within the EC received national VERs and antidumping duties at the EC level as compensation. *Multinational production* has a statistically significant negative effect on nontariff barriers. *Scale economies* and *market size* are weakly significant. The positive sign for *scale economies* is consistent with the expectation that industries with large returns to scale tended to be protectionist. *Market size* suggests that industries in which the EC market was small compared to MES received less protection than industries with large markets.

An examination of marginal effects shows the relative importance of the different variables. The analysis evaluates changes in the probability that an industry receives no protection (nontariff coverage equals 0) as one independent variable changes from low to high (one standard deviation below to one standard deviation above its mean). *Intra-EC trade* exhibits the strongest marginal effect: the probability of no trade protection declines by 17.3 and 15.1 percentage points in the two models as *intra-EC trade* shifts from low to high levels. *Multinational production* also has large effects, as the probability of no nontariff barriers increases by 12.8 in model 1 and 12.1 percentage points in model 2. Smaller markets relative to MES raised the probability of no trade protection by 10.1 and 15.5 percentage points, respectively. None of the other variables produces a change in this probability of more than 5 percentage points.

25. *Multinational production, intra-EC trade, national concentration,* and *EC concentration* are from Davies and Lyons 1996. *Scale economies* is from Commission of the European Communities 1997. *Import competition* and *export dependence* were compiled from Eurostat, *Panorama of EU Industry* (various years).

26. Tobit is an appropriate method because the dependent variable, *nontariff barriers,* is censored in that it cannot be less than zero or greater than one. The Tobit results differ little from OLS regression results, except that t-statistics are slightly smaller for *scale economies* and *market size.*

TABLE 26.   Tobit Results for EC Nontariff Barriers

Variable	Nontariff Barriers in 1992	
Market size	−6.27*	−10.20*
	(3.30)	(5.65)
Scale economies	0.06*	0.07*
	(0.03)	(0.04)
Multinational production	−0.71**	−0.70***
	(0.27)	(0.25)
Import competition	−0.24	−0.13
	(0.34)	(0.35)
Export dependence	−0.54	−0.55
	(0.50)	(0.51)
Intra-EC trade	0.95***	0.86**
	(0.33)	(0.32)
EC concentration	1.11	
	(1.49)	
National concentration		0.98
		(0.76)
Constant	−0.07	−0.06
	(0.13)	(0.13)
Log likelihood	−12.95	−12.23
Model χ^2	22.43***	23.82***
Pseudo R-squared	0.46	0.49

Note: Cell entries are Tobit regression coefficients, with standard errors in parentheses. $N = 51$.
***$p < .01$ **$p < .05$ *$p < .10$

Thus, the Tobit models point in the same direction as the case studies. Industries generally received more trade protection when scale economies were more significant. Though production sharing cannot be estimated directly, trade protection was lower when firms generated more sales outside their home markets. Finally, exposure to competitive pressure within the EC appears to have been a stronger determinant of nontariff barriers than the pattern of trade with countries outside the EC.

European Protectionism after 1992

Industries with Economies of Scale

The completion of the single market had especially profound implications for trade in automobiles. The abolition of national quotas threatened to increase Japanese market shares in Italy and France from 2–3 percent to 20 percent, so the smaller mass producers (Fiat, Renault, and PSA Group) were likely to experience adjustment costs. In 1993 ACEA lobbied, successfully, to have the VER with Japan revised to one million vehicles per year and extended through the decade. At the end of 1999 the VER was phased out and automakers lost anti-dumping suits against Japan and South Korea. Though the French government granted Renault and PSA an enormous €400 million subsidy and tariffs continued at 10 percent for cars (16 percent for trucks and 22 percent for buses), the EU automobile market at least was freed of quantitative restrictions (Messerlin 2001, 286–88).

Producers of consumer electronics and semiconductors also sought protection against Japan. Thomson chief executive Alain Gomez advocated 30–50 percent tariff hikes for a five-year period to ease the single market's completion (Tyson 1992, 248 n. 70). Corporate leaders backed EC quotas or the continuation of national trade restrictions in an effort to push the European Commission in a more protectionist direction in its July 1991 policy guidelines for the electronics industry (Cawson et al. 1990, 274–75). With color television patents set to expire, firms also sought new standards for high-definition television (HDTV) to block entry by Japanese multinationals. Tyson (1992, 241) elaborates:

> the Europeans are using Community rather than national standards and promotional subsidies to encourage Community rather than national champions in HDTV. . . . Philips and Thomson . . . have staked their future on the HDTV struggle and have used their strong ties with national governments, Community officials, and European trade associations to shape Europe's HDTV policy.

All the while, companies continued to pursue antidumping duties, which they believed were more effective than VERs at limiting imports.[27] In semiconductors, a wave of dumping cases led to an agreement with Japan on exports restraints and floor prices for dynamic random-access memories in 1990, which was renewed in 1998.[28] Firms also initiated antidumping complaints against Asian producers of photocopiers, microwave ovens, weighing scales, and a number of other electronic goods.

However, FDI in Europe complicated protectionist campaigns in automobiles, consumer electronics, and semiconductors. The 1992 program offered Japanese and South Korean transplants free access to the internal

27. In 1992, Philips and Grundig launched antidumping complaints against Japanese CD players exported through Singapore, Taiwan, and Malaysia; three years later, Philips sought dumping duties against VCRs exported from Korea and Korean firms in Singapore.

28. The EC reduced tariffs on many types of memory chips from 14 percent to 7 percent in 1996. Still, the European Commission had ongoing disputes with the United States over the phasing schedule for these duties, and it continued to resist a move to zero tariffs.

market precisely as trade restrictions were being phased out at the national level and harmonized across the EC. Moreover, Japanese and South Korean affiliates in Europe began to import intermediate components to circumvent EC restrictions on finished goods from Asia. At first, EC firms sought tough rules of origin to block new investors from sharing in the benefits of completing the single market, as hypothesis 7 anticipates. But as time went on and Asian transplants increased local content, rules of origin became ineffective; companies had to find other ways to restrict the production and sales of these affiliates or end their protectionist lobbying altogether.

In the most prominent debate over rules of origin, Renault and PSA Group pressed the French government to treat Nissan Bluebirds manufactured in Britain as Japanese imports on the grounds that these cars failed to attain 80 percent EC content.[29] After Britain formally complained, the European Commission ruled that 65 percent EC content was sufficient to avoid tariffs. In another case, Philips and Grundig insisted in 1985 that Japanese factories in the EC count under the VER on videocassette recorders. This led to a commission directive that transplants with less than 45 percent EC content would count under a separate quota of 1.1 million kits imported for local assembly (Cawson et al. 1990, 311; Tyson 1992, 224 n. 17, 229). The commission later extended the 45 percent standard to computer printers, photocopiers, and several other consumer electronics.[30] In semiconductors, EECA lobbying resulted in new technical requirements in 1989: in place of rules mandating local assembly and testing (10–15 percent of value added), the commission stipulated that wafer fabrication (or "diffusion," generally 60 percent of value added) had to be performed in the EC. Finally, procurement directives required 50 percent EC content in manufacturing and R&D to receive public contracts for telecommunications gear, computers, and power-generating equipment (U.S. Congress 1991, 198–99).

Antidumping was a second area that European manufacturers used to combat foreign entry. In 1987, the Committee of European Copier Manufacturers (CECOM) complained that Japanese affiliates were importing photocopier parts and components for assembly in Europe to circumvent antidumping duties on complete photocopiers. This suit led the European Commission to issue an anticircumvention order mandating 40 percent EC content—though this figure was less than the 60 percent that Philips, Grundig, and several other

---

29. PSA chairman Calvet characterized Britain as "a Japanese aircraft carrier just off the coast of Europe" (McLaughlin and Jordan 1993, 144).

30. "Access to the European Market: Some Original Ideas on the Limits to Free Trade," *Financial Times*, February 10, 1989, 13.

firms sought (Tyson 1992, 230).[31] This "screwdriver assembly" rule effectively required foreign multinationals to meet EU content targets to avoid paying dumping penalties on captive imports of subassemblies from a corporate parent located outside Europe.

But rules of origin and screwdriver assembly provisions began to lose their utility as Asian multinationals expanded their European factories and induced suppliers to move offshore. Companies in electronics and telecommunications soon recognized that "in the long run there was little protection to be gained from tariffs or other protective devices given that foreign competitors could rapidly circumvent them via inward investment."[32] Moreover, inward FDI inspired joint ventures and strategic alliances between Asian and European companies, which made the commitment of resources to protectionist lobbying more difficult to justify.[33] In a few cases this split the united front that industries once presented: for example, a dumping complaint by Philips against videocassette recorders from Singapore targeted Thomson, which imported 1.5 million of these items in a joint venture with Toshiba.[34] In other cases, acquisitions of EU companies by their Japanese rivals diluted industry pressure for protection.[35] Over time, it became impossible to block entry into the EU market with traditional protectionist measures against trade. European companies had to target the transplants directly or leave them alone.

But the only serious effort to limit the activities of foreign multinationals was in the automobile industry. As early as 1989, Italy's foreign minister complained that Japanese FDI "would undermine the Community's attempt to negotiate a car export restraint agreement with Tokyo."[36] By 1993, Honda surpassed 80 percent EU content, while Toyota reached 60 percent with a further

---

31. The next year, CECOM accused Ricoh of assembling Japanese photocopier components at its U.S. affiliate and then exporting them to the EC. The European Commission subsequently ruled that the country of origin should be determined based on the location where "technically sophisticated components, such as the various printed circuit boards, lenses, various motors and high-voltage generators" were manufactured (U.S. Congress 1991, 200).

32. Sharp (1991, 73) concludes that this realization "led inexorably to the view that to compete successfully, even *within* Europe, these erstwhile national champions needed to set their sights on global markets and global competitiveness."

33. This helped to moderate pressure for idiosyncratic HDTV standards (Cawson et al. 1990, 373–74).

34. "Brussels to Probe East Asian VCR Dumping Claim," *Financial Times,* April 19, 1995, 8.

35. Of the five firms that filed the dumping claim for photocopiers, Develop sold its business to Minolta, Tetras sold shares to Canon, and Olivetti established a joint venture with Canon. This left only Xerox and OCE to pursue the suit to completion (Organization for Economic Cooperation and Development [OECD] 1994, 57–58).

36. "Italy Hits at Britain over Japanese Car Plants," *Financial Times,* February 1, 1989, 6.

boost to 80 percent anticipated; overall, Japanese transplants produced half a million vehicles in Europe, and they forecasted 2 million by the year 2000. In negotiations with Japan, ACEA pushed to have the transplant production included in the VER. But this proposal achieved only partial success: the agreement merely included an ambiguous statement that Japan's transplant sales were expected not to surpass 1.2 million units.[37]

In industries in which inward FDI was less of a consideration, lobbying groups could seek more traditional protectionist measures. In steel, firms responded to the liberalization of the VER program with antidumping claims on plates, sheets, pipes, tubes, and ferroalloys. A surge in imports from Eastern Europe and the former Soviet republics also inspired German firms to join French and Italian producers to push the European Commission for quotas (Hayes 1993, 77). This resulted in quantitative restraints on Russian and Ukrainian steel—other than automobiles, the only significant case of quotas in the single market. When the quotas were converted to surveillance measures in 1996, auto-limitation arrangements covered 10 percent of imports, down slightly from 15 percent in 1988 (Messerlin 2001, 276–78).

The transition to the single market touched off less protectionist lobbying in chemicals. Producers such as ICI worried that their domestic markets "could be very attractive to non-European producers" with the removal of national trade barriers (Ghellinck 1991, 348). In particular, chemical companies objected to new rules that would grant more weight to the views of importers, consumers, and upstream industries in antidumping decisions.[38] The International Rayon and Synthetic Fibers Committee sought antidumping duties against staple fibers from Belarus and polyester yarns from Indonesia, Thailand, and Malaysia and an extension of tariffs on fibers from Taiwan and Turkey, while petrochemicals producers filed antidumping complaints against East European producers of soda ash, polyvinyl chloride, and fertilizers. Still, the chemical industry did not seek the sorts of quantitative barriers applied to automobiles and steel. Moreover, CEFIC consented to tariff cuts on 170 chemical products, a duty reduction of about $20 million annually, as compensation for increased tariffs on certain chemicals in Sweden, Austria, and Finland after their accession to the EU in 1995.

37. France and Italy (home to Renault, PSA Group, and Fiat) viewed this as a firm ceiling; Britain (host to Japanese transplants) regarded it as a forecast. Privately, British officials expected Japanese transplants to sell two million vehicles once they reached full capacity. The VER also did not address EC sales by Japanese transplants in the United States ("The Enemy Within" 1993, 67–68).

38. This was important to the antidumping case for soda ash because glassmakers opposed these duties. Brunner Mond favored dumping penalties, but Solvay withdrew its support.

Industries with Constant Returns to Scale

In industries that lacked scale economies, protectionist lobbying was most intense for textiles, apparel, and footwear, products with varying levels of trade protection at the national level. Even so, these pressures rarely led to tougher measures against outside trade. In footwear, 104 national VERs and quotas were abolished on schedule by 1992; the remaining 30 were transformed into twelve EU quantitative restrictions, mostly against imports from China, South Korea, and Taiwan (WTO 1995b, 101–2). On balance, Europe became more open to trade in labor-intensive and resource-intensive industries after completing the single market. External quotas in 2000 were limited to Chinese footwear, tableware, and kitchenware, with surveillance measures on toys and bicycles (WTO 2001, 55).[39]

Some liberalization occurred in textiles and apparel as well. Under the 1992 program, 80 of the 110 national quotas and VERs were folded into twelve EU quotas. The Uruguay Round Agreement on Textiles and Clothing (ATC) subsequently established schedules to phase out quotas in four stages ending in 2005. The EU also eliminated quotas against Turkey and ten European countries in 1996–98. By 2001, liberalization covered one-third of all product categories—though only 5.4 percent of restricted imports, as the most sensitive products were delayed until 2005 (WTO 2001, 53–54). Messerlin (2001, 292–93) notes that while few categories remained to be liberalized in Germany (39 percent), ATC commitments in labor-intensive products back-loaded quota elimination for Greece (88 percent), Portugal (77 percent), and Italy (53 percent).

Analysts have questioned whether the ATC will trigger a spate of new restrictions at the final hour. Since 1994 there have been more antidumping claims, though success rates have been low, and producers of cheap, standardized articles still need quotas to keep out imports from China and Asia (Messerlin 2001, 293–94). Even so, Brenton (2002, 216–17) argues that a return to the protectionism of the MFA era is unlikely: "in Europe the clamor for protection has not been heard. EC industry, following substantial outsourcing, appears resigned to the death of the MFA and is devoting its efforts to opening export markets in the developing countries whose quota access to the EC will

39. There also remained "massive production subsidies" (particularly in France) for newsprint and lumber, tough antidumping measures on lumber and cement, and technical regulations in these industries that limited intra-EC and outside trade. In these three cases—newsprint, lumber, and cement—delays also occurred in harmonization and mutual recognition under the single-market program (Messerlin 2001, 263–68).

be liberalized." Most EC firms shed low-skill production and enhanced productivity by specializing in high-end items, developing vertical linkages with foreign suppliers, and expanding outward-processing trade (Hine and Padoan 2001, 69). These trends made it possible to liberalize Europe's external trade, even if the end of textile and apparel quotas was delayed until the final hour.

Politics and Institutions in EC Trade Policy

Lobbying and Industry Concentration

Before 1992, interest groups seeking to influence trade policy primarily assembled in national capitals because there was limited scope for EC-wide import regulation (outside of agriculture and steel) and the important policy decisions occurred in the Council of Ministers, which was composed of representatives of the member states. The European Commission could not effectively monitor or control national trade policies, so local authorities enjoyed wide latitude to exercise administrative discretion. In this institutional environment, lobby groups that wanted nontariff barriers on outside trade or Article 115 measures against EC members needed to persuade only their home governments.[40] This system especially favored domestic industries led by national champion firms. National champions often bargained directly with government ministries to obtain the relief they desired, rather than lobbying through industry-wide trade associations. As a result, Fiat, Renault, and Leyland (automobiles), Philips and Thomson (consumer electronics), and British Steel, Usinor, Sacilor, and Finsider (steel) had considerable clout with their home governments.[41] Even industries with large numbers of firms, notably in textiles, apparel, and footwear, could successfully mobilize national campaigns for quantitative restrictions and Article 115 measures before the single market was completed.

However, the Single European Act fundamentally altered trade policy-making. Member states lost the authority to employ national quotas and VERs as

40. National quotas and Article 115 measures required the European Commission's authorization, but not the approval of the Council of Ministers. However, the commission sometimes was not aware (much less supportive) of the import barriers in effect at national borders (Schuknecht 1992, 74–75).

41. In Thomson's case, "The firm was much more able to dictate the stance of the [French Industry] Ministry on such matters as trade policy than vice versa." Philips, though it was Dutch, also wielded influence in national capitals because it operated large factories in each member state (the firm produced VCRs in France and CD players in Belgium, and it delayed closing its TV factory in Britain in part to maintain the sympathy of the British government). Generally these two firms, as well as other large companies, were more active in trade policy than national industry associations (Cawson et al. 1990, 270–71, 322–23).

Brussels took control over quantitative restraints and abolished Article 115 measures. These changes reshaped institutional structures and the distribution of power over trade policy. Though the Council of Ministers continued to make many important decisions—which meant that lobby groups needed to retain influence with their home governments to have their interests represented in the council—the single-market program strengthened the European Commission as the agency responsible for executing unified trade measures.

These institutional changes channeled protectionist pressures from the national level upward to the European Commission.[42] Industry groups increasingly organized EU-wide to advance their interests in Brussels, which spurred the creation of Euro-groups such as ACEA and its predecessor, CCMC (automobile industry); EUROFER (steel); Comitextil (textiles and apparel); EACEM (consumer electronics); CEFIC (chemicals); and the Committee of Professional Agricultural Organizations (Mazey and Richardson 1993, 4–7). In Brussels, according to Schuknecht (1992, 52), "Well-organized and cohesive interest groups with significant political and economic weight are relatively over-represented." Yet many EU groups have suffered from insufficient resources and internal divisions between their constituent national associations, as differences in factor costs and product niches generate national and sectoral cleavages. As a result, Euro-groups tend to be slow, indecisive, and reactive more than proactive toward the European Commission, so "they are often rather ineffective, and leading multinationals have become increasingly exasperated with them" (Grant 1993, 31).

Table 26 shows that neither regional nor national concentration significantly affected nontariff barriers in 1992.[43] But anecdotal evidence suggests that organized pressures since then have been greatest in concentrated industries such as automobiles, consumer electronics, steel, and chemicals, in which large companies operate throughout the EU and national champions dominate. Euro-groups in these industries are composed of a handful of multinational companies, but the leading firms (whether European or foreign owned) generally retain their own representation in Brussels to conduct lobbying. Industries with large companies exert pressure at the EU level effectively because they are better able to mobilize lobbying resources and they face fewer disadvantages to collective

42. An exception is the telecommunication industry: "The large firms continue to see their interests as best protected through direct contact with the governments who are their main customers; they are large enough not to need the umbrella of a body to represent the aggregate of sectoral interests" (Cawson et al. 1990, 357).

43. However, studies such as Tharakan and Waelbroeck 1994 find that large firms and concentrated industries have had more success in the European Commission's antidumping investigations.

organization. For example, large firms can more easily bear the expense to maintain a well-staffed and -equipped office for political activities or to pursue trade remedies, such as antidumping claims, which in the early 1990s cost upwards of 100,000 ECU (Grant 1993, 30–35). So long as the leading firms share common interests, these groups wield considerable clout in Brussels.

It helps large companies that the European Commission has exclusive authority in external trade policy. The Directorates General can unilaterally impose provisional trade remedies without the Council of Ministers' approval, and many "[d]eals are done 'behind closed doors' between bureaucrats" (McGuire 1999, 81). Though the commission started to hold occasional public hearings on private-sector trade issues in 1998, it still deals with lobby groups mostly through informal meetings, which are private and confidential. Because the European Parliament has no formal role in external trade policy other than to approve foreign trade agreements, most political pressure on trade issues is exerted out of public view (WTO 2001, 22–23).

Two examples demonstrate the influence of large firms in concentrated industries. The first is the success of protectionist lobbying in consumer electronics, which reflects the pressures individually brought to bear by the two leading firms, Philips and Thomson. Producers began lobbying for EC-wide import restraints on home electronics such as VCRs early in the 1980s, before the concentration of authority over trade in the European Commission. Yet the EACEM remained a weak organization that functioned largely to legitimate the policy stances that Philips and Thomson espoused (Cawson et al. 1990, 219–21). Philips, in particular, became active and powerful in Brussels: "many EEC officials concede that Philips was among the most persuasive lobbyists at the European Commission, maintaining an impressive organization in Brussels devoted to that task" (Cawson et al. 1990, 323).[44] The firm's ability to overcome the German government's typically liberal inclinations in the Council of Ministers spawned the maxim "When Philips goes to Brussels, all the doors fly open" (Cawson et al. 1990, 293).

A second example is the automobile industry. The larger EU firms, including Ford and GM, maintain offices in Brussels and rely on these lobbying arms more than industry Euro-groups to advance their interests. However, divisions based on national orientation and product niche prevented automakers from

44. Notably, the VER on videocassette recorders from Japan "demonstrated the extraordinary political power which Philips was able to exert both in Brussels and the national capitals of EEC member states" (Cawson et al. 1990, 372).

adopting a common position on technical standards and other aspects of the single-market program. This changed when PSA Group was excluded from negotiations with Japan in 1990, and Ford and GM were invited to join the new, more unified trade group, ACEA (McLaughlin and Jordan 1993, 137–46). Holmes and Smith (1995, 131) emphasize "the ability of the car producers (excluding Peugeot) in Europe to agree and commit to a common political position through ACEA . . . and negotiate with the Commission" as a critical factor in the establishment of the VER.[45] With the addition of Ford and GM, ACEA had a formidable lobbying presence in Brussels dominated by multinational firms in a highly concentrated industry.

By comparison, industries with lots of small firms lobby primarily through Euro-groups. Despite a few notable exceptions, such as Comitextil and the Committee of Professional Agricultural Organizations,[46] these industries tend to lack influence over trade policy. Small firms, especially those oriented toward national markets, face severe disadvantages in EU-wide collective action. They are poorly organized at the European level and frequently immobilized by disagreements among the national associations within the Euro-group. Large, diffuse industries—textiles, apparel, and footwear, for example—have rarely filed antidumping suits. With Article 115 restraints now banned and VERs like those for automobiles and steel apparently beyond reach, small footwear producers and other politically weak industries instead have sought more modest actions such as surveillance measures and informal industry-to-industry arrangements.

Qualified Majority Voting

In the EU since 1992, it not only has been more difficult to mobilize industry coalitions now that groups must lobby in Brussels rather than national capitals; institutional rules in the Single European Act have also made it harder to reinstitute trade protection EU-wide once it was lost in national markets. Specifically, new voting procedures in the Council of Ministers (which ratifies the European Commission's foreign trade agreements and antidumping actions) required a qualified majority of fifty-four out of seventy-six votes.[47] The

45. These authors conclude: "Member governments are ill-placed to oppose policies which they are assured to have the support of the European industry."

46. These two groups are well organized and powerful at the European level despite the industrial and geographic diffusion of their membership. See Grant 1993, 37–41.

47. These are the voting figures for the Council of Ministers before the Amsterdam (1999) and Nice (2004) treaties entered into force.

previous system relied on unanimity to pass legislation, so each member state effectively enjoyed veto power—though vetoes rarely blocked new trade barriers since most trade decisions occurred in national capitals rather than Brussels (and if the Council of Ministers did veto trade protection, countries could still restrict imports unilaterally). Once the European Commission's trade powers expanded, however, a coalition of Germany (ten votes), Britain (ten), and the Netherlands (five) or Denmark (three) could block protectionist actions in the Council of Ministers. Since the countries most supportive of restricting imports held only half of the council's votes,[48] protectionist measures needed broad appeal to secure the requisite support (Hanson 1998).

Through qualified majority voting, EU institutions in Brussels aggregate member state preferences to reach policy decisions. Since policy outcomes are a compromise of national interests, it is necessary to know which states, or coalitions of states, are most influential and what their preferences are. Historically, France and Italy have been the most assertive at pushing protectionist policies. Germany and the Benelux countries, on the other hand, have generally preferred less restrictive import policies, and Britain also has leaned toward a liberal import regime.[49]

Decisions made since the move to qualified majority voting suggest that the lobbying positions of concentrated interests in national economies have heavily influenced member state preferences in the Council of Ministers. The VER on Japanese automobiles is one such case, as the positions of national representatives mirrored the interests of the leading firms: Britain (host to Ford, GM, Nissan, Honda, and Toyota) accepted controls on imports from Japan but opposed restraints against the transplants; France, Italy, Spain, and Portugal (home to declining national champions) sought restrictions against imports and transplants alike; Germany initially resisted strict controls on Japan but later adopted a tougher position as specialist automakers began to worry about Japanese competition in luxury models; and Denmark, Greece, Ireland, and Benelux, with no national automobile production, favored open trade policies

48. These countries were France (ten votes), Italy (ten), Spain (eight), Greece (five), and Portugal (five).
49. In several pre-1992 cases, however, Germany relented to protectionist pressures from France and Italy to preserve unity. This made Germany an important swing vote on trade decisions in the Council of Ministers. For example, Germany shifted positions and accepted quantitative limits for steel and textiles in the 1970s. The German minister of economics later explained: "The German Government . . . only agreed to measures regulating imports in the textiles and steel sectors with considerable reservations, in order to avoid the threat of national protection measures and in order to maintain the degree of integration already achieved in the EEC" (Hayes 1993, 74).

but conceded to the member states with stronger interests at stake (Mason 1994, 440–44).[50]

Conclusion: Fortress Europe?

The failure to complete the single market in the first wave of European integration from 1958 to 1973 left national markets separated and production in the EC fragmented. This was particularly damaging to industries with large returns to scale because firms needed to concentrate production to compete with rivals in the United States and Asia. These companies therefore pushed national governments and the bureaucracy in Brussels to remove the remaining barriers to intra-EC trade in the 1992 program.

The single-market initiative in turn had significant consequences—both deliberate and unintended—for EU policy toward outside trade. While the 1992 program was being implemented, protectionist lobbying intensified as several industries sought barriers to external trade as a buffer against increased competition in Europe. Most notably, an EU-wide VER replaced national quotas on Japanese automobiles to ease restructuring and slow down the elimination of excess capacity in the region. Similar motives underpinned pressure from consumer electronics producers for antidumping and anticircumvention restrictions on Asian factories, as well as the steel industry's desire for transitional quotas on Russian and East European steel.

Nevertheless, pessimism about the development of fortress Europe has proved unwarranted. As Europe completed the single market and expanded once more, taking in Sweden, Finland, and Austria, MFN tariffs declined from 6 percent in 1995 to 4.2 percent in 1999, and the EU negotiated further cuts to around 3 percent in the Uruguay Round (WTO 2001, 99). In the decade after 1992, the incidence of antidumping duties dropped, and only restraints on automobiles, steel, and a handful of less significant manufactures survived from the labyrinth of national quotas and VERs that predated the transition to the single market. While new TRIMs discriminated against Asian multinationals, the EU did not take the drastic step of applying the sorts of quotas proposed for Japan's automobile transplants.

Several factors—some at the core of the book's theory and a few outside of

---

50. Hanson (1998, 74–80) argues that the automobile VER was more generous than the national quotas it replaced—a debatable point (according to estimates, the VER redistributed sales among EC markets but was no more open to Japanese imports overall) that overlooks a more significant lesson: qualified majority voting does not prevent new trade barriers when a qualified majority has protectionist preferences.

it—explain the market opening that followed the Single European Act. First, the 1992 program stimulated inward FDI from foreign multinationals seeking to surmount trade barriers and gain scale economies in the larger internal market. While at first this led to political pressure for restrictions against these transplants, over time foreign operations in the EU were "Europeanized." Local production rather than exports to the EU are now the dominant form of foreign entry in automobiles, electronics, and chemicals, so barriers to external trade have been rendered ineffective. Moreover, as European electronics and automobile companies started outsourcing abroad, antidumping measures that targeted screwdriver factories in the EU began to threaten European-owned firms. These trends diminished the incentives for protectionist lobbying in these industries.

Second, many of the industries that obtained national quotas and Article 115 measures before 1986 were too poorly organized and too divided internally to effectively exert protectionist pressure in Brussels. Institutional changes imparted a liberal bias to the making of trade policy by reducing the capacity of protectionist-seeking groups to obtain new trade barriers. The centralization of authority in Brussels helped (or at least did not hinder) only the most concentrated industries, such as automobiles.

Qualified majority voting was a final bulwark keeping the single market generally free of quotas and VERs on outside trade. In cases like the automobile industry, new voting rules did not dilute protectionist preferences in the Council of Ministers because concentrated interests operated factories throughout Europe and wielded clout with member governments. But protectionism has been a losing battle in poorly organized industries that face difficulty prevailing over a qualified majority. Thus, the EU has become more open rather than more protected since 1992.

CHAPTER 6

NAFTA
The Politics in the United States

The United States abstained from the drift toward trading blocs in the 1930s and the years after World War II. As chapter 4 explains, it instead pursued nondiscriminatory trade liberalization through the RTAA and five phases of multilateral negotiations in the GATT up to the Kennedy Round's completion in 1967. The automotive trade agreement with Canada was the first waiver from MFN the United States sought under Article XXIV—and its only one until 1985.

In those intervening two decades, the two main pillars of U.S. trade policy crumbled. The first to fall was the commitment to trade liberalization, as pressure for nontariff barriers erupted in the 1970s. Soon the second pillar, adherence to MFN, was cast aside when the United States began to seek free trade deals with selected countries. These initiatives culminated in agreements with Canada in 1988 and Mexico in 1993.

This shift from multilateralism to regionalism reflected, first and foremost, the changed market interests of firms in industries dependent on large-scale, multinational production. Competitive pressures caused U.S. companies to modify their strategies in two important ways after 1970. First, factories had to be rationalized and streamlined to better take advantage of large returns to scale. Increases in MES levels or failure to keep pace with rivals abroad amplified the need for larger volume in industries producing for the U.S. market; more frequently, overcapacity and duplication in multinational firms manufacturing in the United States, Canada, and Mexico left substantial scale economies unexploited. Companies that had not concentrated production in North America faced serious liabilities when optimal plant sizes grew larger or when foreign firms reached (and sometimes surpassed) U.S. scales of output. Second, firms moved labor-intensive stages of manufacturing out of the United States and outsourced components or final assembly to cut factor costs. As this trend progressed, companies developed regional procurement networks to specialize production across different locations.

In industries restructuring along these lines, firms actively campaigned for free trade agreements. To consolidate manufacturing on a continental scale, producers needed unfettered access to all markets in the region. In addition to free trade, firms also wanted rules to govern FDI, TRIMs, intellectual property, and services. Multilateral discussions on these issues were floundering in the Uruguay Round; regional arrangements offered deeper integration than could be achieved in the GATT. Moreover, restructuring costs left firms vulnerable to foreign competition in the medium term. To provide shelter during reorganization, some industries sought exclusive measures against outside investors and suppliers of imports. Simply stated, many companies needed discriminatory liberalization to restructure manufacturing establishments more efficiently.

As firms with multinational operations and large returns to scale pursued regional free trade, labor-intensive industries, labor unions, and import-competing agriculture bitterly opposed free trade agreements with Canada and especially Mexico. Many of these dissenting groups received prolonged staging periods for tariff elimination, tough rules of origin, expanded Trade Adjustment Assistance, and other special measures to mollify their opposition. But this coalition was too poorly organized and its interests too diffuse to defeat NAFTA.

The evidence in this chapter indicates that NAFTA has promoted multilateral liberalization, at least in the industries that supported it. Most pro-NAFTA industries supported sweeping tariff cuts in the Uruguay Round, and they have continued to push for new trade agreements regionally and in the WTO. In contrast, industries that lobbied against NAFTA generally opposed the Uruguay Round agreements, and they have since lobbied to block further liberalization, whether regional or multilateral. Overall, free trade agreements enhanced the market position of firms in industries with large returns to scale and production-sharing networks. Meanwhile, industries with few opportunities to gain scale economies or outsource labor-intensive tasks saw their economic fortunes decline.

This chapter specifies how scale economies and production sharing influence trade preferences to explain why some industry groups in the United States sought a North American trading bloc while others opposed one. The chapter then addresses the politics of lobbying on the NAFTA treaty. The discussion concludes by evaluating how free trade agreements have affected domestic interests in multilateral liberalization.

From Multilateralism to Regionalism

The U.S. government's conversion from multilateral liberalization to the pursuit of regional initiatives in the 1980s coincided with a series of dramatic external events. Competition from Europe and Japan, along with the emergence of the Asian "tigers," put growing pressure on U.S. industries, as these countries employed advanced manufacturing methods at considerably lower wage levels. The Kennedy Round tariff schedules pushed average duties below 10 percent, while the overvalued dollar sucked in imports and hindered exports, further exposing the U.S. market to foreign competition. Though the dollar's decline with the suspension of gold convertibility raised prices for foreign goods, import penetration continued to grow until it exploded under the Reagan administration's strong dollar policy.

Equally important were trends inside North America, as national responses to economic integration led to disputes between the United States and Canada, then later between the United States and Mexico. Canada's Foreign Investment Review Agency (FIRA), created to screen new investments and regulate foreign-owned firms, started to pressure U.S. multinationals to satisfy performance rules for local content and exports, transfer technology or patents to indigenous firms, hire Canadian management and labor, and conduct more R&D in Canada. This "aggressive application of industrial policy," the Commerce Department complained, threatened to "distort trade."[1] Canada also began to offer generous investment incentives to European and Japanese firms. For example, Michelin received $73 million in grants and low-interest loans to build two tire plants in a depressed area of Nova Scotia. Volkswagen secured tariff rebates on imported parts used in exported vehicles in 1978, an offer later extended to Honda and Toyota. In return for local content and value-added commitments, foreign automakers could collect rebates of up to 100 percent on their imports.[2]

Canada's new regulatory posture provoked threats and occasional retaliation from the United States. The Treasury Department placed countervailing duties on steel-belted radial tires imported from Michelin's subsidiary in Canada—the first time trade remedy laws had been used against investment incentives. The Carter administration demanded consultations to express its

1. Untitled, undated memo, Joint U.S.-Canadian Committees on Trade and Economic Affairs, 1953–72, Box 2, RG 489.

2. Honda achieved full tariff remission status in 1985; Toyota was scheduled to soon follow. In 1987, Toyota and seven other foreign firms received 70 percent rebates on their imports (Fuss and Waverman 1987, 224–25).

disapproval of Canada's tariff rebates to foreign automakers, which were not designated for privileges under the APTA. These disputes peaked as the Reagan administration targeted FDI regulation as an unfair trade barrier. A number of bills in Congress sought to pressure foreign countries to grant reciprocity in investment, and revisions to Section 301 authorized retaliation. Officials in the United States pushed to add TRIMs to the agenda for the next trade round at the 1982 GATT ministerial meeting. The next year, the United States challenged Canada's local sourcing, import substituting, and export performance rules in GATT dispute settlement. When Canada renewed its undertakings with foreign automakers, the U.S. Trade Representative (USTR) concluded that countervailing duties were likely. Though U.S. officials did not know the scale of the probable damage (the remission agreements were confidential), an anti-subsidy complaint was inevitable once foreign-affiliated plants came onstream (Fuss and Waverman 1987, 224–26).

These events occurred as multilateral trade negotiations wallowed. After the Tokyo Round, it took seven years before the Uruguay Round's belated launch. As discussions for a new trade round dragged on, President Ronald Reagan announced that he would instruct "trade negotiators to explore regional and bilateral agreements with other nations" to pursue the broad liberalization in services, intellectual property, and FDI the United States hoped to achieve in the GATT.[3] The United States soon completed its first free trade agreement, with Israel.

With the multilateral process stalled, a Canadian Royal Commission concluded that bilateral negotiations with the United States were the best method to reduce nontariff barriers and resolve investment disputes. Though more than three-quarters of Canada-U.S. trade was duty-free,[4] conflicts persisted over softwood lumber, Atlantic groundfish, and potash. Moreover, the Royal Commission found, industrial policy had failed to reorient the branch factory system, and Canadian manufacturing productivity had declined over the previous decade. Multinationals from the United States and many Canadian firms testified that opportunities to exploit scale economies were considerable if they could sell more of their output abroad. Opening the U.S. economy to Canadian goods, these firms asserted, would allow them to specialize for a larger market.

The Royal Commission's report helped to persuade the Canadian government to seek a free trade agreement with the United States. Canadian officials

---

3. "Remarks at a White House Meeting with Business and Trade Leaders, 23 September 1985," Official Web Site of the Ronald Reagan Presidential Library, http://www.reagan.utexas.edu/resource/speeches/1985/92385a.htm.

4. In the United States, tariffs on imports from Canada averaged 0.9 percent, while Canadian tariffs on U.S. imports averaged 2.4 percent (Royal Commission on the Economic Union 1985 1:263–65).

believed that with mutual free trade, branch plants would specialize for an enlarged continental market instead of downsizing or leaving. Canada's U.S. ambassador explained, "Canadian industry must have open and secure access to U.S. markets to achieve economies of scale and effective rationalization of product lines needed to remain competitive" (Granatstein 1985, 47). In October 1987, the treaty's twenty chapters were completed, and the Canada–United States Free Trade Agreement (CUSFTA) was signed in January 1988.

Relations between the United States and Mexico followed a similar trajectory. From 1962 to 1981, the Mexican government initiated several industrial programs to promote import substitution in capital-intensive activities. After the 1982 debt crisis, protected industries were rapidly exposed to foreign competition to promote macroeconomic stabilization.[5] New measures to generate foreign exchange accompanied import liberalization. The 1983 Automotive Decree required multinationals to export $2.50 for each dollar of imports and imposed domestic content rules of 60 percent. The 1984 Pharmaceutical Decree mandated greater local production of chemical intermediates, more R&D spending, and higher export-to-sales ratios (USITC 1990a, chap. 4, 7–11).

As with Canada, the United States warned Mexico not to extend performance rules in automobiles to other sectors, and when these efforts failed, it pushed to scale back investment controls.[6] Bilateral discussions produced a "Framework of Principles and Procedures for Consultation Regarding Trade and Investment Relations" in 1987. Parallel "Trade and Investment Facilitation Talks" addressed nontariff barriers, FDI, services, and intellectual property (USITC 1990a, chap. 2, 3–6). In the spring of 1990, Mexican president Carlos Salinas de Gortari proposed free trade negotiations. Discussions opened in June 1991 and ended with the signing of the NAFTA treaty in October 1992. When NAFTA entered into force on the first day of 1994, the United States had free trade agreements with countries accounting for one-third of its total trade.

The book's analytical framework illuminates two key incentives for industry groups to seek regional trade liberalization: market pressures to capture unexploited scale economies or to reduce labor costs by expanding regional production sharing. These considerations were critical to political demands in the United States for free trade in North America. The next two sections discuss the sources of each of these motives.

---

5. Mexican tariffs declined from 27 percent in 1982 to 13 percent in 1990. Mexico also dismantled quantitative controls and liberalized FDI to allow full foreign ownership in three-quarters of all industrial activities (USITC 1990a, chap. 4, 3–4).

6. Mexico did not join the GATT until 1985, so these laws could not be challenged in dispute settlement.

Industries with Large Returns to Scale

For a number of reasons, scale economies became more important to U.S. firms after 1970. Normally, firms can exploit large returns to scale without trading blocs if the national market is sufficiently large compared to MES production. The high rate of consumption in the United States, chapter 4 argues, made U.S. producers less interested in trading blocs in the interwar and early postwar periods. To be sure, the United States remained the world's largest market for most goods during the period covered in this chapter. However, production was no longer as effectively concentrated to maximize the scale of output at the plant level.

In a few industries, the failure of domestic demand to keep pace with increases in the MES motivated firms to seek larger markets. In other cases, producers lost their scale advantages over foreign rivals as import penetration fragmented the domestic market, making regional expansion attractive as a complement to national trade protection. But the most significant factor was that U.S. companies with FDI in Canada and Mexico experienced intense pressure to reduce duplication and centralize dispersed production in one location—a strategy that could be implemented only if the barriers separating these markets were eliminated.

In addition to concerns about scale economies, high labor costs propelled U.S. companies to move production outside the United States. As a result, subcontracting and intrafirm trade with Canada and Mexico expanded rapidly. These markets were more attractive locations than Asia or South America because of their geographic proximity, particularly if goods produced close to home received free access to the U.S. market. Offshore manufacturing operations functioned most efficiently when they were closely integrated with plants in the United States. Companies involved in production sharing and intrafirm trade therefore could benefit from the removal of barriers to the movement of goods across the borders linking various stages of manufacturing. In many cases, this amplified the need for regional trade liberalization to gain scale economies; in a few industries with smaller returns to scale, the growth of procurement networks outside the United States created an additional constituency for free trade agreements.

Returns to Scale and MES Production

A large MES compared to home consumption constrains firms in their efforts to expand capacity and reduce unit costs because it is more difficult to find profitable outlets for surplus production. As a result, firms in industries with large MES production levels tend to benefit the most from access to a larger than national market. In addition, large returns to scale impose steep penalties, in terms of higher unit costs, on companies that have not exhausted the potential scale economies. Thus, businesses with a large MES are more likely to support regional trade liberalization the larger the returns to scale. This makes it important to determine which industries have these characteristics.

Previous chapters rely on engineering estimates of the returns to scale in manufacturing different products. However, data available for the United States allow more direct measurement at the industry level. In this method, variations in value added per worker in plants of different sizes provide estimates of the elasticity of unit costs with respect to scale.[7] The results of this measure are consistent with engineering estimates: returns to scale are largest in chemicals, electrical and industrial machinery, motor vehicles, nonferrous metals, and certain consumer goods such as tobacco and grain products; in contrast, textiles, apparel, rubber, plastic, and leather have small and sometimes negative returns to scale.

Proxy measures for MES production, unfortunately, are not so reliable, and time-series data are not available to substantiate the earlier claim that MES levels generally were growing larger. Table 27 presents MES engineering estimates as a share of U.S. consumption, with industries ordered vertically according to the returns to scale. Despite the product coverage limitations in the MES data, these thirty-seven industries accounted for 52.3 percent of domestic sales in 1987.

The area of table 27 inside the dashed line highlights the industries with the strongest incentives to support regional free trade to take advantage of scale economies. The cut point was set at 3 percent because no industries fell between 2 percent and 3 percent; only five (marked with an asterisk) were between 3 percent and 4 percent. The data show that the sectors likely to benefit the most from an increase in market size cluster in the transportation, machinery, electrical, chemical, and primary metal industries. These industries require large fixed investments in plant and equipment or high R&D costs.[8] In

7. For a description of this method, see Chase 2003, 149–51.

8. There is reason to question the estimates of low returns to scale in blast furnace and basic steel, household audio and video equipment, and plastics materials and synthetics. In steel, minimills refining scrap into finished steel achieved higher levels of output per worker than integrated firms. Consistent with this observation, electrometallurgical products (SIC 3313) showed negative returns to scale, while blast furnaces and steel mills (SIC 3312) had positive returns to scale (7.2 percent). Similarly, returns to scale were large (9.3 percent) in household audio and video equipment (SIC 3651) but negative in prerecorded records and tapes (SIC 3652). Finally, plants were larger, but value added per worker lower, in cellulosic manmade fibers (SIC 2823) than in noncellulosic organic fibers (SIC 2824), where returns to scale were 15.3 percent. Thus, refined industry classifications suggest significant economies of scale in segments of all three industries.

TABLE 27.   Returns to Scale and Market Size in the United States, 1987

	MES Less than 3% of Domestic Consumption	MES at Least 3% of Domestic Consumption
Returns to scale		
Large (>14%)	Paperboard mills	Tobacco products
	Bakery products	Agricultural chemicals*
	Grain mill products	Primary nonferrous metals*
	Sugar and confectionery products	Drugs*
	Dairy products	Electronic components
	Paper mills	Computer and office equipment
	Paints and allied products	Farm machinery
	Soaps, cleaners, and toilet goods	Motor vehicles and equipment
Moderate (7–12%)	Beverages	Engines and turbines
	Footwear, except rubber	Communications equipment
	Miscellaneous electrical equipment	Industrial organic chemicals*
	Iron and steel foundries	Household appliances
		Aircraft and parts
		Tires and inner tubes*
Small (<6%)	Carpets and rugs	Blast furnace and basic steel
	Cotton fabrics	Audio and video equipment
	Preserved fruits and vegetables	Plastics materials and synthetics
	Manmade fiber and silk fabrics	
	Yarn and thread mills	
	Meat products	
	Knitting mills	
	Petroleum refining	

Source: Data from U.S. Bureau of the Census 1997.
*The five entries marked with an asterisk were between 3 percent and 4 percent.

contrast, textiles, apparel, rubber, plastic, and leather lacked significant returns to scale, while industries such as paper, processed food, household chemicals, and metal manufactures enjoyed a large domestic market.[9] In short, industries on the lefthand side of table 27 would derive little or no gain from increases in the scale of output. Industries to the right, on the other hand, could benefit from the creation of a larger market through free trade agreements.

It is important to specify the nature of these benefits more clearly. Firms

9. It is possible that the MES data are inaccurate because opportunities to gain scale economies in some of these activities increased with technological changes and the development of capital-intensive and knowledge-based techniques. For example, producers of textiles introduced new methods for designing products, handling materials, and monitoring assembly through the use of computers, automation, and microelectronic technologies. But even if optimal scales were larger than estimated, in most of these cases domestic demand still provided ample room for hundreds of plants in the U.S. market.

with production located primarily in the United States would have opportunities to expand exports through greater market access in Canada and Mexico. If they could gain market shares, either by displacing producers in the region (trade creation) or taking customers from firms outside the region (trade diversion), it would be possible to expand and ride down their cost curves. However, companies with multiple plants in North America did not have to increase market shares to gain scale economies. Rather, they could reduce costs in a wider market by specializing manufacturing facilities and consolidating production for the entire region. Thus, the potential benefits were greatest in industries with large returns to scale *and* multinational operations. It is therefore necessary to consider the effects of FDI in North America.

Foreign Investment and Scale Economies

Increasing returns to scale production in North America was progressively fragmented during the postwar period and could not achieve optimal levels of concentration because national regulations and barriers to regional trade compelled production in multiple locations. In Canada and Mexico, U.S. companies faced high trade barriers, so many established foreign affiliates to locally produce goods that could not be exported from the United States. These "miniature replicas" manufactured the same product line as the parent firm in small factories with short production runs. Unit costs were high; these inefficient operations were profitable only because tariff protection and entry barriers enabled foreign affiliates to charge high prices in the local market.

By the 1980s, small-scale factories in Canada and Mexico had become a severe liability. They had lost much of the tariff protection that initially made local production attractive. Moreover, plants in the United States suffered from excess capacity and intense competition from Asia and Europe. Opportunities to gain scale economies existed if manufacturing facilities could be streamlined and rescaled for the regional market. Pressure to rationalize operations was particularly acute for multinational companies producing goods with large returns to scale in all three countries. As long as barriers to trade segmented the North American market, plants in the region could not be specialized and inefficient product lines closed down.

In Canada, miniature replica production was longstanding, as chapter 4 shows. Throughout Canadian industry, small-scale branch plants manufactured behind high tariff walls. Multinationals from the United States generally resisted market integration between the United States and Canada because tariffs created substantial rents for their branch plants. Neither the multinationals nor the Canadian and U.S. governments wished to modify this relationship before 1970. The exception was automobiles: rents declined when the market available to the branch plants receded after the war, while new regulatory rules disrupted production and raised the threat of U.S. retaliation—causing automakers to push for the APTA.

But after 1970 it became more difficult for the branch plants to prosper while manufacturing diverse product lines for the small Canadian market. Canada retained substantial trade protection in manufacturing after the Kennedy Round, but it accepted deeper tariff cuts in the Tokyo Round in an effort to encourage industry (particularly the branch plants) to specialize and lengthen production runs. Unproductive branch plants were exposed to competitive pressures as lower tariffs were phased in, so they could no longer mark up prices to compensate for high costs (Royal Commission on the Economic Union 1985 1:228–29).

In addition, FIRA was a major irritant for U.S. firms. Though FIRA approved 80 percent of FDI proposals, companies usually had to accept performance requirements in return; a proposal's denial or withdrawal signaled, in effect, that the applicant did not anticipate returns sufficient to justify the undertakings. Because TRIMs were formulated case by case, the commitments of foreign-owned firms often varied.[10] In some cases, new entrants gained an advantage by negotiating less restrictive undertakings than incumbent firms had to satisfy; in others, latecomers were placed at a disadvantage. Moreover, because screening applied to incumbent firms and new entrants alike, multinationals already based in Canada could not escape review unless they eschewed mergers and expanded only in core product lines. As a result, foreign-owned firms could be subjected to a new set of regulations after substantial investment in local production already had been sunk.[11]

Canadian incentives to attract European and Japanese investment were another problem. These measures subsidized rival firms as they developed modern production facilities. Once established, European and Japanese affiliates

10. Some performance requirements were very precise: for example, Apple Computer promised to reach 38 percent Canadian value added in its first year in operation and to increase local content over time according to a schedule imposed by FIRA, and it agreed to sell 80 percent of its products through Canadian retailers and perform 80 percent of its repairs in Canada (Morici, Smith, and Lea 1982, 43).

11. For example, Chrysler was assessed $243 million in back tariffs in 1978 for failing to meet APTA safeguards. In return for a waiver of these tariffs and a $200 million loan guarantee, the firm agreed to invest an additional $5 billion in Canada and to increase Canadian employment to one job for every nine workers it employed in the United States. It also could not close Canadian factories without prior approval (Hufbauer and Samet 1982, 136–37).

not only competed in the Canadian market with the outmoded branch plants but also built substantial export capacity for the U.S. market. In the Michelin case, 90 percent of the firm's Canadian exports went to the United States. Similarly, tariff rebates for Volkswagen, Toyota, and Nissan required the Big Three, already reeling from the energy crisis, to compete with foreign companies that were not bound by the APTA undertakings.[12]

As Canada reduced tariff protection, extracted new commitments from incumbent firms, and courted third-country investors, U.S. multinationals were stuck with sunk costs in inefficient, small-scale affiliates with high local content. A few companies attempted to streamline operations and eliminate duplication between parent factories and branch plants. GE-Canada, for example, closed down several product lines and lengthened production runs to gain scale economies (Royal Commission on the Economic Union 1985 1:323–27, 346–48). Dupont petitioned the Canadian government for a special license to import nylons duty-free so it could phase out certain product types and rescale others for the North American market; when this request was denied, the firm decided that restructuring would not be profitable (Parliament of Canada 1982, 51). The branch plants could not survive in the Canadian market without trade protection, but the alternative, costly investments in restructuring to promote specialization and gain scale economies, was too risky as long as trade barriers existed between Canada and the United States.

In Mexico, U.S. firms faced similar dilemmas. While FDI flooded into Mexico in the decade after the debt crisis, many of these funds went to the maquiladoras, which produced intermediate components and performed labor-intensive assembly.[13] But most U.S. multinationals also operated fully integrated plants in Mexico's interior, with sales oriented exclusively to the domestic market. As the Mexican government opened the economy to foreign competition after the debt crisis, suddenly these affiliates had to compete with imports from lower-cost locations. Moreover, little time was allowed to adjust because trade liberalization and the new industrial decrees came to pass in such a short spell.

---

12. A federal task force, which included the Big Three, the UAW, and parts producers, recommended a framework to require new entrants "to make binding commitments comparable to the commitments now being made by the vehicle manufacturers operating under the APTA." The report concluded (Federal Task Force on the Canadian Motor Vehicle and Automotive Parts Industries 1983, 107): "an effective compliance procedure must be developed by the Canadian government that will ensure that these comparable commitments will be fulfilled by 1987."

13. Inside the maquiladora zone (an area stretching twenty-five miles south of the U.S. border), foreign companies were permitted to fully own their affiliates, and they could earn rebates on import duties for products that were reexported after processing.

Problems were most acute in the industries with special development programs. Multinationals in automobiles, pharmaceuticals, computers, telecommunications, and electronics originally invested in response to the lure of financial incentives and trade protection. Foreign-affiliated factories outside the maquiladoras manufactured diverse product lines on a small scale. Foreign automakers, for example, produced five different models per factory, compared to one or two in home country plants. "Inefficiencies caused by making too many models," the U.S. International Trade Commission (USITC) (1993, chap. 4, 8) noted, "are made worse because the Mexican market is relatively small, thus making it hard to produce enough automobiles to benefit from economies of scale." These firms produced 281,200 automobiles, half of MES output levels; this amounted to just 14,800 cars per assembly line, or 5,300 per model. Elsewhere conditions were similar: five computer firms made 110,000 personal computers, fifty-nine different models in all, and foreign companies produced 752,000 television sets, divided between color and monochrome, less than two-fifths of the MES for each type (Peres 1990, 96–97, 107, 122–23).

Some U.S. firms resisted the policy changes at first. Fourteen multinationals filed suit against the Pharmaceutical Decree for violating intellectual property, and exports-to-sales fell well short of government targets. Computer firms that had invested under the previous industrial regime pushed to continue import permits for five more years because production was still in its "infancy." A few companies gave up altogether: Apple divested from Mexico because it could not meet local content targets, particularly after rival IBM negotiated a more favorable deal with the Mexican government (Peres 1990, 90–91, 103).

But most U.S. multinationals had made commitments to Mexican production that were too large to terminate. For many firms, the solution was to relocate manufacturing or assembly to Mexico—and then export back to the United States. This strategy worked particularly well for firm-specific components with no external market, which could be sold to the parent company at transfer prices. For example, automakers installed thirteen new engine plants with a total capacity of 2.4 million units; 85 percent of this output was exported to the United States (Peres 1990, 116–21).[14] In other cases, firms ended fully integrated production and focused on intermediate goods or final assembly in Mexico. In consumer electronics, Zenith, Matsushita, and Philips stopped manufacturing complete TV sets in Mexico and built large assembly

14. New factories specialized for the U.S. market made existing affiliates more profitable because companies that surpassed export targets were permitted to maintain lower local content and offer more product lines for sale in Mexico.

plants directed to export markets. Computer firms phased out the production of personal computers and specialized in disk drives and components (Peres 1990, 92–93).

This reorientation of corporate strategies to compensate for inefficient scale and low export volumes in Mexican factories was costly and painful. Multinationals from the United States had considerable room to reduce costs if they concentrated production at the regional level, but this could occur only if the policy externalities that had fragmented production in the first place were eliminated. Specializing Mexican affiliates was feasible only if phased-out product lines could be imported from the United States and new capacity dedicated to export had free access to the U.S. market, where tariffs remained in place and administered trade restrictions were a constant threat. Finally, there was the risk that industrial decrees would be revised after capital had been sunk in new production arrangements: as an automobile executive explained, "what one thought was a good deal could turn out badly . . . because of changes in decrees" (Guisinger 1985, 114).

In sum, North American manufacturing was fragmented because trade protection in Canada and Mexico encouraged entry at an inefficient scale, which caused firms to produce in multiple locations. After 1970, foreign competition, activist industrial policies, and market opening exposed U.S. affiliates in the region to outside pressure. In industries with small-scale production and high U.S. ownership in Canada and Mexico—such as computers, automobiles, consumer electronics, telecommunications equipment, home appliances, pharmaceuticals, and petrochemicals (as shown in table 28)—manufacturing could be integrated across borders among the different divisions of multinational firms, allowing companies to capture restructuring benefits from policy changes. Increased certainty and an open market environment would allow multinationals to phase out noncore product lines in foreign plants, expand production runs, and consolidate into fewer locations to maximize scale economies.

Trade and regulatory liberalization raised two problems, however. First, it could not be immediate: a rapid removal of trade barriers would further expose foreign affiliates to competition in once-protected host markets. Liberalization in stages would minimize the disruption and provide breathing room while restructuring took place. Second, trade liberalization could not be multilateral: multinationals would be vulnerable to external competitive pressures while they reorganized their operations. If third-country producers increased exports or invested in the region, North American firms would be pushed up their cost curves. Companies would have few incentives to begin costly restructuring without measures to prevent new entrants from capturing the benefits of trade

TABLE 28. FDI in Industries with Economies of Scale, 1989

Industry	Foreign Production Divided by Total Shipments
High FDI	
Computer and office equipment	53.2
Motor vehicles and equpment	41.7
Communications equipment[a]	34.3
Drugs	32.9
Household appliances	32.6
Tobacco products	30.7
Farm machinery	28.3
Industrial organic chemicals[b]	27.9
Tires and inner tubes[c]	27.1
Electronic components	26.7
Low FDI	
Agricultural chemicals	13.5
Engines and turbines	13.4
Aircraft and parts[d]	2.6
Blast furnace and basic steel[e]	2.0

Source: Data from U.S. Bureau of Economic Analysis 1992; U.S. Bureau of the Census 1997.

[a]Communications equpment and audio and video equipment.

[b]Industrial inorganic chemicals, plastics materials and synthetics, and industrial organic chemicals.

[c]Rubber products.

[d]Other transportation equipment.

[e]Ferrous metals.

liberalization. In short, there needed to be a mechanism to exclude outsiders. Thus, a regional arrangement, not multilateral liberalization, would provide larger gains for industries with large returns to scale.

North American Production Sharing

Restructuring affiliates in Canada and Mexico to gain scale economies often reoriented production from finished goods to intermediate components: factories making a full line of color televisions instead would concentrate in cathode-ray tubes, fully integrated automobile plants began to manufacture engine blocks or transmissions, affiliates producing complete refrigerators shifted to condensers, and so on. These adjustments accelerated the trend toward outsourcing and production sharing in North America. In these strategies, a corporate parent and its affiliates (or original equipment manufacturers and arms-length subcontractors) trade unfinished products, with each division adding value along the way, and the outputs of geographically dispersed operations are brought to one location only at the final assembly stage.

Production sharing generally takes advantage of differences in low-skill labor costs between the United States and developing countries. As import competition from Japan and Asia increased in the 1970s, firms facing cost pressures moved manual tasks to labor-rich areas and vertically integrated across borders to maintain their competitive position. "As domestic labor-intensive production became less and less economical," Grunwald and Flamm (1985, 10) explain, "U.S. firms began to look to other countries, breaking production into stages and carrying out the labor-intensive processes in countries where wages were low." In these arrangements, factories in the United States performed stages that required long production runs, large amounts of capital, or skilled labor, while affiliates in Mexico, South America, the Caribbean, and Asia made labor-intensive parts and assembled finished products.

Policy measures assisted the rise of production sharing. Sections 9802.00.60 and 9802.00.80 of the Harmonized Tariff System (formerly Sections 806.30 and 807.00 of the Tariff System of the United States) established the Offshore Assembly Program (OAP), which allows firms exporting products for foreign processing to pay tariffs only on the value added abroad (not U.S. content) when these goods reenter the United States. As U.S. multinationals invested in export-processing zones in Asia, Mexico initiated the Border Industrialization Program in 1965 to attract manufacturing into the border region. Firms that combined these privileges with OAP could send a product to the maquiladoras and then return it to the United States, paying tariffs only on the value added in Mexico. As a result, intermediate goods trade between the United States and Mexico expanded dramatically. OAP imports from Mexico were one-fifth those from Hong Kong and one-quarter those from Taiwan in 1966; by 1970, Mexico's OAP trade doubled Hong Kong's and quadrupled Taiwan's (Grunwald and Flamm 1985, 137).

At about the same time, U.S. multinationals began to rationalize product lines between parent factories and the branch plants in Canada. In this case, production-sharing motives were different than in Mexico—Canadian branch plants moved to a narrower range of products for the combined Canada-U.S. market to exploit scale economies; Mexican maquiladoras specialized in manufacturing processes with high labor content and few economies of scale. But the effects were similar: the development of a regional supply network and growing cross-border trade. Policy initiatives such as the APTA assisted this trend, and OAP trade with Canada was substantial in office machinery, engines, tractors, and other types of machinery.

With the market-opening measures in Mexico after the debt crisis, multinationals started to rearrange affiliates in Mexico's interior by reducing product lines, lengthening production runs, and reorienting sales to the regional economy. This further increased production-sharing trade in North America. By 1987, Mexico and Canada accounted for 60.3 percent of OAP trade and 44 percent of the foreign content of this trade. Under the APTA, another $28.1 billion (equal to 41 percent of OAP trade) entered the United States from Canada. Overall, 60.5 percent of the intrafirm trade of U.S. companies involved Mexico and Canada.[15] These figures help to explain why some firms would be interested in trade liberalization and policy harmonization regionally more than multilaterally.

The industries most active in developing regional supply chains had technological features conducive to offshore manufacturing: production techniques divisible into stages that could be performed at different times and locations, low-skill components and processes that could use cheaper foreign labor, and low weight-to-value ratios for intermediate goods, which create low shipping costs between separate locations. The semiconductor industry was the first to move abroad, starting in 1961 with Fairchild Semiconductor's establishment of an affiliate in Hong Kong, as foreign assembly and packaging helped to reduce factor costs and enhance price competitiveness. Offshore manufacturing also expanded in electrical items such as radios, televisions, personal computers, and home appliances, where firms could match long production runs in the United States with cheap foreign workers for labor-intensive soldering, assembly, and testing. The manufacture of components for automobiles, machinery, and instruments moved abroad in this period as well.

The first column of table 29 presents the intrafirm trade of U.S. companies as a share of domestic sales in 1987. Manufacturers of computers, automobiles, consumer electronics, and electronic components engaged in the largest amounts of intrafirm trade. Trade with foreign affiliates was less common in paper, nonmetallic minerals, plastics, furniture, and lumber. Leather, apparel, and textiles recorded large increases in intrafirm trade in the 1980s, but levels remained low relative to total sales.

The second column of table 29 reports OAP trade as a percentage of total sales. Most of this trade was concentrated in the five industries heavily engaged in intrafirm trade—particularly automobiles and consumer electronics. In addition, however, the leather, apparel, and furniture industries registered no-

---

15. The figures in this paragraph are from the sources for tables 28 and 29.

TABLE 29.   Intrafirm Trade and Offshore Assembly, 1987

Industry	Intrafirm Trade as a Percentage of Total Shipments	OAP Trade as a Percentage of Total Shipments[a]
High		
Computer and office equipment	27.6	2.7
Motor vehicles and equipment	24.3	20.7
Household audio and video equipment	23.5	8.5
Electronic components	22.6	4.9
Farm machinery	10.4	2.9
Construction machinery	9.3	1.7
Industrial inorganic chemicals	8.7	0.0
Drugs	6.7	0.0
Household appliances	5.7	0.6
Industrial organic chemicals	5.1	0.0
Plastics and synthetics	5.1	0.0
Low		
Paper and allied products	1.6	0.0
Leather and leather products	1.4	2.3
Apparel	1.1	0.8
Stone, clay, and nonmetallic minerals	0.9	0.1
Plastics products	0.9	0.1
Textiles	0.6	0.1
Furniture and fixtures	0.6	0.8
Lumber and wood products	0.5	0.1
Ferrous metals	0.2	0.1

Source: Data from U.S. Bureau of Economic Analysis 1992; U.S. Bureau of the Census 1997.

[a]Foreign content of OAP trade with Canada and Mexico in 1987. Data provided courtesy of the authors of Feenstra, Hanson, and Swenson 2000.

table levels of OAP trade despite little intrafirm trade.[16] Moreover, outsourcing was growing rapidly in these industries: over the next five years to 1992, OAP trade increased 231 percent in apparel and 175 percent in leather.

Production sharing and outsourcing also were concentrated in North America. Among the industries with high levels of outsourcing, at least one-third of OAP trade occurred with Mexico and Canada in every case except

16. There is overlap between OAP trade and intrafirm trade, yet the two measures differ in important ways. First, OAP trade includes subcontracting between unaffiliated parties in addition to trade between affiliated firms. When firms do not own their suppliers, OAP trade picks up cross-border production not accounted for in intrafirm trade. Second, OAP trade crosses the U.S. border twice, once leaving and again reentering the United States. Thus, it does not capture production-sharing arrangements that involve one-way movements of goods (from the parent to affiliates or from affiliates to the parent). Thus, the two datasets are best used in conjunction with one another; not all intrafirm trade enters under OAP provisions, nor does all OAP trade remain within the firm, even if there are incentives to combine the two.

apparel and leather, where firms preferred to outsource to Asia. Industries with substantial intrafirm trade outside North America (computer and office equipment, electronic components, farm and garden machinery, drugs, industrial chemicals, and instruments) traded intensely with regional affiliates as well. In most cases, the North American operations of U.S. multinationals were not closely integrated with affiliates outside the region.[17] Thus, industry interests in free trade between parent firms and their affiliates outside North America were not as widely distributed as those for liberalizing trade with Mexico and Canada.

In sum, the growth of production-sharing networks in North America made the United States, Canada, and Mexico highly interdependent in manufacturing, not merely consumption. These production linkages were concentrated in a few industries, so the private risks fell on a handful of U.S. multinationals. Five firms—Chrysler, GM, Ford, IBM, and Volkswagen—shipped one-fifth of Mexico's foreign sales in 1990. Chrysler, GM, and Ford, respectively, exported 42 percent, 36 percent, and 31 percent of their Mexican production, of which 91 percent, 100 percent, and 100 percent went to the United States. IBM sold 95 percent of its Mexican output abroad (U.S. General Accounting Office 1992).

Though the maquiladora zone in Mexico and OAP provisions in the United States had reduced barriers to production-sharing trade, multinationals still had to pay tariffs on Mexican content in both countries. Moreover, it was difficult to reorganize corporate activities because only plants in the border region received maquiladora privileges and the maquiladoras could not sell in the domestic market, so they were cut off from plants in Mexico's interior. Finally, production-sharing arrangements, once established, were vulnerable to antidumping actions in the United States, new regulations on foreign investors in Mexico and Canada, and trade disputes between these countries. A regional arrangement would solve these lingering problems and allow multinational companies to extend and more closely integrate North American production networks.

Nationally Oriented Industries with Small Returns to Scale

Industries with few scale economies and negligible production sharing have little to gain from regional trade liberalization: longer production runs do not reduce unit costs, and technology makes moving abroad to cut labor expenses

---

17. An exception is chemicals, particularly pharmaceuticals, industrial chemicals, plastics, and synthetics, as companies exported ingredients to Europe but had little scope for offshore processing in low-wage areas. In computers, consumer electronics, and electronic components, firms conducted substantial trade with affiliates in Asia in addition to Mexico and the Caribbean.

difficult. Still, some can expect to be harmed more than others. Preexisting trade patterns and protectionist barriers provide insights into trade preferences because industry groups are likely to oppose free trade agreements if they anticipate increased import penetration and to support it if they expect new export opportunities.

Table 30 shows the industries with the highest rates of import penetration from Canada and Mexico—the ones most likely to oppose free trade agreements. Canadian competition concentrated in natural resources and resource-intensive manufacturing: nonferrous metals, paper, lumber, furniture, and steel. These industries enjoyed some natural protection because of high transport costs in goods with high weight-to-value ratios. But import penetration was especially severe in northern U.S. markets near the border, and Canada was the main source of competition in nonferrous metals, paper, and lumber.

As the last column in table 30 illustrates, the U.S. market already was open to Canadian trade in the industries that faced the most competition: tariffs were low and, aside from countervailing duties on softwood lumber, few non-tariff barriers existed. Moreover, there were large disparities in market access, as Canadian duties on paper (5.2 percent), processed wood (8 percent), and furniture (10.3 percent) exceeded U.S. rates by a factor of at least three. Only in steel and nonferrous metals was the Canadian market more open than the U.S. market. Canada's strong position in these two industries suggests that U.S. producers were not likely to reap large gains from trade creation under a free trade agreement.[18] Thus, incentives to oppose free trade were most salient in steel and nonferrous metals, despite large returns to scale, and also lumber.

Import penetration from Mexico was most significant in leather goods, apparel, glass and glassware, and rubber products. Compared to the case of Canada, however, a very different pattern emerges. Mexican imports surpassed 2 percent of consumption in only one manufacturing industry, leather: Asia, not Mexico, was the principal source of competition.[19] Yet these were the most labor-intensive industries in the United States, and they were significantly protected: tariffs on leather products were 8.9 percent, and export restraints applied

18. Canada's status as one of the few major producers outside the multilateral steel arrangement was an additional threat to U.S. steel companies, which had only tariffs to protect them against Canadian goods.

19. Import penetration also was severe in food products such as fruits and vegetables. Mexico has abundant arable land for tropical produce, and proximity to the United States reduces transport time for goods with limited shelf life. In addition, tomatoes, cucumbers, broccoli, radishes, onions, and the like require picking, trimming, and packing by hand. This labor intensity makes U.S. farmers susceptible to low-wage competition from Mexico; indeed, many U.S. firms have relied on migrant Mexican workers to perform these tasks (U.S. Congress 1992, 197).

to South Korean footwear; apparel tariffs averaged 18.0 percent, and the MFA covered 80 percent of imports; in rubber and glass products, tariffs were 7.7 percent and 7.0 percent, respectively. Even so, all had experienced steady import growth after the Kennedy and Tokyo Round tariffs cuts. Most exports to Mexico were semifinished products in need of further processing before returning to the United States. Since producers in these industries faced price pressures from low-wage areas generally and depended on barriers to imports originating both inside and outside North America, they had powerful reasons to fight free trade agreements.

To complicate matters a bit, it is worth noting that outsourcing trade was on the rise in the apparel and leather industries, as table 29 illustrates. Because of this trend, these two industries were becoming increasingly bifurcated. In

TABLE 30.   Import Competition from Canada and Mexico

Industry	Imports from Canada	Imports from All Countries	U.S. Tariff Rate[a]
Nonferrous metals	7.4	15.5	1.1
Paper and allied products	6.4	8.3	0.5
Lumber and wood products	5.0	7.4	1.7
Furniture and fixtures	2.7	11.0	2.7
Ferrous metals	2.3	12.2	4.2
Rubber products[b]	1.9	18.0	7.7
Glass and glassware	1.6	9.1	7.0
Leather and leather products	0.9	49.0	8.9
Miscellaneous manufacturers	0.8	35.2	3.6
Apparel	0.5	28.7	18.0
Textiles	0.1	7.4	13.1

	Imports from Mexico	Imports from All Countries	U.S. Tariff Rate[a]
Leather and leather products	3.1	49.0	8.9
Apparel	1.5	28.7	18.0
Glass and glassware	1.4	9.1	7.0
Rubber products[b]	1.4	18.0	7.7
Furniture and fixtures	1.3	11.0	2.7
Miscellaneous manufactures	1.1	35.2	3.6
Nonferrous metals	0.9	15.5	1.1
Ferrous metals	0.7	12.2	4.2
Textiles	0.4	7.4	13.1
Lumber and wood products	0.3	7.4	1.7
Paper and allied products	0.3	8.3	0.5

Source: Data from USITC Trade DataWeb, http://dataweb.usitc.gov; U.S. Bureau of the Census 1997.
[a]Duties collected divided by total imports.
[b]Excludes tires and inner tubes.

apparel, for instance, large producers of standardized products such as blue jeans and underwear left technology- and skill-intensive cutting, finishing, pressing, and laundering in the United States but moved high-volume sewing operations abroad or subcontracted to independent firms; smaller manufacturers of "fashion-sensitive goods" such as women's wear continued to sew entire garments with U.S. labor (U.S. Congress 1992, 175–82). Multinational companies therefore had motives to support free trade agreements that were not salient to small, nationally oriented firms.

Finally, industries facing little Mexican competition were not likely to have a strong position on free trade. Though the U.S. textile industry was heavily protected, it was North America's most efficient producer of yarns and fabrics; Mexican costs, despite low wages, were 25–150 percent higher (Hufbauer and Schott 1992, 267). In steel, U.S. quotas limited Mexico's import share with or without tariffs. In both cases, greater access to the Mexican market would more than offset the elimination of U.S. tariffs, particularly if the textile MFA and the multilateral steel arrangement remained in place.[20] Incentives to oppose free trade with Mexico therefore were not as great as in glass and rubber, nor were the sorts of cleavages anticipated in apparel and leather likely to surface.

U.S. Labor Unions

Two calamities hit U.S. labor unions after 1970. First, wage gaps between skilled and unskilled workers widened as trade exposure increased and firms moved production offshore. Second, heavy job losses hit labor unions as some employers restructured and downsized, while others went out of business altogether. In response to rising unemployment in import-sensitive sectors, the American Federation of Labor and Congress of Industrial Organizations (AFL-CIO) turned against trade liberalization in 1969. Since then, labor unions have campaigned against tariff cuts, FDI, and reverse imports (that is, domestic sales of products manufactured abroad by U.S. multinationals).

With trade liberalization, whether regional or global, workers could expect more of the same: growing wage inequality and localized unemployment. In industries where firms produced labor-intensive goods primarily with domestic labor, the principal threat was import competition. In these cases, labor unions shared a common interest with their employers, so labor and capital were likely to join together against regional free trade. When firms are multinational,

20. USITC 1990a, chap. 2, 5–6. These quotas had been modestly liberalized on a bilateral basis in 1985 and 1988.

however, restructuring occurs across borders. The costs of these adjustments are externalized to workers, particularly unskilled labor in high-wage countries. Thus, production sharing will tend to split the preferences of businesses and labor unions: workers have incentives to oppose free trade agreements to prevent firms from moving labor-intensive processes abroad. Either way, U.S. labor unions had strong motives to lobby against free trade with Canada and especially Mexico.

Domestic Groups and Regional Trade Liberalization

In the United States, trade lobbying occurs in three phases. In the first phase, Congress must delegate to the president the authority to begin negotiations. At this point, interest groups mobilize to pressure Congress to grant or deny delegation and to influence the specific terms the president must satisfy in using this authority if approved. In the second phase, interested parties present their negotiating objectives to the agencies responsible for formulating trade strategy and conducting negotiations, the USTR and the USITC. This gives private actors an opportunity to push for treaty provisions favorable to their interests. Finally, the fast-track provisions of the 1974 Trade Act introduced a third phase of lobbying: once a treaty has been negotiated, Congress must approve or reject it. This enables interest groups to influence the chances of ratification based on the extent to which a trade agreement's terms satisfy their objectives.

Statutory procedures ensure that domestic interests have opportunities to wield influence at each of these three stages through a formal advisory framework of private-sector committees. These private-sector advisory groups provide information and advice to the executive branch and Congress, both of which must consult regularly during and after trade negotiations. This allows firms, trade associations, and labor unions to present their concerns and propose remedies; it also helps trade negotiators learn what terms must be included to dissuade certain groups from trying to block a trade agreement (O'Halloran 1994, 144–45).

Private actors have numerous informal means to influence policy: they can meet with USTR and USITC officials, or they can contact members of Congress, who can exert pressure on executive agencies. Fortunately, many channels of influence are public: Congress convenes hearings before trade negotiations start and after they are finished; USTR and USITC reports provide additional insights into communications between private actors and trade negotiators. Testimony and written submissions by organized groups regarding their objectives in trade negotiations and their views of the completed treaties provide a basis to evaluate industry preferences on North American free trade.

Ordered Probit Analysis

The ordered probit analysis in table 31 examines industry preferences on free trade with Mexico and Canada. The units of analysis are three-digit SIC codes. The dependent variable is coded as "1" if industry groups supported free trade, "−1" if they opposed free trade, and "0" if industry groups did not lobby. Industries are coded as not lobbying unless a trade association (or at least two firms responsible for 25 percent of industry sales or more) testified or submitted material for the record in a congressional or USITC hearing (see Chase 2003, 154–55).

The models employ the measure of *returns to scale* previously described (see table 27) to estimate the importance of scale economies. For production sharing, models 1 and 3 use *intrafirm trade,* and models 2 and 4 use *OAP trade* with Mexico and Canada (see table 29). All models include *import competition* and *export dependence* as proxies for factor costs.

TABLE 31.   Ordered Probit Estimates for NAFTA and CUSFTA Lobbying

Variable	NAFTA Lobbying		CUSFTA Lobbying	
	(1)	(2)	(3)	(4)
Returns to scale	4.93***	4.74***	3.04***	2.93***
	(1.17)	(1.14)	(1.06)	(1.04)
Intrafirm trade	10.28***		11.85***	
	(3.11)		(3.00)	
OAP trade		30.60**		35.99**
		(13.97)		(14.72)
Import competition	−3.98***	−3.27***	−2.57***	−1.90***
	(0.83)	(0.76)	(0.73)	(0.68)
Export dependence	3.66**	5.48***	−2.11	0.53
	(1.58)	(1.45)	(1.56)	(1.38)
Threshold 1	−0.44	−0.41	−1.02	−0.92
	(0.19)	(0.19)	(0.20)	(0.20)
Threshold 2	0.91	0.91	0.74	0.74
	(0.20)	(0.20)	(0.19)	(0.19)
Log likelihood	−117.05	−120.61	−116.70	−122.47
Model χ^2	56.56***	49.44***	34.38***	22.83***
Pseudo R-squared	0.19	0.17	0.13	0.09

Note: Cell entries are maximum likelihood estimates obtained using ordered probit analysis, with asymptotic standard errors in parentheses. $N = 134$.

***$p < .01$ **$p < .05$ *$p < .10$

In the analysis of NAFTA lobbying in model 1 and model 2, all variables are correctly signed and statistically significant. The coefficients for *returns to scale, intrafirm trade,* and *OAP trade* confirm that concentrating production and expanding regional procurement were important considerations for NAFTA supporters. *Export dependence* also increases support for free trade with Mexico; *import competition* is associated with opposition to NAFTA.

The results are similar in model 3 and model 4, which evaluate industry positions on the CUSFTA treaty. The coefficients for *returns to scale* and *import competition* are smaller but still significant. *Export dependence* is no longer statistically significant; it even has an incorrect negative sign in model 3.

The substantive importance of these variables is more apparent when maximum likelihood coefficients are translated into predicted probabilities of industry support for free trade. Table 32 shows predicted probabilities of support for NAFTA (based on the averages of model 1 and model 2) and CUSFTA (based on the averages of model 3 and model 4). When returns to scale are large and production sharing is significant, predicted support is 64.3 percent for NAFTA and 55.3 for CUSFTA. Industries with large returns to scale but little production sharing lobbied for NAFTA 39.5 percent of the time and CUSFTA 27.4 percent of the time. The figures are similar when production sharing is significant but returns to scale small, 28.4 percent for NAFTA and 32.9 percent for CUSFTA. Support is lowest, 11.4 percent and 12 percent, respectively, when returns to scale are small and production sharing is minimal. These findings strongly support hypothesis 1 and hypothesis 3.

The data analysis provides a compelling snapshot of industry lobbying for regional free trade. Among industries with similar economic characteristics,

TABLE 32. Predicted Probabilities of NAFTA and CUSFTA Support

	Production Sharing	
Returns to Scale	**High**	**Low**
Large	(1)	(2)
	NAFTA: 64.3%	NAFTA: 39.5%
	CUSFTA: 55.3%	CUSFTA: 27.4%
Small	(4)	(3)
	NAFTA: 28.4%	NAFTA: 11.4%
	CUSFTA: 32.9%	CUSFTA: 12.0%

Note: Cell entries are predicted probabilities from the models in table 31, minus and plus one standard deviation of returns to scale and production sharing, holding other variables constant at their mean values.

however, the motives for free trade, or the mechanisms sought to cushion the blow of liberalization, sometimes differed. It is therefore worth taking a deeper look at how industry groups justified their positions on free trade with Mexico and Canada.

Multinational Firms with Large Returns to Scale

Firms and trade associations in industries with large returns to scale and investment in Canada provided the strongest support for CUSFTA. Most enthusiastic about free trade were producers of automobiles, computers, electronic components, consumer electronics, telecommunications equipment, home appliances, industrial chemicals, plastic and synthetic materials, and farm and construction machinery. At the outset of negotiations, representatives of these industries emphasized that while they wished to see tariffs eliminated between the United States and Canada, tariff cuts alone would not win their support. Instead, multinational companies wanted a comprehensive arrangement that removed tariff and nontariff barriers, liberalized foreign investment rules, opened procurement markets, and protected intellectual property.

A major concern was Canada's treatment of FDI. Though the Conservative government had scaled back screening and assigned FIRA a more welcoming name, Investment Canada, this relaxed stance could be reversed with little warning. Interviews with Canadian affiliates indicated that "the lack of consistent, long-term government economic policies made it difficult . . . to engage in long-range planning. A stable policy environment was preferred" (Daly and MacCharles 1986, 79). Companies would restructure only after receiving credible assurances of policy liberalization—otherwise, long-term plans would be vulnerable to a resurgence of the regulatory activism of the 1970s. Therefore U.S. multinationals sought to end screening and abolish TRIMs to "provide assurances against a return to the FIRA-based deterrence environment," as an executive of Procter and Gamble put it (U.S. Senate 1987, 308).

Regulatory certainty was especially important to automotive firms. New rules requiring Canada to end export-based duty remissions and phase out tariff rebates for foreign multinationals were integral to the support of the Motor Vehicle Manufacturers Association (MVMA). Trade groups such as the Chemical Manufacturers Association and the Computer and Communications Industry Association also cheered the elimination of export performance and local content requirements (U.S. House of Representatives 1988, 349–50, 662, 751).

Intellectual property was another concern of U.S. multinationals. Efforts in the GATT to improve the protection of copyrights, patents, and trademarks were floundering. Fearing that the Uruguay Round would adopt weak standards, producers of chemicals, computers, communications equipment, and electronic components pushed for strong intellectual property rules in the CUSFTA talks. When the treaty included many of the desired provisions, the American Electronics Association expressed hope that it would "set a critically important example of multilateral negotiations going on in the GATT" (U.S. House of Representatives 1988, 316). Public procurement also was an issue, particularly in telecommunications, as AT&T, GTE, and Rockwell International had filed a complaint with the USTR prior to the negotiations on discriminatory practices favoring Bell-Canada. These firms approved of provisions in the CUSFTA treaty that opened procurement markets to producers unable to qualify under the strict criteria then in force (U.S. House of Representatives 1986, 510–13; U.S. Senate 1987, 7–8).

While multinational companies favored free trade and comprehensive rules for FDI, their support for the CUSFTA treaty was contingent on transitional protection and measures that discriminated against producers outside North America. Several firms emphasized that they had structured investments to comply with regulatory mandates in a protected market and they did not want new entrants to establish modern facilities in the region to capture free trade benefits. Moreover, once trade protection was gone, branch plants would be at a competitive disadvantage until they were reorganized or closed. Multinationals therefore sought exclusive provisions, restrictions on outsiders, and transitional protection to place limits on external competition during the period when investments were being restructured.

The most important entry restrictions were origin rules that mandated 50 percent North American content to receive CUSFTA treatment. Canadian negotiators proposed a 35 percent requirement so foreign multinationals would not be deterred from making new investments. However, firms in automobiles, electronics, machinery, and chemicals insisted on tougher safeguards to prevent European and Asian companies from setting up screwdriver factories to earn free trade privileges. For example, Zenith and GE insisted on 50 percent local content to block Asian firms from expanding production of "snap-together" television receivers in Canada. Automakers also backed the 50 percent rule, though they preferred a 60 percent standard.[21]

21. Labor unions and suppliers of auto parts, picture tubes, and electronic components pushed for origin rules higher than 50 percent because they feared that Japanese, European, and North American multinationals would increase subcontracting outside the region. Original equipment manufacturers, however, opposed stringent limits that would hinder their ability to outsource production. U.S. House of Representatives 1988, 344–45; U.S. Senate 1986, 306–8.

In addition, special provisions were negotiated for automotive trade so that the Big Three's long-standing production arrangements would not be upset. Officials in the United States initially proposed that free trade in automotive products apply only to Canada-U.S. trade so that foreign automakers could no longer earn tariff rebates and export-based duty remissions through separate undertakings with the Canadian government. However, this position ran afoul of the MVMA, which told negotiators it was "extremely alarmed" by the proposal (Wonnacott 1988, 105–7). Automakers also urged Congress to block any deal that changed "existing trade arrangements on which MVMA member companies have structured long-term competitive strategies" (U.S. Senate 1987, 232). As a result, negotiators agreed that the Big Three could continue duty-free imports of non-U.S. parts into Canada as long as they adhered to the safeguards specified in the 1965 letters of undertaking. These provisions allowed the Big Three to maintain their special treatment, while they also made Japanese and European multinationals ineligible for the same privileges.

Finally, the CUSFTA treaty included phase-out periods of up to ten years for eliminating trade barriers. Producers did not need transition periods to open the U.S. market to Canadian goods because their factories in the United States already produced on a large scale. But Canadian affiliates with high unit costs would suffer if they were exposed to free trade too quickly. Whirlpool, for instance, argued that rapid tariff elimination "would be unreasonable and not economically or politically acceptable to Canadian appliance manufacturers" (U.S. House of Representatives 1988, 770). To mitigate adjustment costs and prevent a flood of imports into the Canadian market, U.S. multinationals pushed to eliminate trade barriers gradually to allow the branch plants time to reorganize before facing free trade conditions.

As with the free trade agreement with Canada, the most enthusiastic advocates of free trade with Mexico were industries seeking to concentrate production and expand regional supply networks. Producers of automobiles, computers, consumer electronics, telecommunications equipment, farm and construction machinery, pharmaceuticals, and chemicals were the NAFTA treaty's strongest supporters. Representatives of these industries suggested that free trade with Mexico would facilitate changes in the structure of manufacturing in the region, helping to reduce unit costs and enhance the competitive position of firms. Companies especially welcomed opportunities to gain scale economies and outsource labor-intensive components to Mexico.

Multinationals from the United States wanted more than tariff-free trade, however. To accommodate the restructuring they desired, these firms also sought to end industrial and regulatory policies that forced multinationals to purchase high-cost local inputs or sell unprofitable exports; freer access to government procurement markets, which were biased in favor of national firms; fewer equity restrictions on FDI; and improved standards for intellectual property protection. Emphasis varied with the level of regulation (most onerous in motor vehicles, computers, electronic equipment, and pharmaceuticals), dependence on R&D (particularly great in pharmaceuticals, computers, and electronic components), and the importance of government procurement (highest in telecommunications and petroleum equipment). The Uruguay Round at the time had not effectively addressed these issues—and many firms hoped the NAFTA treaty would provide a model for improved trade laws in the GATT.

As part of the NAFTA treaty, U.S. multinationals pushed vigorously to get rid of investment restrictions and performance requirements in Mexico. Before the negotiations began, automobile firms demanded an end to Mexico's trade-balancing and local content requirements. Other industries, including computers, organic and petroleum-based chemicals, and farm and construction machinery listed liberalized regulatory rules as preconditions for their support for a free trade agreement (U.S. House of Representatives 1991, 181–83, 188–90, 792, 945–46). When the draft treaty was released, the Chemical Manufacturers Association asserted that its treatment of FDI "breaks new ground" (U.S. House of Representatives 1992b, 477). The Motor and Equipment Manufacturers Association hailed the phasing out of performance requirements as "the single most significant accomplishment of the NAFTA automotive negotiations" (U.S. House of Representatives 1992b, 300).

Enhanced protection of intellectual property was another important feature of NAFTA. The chemicals and electronics industries advocated a free trade agreement to strengthen patents on new chemicals, protect against software piracy, and prevent the unfair use of inventions (U.S. House of Representatives 1991, 181–83; 1993b, 769). The pharmaceuticals industry conditioned its support on the enactment of "adequate, world-class" patent laws in Mexico (USITC 1990b, chap. 2, 19). Finally, firms in telecommunications and petroleum equipment sought provisions for more open government procurement (U.S. Senate 1992, 194–96). As one telecom firm asserted, "a comprehensive FTA agreement would open markets reciprocally for both the United States and Mexico, permitting manufacturers . . . to increase their competitiveness and economies of scale" (USITC 1990b, chap. 2, 9).

While U.S. multinationals enthusiastically supported the NAFTA negotiations, they also sought exclusive provisions in the final treaty and prolonged periods for the phase out of tariff protection in Mexico. These firms emphasized to the USITC (1990b, chap. 2, 7) that Mexican industrial programs had left them with large sunk costs in poorly specialized, inefficient-scale factories. Computer producers complained that they had "high costs imposed on them by the Computer Decree that would not be borne by new competitors." The Automobile Manufacturers Association similarly noted that Mexican affiliates that "operate at less than maximum scale of efficiency" were at a disadvantage (U.S. House of Representatives 1993a, 150). While U.S. companies wanted to rid themselves of these vestiges of import substitution, they needed to make sure that outsiders could not gain market shares at the expense of Mexican affiliates.

In particular, firms pushed for gradual movement to free trade to shelter their Mexican affiliates during the transition to free trade and minimize the disruption to foreign plants. For example, computer producers IBM, Hewlett-Packard, and Data General were "strongly supportive of an FTA," but they wanted "some phase-in of tariff reductions to prevent dislocation to their Mexican operations" (USITC 1990b, chap. 2, 7). Automakers also requested long tariff phaseouts for their affiliates (U.S. House of Representatives 1993a, 146–47). In home appliances, GE and Whirlpool (which owned factories in Mexico) sought to delay exposure to free trade, while Amana and Maytag (which did not own factories in Mexico) pushed to accelerate the schedule for tariff elimination (USITC 1993, chap. 16, 2 n. 3).

Multinationals from the United States also sought discriminatory measures in the NAFTA treaty to block new entrants from seizing market shares. These companies feared that competitors would build integrated, state-of-the-art production facilities in North America while they attempted to restructure. Automakers, for example, pushed to delay NAFTA treatment for firms that had not invested in Mexico under its Automotive Decrees.[22]

While these sorts of restraints on FDI were not incorporated into the final treaty, rules of origin were crafted to ensure that new entrants would not be able to share in the benefits of free trade without having to pay the same restructuring costs. Without discrimination to ensure excludable benefits for incumbents, established investors most likely would not have supported regional free trade so enthusiastically. Automakers received a 62.5 percent origin rule to force Asian companies to source inputs locally in return for free trade privileges. Other provisions required that televisions traded under NAFTA include

---

22. Specifically, they sought provisions to require new investors to comply with Mexico's value-added and trade-balancing requirements for five years, and they wanted future entrants to have to wait ten years to gain the free trade privileges that incumbent firms (the Big Three, plus Volkswagen and Nissan) would receive immediately ("Vehicle Dispute Drives a Wedge through NAFTA Talks," *Financial Times,* October 25, 1991, 6).

picture tubes manufactured in North America. Only the global supply operations of certain large multinationals, which did not want their outsourced products excluded from free trade treatment, acted as a brake on the trend toward tough rules of origin. For instance, IBM "had a fit" over proposals that would have required North American production of motherboards, screens, and hard drives for personal computers (Cameron and Tomlin 2000, 90). And GM endorsed lower rules of origin than did Ford and Chrysler (60 percent versus 70 percent) so that its joint ventures with Toyota and Suzuki would not be disadvantaged (Hufbauer and Schott 1992, 162–70).

Nationally Oriented Industries with Large Returns to Scale

Most industries with large returns to scale but little production in Canada did not lobby on CUSFTA. Those that did generally were not as enthusiastic about it as multinational firms. Though free trade opened the Canadian market to U.S. goods, it also exposed producers in the United States to competition from Canada. Where the U.S. market was well protected and producers in Canada already had attained a large scale, this was an unattractive proposition. Moreover, a comprehensive arrangement covering FDI, government procurement, and intellectual property offered firms with purely domestic operations few additional benefits.

The steel industry was split over free trade with Canada. In August 1987, AISI sought an exemption from trade negotiations because producers "strongly opposed steel trade liberalization talks with Canada (or with any other country) as long as the U.S. and the world steel crises continue unresolved." Though the group conceded that free trade was not likely to increase import competition, it wanted to leverage the talks into an extension of steel VERs. The AISI remained "skeptical" of CUSFTA in April 1988 because Canada had not joined the new multilateral steel program. Nevertheless, nine large firms in the National Steel Producers Association testified more favorably. In their view, high Canadian tariffs meant that Canada's refusal to negotiate quotas with foreign countries should not derail efforts to liberalize trade bilaterally. The Specialty Steel Industry Association also did "not object" to the CUSFTA treaty because free trade would alleviate market access disparities that firms believed had exacerbated the unfavorable balance in mutual steel trade (U.S. Senate 1989b, 4–57).

Nonferrous metals producers presented a more unified front against CUSFTA. The Nonferrous Metals Producers Committee complained about inadequate disciplines against Canadian subsidies and suggested that dispute settlement rules would undermine the use of unfair trade laws to combat this subsidization. Firms in lead and zinc alloys opposed free trade even more intensely, arguing that they could not survive beyond the third year of the treaty's ten-year tariff phasing schedule (U.S. House of Representatives 1988, 283–99).

As NAFTA negotiations got underway, however, these industries took a more favorable position because Mexican competition was less intense and producers south of the border had not reached comparable scales of output. Steelmakers even recommended free trade with Mexico in their CUSFTA testimony. As negotiations proceeded in 1991, the AISI signaled the USTR that it backed NAFTA as long as the treaty did not weaken U.S. trade remedy laws. Steel companies especially wanted the Mexican government to liberalize procurement in the petroleum sector and eliminate duty drawbacks on exports by foreign steel firms in Mexico (Hufbauer and Schott 1992, 250).

Nonferrous metals producers also supported free trade with Mexico to eliminate disparities in Mexican and U.S. tariffs. The Nonferrous Metals Producers Committee and the Aluminum Association viewed the NAFTA negotiations as an opportunity to redress their complaints with the CUSFTA treaty (U.S. House of Representatives 1991, 748–50, 915–25; 1992b, 568–71). Though the Committee on Pipe and Tube Imports objected to (and petitioned to accelerate) lengthy tariff phaseouts for Mexico, it endorsed the opening of Mexico's procurement market (U.S. House of Representatives 1992b, 485–89). As a result, these groups were more favorable to free trade with Mexico than they had been with Canada.

Industries with Constant Returns to Scale

Industries intensively using natural resources were the most active lobbies on the CUSFTA treaty. The lumber industry predictably opposed free trade with Canada. A bevy of trade associations—the Coalition for Fair Lumber Imports, the Northwest Independent Forest Manufacturers, the Inland Forest Resource Council, and the American Plywood Association—demanded that Canada eliminate "stumpage rates," which enabled producers to purchase timber at low prices. When the CUSFTA treaty failed to address timber subsidies to their liking, these groups opposed its passage (U.S. Senate 1986, 58–76, 210–14; U.S. House of Representatives 1988, 331–36).

The furniture and paper industries, however, backed free trade with Canada. From the standpoint of hypothesis 4, this is puzzling given that these two industries already faced intense import competition from Canada. The congressional testimony of representatives of these industries suggests that import-competing industries with little trade protection have less to lose from regional trade liberalization—and they may have incentives to join with advocates of free trade agreements when foreign trade barriers are high. Though the U.S. furniture industry had faced import pressures and declining employment over the previous decade, the American Furniture Manufacturers Association blamed Canada's high tariffs for the bilateral deficit in furniture trade. The American Paper Institute also was unconcerned with Canadian import competition because Canada's tariffs were two to three times higher than U.S. rates. In addition, furniture producers expected lower timber prices due to free trade in lumber (U.S. Senate 1986, 77–78; 1989a, 91–93).

Of the major labor-intensive industries, only the American Textile Manufacturers Institute (ATMI) openly opposed free trade, as representatives argued that the Canadian market was too small to yield benefits sufficient to compensate for opening the U.S. market (U.S. House of Representatives 1988, 620–21). Other industries with constant returns to scale did not lobby, as producers of glass and glassware, rubber and plastic products, leather goods, ceramics, and apparel took no position on the CUSFTA treaty.

If these industries appeared indifferent to free trade with Canada, they made it known that they staunchly opposed free trade with Mexico. Lobbying against NAFTA concentrated in labor-intensive manufacturing and temperate agriculture, reflecting differences between the United States and Mexico in endowments of unskilled labor. Industry groups highlighted Mexican wage levels in arguing that lower living and regulatory standards would attract labor-intensive production from the United States under free trade. Increased import competition was the principal concern of these producers. The textile and apparel industries, the ATMI explained, "together suffer an unremitting and oppressive burden of imports into their home market . . . [and] Mexico has been a contributor to this injury" (U.S. House of Representatives 1991, 763). "With so very little of our market left," the Footwear Industries of America argued, "we must strongly oppose an FTA with Mexico, which would lead to a further erosion of our market" (U.S. House of Representatives 1991, 843).

Labor-intensive industries started by seeking special exemptions in the NAFTA negotiations. The Work Glove Manufacturers Association demanded that fabric gloves be excluded on the grounds that these products were exempt from the Generalized System of Preferences (GSP) and the Caribbean Basin Initiative and because they had received the ten-year maximum phasing schedule under CUSFTA due to import sensitivity (U.S. Senate 1991, 504). The glassware industry likewise argued that the USITC's prior rejection of GSP status for Mexican and South American household glassware justified taking these products off the table for the NAFTA talks (U.S. House of Representatives 1991, 855–61). Trade associations in leather goods, ceramic floor and wall tiles, and brooms and brushes also strenuously opposed tariff reductions under NAFTA.

In textiles and apparel, a few pressure groups dropped their opposition to free trade with Mexico after the NAFTA treaty incorporated stringent rules of origin. A key concern of these industries was that foreign producers would use Mexico as an "export platform" to circumvent U.S. quotas under the MFA. Early in the talks, the ATMI and other trade associations opposed NAFTA because the absence of "effective customs enforcement" would give Asian firms investing in Mexico a back door into the U.S. market (U.S. House of Representatives 1991, 764).

The solution that these industries favored was stringent rules of origin, which would divert trade and thereby stave off outside pressures for adjustment as long as external barriers remained in place. Textile firms advocated a "yarn forward" origin rule to force production to stay in the region by granting tariff-free treatment only to fabrics made from North American yarn (U.S. House of Representatives 1992b, 278–81, 562–63). Once Mexico and Canada accepted these provisions, the majority of ATMI members voted to support NAFTA. In contrast, the Association of Importers of Textiles and Apparel—an early supporter of free trade with Mexico—denounced NAFTA as "a North American protection agreement" because it penalized firms sourcing fabrics in Asia (U.S. House of Representatives 1992b, 287–88).

The apparel industry remained more divided over NAFTA, however. Garment producers pushed for "fabric forward" origin rules to require that finished clothing use North American yarn and fabric, along with safeguards against import surges. When the final treaty and its side agreements included these terms, apparel companies that could outsource to Mexico adopted a more favorable position. Yet the Apparel Manufacturers Association reported, "Supporting NAFTA was not an easy decision for our organization and some members, frankly, still disagree" (U.S. House of Representatives 1993a, 581). Small shops that produced mostly in the United States continued to oppose free trade with Mexico. Thus, the National Knitwear and Sportswear Association (which represented smaller firms) denounced NAFTA as "a bad agreement" (U.S. House of Representatives 1993a, 117). The Work Glove Manufacturers Association also refused to reconsider its opposition.

Labor versus Business

Every labor union that testified to Congress opposed the CUSFTA and NAFTA treaties. Since business groups and labor unions only united against free trade agreements, but never in favor, political cleavages between capital and labor were neither purely factor based nor sector based. This is a puzzle for standard trade theories, which predict one or the other type of cleavages (not both). Yet labor lobbied as a factor of production, while capital lobbied as sectors.

Labor groups unanimously objected to CUSFTA, even though opposition from industry groups was rare. In industries with production sharing, labor unions argued that free trade would enable foreign-owned firms to establish production in the region. Labor unions in consumer electronics contended that Asian firms such as Mitsubishi would launch an export assault from Canada, leading to more layoffs for U.S. workers.[23] The UAW even sought a U.S.-content rule (which negotiators rejected) to discourage Honda, Toyota, and Hyundai from expanding assembly operations in Canada. In addition, unions argued, U.S. companies would increase outsourcing if intermediate products obtained abroad could be traded freely between the United States and Canada. Thus, the UAW objected to the 50 percent origin rule because automobile firms could manufacture the power train, the most expensive component, outside North America and still qualify for free trade (U.S. House of Representatives 1988, 338–41). Electronics workers likewise complained that TV manufacturers importing picture tubes and components from Asia could still achieve 50 percent content.

In labor-intensive industries such as apparel, textiles, leather, and plastic goods, labor groups stressed basic concerns about import penetration. The unions did not claim that Canada had an advantage in low-wage activities. Instead, they emphasized the threat of increased imports from outside the region "to take advantage of an enlarged market and the inability of Customs to properly monitor the trade flows across our huge border." The Amalgamated Clothing and Textile Workers Union declared that free trade would "hurt workers on both sides of the border" (U.S. House of Representatives 1988, 611). But the larger problem for unions was the extension of free trade to countries other than Canada. As the AFL-CIO noted, workers were "concerned that this proposed agreement will be used as a blueprint for bilateral negotiations with

---

23. The Committee to Preserve American Color Television asserted: "free trade arrangements are not appropriate where the conditions of trade are such that third countries not party to the free trade arrangement will benefit. . . . Japan has a substantial stake in the proposed United States-Canada free trade arrangement and will receive substantial benefits from it" (U.S. Senate 1986, 177).

other countries as well as the Uruguay Round" (U.S. House of Representatives 1988, 162). Apparel and textile unions especially feared that CUSFTA signaled the end of the MFA and future trade concessions for Mexico, Japan, and other Asian countries. The International Leather Goods, Plastics, and Novelty Workers Union declared: "the cumulative effects of this duty-free trade will kill us" (U.S. House of Representatives 1988, 174). In short, labor unions were girding for larger battles ahead—a free trade agreement with Mexico and multilateral liberalization in the GATT.

Thus, it is not surprising that labor unions joined labor-intensive employers in an unremitting campaign against NAFTA. In industries in which companies engaged in production sharing, workers feared job losses to foreign countries. In these cases, labor unions emphasized their concern with H. Ross Perot's "giant sucking sound" of U.S. jobs moving to Mexico. Where outsourcing was less significant, however, unions and their employers embraced protectionism equally. Both suffered from import competition in labor-intensive products, so both benefited from trade restrictions. In these cases, labor unions objected not to the migration of U.S. companies abroad but to the pain of import competition unleashed through trade liberalization under the GATT, the GSP, the Caribbean Basin Initiative, and free trade agreements with Israel, Canada, and Mexico. Business associations in these industries echoed their complaints.

The Politics of Free Trade

The preceding analysis demonstrates that industries with large returns to scale and production-sharing arrangements supported free trade agreements. This discussion generally supports the book's hypotheses about the specific motives for firms to seek trade liberalization regionally instead of globally. But it is also important to understand how domestic preferences influence national policy choices. Thus, the book's secondary objective is to explain how economic considerations filter through political processes to affect policy outcomes.

Only one-third of all manufacturing industries publicly supported NAFTA. To be sure, the pro-NAFTA lobby received significant support from nontradable services such as banking, finance, insurance, telecommunications, and computer software—but the free trade coalition was numerically inferior in manufacturing. However, industry groups vary in their capacity to organize. Table 33 demonstrates that the pro-NAFTA industries were more concentrated in terms of output (share of sales by the twenty largest firms) and employment (percentage of workers in plants with more than one thousand employees) than the

industries that did not lobby. Because concentrated groups can more easily absorb the costs and internalize the benefits of political activity, they are less prone
to free riding. NAFTA opponents were modestly concentrated in terms of sales,
but not employment (because they operated small plants). However, NAFTA
opponents were more localized geographically than NAFTA supporters and
groups that did not lobby. Presumably this spatial concentration increased political pressure on executive agencies and Congress to add provisions favorable
to these industries, even if it did not defeat NAFTA altogether.

This suggests that in addition to organizational abilities across industries,
the actual content of the NAFTA treaty is important to understanding why it
was ratified. Specific provisions in the final treaty and its side agreements were
critical to blunt anti-NAFTA pressure. To minimize domestic opposition, the
USTR negotiated tariff phaseouts of up to fifteen years to delay free trade in
import-sensitive products, stringent rules of origin for products with large
U.S.-Mexico tariff differentials, and safeguards against import surges. Table 33
confirms that industries that lobbied against NAFTA received tariff-phasing
schedules four to seven times longer than industries that favored free trade or
did not lobby. Moreover, prolonged phasing schedules, tariff-rate quotas, and
escape clauses helped to neutralize powerful agricultural opposition in sectors
such as sugar, peanuts, and winter fruits and vegetables (Orden 1996). Finally,

TABLE 33.   Economic and Political Characteristics of Lobby Groups

Variable	Lobbied for NAFTA	Did Not Lobby	Lobbied against NAFTA
Group preferences			
Returns to scale	0.127***	0.075	0.036*
Foreign production	0.210***	0.120	0.090
Intrafirm trade	0.045**	0.018	0.026
OAP trade	0.012	0.006	0.007
Import competition	0.120	0.135	0.230**
U.S. tariff rate	0.025	0.028	0.094***
Ability to organize			
Sales concentration	0.704**	0.623	0.693*
Employment concentration	0.267***	0.146	0.087
Geographic concentration	0.426	0.414	0.492***
Policy outcomes			
NAFTA phasing	0.888	0.516	3.938***
Number of industries	46	55	36

Note: Significance levels are based on a two-tailed *t*-test for equality of means, with "did not lobby" as the
comparison group.
***$p < .01$ **$p < .05$ *$p < .10$

the side agreements, by dividing the environmental lobby, muted pressure on members of Congress to vote against NAFTA.

NAFTA and External Trade

The pursuit of regional arrangements in U.S. policy coincided with rising protectionism and threats of retaliation against countries that maintained allegedly unfair trade barriers. During the dollar's appreciation after 1981, industries turned en masse to trade remedy laws, which had just been revised to favor complainants. Forty-four antidumping and thirty-five countervailing duty claims were filed per year in the decade up to 1990, and more than half of these cases won affirmative decisions for import relief.[24] Many others were withdrawn once foreign governments agreed to export limits, as negotiated trade restraints emerged in steel, machine tools, automobiles, semiconductors, videocassette recorders, microwave ovens, televisions, footwear, textiles, and apparel (GATT 1992 1:114–17). These shifts in U.S. trade policy are widely viewed as the inspiration for Canada and Mexico to pursue free trade agreements to ensure unfettered access to their largest export market.

Though the NAFTA treaty included protectionist elements, trade and investment diversion were not primary objectives. NAFTA established a low common external tariff for computers and semiconductors (U.S. Department of Commerce 1993, chap. 9, 3). As NAFTA was being implemented, Canada cut tariffs on automobile engines and parts from 9.2 percent to 2.5 percent. Supporters of NAFTA in electronic components, computers, chemicals, and farm and construction machinery sought only mild restrictions, if any, on foreign firms. There were exceptions to be sure, such as provisions that prohibited Mexico and Canada, for ten years, from reducing tariffs on picture tubes without U.S. approval (U.S. Department of Commerce 1993, chap. 5, 2–3).[25]

Evidence from lobbying activity suggests that U.S. industry exerted less pressure for protectionism after NAFTA. The reports of industry-sector advisory committees show that most NAFTA supporters strongly backed the Uruguay Round agreements. Many of these industries thought NAFTA would improve the chances for success in the Uruguay Round because it could pro-

24. Legislative changes eased the standards for determining injury from imports and the methods for calculating dumping margins. See Destler 1995, 145–52.

25. Suppliers such as Corning hoped NAFTA would halt the explosion of Japanese and South Korean imports via Mexico. Still, these firms sought tariff cuts in the Uruguay Round because trade protection was not viable as long as foreign multinationals could invest around restrictions at the North American border (U.S. Senate 1994, 69–70).

vide a model for the GATT in areas such as services, TRIMs, intellectual property, national standards, technical barriers, and dispute settlement (USTR
1994). The chemical industry accepted deep cuts in U.S. tariffs because the
Uruguay Round would "have many times the benefit of any regional trade
agreement" (U.S. House of Representatives 1994b, 100) as long as "free riders"
could be persuaded to join in multilateral liberalization (U.S. House of Representatives 1994a, 255). Producers of construction and farm machinery also
pushed for tariff reductions in the GATT. The automobile industry supported
the Uruguay Round agreements and advocated NAFTA provisions for the
staged removal of TRIMs "as the standard for our talks with other countries"
(U.S. House of Representatives 1994a, 291). In these and other cases, protectionist tendencies moderated after the NAFTA treaty.

By comparison, industries that opposed NAFTA also opposed multilateral
trade negotiations in the GATT. Textile and apparel lobby groups fought proposals to end the MFA because liberalization would enable Asian countries to
"capture whatever markets Mexico might have gained under NAFTA" (U.S.
House of Representatives 1992a, 172). Textile producers also objected to
Uruguay Round cuts in Canada's MFN tariff rate (U.S. House of Representatives 1992b, 280–81). Glassware producers told Congress that they opposed
not only the NAFTA treaty but also the Uruguay Round and all other reductions in trade barriers (U.S. House of Representatives 1991, 854–63, 903–14).
Along with producers of leather goods, rubber and plastic products, and ceramics, these industries sought broad exemptions and prolonged phase-in periods for tariff cuts. Free trade agreements subjected labor-intensive producers to even tougher import competition, inciting more intense protectionist
pressures.

Data on tariff changes in the Uruguay Round support this anecdotal evidence. Table 34 presents two sets of OLS regression results: models 1 and 2 analyze tariff rates in 2000; models 3 and 4 examine tariff changes from 1992 to
2000.[26]

In the book's theory, industries with relatively large-scale production and
large returns to scale should have less trade protection at any given time, and
trade protection should be declining in industries that are gaining scale economies (hypothesis 5). Because changes in relative scale are difficult to calculate,
the analysis uses *returns to scale* to distinguish the industries most likely to ex-

26. The dependent variable is duties collected divided by imports from all countries other
than Mexico, Canada, and Israel so that the effects of free trade agreements will not bias the evaluation of multilateral trade policies. Tariff data are from the USITC Trade DataWeb,
http://dataweb.usitc.gov.

TABLE 34.   OLS Regression Results for U.S. Tariffs

Variable	Tariff in 2000		Change in Tariff, 1992–2000	
	(1)	(2)	(3)	(4)
Returns to scale	−0.13***	−0.13***	−0.75**	−0.73**
	(0.04)	(0.04)	(0.33)	(0.34)
Intrafirm trade	−0.23***		−1.32**	
	(0.06)		(0.55)	
OAP trade		−0.83***		−0.96
		(0.31)		(2.90)
Import competition	0.13***	0.11***	0.50***	0.33*
	(0.02)	(0.02)	(0.19)	(0.18)
Geographic concentration	0.13***	0.15***	0.57**	0.62**
	(0.03)	(0.03)	(0.27)	(0.27)
Industrial concentration	0.04**	0.04**	0.46***	0.38**
	(0.02)	(0.02)	(0.17)	(0.17)
NAFTA phasing			0.03***	0.03***
			(0.01)	(0.01)
Constant	−0.04***	−0.05***	−0.89***	−0.91***
	(0.01)	(0.01)	(0.13)	(0.14)
F-ratio	19.47***	16.65***	8.39***	7.12***
Adjusted R-squared	0.41	0.37	0.25	0.22

Note: Cell entries are OLS regression coefficients, with standard errors in parentheses. $N = 134$.
***$p < .01$ **$p < .05$ *$p < .10$

perience cost reduction from regional free trade. Industries heavily involved in *intrafirm trade* or *OAP trade* also should have low, and declining, levels of trade protection (hypothesis 6). Since import penetration should stimulate protectionist pressure (hypothesis 4), industries facing *import competition* will tend to receive high tariffs and tariff increases (or at least smaller than average tariff cuts). The analysis controls for collective action costs by including *industrial concentration* and *geographic concentration,* both of which should be positively associated with trade protection.[27]

In models 1 and 2, all variables are statistically significant with the correct signs. Scale economies lead to lower tariffs; tariffs decline in both models by 1.1 percentage points with each one standard deviation increase in *returns to scale.* Production sharing also produces lower tariffs, though the effect is greater for *intrafirm trade* (1.3 percentage points) than *OAP trade* (0.8 percentage points). *Import competition* is associated with higher tariff rates, as tariffs rise by 2.1

27. Industrial concentration is measured as the percentage of industry sales by the twenty largest firms. The geographic concentration variable is from Busch and Reinhardt (1999), and it is available at http://userwww.service.emory.edu/~erein/research/#geocon.

percentage points (model 1) and 1.8 percentage points (model 2). Tariffs also increase with *geographic concentration* and *industrial concentration.*

Models 3 and 4 include an additional control variable, *NAFTA phasing,* which is the number of years to tariff elimination in the NAFTA treaty (see Chase 2003, 160–61, for a description). The analytical approach suggests that industries liberalized rapidly in NAFTA would have been more likely to experience cost reduction, while those for which free trade was delayed would have had less impetus to restructure. Industries with shorter phasing schedules therefore should have greater liberalization in external tariffs, while industries with long phasing schedules should receive smaller tariff cuts.

The results show that industries with delayed tariff phaseouts were liberalized less after the Uruguay Round, while deeper tariff cuts occurred in industries that were rapidly exposed to free trade under NAFTA. Holding other variables constant at their mean values, a one standard deviation increase in *NAFTA phasing* increases tariffs by 8.1 percent in model 3 and 9.2 percent in model 4. *Import competition* also increases tariffs, though the effect is greater in model 3 (8 percent) than model 4 (5.3 percent). *Geographic concentration* and *industrial concentration* likewise have positive effects on tariff changes.

At the same time, industries with large returns to scale experienced larger tariff cuts. All else equal, tariffs dropped by 6.1 percent and 6 percent in the two models with each increase of one standard deviation in *returns to scale.* This supports the expectation that industries with large returns to scale—particularly those that were liberalized rapidly in NAFTA—were able to gain scale economies and reduce unit costs. *Intrafirm trade* had a negative effect on tariff changes as well, as tariffs dropped by 7.1 percent with each incremental increase. *OAP trade* was negatively associated with tariff changes, though the effects were neither statistically significant nor substantively large.

Conclusion: Multinationals and NAFTA

Technological changes after 1970, along with Mexican and Canadian trade and industrial practices, encouraged the pursuit of regional free trade in industries such as automobiles, computers and office equipment, electronic components, telecommunications, chemicals, and farm and construction machinery. Once Canadian and Mexican tariffs declined, U.S. multinationals that had invested in inefficient-scale facilities to serve protected markets became vulnerable to foreign competition. With these "miniature replica" factories a major burden, multinational companies could benefit from streamlining operations, specializing plants for particular product lines, and closing down inefficient production. Many firms also had outsourced intermediate manufacturing to Mexican maquiladoras, which increased intrafirm trade across North American borders. As production sharing expanded, so did the incentives to eliminate the remaining barriers to cross-border trade and investment. These two trends gave rise to political pressure in the United States for free trade with Canada and Mexico.

Free trade agreements also helped to enhance the competitive position of many U.S. companies by making it easier to take advantage of scale economies and extend regional supply chains. Most supporters of NAFTA favored liberalization in the GATT, while opponents of free trade with Mexico fought the Uruguay Round with equal vigor. Evidence to date therefore suggests that regional arrangements in North America have promoted multilateral liberalization rather than inhibiting it.

CHAPTER 7

Reluctant Regionalism
Japan and Asia

While Europe and North America have implemented significant initiatives to liberalize regional trade in recent years, trading blocs have not formed in Asia.[1] One important factor in this trend is that until recently Japan remained a committed member of the "friends of Article I club" (Scollay and Gilbert 2001, 4 n. 7).[2] Finally, in 2001, Japan concluded the Japan-Singapore Economic Partnership Agreement (JSEPA), its first regional arrangement. That year Japan's Ministry of Economy, Trade, and Industry (METI), in its annual white paper, raised the prospect of future agreements with South Korea, Mexico, and Chile. At the 2002 ASEAN summit, Japan proposed discussions for a free trade area with Southeast Asia.[3]

Japan's conversion to regionalism has been slow, and it is incomplete. To be sure, factors that would motivate domestic groups to seek regional arrangements have gained importance of late. Most significant, Japanese multinationals have invested extensively in ASEAN countries. Over time, many of these investments have been integrated into cross-border production networks linking ASEAN countries more closely with one another and (occasionally) Japan. Japanese companies recently have developed offshore procurement bases in coastal China as well; as production sharing expands and reverse imports into Japan increase, firms have incentives to push to abolish the remaining barriers to entering the Chinese market and exporting back to Japan. Thus, growing trade linked to FDI and foreign production is integrating the Japanese econ-

---

1. The ASEAN Free Trade Area (AFTA) is scheduled for completion by 2005, but to date many details of this arrangement have not been formalized, product coverage is limited, and final implementation remains uncertain.

2. This moniker refers to the MFN commitment in GATT Article I.

3. "Japan Softens Stand on Asian Free-Trade Pact," *Financial Times*, September 14, 2002, 7.

222

omy more closely with labor-rich Asia. This trend has created interests in further liberalization, guarantees for investment, and semiformal agreements and institutions to manage these "economic partnerships," as the Japanese government calls them.

Weighed against the factors pushing Japan closer to Asia are forces that continue to pull the two areas apart. Foremost are ongoing pressures for trade protection. Japan's agricultural market is hermetically closed despite commitments in the Uruguay Round to liberalize. It is no surprise that Singapore, which has almost no domestic agriculture, was selected to launch Japan's experiment with regional arrangements. In the manufactured products that Asia exports, Japanese industry is protected with high tariffs (footwear and leather), actual or threatened nontariff barriers (textiles and apparel), and keiretsu ties and cartel practices (basic materials such as steel, nonferrous metals, petrochemicals, and cement). Domestic resistance to opening this market, regionally or multilaterally, remains strong.

A closer look further suggests that incentives for a trading bloc in Asia are not broadly distributed in Japan. Only a handful of industries, such as electronics and precision instruments, have developed production-sharing networks conducive to the formation of regional arrangements. In other industries with FDI in Asia, producers are divided in their preferences (textiles and apparel), or they oppose liberalization between Japan and the region (automobiles). In contrast to production sharing in North America and Western Europe, offshore manufacturing by Japanese firms rarely involves reverse imports into the home market; FDI integrates Asian economies more closely with one another, but not always with Japan. And even as production relationships become more tightly linked in the Asian region, sales of finished goods remain oriented to Western markets. External dependence raises the risks that regional arrangements in Asia will provoke protectionist responses elsewhere.

Thus, Japan's pursuit of regional arrangements has been delayed and tentative, and it is likely to remain so. The trade agreement with Singapore minimized the potential domestic resistance in Japan. When (or if) discussions proceed with South Korea, China, and ASEAN, the costs for protected Japanese producers rise while the benefits for companies that have established production offshore remain diffuse and limited. In Southeast Asia, Japanese companies are likely to show greater interest in AFTA than in free trade between ASEAN and Japan. In short, the book's analytical framework does not anticipate the formation of a yen bloc in Asia or a significant burst of regional initiatives from Japan.

Scale Economies and Postwar Japan

Japan achieved its postwar economic development without the assistance of a trading bloc—a feat the country could not accomplish before World War II, as chapter 3 shows. In the years after the war, a major concern for U.S. officials was "the terrific problem of how the Japanese are going to get along unless they again reopen some sort of empire toward the south," as George Kennan put it in a 1949 State Department meeting. The Central Intelligence Agency concluded, "Japan for normal economic functioning on an industrial basis, must have access to the Northeast Asiatic areas—notably North China, Manchuria, and Korea," and without these markets and raw materials sources there was "no hope of achieving a viable economy" (Cumings 1984, 18). Industrialists in rebuilding industries such as cotton spinning "openly bemoaned the loss of Japan's colonial market in Manchuria, Korea, and China" (Uriu 1996, 47). But the U.S. military occupation and the migration of Japan's former colonies (except for Taiwan) to the Soviet camp ruled out any initiative to reconstitute the prewar Co-Prosperity Sphere, even in a more benign form.

How did Japanese industry develop after the war shorn of its prewar empire? One prominent thesis is that producers specialized in goods with smaller returns to scale. In this argument, Japanese firms developed "flexible manufacturing strategies" to produce differentiated goods in small batches instead of standardized articles in long production runs. In automobiles, for example, the Kanban system of "lean production" permitted the design of larger varieties of bodies and engines relative to total volume to differentiate production. Rather than building large, vertically integrated enterprises, manufacturers outsourced components to independent suppliers who provided parts through "just-in-time" delivery systems. Though this method sacrificed scale economies, it also minimized excess capacity and focused on cost savings through higher product quality, lower inventories, and less downtime for machinery and equipment (Friedman 1988, 9–23, 156–60).

If true, this would have alleviated the need for a large captive market to sustain mass production. However, after accounting for higher rates of subcontracting, Japanese industry generally has produced on a scale comparable with industries in the United States and Europe since the 1970s. In 1986, for example, Japanese automakers assembled 231,321 vehicles per plant, compared to 197,498 for plants in the United States (calculated from METI 1988; U.S. Bureau of the Census 1997). In fact, Toyota assembled 337,220 vehicles on average in its Japanese factories in 2001—very close to the MES of 500,000 units (United Nations Conference on Trade and Development [UNCTAD] 2002,

133, 286). Chapters 5 and 6 present evidence that the cost advantages of Japanese companies in TVs and VCRs also inhere in production runs up to three times longer than those of U.S. and European firms. Thus, while production is less vertically integrated in Japan, it is not the case that the scale of output is smaller in parts-intensive, assembly-based automotive equipment, consumer electronics, and electrical appliances.

Japanese companies were able to attain high rates of output for two important reasons. First, the Japanese economy was integrated into an "American-managed free trade regime" early in the postwar period. This promoted "trade triangles" in which firms acquired raw materials from Asia and manufactured finished products for export to the United States (Cumings 1984, 16–19). An open U.S. market enabled Japanese products from transistor radios to televisions, automobiles, and integrated circuits to achieve rapid export penetration once they gained an initial price advantage. In televisions, for example, "Japanese firms had the advantage of the large combined [National Television Standards Committee] markets in Japan and the United States in which to exploit scale economies" (Cawson et al. 1990, 224).[4] Specializing for markets in the West thereby enabled Japanese companies to achieve globally competitive scales of production.

Second, once reconstruction was completed and living standards improved, Japan had a national market second only to the United States in size and wealth (Johnson 1982, 15–16). Along with "free access to overseas markets, which multiplied the returns to scale," Japan also "had the good fortune . . . of having a large and rapidly growing domestic market" (Okimoto 1989, 25). Because Japan's market was larger than any in Europe, the country was not limited to one or two national champions; instead, there was room for several world-class firms (Okimoto 1989, 107).

Exports to North America and Europe eventually allowed Japanese companies to grow larger and develop greater capacity than the domestic market alone could support. Since 1990, transport equipment, electrical machinery, and industrial machinery have accounted for more than 70 percent of Japan's exports; just three product groups (automobiles and parts, electronic circuits and tubes, and audio and video equipment) routinely comprise one-third of all exports. Mostly these exports leave the Asian region for markets in the West. Because of low incomes in Asia and import substitution, Japan has never enjoyed a comparable market in the region. As a result of these historic trading

4. The National Television Standards Committee established the transmission standard for the United States in 1953.

patterns, the trend toward trading blocs in other regions naturally generated anxiety in Japan but produced little enthusiasm for Japan to seek regional arrangements of its own, at least until firms began moving offshore.

Japanese FDI and the East Asian Region

Japanese firms were slower than U.S. multinationals to invest in East Asia due to limits on capital outflows that persisted into the 1970s (Encarnation 1992, 149–51). As balance of payments surpluses led to the relaxation of capital controls and yen appreciation increased wage costs in Japan, companies responded to the lure of cheap labor in the newly industrialized economies (NIEs): South Korea, Taiwan, Hong Kong, and Singapore. Though some foreign affiliates targeted protected local markets, most were export platforms for apparel and electronic devices destined for Western markets. A second wave of FDI in the four years to 1982 focused on Southeast Asia, where Thailand, Malaysia, and Indonesia offered new export incentives with lower wage and currency costs than the NIEs.

The movement of Japanese companies offshore resumed and accelerated as the yen strengthened after the 1985 Plaza Accord. By 1989, Japanese FDI reached 5.9 percent of gross domestic product (GDP), compared to only 1 percent in 1980. Almost three-quarters of FDI between 1986 and 1989 went to North America and Europe, as industry responded to trade frictions and the trend toward trading blocs by opening manufacturing outlets in these markets, while Japanese banking and real estate took advantage of the strong yen to accumulate foreign financial assets and property. Though East Asia's share of Japanese FDI declined, average annual outflows increased sixfold. While the fastest growth occurred in finance, real estate, services, and infrastructure, FDI also increased significantly in manufacturing.[5]

Analysts observing the growth of Japanese FDI in East Asia expected that this trend would lead to the creation of regional institutions to manage trade, technology transfer, and dispute settlement among nations. A 1989 *Economist* survey suggested that the relocation of Japanese companies to East Asia was forming a de facto yen bloc in the region.[6] According to Bernard and Ravenhill (1995, 171), the factors "driving the process of economic integration in East Asia" included "the globalization of production networks; increased intergovernmental disputes over bilateral economic relationships; and the rapid pace of technolog-

---

5. The preceding two paragraphs draw from Urata 1993, 275–79.
6. "The Yen Block" 1989.

ical change." Several studies viewed this integration process pessimistically. According to Hatch and Yamamura (1996, 159, 163), the "emerging production alliance" represented "the regionalization of Japan's vertical or supply keiretsu." In this line of reasoning, the extension of Japanese networks of suppliers and distributors into East Asia, tight control over advanced technology, and foreign assistance tied to the purchase of Japanese goods raised entry barriers for Western firms and threatened to close the region to foreign business (Taylor 1995; Islam 1993). A prominent conventional wisdom therefore suggested that Japan was reconstituting its interwar Co-Prosperity Sphere, or at least a modern variant without formal institutional structures and openly aggressive behavior.

Still, myriad factors inhibited the development of an East Asian trading bloc, until recently. First, production sharing was not as extensive as in North America or Europe. To be sure, Japanese trade in intermediate components with East Asia expanded after 1985. Bernard and Ravenhill (1995, 177, 183) note the emergence of a "supply architecture . . . built around ongoing Japanese innovation of components, machinery, and materials" and conclude: "Malaysia, Thailand, and coastal China have all become linked to production in Northeast Asia, so that we may now speak of *regionalized* manufacturing activity in a number of industries." But the UNCTC (1991, 51) points out that intrafirm trade in East Asia was low compared to other regions. Moreover, this trade flowed in one direction—from Japan, where the supply of "core technologies" and advanced components was centralized, to East Asia (Bernard and Ravenhill 1995, 178). As Japanese subcontractors followed original equipment manufacturers into the region, East Asian affiliates became less dependent on Japan, so trade declined as procurement networks expanded (Doner 1993, 172–73; Hatch and Yamamura 1996, 158–63).

Second, Japanese companies rarely used foreign plants to service the home market. Historically, U.S. affiliates in East Asia shipped one-third of their production back to North America, while Japanese affiliates sold primarily to third countries outside the region (Encarnation 1992, 157–58, 174–76). In the late 1980s, Japanese producers of home appliances such as electric refrigerators and air conditioners began to source more domestic sales from Thailand and Malaysia. In addition, Matsushita, Sanyo, and others transferred low-end consumer electronics production to Malaysia and Thailand after 1989. Yet companies did not terminate production of these items in Japan, and reverse imports of other products from East Asia were uncommon. In an ideal-type product cycle, "a more self-contained yen bloc would have emerged as exports of final manufactured products flowed back to Japan from other countries in East Asia" (Bernard and Ravenhill 1995, 185–86, 200).

Finally, even as the East Asian region became "increasingly integrated in terms of production," it remained "outward-oriented in terms of trade" (Doner 1993, 160). While Japan's North American and European affiliates manufactured and distributed finished products inside these regional markets, as recently as a decade ago factories in East Asia operated principally as export platforms to assemble intermediate goods for sale outside the region (Urata 1993, 283–85). Imports of Japanese technology and components for assembly, finishing, and sale abroad produced "trade triangles" in which East Asia ran trade deficits with Japan, offset in part by surpluses with the United States. Triangular trading patterns, and the technological dependence that created them, produced tension in Japan's relations with South Korea, Taiwan, and ASEAN countries (Bernard and Ravenhill 1995, 200–3). Moreover, Japanese companies and their East Asian affiliates could not afford to jeopardize access to markets outside the region. The risk of retaliatory protectionism in North America or Europe therefore limited the potential benefits of regional arrangements.

These considerations help to explain why an East Asian trading bloc did not emerge in the decade after 1985, when Japanese companies were establishing production in the region. The question remains whether past trends have continued into the present or changed and whether incentives for regional arrangements have grown stronger in Japan of late. The book's analytical framework anticipates that domestic pressure to liberalize regional trade and investment will intensify when production sharing becomes more broadly distributed at the industry level, intrafirm trade increases, and corporate strategies rely not only upon free access to the region from Japan but also free access to Japan from the region. Until these conditions are satisfied, the critical mass of political support in Japan will fail to develop.

To illuminate recent developments, the next section examines data on Japanese production, investment, and trade. The analysis reveals strong motives for producers of electrical equipment, industrial machinery, and precision instruments to seek regional arrangements; weak incentives for companies in the automotive industry; and mixed interests for firms manufacturing textiles and apparel. The section that follows presents case studies of these three groups of industries.

Production Sharing in Japanese Industry

The previous section identifies factors that have limited the incentives for Japanese firms to seek regional arrangements: overseas production was established only in the 1980s, and remained at an early stage of development by the mid-1990s; export specialization for Western markets raised the risks of retaliation; production-sharing arrangements were concentrated in a small number of industries; and companies rarely reverse imported, so cross-border production networks failed to integrate Japan with the East Asian region.

In recent years, the movement of Japanese companies offshore has continued and accelerated—further linking production in the region while raising concerns about the "hollowing out" of Japanese industry. In 1995, according to the Japan External Trade Organization (JETRO), the overseas production ratio was 8 percent for Japan, 16 percent for the EC, and 26 percent for the United States.[7] By 2000, Japan's overseas production ratio had reached 13.4 percent. Between 1990 and 2000, employment in Japanese manufacturing declined 13 percent, from 15.2 million to 13.2 million, while employment in Japan's foreign manufacturing affiliates more than doubled, from 1.2 million to 2.8 million. Reverse imports, displayed in figure 3, soared to ¥5.6 trillion, a threefold increase over ten years (METI 2002b, 1; JETRO 2002, 21).

Data at the industry level show, however, that not as much has changed as the figures detailed in the preceding may suggest.[8] Table 35 shows modest growth in Japan's intrafirm trade as a percentage of domestic sales. Yet intrafirm trade surpassed 7 percent of sales in only four industries: precision instruments, electrical machinery, transport equipment, and industrial machinery. Other industries engaged in little intrafirm trade, suggesting that Japanese production sharing with other countries was trivial. Moreover, intrafirm trade was mostly exports of technology, parts, and components from Japan. Japanese multinationals rarely used their foreign affiliates as procurement sources, as imports accounted for only 13.3 percent of intrafirm trade in 2000 and the industries with the highest intrafirm trade ratios showed the least propensity to import.

The figures on reverse imports in table 36 confirm that foreign affiliates were not major suppliers for Japanese production. Reverse imports accounted for only 1.8 percent of industry sales in 2000, up from 1.5 percent in 1997. Offshore procurement was most significant in precision instruments at nearly 10 percent of sales. Electrical machinery and industrial machinery registered

7. JETRO 1995, 20. This figure is the sales of foreign affiliates divided by domestic sales.

8. This analysis is based on survey data in METI 2003. Because METI lacks a legal mandate for these surveys, company responses are voluntary, so problems of sampling and coverage exist (see Ramstetter 1996). The dataset covers 89.7 percent of industry sales in 1999, the most recent year for which comparable Census of Manufacturing data are available. The data are tabulated quarterly, so the analysis compares the earliest four quarters (fourth quarter 1996–third quarter 1997) with the latest four quarters (second quarter 2000–first quarter 2001).

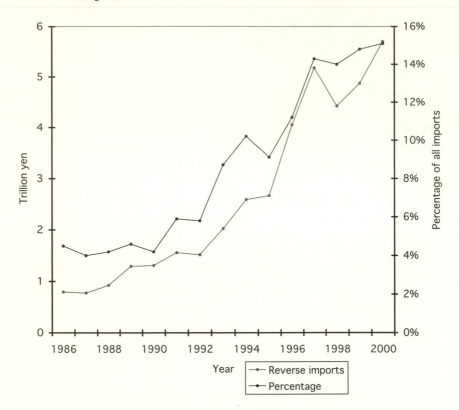

Fig. 3. Reverse imports in Japanese manufacturing, 1986–2000. (Data from METI, various years, "Survey of Overseas Business Activities," http://www.meti.go.jp/english /statistics/data/h2c4tope.html.)

modest amounts of reverse imports, while offshore purchases were growing in ceramics, stone, and clay. In industries with substantial production overseas, imports from foreign affiliates were notably scarce in transport equipment and chemicals.[9]

The data in tables 35 and 36 include all Japanese affiliates in all regions. But the trade and investment patterns of Japanese companies in East Asia are most

9. To place these findings in context, in 1989 the United States reverse imported twice as much as a share of GDP, 3.6 percent. Reverse imports were greatest in transport equipment (11 percent of shipments), electrical machinery (6.9 percent), industrial machinery (6.1 percent), and chemicals (3 percent). Companies in the United States reverse imported significantly less than their Japanese counterparts only in precision instruments (2.2 percent). Figures were calculated from U.S. Bureau of Economic Analysis 1992 and U.S. Bureau of the Census 1997.

TABLE 35. Japanese Intrafirm Trade

Industry	Intrafirm Trade as a Percentage of Total Shipments			Intrafirm Imports as a Percentage of Total Intrafirm Trade
	2000	1997	1989	2000
Precision instruments	30.0	24.3	21.1	17.0
Electrical machinery	23.1	17.8	15.6	13.5
Transport equipment	20.0	15.4	13.3	5.0
Industrial machinery	16.5	12.4	10.3	18.7
Nonferrous metals	6.8	3.6	2.2	29.8
Other manufacturing	6.6	5.9	7.9	31.4
Ceramics, stone, and clay	5.6	3.3	n.d.	23.8
Chemicals	5.1	3.6	2.5	14.3
Metals	3.6	2.2	n.d.	24.2
Textiles	1.9	1.2	1.5	59.0
Wood, pulp and paper	1.3	1.1	3.8	87.6
Food and tobacco	1.2	1.4	1.1	78.3
Iron and steel	1.2	0.6	0.3	28.7
All industries	12.1	10.6	9.9	13.3

Source: Data from METI 2003.
Note: n.d. = no data.

TABLE 36. Reverse Imports and Overseas Production Ratios in Japan

Industry	Reverse Imports[a]		Overseas Production Ratios[b]	
	2000	1997	2000	1997
Precision instruments	9.9	10.5	27.1	24.4
Electrical machinery	3.9	3.5	30.4	28.3
Industrial machinery	3.3	2.9	23.2	22.8
Ceramics, stone, and clay	2.2	1.0	25.4	16.6
Textiles	1.9	1.8	17.2	17.3
Wood, pulp and paper	1.5	1.1	7.2	5.7
Metals	1.0	1.2	7.1	7.2
Food and tobacco	0.8	0.9	7.0	7.5
Nonferrous metals	0.7	0.4	9.4	7.9
Other manufacturing	0.5	0.5	9.5	11.5
Chemicals	0.4	0.5	11.9	11.1
Transport equipment	0.3	0.2	35.9	26.2
Iron and steel	0.1	0.1	7.1	7.2
All industries	1.8	1.5	22.5	19.4

Source: Data from METI 2003.
[a]Exports of Japanese foreign affiliates to Japan divided by total shipments of Japanese parents.
[b]Sales of Japanese foreign affiliates divided by total shipments of Japanese parents.

relevant to the incentives for regionalism. Historically, Japanese affiliates in North America and Europe have relied heavily on their corporate parents in Japan for technology, parts, and components, while they have rarely established export ties back to Japan. East Asian affiliates, however, have been more extensively integrated with Japanese production. Moreover, Japanese affiliates have increased their local procurement in the region and exports back to Japan since the Asian financial crisis. In 2000, East Asia accounted for 80 percent of ¥5.6 trillion in Japanese imports from foreign affiliates. Included in this total was ¥740.7 billion imported from China, up from ¥285.3 billion in 1996 (METI 2002b, 10–11).

Tables 37–39 examine the sales and trade of Japan's East Asian affiliates in the five industries with the most overseas production in the region: precision instruments, electrical machinery, industrial machinery, textiles and apparel, and transport equipment.[10] Table 37 shows the sales destinations of East Asian affiliates in different areas to illustrate their varied functions. Some are market-seeking investments that sell primarily in host countries, as with transport equipment in ASEAN and the NIEs, and textiles and apparel in the NIEs. Other foreign affiliates serve as procurement sources for Japanese factories: precision instruments, industrial machinery, transport equipment, and textiles and apparel in China; industrial machinery and precision instruments in ASEAN; and precision instruments in the NIEs. Finally, there are export platforms, such as electrical machinery in all three areas, industrial machinery in the NIEs, and textiles and apparel in ASEAN.

Three generalizations lead to expectations about the trade preferences of Japanese multinationals. First, high affiliate sales to Japan strengthen the motives for regional trade liberalization to facilitate two-way trade flows for offshore procurement. Second, export platforms raise the risks of retaliation due to dependence on sales to third countries. Third, affiliates oriented toward local markets benefit from import barriers in host countries, which reduces the incentives for regional integration.

Applying these generalizations, table 37 points to four conclusions. First, large sales shares to Japan imply that production-sharing networks were most fully developed in precision instruments (in all three areas) and industrial machinery (China and ASEAN, but not the NIEs). Hypothesis 3 predicts the strongest support for regional trade liberalization in these two industries. Second, foreign affiliates in electrical machinery operated primarily as export platforms, secondarily as offshore suppliers; the sales orientation toward third

10. These data cover the fourth quarter 2001 through the third quarter 2002.

countries rather than Japan should temper the motives for regional arrangements. Third, offshore production of textiles and apparel served Japanese customers from China, third markets from Southeast Asia, and local consumers in the NIEs, again pointing to mixed incentives for regional arrangements. Fourth, transport equipment affiliates were oriented to host markets, where they benefited from continued trade protection—except in China, where Japanese companies were expanding offshore procurement.

TABLE 37.   Sales of Japan's East Asian Affiliates, 2002

Industry/Area	Percentage of Sales in Host Country	Percentage of Sales to Japan	Percentage of Sales to Third Countries
China and Hong Kong			
Precision instruments	28.7	63.3	7.9
Electrical machinery	28.9	28.8	42.3
Industrial machinery	19.7	56.2	24.1
Textiles and apparel	43.6	47.1	9.4
Transport equipment	33.4	48.2	18.3
ASEAN[a]			
Precision instruments	28.6	55.5	15.9
Electrical machinery	16.2	31.9	51.9
Industrial machinery	25.4	56.9	17.7
Textiles and apparel	45.3	14.0	40.6
Transport equipment	79.7	7.0	13.2
NIE[b]			
Precision instruments	12.4	80.3	7.3
Electrical machinery	44.4	19.7	35.9
Industrial machinery	47.3	13.6	39.0
Textiles and apparel	70.1	0.8	29.1
Transport equipment	88.3	3.5	8.2

Source: Data from METI 2003.
[a]Indonesia, Malaysia, Philippines, and Thailand.
[b]Singapore, South Korea, and Taiwan.

TABLE 38.   Intrafirm Trade of Japan's East Asian Affiliates, 2002

Industry	Percentage of Sales Exported to Japanese Parents			Percentage of Sales Imported from Japanese Parents		
	China	ASEAN	NIE	China	ASEAN	NIE
Precision instruments	29.6	28.8	32.3	16.8	10.4	10.3
Electrical machinery	17.8	22.8	15.8	10.8	9.5	17.3
Industrial machinery	50.8	7.9	21.5	18.3	5.4	13.1
Textiles and apparel	29.8	6.1	0.7	16.7	6.8	13.7
Transport equipment	46.2	4.9	0.8	30.5	15.7	16.6

Source: Data from METI 2003.

The intrafirm trade of Japan's East Asian affiliates in table 38 supports these generalizations. Foreign affiliates were most closely integrated with Japanese production in precision instruments, followed by electrical machinery and industrial machinery. In textiles and apparel and transport equipment, only Chinese affiliates had production-sharing links with Japanese parents.

These figures also suggest that the triangular trade patterns associated with the initial movement of Japanese firms into the East Asian region were disappearing. Foreign affiliates were no longer so heavily dependent on Japanese parents for technology, parts, and components, while Japanese parents used East Asia as a source of inputs and supplies more frequently. As table 39 shows, only Japanese affiliates in the NIEs ran deficits in intrafirm trade with Japan; ASEAN and China enjoyed large surpluses as a result of Japanese FDI (despite the deficit in the transport equipment trade of ASEAN countries).

Changing patterns of Japanese production, trade, and procurement also affected the trade of East Asian countries with one another as Japanese companies integrated the activities of affiliated firms and developed local suppliers. Intraregional trade in East Asia, excluding Japan, was mostly electrical and electronic equipment (31.6 percent), machinery (15.9 percent), and chemicals (11 percent). By comparison, intraregional trade was minuscule in motor vehicles (0.5 percent), motor vehicle parts (0.4 percent), and other transport equipment (1.3 percent). Generally, the data show growing procurement in East Asia for intermediate components incorporated in finished products ultimately sent outside the region. For example, the share of East Asian exports sold inside the region was high for inputs such as electronic tubes and semiconductors (68.1 percent), integrated circuits (58.7 percent), other electronic parts (51.2 percent), and parts for computers and peripherals (46.3 percent). By comparison, finished goods were exported outside the region, particularly audio equipment (85.2 percent extraregional exports),

TABLE 39.   Intrafirm Trade Balances of Japan's East Asian Affiliates, 2002

Industry	All Asia	China	ASEAN	NIE
All manufacturing	574,971	315,610	343,201	−72,535
Electrical machinery	513,799	128,746	411,361	−26,368
Industrial machinery	169,345	149,962	5,969	13,158
Precision instruments	73,886	32,199	24,025	16,728
Textiles	9,124	13,132	−1,475	−3,647
Transport equipment	−195,889	12,664	−134,262	−55,677

Source: Data from METI 2003.
Note: Amounts are million Japanese yen.

video equipment (80.5 percent), and computers and peripherals (72.8 percent). Similar divisions existed in textiles and apparel: 52 percent of textile and fiber exports remained in the region, while 83.1 percent of clothing exports left Asia (JETRO 2003, 8–9).

To sum up, today production sharing by Japanese companies in the East Asian region is most developed in precision instruments, electrical machinery, and industrial machinery—notably photographic and optical equipment, consumer electronics, semiconductors and integrated circuits, and computers and peripherals. More so than in other branches of East Asian industry, "firms in the region are increasingly linked across borders in complex and ongoing relationships that extend beyond the boundary of the firm and span the entire value-chain in the given activity" (Borrus, Ernst, and Haggard 2000, 1). In these sectors, intrafirm trade is substantial, reverse imports are becoming significant, and triangular trading patterns have disappeared. These cross-border production networks integrate Japanese capital and technology, the managerial skills and know-how of firms from Taiwan and South Korea, and the labor pool available in Southeast Asia and China.

In other industries with high levels of FDI, notably textiles and apparel, transport equipment, and chemicals, production sharing remains in its infancy. In these sectors, intrafirm trade is less significant (except in transport equipment), intraregional trade is small, reverse importing into Japan is uncommon, and triangular trading links persist. Japanese affiliates in East Asia tend to service local markets or operate as export platforms; neither function integrates the region more closely with Japan.

In all of these industries, barriers to regional trade and investment inhibit further specialization along the value chain. East Asian countries retain high tariffs on many manufactured articles conducive to production sharing. METI points to high bound tariff rates in Malaysia on transport equipment (22.6 percent), textiles (21.5 percent), and electrical equipment (30 percent maximum); in Indonesia on transport equipment (30.6 percent), textiles (27.8 percent), and electrical equipment (26.1 percent); and in Thailand on transport equipment (47.6 percent) and electronics (31.6 percent).[11] Also, the AFTA Temporary Exclusion List delays trade liberalization for transport equipment, electronics, and machinery in certain ASEAN countries. Moreover, regional disputes threaten to disrupt production-sharing trade: China, for example, imposed 100 percent tariffs on Japanese automobiles, air conditioners, and cellular telephones in response to Japanese safeguards on certain agricultural goods

11. METI 2002a, 191–98. In practice, applied tariff rates tend to be lower than these figures.

in 2001.[12] Finally, equity restrictions, TRIMs, and other regulatory rules create persistent uncertainties for foreign investors in the East Asian region.

But the elimination of these barriers would have very different effects in different industries, as the following section illustrates. In electrical, electronic, and photographic equipment, regional integration would allow Japanese companies to further rationalize East Asian production by restructuring high-cost "mini-Matsus," that is, small factories manufacturing full product lines for host markets.[13] Specifically, foreign affiliates could be specialized to perform discrete steps along the supply chain to eliminate duplication and gain scale economies.

In other sectors, however, adjustment to regional free trade would be difficult. In "areas like automobiles, chemicals, textiles, or foodstuffs," Legewie (2000, 89) notes, "the remaining tariff walls still limit the scope for further production concentration or confine it to the area of parts and components." While regional trade liberalization would open up such opportunities, East Asian affiliates generally are less prepared to face tough competition. Moreover, multinational companies earn substantial rents in protected regional markets, and resistance to opening the Japanese market is stronger. Under these circumstances, incentives to form a regional arrangement are low.

Regionally Oriented Industries

As Japanese companies expand production in East Asia, increasingly they organize their activities on a regional basis. Leaders in this regionalization of production include Matsushita, which has moved to streamline its regional operations, centered in Malaysia, where the firm accounts for 4 percent of the manufacturing workforce, and Toyota, which has strengthened its production and supplier base in the region, particularly in Thailand, through its "Toyota Cooperation Club" (UNCTAD 2001, 146–47). These strategies have created local industrial agglomerations, such as electronics around Penang, Malaysia, and automobiles along Thailand's eastern seaboard; in some cases, production linkages extend back to Japan.

There is anecdotal evidence that this trend has raised Japanese industry's interest in regional arrangements to liberalize trade and safeguard FDI. The proposed AFTA, according to Hatch and Yamamura (1996, 35), "was enthusiasti-

12. "Japan Call to China on Tariffs," *Financial Times*, June 23, 2001, 8.
13. The term refers to affiliates of Matsushita, which was among the first Japanese electronics firms to invest in local production in East Asia. In the late 1990s, Matsushita still produced televisions at seven different locations in Asia (not including China, where it has established assembly plants more recently), a severe drain on economies of scale (Legewie 2000, 87).

cally received by Japanese multinationals." Strong support for an expanded regional role exists in "important sections of Japan's business community, which have been closely involved in talks on bilateral arrangements," the *Financial Times* reports.[14] Recently these pressures have been extended to China, as METI (2002a, 102) notes: "Among the Japanese companies that have entered China, an extremely large number have been calling for greater transparency of policies and measures, as well as consistent and fair implementation for all trade-related policies and measures."

A deeper look at the incentive structures in Japanese industry suggests that support for a regional arrangement in East Asia is less extensive than it might appear, however. Regarding AFTA, Ravenhill (1995, 856) observes: "Many foreign investors favored liberalization of intraregional trade and welcomed the prospect of producing for a region-wide market. Others, who had committed themselves to high-cost, small production runs under import substitution regimes and local content requirements, were less enthusiastic." The case studies in this chapter suggest that Japanese firms in electronics, electrical machinery, and precision instruments have reasons to embrace the welcoming approach to regional trade liberalization. Elsewhere, lack of enthusiasm tends to prevail. In the automobile industry, Japanese multinationals have sunk considerable capital in production strategies oriented to tariff-protected host markets, and liberalizing this trading environment would be costly. In textiles and apparel, large firms, particularly garment manufacturers, have developed production-sharing networks that would benefit from more open markets in both the region and Japan, but nationally oriented textile producers have mobilized to push for new barriers to imports, a sign of growing industry divisions over trade.

Electronics: FDI-Led Regional Integration

Electronic equipment was a leading export item in Japan's postwar development, as producers penetrated foreign markets with transistor radios in the 1960s and proceeded to establish dominant positions in televisions and audiovisual equipment, integrated circuits, and photographic and optical equipment. In 1985, Japan controlled close to 90 percent of world markets for VCRs, photocopiers, and 256K and 1MB memory chips. By 1990, office machines, telecommunications equipment, and other electrical machines accounted for 29 percent of Japan's exports, for the first time surpassing automotive products and other transport equipment (WTO 1998b, 159).

14. "Japan Aims for South Korea Trade Deal," *Financial Times*, November 3, 2000, 6.

In 1985, table 40 shows, Japanese firms depended on sales abroad and strongly preferred exports to foreign production. The leading companies exported 20 to 50 percent of sales, and exports from Japan exceeded foreign production in every case—often by a factor of three or more. When companies had established East Asian production—which was not often—these investments served one of two purposes. First, cheap labor and regulatory incentives in export-processing zones attracted assembly-based manufacturing destined for foreign markets. Second, Japanese companies established "mini-Matsus" to manufacture "simple products like batteries, radios, electric fans, rice cookers and other low-end home appliances, small TV sets and some related components" for protected host markets in Southeast Asia (Ernst 2000, 82).

After 1985, electronics companies rapidly transferred manufacturing functions from Japan to East Asia. The yen's rise after the Plaza Accord, followed by another round of appreciation after 1990 and the collapse of the bubble economy in Japan, "forced firms to cut costs at every stage of the value-chain" (Ernst 2000, 93). While previously East Asian affiliates manufactured a full range of household items, processes gradually were specialized across countries. Because the strong yen made components imports from Japan expensive, firms persuaded their suppliers to move offshore or developed local procurement sources. To compete more effectively with South Korean producers that had gained a price advantage from exchange rate movements, companies such

TABLE 40. Export Dependence of Electronic and Photographic Equipment Companies

Company[a]	Exports from Japan as a Percentage of Total Shipments		Exports from Japan Divided by Sales of Foreign Affiliates	
	1985	2001	1985	2001
Hitachi	19.9	12.4	1.6	0.5[b]
Matsushita Electric	25.2	19.9	3.6	0.7
Sony	53.5	26.8	2.6	1.3
Toshiba	21.8	21.2	3.6	0.7
Fujitsu	20.1	11.2	3.0	0.8[b]
NEC	27.2	12.9	4.5	
Mitsubishi Electric	23.7	16.3	1.9	1.0
Canon	44.9	47.0	1.7	1.6
Sanyo Electric	42.3	19.3	13.6	0.9[b]
Sharp	49.5	29.6	7.3	
Fuji Photo Film	31.2	23.3		0.4
Ricoh	33.7	19.5		1.3[b]

Source: Data from UNCTC 1988, 533–45; UNCTAD 2002, 47.
[a]Descending order of total sales in 2001.
[b]Based on sales of foreign affiliates in 1996.

as Matsushita established "global export platform mega-plants" in Southeast Asia to maximize scale economies (Ernst 2000, 89).[15]

As part of this process, companies increasingly relied on East Asian affiliates as procurement sources for Japanese production. The share of intermediate components in imports increased by 50 percent or more for computers and peripherals, electrical appliances, telecommunication equipment, and heavy electric machinery (WTO 1998b, 109). In addition, firms began to reverse import finished goods: for example, reverse-imported color televisions into Japan jumped from 1.7 million in 1989 to 6 million in 1994, and increases also occurred in audiovisual equipment and computer products. To reduce frictions over Japan's large trade surpluses, Matsushita issued plans in 1989 to import 10 percent of the components for its Japanese production. When the firm achieved its ¥420 billion target two years early in 1991, it established a goal of ¥600 billion for 1993. Toshiba also sought to double imports to ¥200 billion and increase foreign production from ¥300 billion to ¥500 billion by 1992. These changes reduced exports relative to output in Japan and boosted foreign production, as table 40 illustrates. As imports climbed, firms shifted from consumer electronics to higher-margin industrial electronics and electronic components. With the large share of intrafirm trade and outsourcing in imports, there were no calls for trade protection (Yoshimatsu 2000, 92–99).

The regionalization of Japan's electronics industry not only has integrated East Asia into Japanese production but also has promoted trade and production linkages among East Asian countries. Specialization in the region has operated in tiers, with Japan at the top; the four NIEs on the second rung; Malaysia, Thailand, Indonesia, and the Philippines third; and finally China and Vietnam. These development patterns have been "highly conducive to the emergence of regional production networks" because they "created unusually heterogeneous production capabilities and thus a high degree of intra-regional complementarity" (Borrus, Ernst, and Haggard 2000, 12–13). At the same time that these regional production networks provide a motive to open markets further, the legacy of import substitution—an ongoing industrial dualism in which mini-Matsus coexist with modern, large-scale export platforms—suggests that regional trade liberalization would create opportunities for multinational companies to enhance productivity through economies of scale.

15. The responses of individual firms varied. Matsushita regionalized aggressively, as its affiliates quickly shifted from host markets to "export platform production . . . on a massive scale." In contrast, Sony concentrated most of its overseas production in North America and Europe, while in East Asia it moved abroad more tentatively. Today, Ernst concludes, "Sony's Asian production networks are still relatively underdeveloped." Small firms such as Sanyo, Aiwa, and Uniden were the first to establish outsourcing arrangements in East Asia, during the late 1970s (Ernst 2000, 91–93).

At least until recently, these incentives apparently had not reached a critical mass. According to Ernst (2000, 90), while electronics companies "have been more substantially exposed to international production" than other branches of Japanese manufacturing, "they still lag behind their American and European counterparts." Ernst (2000, 82–86) and Guerrieri (2000, 44–50) also note the persistence of triangular patterns in East Asian electronics trade into the late 1990s—evidence that Japanese production networks remained "highly centralized" and closed to outsiders. Yet the latest data, presented earlier, suggest that trade triangles are gone, reverse imports have grown, and procurement has opened up. These trends suggest large benefits for Japanese companies from regional trade liberalization.

The JSEPA treaty is consistent with these imputed interests. Electronics and components account for 45 percent of Singapore's manufacturing, an extreme level of specialization. More than 40 percent of the industry's employees work in Japanese affiliates (WTO 2000a, 89). Singapore also is the world's third-largest exporter of office and telecommunication equipment, after the United States and Japan, and the sixth-largest importer.[16] Though tariffs on Japan-Singapore IT trade had been phased out under the WTO, the JSEPA treaty went further, eliminating nontariff barriers and easing administrative and customs burdens. The arrangement also established liberal rules of origin, in recognition that "companies are typically tightly integrated into an intricate supply chain network throughout the region" (Joint Study Group 2000, chap. 2, 5).

Even greater gains could be reaped from regional arrangements with countries that previously practiced import substitution, where tariffs are higher and restrictions on Japanese affiliates greater. For example, while most electronics can be imported into Indonesia duty-free, televisions and TV components must pay 20 percent tariffs (WTO 1998a, 110). Such barriers exist throughout Southeast Asia. Without these nuisances, Japanese companies could assimilate their domestic operations, mini-Matsus, and newly established export platforms into a unified multinational structure to specialize production and gain scale economies. Thus, pressure from the electronics industry for regional arrangements is likely to continue to gain strength.

Automobiles: Building a Regional Fortress

Japan's automotive industry, like its electronics industry, has been highly export oriented. Table 41 shows that the four leading automakers exported 43–66

16. "Information Technology (IT) Products: Free Trade for a Dynamic Trade Sector," WTO, http://www.wto.org/english/thewto_e/minist_e/min01_e/brief_e/brief10_e.htm.

TABLE 41.   Export Dependence of Automotive Companies

Company[a]	Exports from Japan as a Percentage of Total Shipments		Exports from Japan Divided by Sales of Foreign Affiliates	
	1985	2001	1985	2001
Toyota	43.0	30.8	8.6	0.5
Honda	53.1	27.4	4.0	
Nissan	48.9	25.0		0.6
Mazda	66.3	33.9	34.9	0.6
Nippon Denso	13.3	15.8	0.8	
Isuzu	58.6	31.1	45.1	5.5
Suzuki	44.0	39.3	3.3	3.4[b]
Daihatsu	16.7		1.4	
Fuji Heavy Industries	59.9	30.1		1.1[b]
Kawasaki Heavy Industries	41.0	34.4	10.5	
Yamaha Motor	67.8	50.7	10.8	0.7

Source: Data from UNCTC 1988, 533–45; UNCTAD 2002, 47.

[a]Descending order of total sales in 2001.

[b]Based on sales of foreign affiliates in 1996.

percent of their sales in 1985. Even the largest companies centralized production in Japan, with little output abroad. VERs by the United States and the EC caused Japanese automakers to begin manufacturing in North America and Europe in the 1980s. By 2001, all except second-tier producers Isuzu and Suzuki generated more sales abroad than they exported from Japan.[17] But even as companies transferred capacity overseas, East Asia was not an important destination for FDI: North America accounted for 65 percent of foreign affiliate sales, Europe 13.1 percent, and East Asia only 11.5 percent (METI 2003).

Unlike the electronics industry, Japan's East Asian automotive affiliates produce for host markets exclusively. Table 37 shows that in the four ASEAN countries, which accounted for three-quarters of affiliate production in the region, 79.7 percent of sales were made locally in 2002; in the NIEs, which accounted for one-fifth of Japan's East Asian production, 88.3 percent of sales were domestic. These figures were down slightly from 1997, when 86.1 percent of ASEAN and 91.5 percent of NIE sales were local. Though affiliates in the two areas imported one-sixth of their sales from Japan, they almost never exported back to Japanese parents (see table 38).

The reason for these patterns of production and trade is simple: high tariffs

17. Even so, Japan exported 4.4 million of the 10 million automobiles it produced in 1998. Japanese companies manufactured an additional 2.4 million vehicles in the United States and 910,000 in the EC that year (WTO 2000b, 91).

TABLE 42.   Automotive Policies in Southeast Asia

	Tariffs (%)		Local Content Rules (%)	
Malaysia	*Import duties*		Passenger cars	45–60
	Completely knocked down	42		
	Completely built up[a]	200		
	Excise taxes			
	Passenger cars	25–65		
	Motorcycles	10–20		
	Other vehicles	0–45		
Indonesia	*Import duties*		Tariffs on automobile parts vary	
	Passenger cars	200	inversely with local content, from	
	Jeeps	100	100% (20% local content or less)	
	Other vehicles	0–100	to 0% (60% local content or	
			more); for commercial vehicles,	
	Built-up vehicle surcharge		tariffs range from 40% (20% lo-	
	Passenger cars	100	cal content or less) to 0% (40%	
	Other vehicles	40	local content or more).	
Thailand	*Import duties*		Passenger cars	54
	Completely knocked down	22	Motorcycles	70
	Completely built up	80	Other vehicles[b]	60–100
			Automobile engines[c]	20–70
	Excise taxes	37–50	Motorcycle engines[c]	30–80

Source: Data from WTO 1997, 104–7; WTO 1998a, 68–69, 112–15; WTO 1999, 62, 99.
[a]Limit 80 per company.
[b]Exact figure depends on size and type of vehicle.
[c]Local content requirement increases by 10% each year after production begins.

and local content rules forced Japanese firms to manufacture locally to access national markets, particularly in Southeast Asia. Table 42 summarizes automotive policies in Malaysia, Indonesia, and Thailand. In each case, completely built-up cars are subject to high tariffs, import licensing, and other surcharges and excise taxes; completely knocked-down vehicles, though less heavily taxed, face significant barriers as well.[18] Automobile assemblers also must satisfy local content rules to avoid sanctions (Malaysia), earn corporate tax exemptions (Thailand), or secure import tariff rebates (Indonesia).

Because foreign affiliates have been oriented to host markets, unexploited scale economies are substantial. Most plants manufacture less than 10,000 vehicles, and few models sell more than 5,000 units. In 1993, Thailand produced 419,861 automobiles, trucks, and buses, up from 98,148 in 1987, and Japanese

18. Even Singapore imposed uncharacteristically high tariffs of 41 percent on motor vehicles and 12 percent on motorcycles (WTO 1996, 77).

affiliates contributed more than 90 percent of this output. Divided among twelve assemblers and thirty-five models, this amounted to 35,000 vehicles per firm and 12,000 per model (WTO 1995c, 105). In Malaysia, where Japanese affiliates coexist with national firms Proton (a joint venture with Mitsubishi) and Perodua (a joint venture with Daihatsu), output per company was 14,983 (WTO 1997, 104).

To expand volume and eliminate duplication in parts manufacturing, Japanese companies have pushed for regional liberalization in ASEAN. In 1988, ASEAN adopted the Brand-to-Brand Complementation (BBC) program, which provided tariff preferences for automotive parts traded among designated producers located in different ASEAN countries. The BBC, Ravenhill (1995, 852) writes, originated "at the behest of Japanese automobile companies which by then had established a dominant position in the Southeast Asian market." Mitsubishi Motors, which owned factories in Thailand, Indonesia, and the Philippines, in addition to its Proton joint venture in Malaysia, proposed the idea in 1987 to the ASEAN Committee on Industry Materials and Energy in an effort to integrate production regionally and reduce overhead. Mitsubishi's plan involved 90 percent tariff rebates on imported parts, plus local content credits for exports from ASEAN, so that the firm could centralize components manufacturing and reduce regulatory compliance costs. In the final plan, ASEAN countries reduced tariff preferences to 50 percent and limited these benefits to automotive assemblers, which had to submit formal proposals to gain approval. Indonesia initially refused to participate in the BBC. Even so, companies lined up to submit plans, beginning with Mitsubishi, followed by Toyota, Honda, Nissan, and the Swedish automaker Volvo (Machado 1994, 313–18).

The BBC scheme opened up opportunities for Japanese companies to develop regional production networks. In addition, firms needed to gain scale economies not only in assembly but more significantly in parts such as alternators, distributors, and starter motors because national markets in Southeast Asia were a small fraction of MES. Automotive assemblers straining to meet local content rules pressured their suppliers to begin production in ASEAN. This increased procurement within the region and reduced imports of parts and components from Japan. For example, Toyota integrated its three plants in Thailand with factories in Indonesia, Malaysia, and the Philippines to centralize production of intermediate components: diesel engines and pressed parts were sourced in Thailand, gas engines in Indonesia, transmissions in the Philippines, and steering gears and automotive electronics in Malaysia; a trading center in Singapore monitored and coordinated the transfer of these components across factories. Subsequently, Toyota's intra-affiliate trade in ASEAN soared from ¥1.6 billion in 1992 to ¥15.5 billion in 1994, and then to ¥35.6 billion in 1996 (Yoshimatsu 2002, 131–32; Hatch 2004, 160–65).

Because of the development of regionally oriented production and supply systems in Southeast Asia, Hatch (2004, 161) writes, Japanese automakers "have . . . endorsed the ASEAN Free Trade Agreement." The January 1992 ASEAN summit envisioned AFTA by 2007, with 0–5 percent tariffs under the Common Effective Preferential Tariff. Due to these plans, the BBC program was deemed unnecessary and scheduled for termination. But companies had sunk substantial capital in anticipation that reorienting their operations from a national to a regional basis would continue to earn them special privileges. Thus, "MNCs and their local affiliates opposed the scrapping of the BBC scheme. . . . The Japanese government and the Japanese Automobile Manufacturers Association (JAMA) also opposed the scrapping." Nippon Denso, the largest automotive components producer in Japan, not only lobbied to retain the BBC program but also sought to extend it from assembly to parts (Yoshimatsu 2002, 131–32).

Pressure from assemblers and parts producers led to the establishment of the ASEAN Industrial Cooperation (AICO) program to replace the BBC scheme in 1996. Under this arrangement, firms located in different ASEAN countries could form AICO partnerships (provided that ASEAN nationals held 30 percent of the equity) to gain 0–5 percent preferential tariffs on their mutual trade, local content accreditation for parts imported from one another, and additional incentives. After the financial crisis, a temporary waiver of the equity rule and the program's extension to intra-affiliate trade eased AICO eligibility. These changes reflected "demands from the private sector," as Japanese companies and JAMA pushed to eliminate restrictive provisions and speed the implementation of the program.[19] Approvals soared from 2 in 1998 to 101 in 2003.

Though firms outside the automotive industry can earn AICO privileges, table 43 shows that automakers have accounted for 87.2 percent of approved proposals since its inception. Moreover, Japanese-affiliated companies have earned nine out of every ten AICO approvals for automotive products, led by Toyota and Honda with twenty-seven each. Over the last five years, Honda

---

19. Multinationals opposed the equity rule in the AICO plan, as some had to boost the stakes of local investors to qualify. Toyota employed an "umbrella" method of applying on behalf of its suppliers (which therefore would not have to meet the requirement), but ASEAN countries reaffirmed the 30 percent equity requirement in 1997. With the onset of the financial crisis, however, this rule became self-defeating since local firms needed greater foreign participation in their capital structure to survive the downturn. See Yoshimatsu 2002, 132–34, 138–41.

TABLE 43.   AICO and Japanese Companies

By Product Category	Number of Approvals	Share of Approvals
Automobile assembly	74	73.3
Automobile components	14	13.9
Electronic and electrical products	5	5.0
Food processing	5	5.0
Machinery	2	2.0
Glass	1	1.0

By Company	Number of approvals[a]	Share of Approvals
Toyota	27	26.2
Honda	27	26.2
Nippon Denso	7	6.8
Nissan	5	4.9
Volvo (Sweden)	5	4.9
Nestlé (Switzerland)	4	3.9
Goya (United States)	4	3.9
Yamaha Motor	3	2.9
Mitsubishi Electric	3	2.9
Mitsubishi Motors	2	1.9
Sony	2	1.9
Isuzu	2	1.9
Ford (United States)	2	1.9
All others (1 approval each)	10	9.8

Source: Data compiled from "Approved AICO Applications as of 10 February 2003," ASEAN Secretariat, http://www.aseansec.org/6398.htm.

[a]Total adds to 103 because two projects include more than one foreign-owned firm.

saved ¥6 billion on import tariffs and another ¥4.6 billion by eliminating duplication; the company expanded ASEAN sourcing from 4.8 percent to 20.8 percent of inputs and cut imports from Japan to 34.9 percent from 55.4 percent (Yoshimatsu 2002, 142).

Despite their enthusiasm for ASEAN trade liberalization, Japanese automakers have opposed opening the region to outside imports. A Thai Board of Investment report notes, "Japanese manufacturers and their Thai joint venture partners have a formidable store of vested interests and carry tremendous influence in policy-making circles. Liberalization policies directly threaten the comfortable operating environment they have constructed over the past twenty years."[20] Surveying recent events, Hatch (2002, 253) writes:

20. "World's Car Makers Prefer the Thai Tiger: An Opening Market in a Sea of Protection Makes Thailand the Region's Leader," *Financial Times*, November 9, 1994, 4.

Japanese automakers likely cooperated in a bid to keep non-Japanese automakers from gaining a foothold in Southeast Asian markets. Organized around groups such as the Thai Automotive Industry Association and the Association of Indonesian Automotive Industries, Japanese automakers lobbied to maintain restrictive measures such as a relatively high tariff on imports from outside ASEAN and domestic content requirements that impede market entry.

Lately Japanese companies have resisted U.S. pressure to open up automotive trade in the region. Toyota has argued that the liberalization of ASEAN automotive policies should be phased in over long periods to allow established companies time to adjust. Thai parts producers, including affiliates of Nippon Denso, lobbied to increase tariffs on completely knocked-down vehicles from 20 percent to 33 percent in 1999. Takashi Imai, head of Keidanren, succinctly expressed the views of Japanese automakers: "all ASEAN companies would go into bankruptcy if tariffs were removed all at once. Accordingly, tariffs should be removed gradually, targeting the year 2010 or 2020. But, it is better to remove tariffs within the ASEAN region" (Yoshimatsu 2002, 142–43).

Because production linkages between Japanese plants and East Asian affiliates are limited, it is even doubtful that Japanese automakers would want a regional arrangement between ASEAN and Japan. Though Toyota, Honda, and Nissan implemented import expansion programs starting in 1989, these plans focused on reverse importing from the United States to defuse UAW pressure for local content rules on Japanese affiliates and antidumping actions by the Big Three. In 1997 North America accounted for 36 percent of the minuscule total of automotive products reverse imported into Japan, compared to just 40 percent for ASEAN.[21] After the financial crisis, Toyota, Honda, and other firms expanded Southeast Asian procurement to assist foreign affiliates and keiretsu suppliers. As a result, reverse imports from ASEAN more than doubled in 1997–2002, from ¥33.4 billion to ¥87.2 billion.[22] But these increases came off low base amounts, and overall sourcing from the region remains insignificant as a proportion of output in Japan.

Thus, Japanese automakers have shifted from national to regional strategies, premised on the expectation of continued liberalization in ASEAN and the preservation of external barriers against outside competitors. Toyota Motor Thailand, which already acquires 79 percent of its inputs from Toyota-affiliated

21. Mostly these were Honda Accords produced in Ohio. See Yoshimatsu 2000, 66–71, 79–82.
22. Over the same period, reverse imports from China and Hong Kong soared from ¥8.6 billion to ¥39 billion (METI 2003).

companies and Japanese joint ventures in the region, seeks to achieve 100 percent local procurement by the time AFTA automotive commitments are implemented in 2005 (UNCTAD 2001, 146). Japanese firms also have raised their equity stakes in joint ventures in anticipation that protected national markets soon will be opened to regional trade.[23] In the meantime, barriers to entry have been increased as Thailand extended local content rules and raised tariffs on completely built-up autos and Malaysia and the Philippines introduced new tariffs on automobiles and parts during the financial crisis. For Japanese companies ensconced inside their ASEAN fortress, the continued separation of East Asia's automotive industry from the outside world merely extends their dominance in the region.

Textiles and Apparel: Protectionists versus Regionalists

Labor-intensive manufactures are the most heavily protected activities in Japan after agriculture. Japan imposes its highest tariffs on footwear (51.4 percent), leather products (12.6 percent), and clothing (10.9 percent).[24] Despite these restraints, employment in textiles, apparel, and fibers declined by one-third to 825,000 in 1996 from 1.2 million in 1985, as twenty-one thousand factories closed in barely a decade. In textiles and apparel, Japan shifted to a net import basis in 1987, and imports soared from 16.3 percent of consumption in 1980 to more than 50 percent after 1993 (Yoshimatsu 2000, 133). A key factor has been the growth of Chinese competition.[25] Even in capital-intensive synthetic fibers, Taiwan, South Korea, and China have moved ahead in polyester staple and filament, leaving Japan in the lead only in acrylic. Thus, "Japanese textile producers have been apprehensive about the rapid increase in the production capacity of their Asian neighbors" (Yoshimatsu 2000, 157).

Larger companies began to move offshore in the 1970s. In fact, they were among the first in Japan to do so, as textiles and apparel (including synthetic fibers) accounted for 40 percent of Japan's FDI stock in East Asia in 1974. The two leading firms, Toray and Teijin, were responsible for almost all of this

23. Daihatsu, now part of Toyota, increased its share of Perodua, Malaysia's second-largest automaker, from 25 percent to 51 percent. This move came in preparation for the cut in Malaysian auto tariffs (delayed to 2005) from as high as 300 percent to no more than 5 percent ("Daihatsu Control of Perodua Stirs Malaysian Resentment," *Financial Times*, September 5, 2001, 31).

24. WTO 2000b, 141–43. Tariff-rate quotas apply rates as high as 60 percent on overquota imports of footwear and leather products.

25. Among Japan's twenty fastest growing import categories in 2000, China's import share surpassed 70 percent in seven categories: tee shirts, women's formalwear, women's blouses and shirts, sweaters and jerseys, men's formalwear, men's shirts, and sportswear (JETRO 2001, 20).

investment. But rather than transferring capacity out of Japan or increasing regional procurement, the big two sought to maintain their markets for fiber exports by integrating into weaving, processing, and finishing.[26] Moreover, import licensing discouraged apparel firms from developing offshore supply chains. In the 1980s, Dore (1986, 196–97) noted that METI had approved a few licenses for outward processing in China but added: "generally the procedure is sufficiently cumbersome to be an effective deterrent."[27] Producers in Hong Kong, Taiwan, and South Korea were too advanced to require Japanese technology or materials. Thus, FDI did little to integrate East Asia more closely with Japan.

Meanwhile Japanese lobby groups pushed for trade protection as the industry faced growing import competition. The Japan Textile Industry Federation and the Japan Spinners Association sought MFA quotas against South Korea and Taiwan as early as 1973, and the Japan Cotton and Synthetic Fiber Weaving Association began to push for import limits on Chinese cotton fabrics in 1975. Protectionist pressures intensified with escalating imports, as at least four industry associations petitioned for MFA quotas in 1985–88. Unable to win lasting protection, despite lobbying the Liberal Democratic Party (LDP) to pressure METI, lobby groups turned to unfair trade laws. Between 1982 and 1993, METI investigated just seven antidumping and countervailing duty cases—four involved textiles and apparel. These claims resulted in VERs on cotton yarn from South Korea and raw silk and silk fabrics from South Korea and China (Yoshimatsu 2000, 135–40).

Finally METI relented and organized hearings to prepare for MFA restrictions, resulting in guidelines for their application in 1994. Though small, nationally oriented yarn, fiber, and knitwear producers were the most enthusiastic, large companies with overseas operations also backed the protectionist cause at first (Yoshimatsu 2000, 141–43). As pro-MFA pressures gained strength, a Teijin executive complained that without trade barriers, "the textile and clothing industries will be sacrificed."[28] Large textile companies continued

---

26. Uriu 1996, 157–60. In contrast, apparel producers never had important markets in East Asia. These firms were smaller, short of funds, and lacking in firm-specific proprietary advantages, so their FDI was low. Foreign affiliates operated primarily as low-wage export platforms to service third countries.

27. METI rarely granted these licenses "in view of the effects on domestic industry." Dore (1986, 202–3) concluded: "Importing is, to begin with, a slightly disreputable activity and has become more so as the industry has got into worse trouble."

28. "We want the government to limit imports, but they are hesitating. Personally, and in the industry as a whole, we are very dissatisfied with the government," a Kurabo official explained ("Hanging on by a Thread: Tariff Barriers and Low Foreign Labor Costs Are Driving Japanese Textile Production Offshore," *Financial Times*, July 6, 1993, 19).

to restrain reverse imports because, a Toray official noted, these "would lead to serious damage to the Japanese textile industry" (Yoshimatsu 2000, 150–52). Apparel producers, however, opposed import restraints because they depended on outward-processing agreements and joint ventures with foreign subcontractors for the bulk of their inputs (Yoshimatsu 2000, 130–31, 143–46).

Ongoing shifts in production and trading patterns have further fractured the textile, apparel, and fiber industry. Over the last decade, companies such as Toray and Toyobo have started reverse importing from Asia, while others have withdrawn from foreign manufacturing (Yoshimatsu 2000, 147–52). Producers with offshore factories, particularly in China, resisted broader quotas on Chinese textiles in the mid-1990s. Thus, one report noted, "the industry calls for protection have generally come from smaller apparel [fabric] makers."[29] Even today, there is no consensus on trade policy because many companies outsource production in the region.[30]

Just as these divisions have blocked the negotiation of trade restraints with China, so too they make it difficult to open the Japanese market to East Asian fabrics and fibers. Even as larger textile companies move production offshore to adjust to cost pressures, small producers of standardized fabrics and knitwear can survive only if the domestic market is protected. Though firms facing import competition thus far have been reluctant to file for quotas under the new policy, no doubt they would mobilize more actively if faced with the prospect of losing present tariffs. Moreover, their competitive position continues to decline. This suggests that regional trade liberalization likely will remain controversial in Japan's textile and apparel industry.

Nationally Oriented Industries

While regionally oriented industries in Japan have had some incentives to support East Asian integration, there are strong reasons for nationally oriented industries to oppose the opening of the Japanese market, both regionally and multilaterally. Protectionism in Japanese agriculture is the most significant barrier to regional arrangements involving Japan. Keiretsu ties and cartel behavior in Japan's basic materials industries are a second major problem for regional trade initiatives.

Because of trade frictions and international pressures, multinationals and

29. "Japanese Mull China Offer to Restrain Textile Exports," *Journal of Commerce*, December 7, 1994, 3A.
30. "Low Prices Have Become the Fashion," *Financial Times*, January 16, 2001, 36.

other large firms in Japan began to push the government to open trade and ease customs and certification procedures around 1982. Working through Keidanren, a federation of 120 industry associations including JAMA, the Electronic Industries Association of Japan, and the Japan Iron and Steel Federation, these companies "exercised their considerable political and economic power to liberalize economic institutions" (Yamamura 1994, 41). Keidanren and individual firms argued that trade friction threatened to provoke foreign retaliation against Japanese products and affiliates. After 1990, this lobbying also focused on domestic deregulation and opening the economy to FDI. At first such pressures faced bureaucratic resistance from METI and the Ministry of Finance, but over time these agencies became more favorable to liberalization and reform (Yoshimatsu 1998, 329–38; Yamamura 1994, 38–41).

Despite unsuccessful efforts to promote liberalization in agriculture, pro-trade industry groups have pushed more aggressively in recent years, particularly on heavily protected products such as rice and grains (Yoshimatsu 1998, 338–41). According to Yamamura (1994, 42):

> [M]ultinational firms, the largest financial institutions, Keidanren, and other major economic organizations became eager to diffuse trade friction and became willing to exercise their considerable power over the LDP cabinets and party leaders . . . to "sacrifice" rice farmers despite vociferous opposition from Diet members dependent on farm votes.

Yet the pace of change remains slow in Japan, and both the willingness of industry groups to expend resources to promote change and their influence within the policy process are limited. As a result, branches of the Japanese economy, notably agriculture and basic materials, are still closed to imports from the region and the world.

Agricultural Protectionism

Farmers are the most protected group in the Japanese economy. Agriculture's political strength resides in the effectiveness of farm lobbies, their influence within the LDP, and (until recently) the single nontransferable vote electoral system. Nowhere is this more apparent than in the import regime for rice. Japan imported just 0.8 percent of its rice consumption in 1999. The "virtual ban on rice imports" amounted to an implied nontariff barrier of 737 percent. Though quantitative controls were converted to tariff-rate quotas, the WTO concluded that this was not likely to increase imports because of the prohibitive ¥351.2 per kilogram tax on overquota imports. In addition to rice, implied nontariff barriers exceeded import prices for tea and roasted coffee (707 percent), wheat (478 percent), soybeans (424 percent), tobacco (241 percent), dairy products (229 percent), oats (141 percent), processed vegetables (139 percent), raw sugar, beef, and oranges (Sazanami, Urata, and Kawai 1995, 21–24). Recently, the WTO (2000b, 83–85) reported high tariffs on dairy products (68.1 percent), grains (33 percent), vegetables (32.1 percent), sugar and confectionery (30.6 percent), oils and seeds (26.4 percent), and preparations of cereals, flour, and starch (22.8 percent). Moreover, specific tariffs and tariff-rate quotas apply to many of these product categories.

Political opposition to opening Japan's agricultural market made Singapore an attractive choice for the country's first bilateral arrangement. Singapore has no rice production, and agriculture contributes only 0.1 percent of its GDP and 2 percent of its exports. As a result, agriculture, forestry, and fisheries accounted for only 1.9 percent of Japan-Singapore trade in 1999, and 0.5 percent of Japan's agricultural imports came from Singapore (Joint Study Group 2000, chap. 2, 3–4). Even so, the Ministry of Agriculture, Forestry, and Fisheries, under pressure from the farm lobby, protested trade liberalization for cut flowers and ornamental fish.[31] In the end, agricultural imports into Japan were excluded from the JSEPA treaty.[32]

The farm lobby has demanded a blanket exemption from all trade agreements, so future bilateral or regional deals risk angering agricultural groups. Because Singapore has little agriculture, the JSEPA treaty covered 94 percent of Japan's imports. If Japan were to attempt a free trade agreement with, say, Thailand—Asia's leading rice exporter, with 20 percent of the world market (WTO 1999, 82)—this could run afoul of the Article XXIV requirement to liberalize "substantially all trade." Studies suggest that even free trade with South Korea would create severe adjustment costs for Japanese farmers. Thus, Scollay and Gilbert (2001, 43, 47) conclude:

> [Such an arrangement] would bring together two countries known for their fierce resistance to agricultural trade liberalization within the WTO, fueling suspicions that they may see a bilateral FTA as a way to pursue the benefits of trade liberalization in a framework that would allow the exclusion of all sensitive agricultural and other natural-resource-based products.

31. "Japan's Dream of a Free-Trade Future Stumbles over Farming," *Financial Times*, July 11, 2001, 12.
32. "Japan Agrees Trade Accord with Singapore," *Financial Times*, October 15, 2001, 17.

In the case of Mexico, the *Financial Times* reports, "Japanese manufacturers badly want an FTA,"[33] yet JETRO (2000, 9) concluded that free trade would "lead to an overall collapse of the existing systems and have a far-reaching impact on domestic production." Agriculture also has been a source of trade friction with China, as efforts to mobilize the farm vote in 2001 elections through safeguard actions on shiitake mushrooms, leeks, and tatami rushes (used for mat-making) provoked retaliation against certain Japanese manufactures.

While Japanese industry recently has warmed to the idea of regional and bilateral trade deals, there are limits to how far industry groups will go to impose change on the farm sector. For example, Keidanren chairman Takashi Imai called import restraints on Chinese agricultural goods "very foolish" but added: "Rice is very important to Japan's economy and society. We have to consider the need for self-sufficiency."[34] Though there are signs that Japanese officials may be willing to include farm goods in future trade discussions to avoid being left out of the trend toward trading blocs,[35] it remains doubtful that they will be able to negotiate comprehensive trade agreements when liberalizing agriculture carries such high political costs.

Basic Materials: Keiretsu Ties

Another barrier to Japan's participation in regional arrangements exists in basic materials such as steel, nonferrous metals, petrochemicals, and cement. East Asian countries have developed price advantages and export potential in these industries as they have gained access to modern technology and built large-scale capacity. Yet inside Japan, industrial collusion and keiretsu ties, which often induce users of basic materials to buy high-cost domestic output instead of cheaper imports, limit market access for producers in the region.

Japanese basic materials industries lost competitiveness due to the post-1973 oil crisis (which increased energy costs and raised prices for petroleum-based raw materials), the yen's appreciation, and the growth of competing production in developing countries. All of the industries listed in the preceding have been covered under METI cartel laws, ostensibly to promote adjustment, as all suffer high costs and charge prices in the domestic market well above import prices. Yet only the aluminum industry had been exposed to import competition by the early 1990s; steel, petrochemicals, and cement continued to

33. "Japan's Dream of a Free-Trade Future Stumbles over Farming," *Financial Times*, July 11, 2001, 12.

34. "Seoul Cool on NE Asian Trade Zone Plan," *Financial Times*, November 8, 2001, 13.

35. Ibid.

record trade surpluses. Unlike in aluminum, where foreign affiliates supply most imports into Japan, Japanese-owned steel and petrochemical plants abroad also do not reverse export (Tilton 1996, 9–11, 38–47, 58–66, 138–39; Uriu 1996, 178–85).

Moreover, consumers of basic materials traditionally have been reluctant to purchase supplies from foreign sources. The rise of low-cost steel manufacturing in South Korea and Taiwan led to informal VERs in the mid-1980s between the Japan Iron and Steel Federation and producers in the region, and Japanese distributors selling foreign steel were threatened with retribution (Wolff 1990, 151–52). When automakers prepared to shift to imports as steel prices escalated with the yen's appreciation, steel producers countered that they had an obligation to buy domestic steel. A few automobile firms and smaller shipbuilders moved some of their procurement to South Korea after Nippon Steel raised prices in 1994. But most steel consumers, fearing retaliation, declined to buy cheaper imports (Uriu 1996, 228–29; Tilton 1996, 179–88). Keiretsu groups and government officials likewise sought to block cement imports from South Korea and Taiwan, as producers in these countries gained price advantages (Tilton 1996, 101–15). In addition, Sazanami, Urata, and Kawai (1995, 26) calculated substantial nontariff barriers for industrial materials such as caustic soda, methane derivatives, soda ash, and sheet glass.

Thus, regional integration between Japan and East Asia requires not only external treaties to reduce tariffs and nontariff barriers but also internal measures to complete the destruction of the keiretsu system that blocks foreign goods from entering Japan. East Asian countries have little to gain from regional arrangements with Japan if their exports cannot penetrate informal cartels and interlocking linkages between producers, suppliers, and distributors. Yet these business structures persist, in part, to exclude competing products, and basic materials industries have resisted their elimination. While regional trade liberalization could, in theory, provide a commitment mechanism to spur faster reform in Japan, in practice such a policy would have to overcome political opposition from industries that have benefited from informal means to close the Japanese market.

Conclusion: A Yen Bloc in East Asia?

This chapter's analysis of FDI by Japanese companies in East Asia suggests that, until recently, delays in creating regional procurement networks inhibited regional integration initiatives. Despite dramatic changes over the last decade, even today production-sharing linkages in East Asia are less broadly distributed and not as developed as those of U.S. firms in North America or European firms in the EU. In Japan, intrafirm trade, regional procurement, and reverse importing are common only in electronics, electrical machinery, and photographic and optical equipment. Particularly in the automotive industry, Japanese FDI has promoted the integration of East Asian countries with one another but not with Japan, and companies have an interest in preserving this ASEAN fortress. In other cases such as textiles and apparel, divisions between regionalists and protectionists have stalemated industry lobbying on trade issues. Finally, export-oriented industries have a great stake in access to North American and European markets that could be harmed by the creation of a trading bloc in East Asia.

While the incentives to support regional arrangements in East Asia are limited, resistance to market opening remains strong in agriculture and basic materials. Japan therefore has not pursued regional arrangements with much enthusiasm, though it has taken tentative steps like the JSEPA treaty. The book's analytical framework suggests that grander initiatives for free trade with South Korea, China, or ASEAN are not likely to gain much traction. As the rest of the world moves toward trading blocs, Japan probably will remain a reluctant regionalist for the foreseeable future.

CHAPTER 8

Multinationals and the
New Regionalism

Trading blocs were popular instruments of trade policy throughout the twentieth century, from the imperial systems of the interwar period to the customs unions and free trade areas formed in Western Europe and North America. Today these arrangements are even more widespread, often linking together countries that lack a common "regional" bond (such as the United States and Singapore, Mexico and the EU, South Korea and Chile). With the WTO stalled since the Cancun walkout, the most vibrant and comprehensive proposals of late to open trade and liberalize investment have been regional and bilateral initiatives—EU enlargement, discussions to link NAFTA and Mercosur into a Free Trade Area of the Americas, the "ASEAN+3" forum in Asia, and the determination of countries such as Chile, Mexico, and Singapore to follow a bilateral track to freer trade.

This burst of regional and bilateral activity has puzzled scholars and policy analysts. Theoretical work recognizes that domestic politics plays a key role in the political economy of trade. But standard trade models cannot explain enthusiasm for regional arrangements, and there have been few theoretically motivated attempts to evaluate a large number of historical or contemporary cases. According to Mansfield and Milner (1999, 604), "there is a lack of empirical evidence indicating which domestic groups support regional trade agreements, whose interests these agreements serve, and why particular groups prefer regional to multilateral trade liberalization." Because the domestic sources of trading blocs remain unclear, existing assessments of the implications for the world trading system rest on conjecture rather than systematic analysis. As Mansfield and Milner (1999, 604) note, "we know little about whether, once in place, regional arrangements foster domestic support for broader, multilateral trade liberalization or whether they undermine such support."

This book addresses these issues through an analytical explanation of how the trade preferences of domestic groups filter through political processes to influence national policies toward regional and global trade. The framework begins with domestic actors—firms and industry associations—and builds upward to derive expectations about policy. The main analytical task is to explain how technological and market factors affect the policy preferences of domestic actors. From there, the approach considers preference aggregation to illuminate how collective action and the design of state institutions affect the ability of domestic groups to obtain the policies they seek.

The Argument

Simply put, states establish regional arrangements in response to pressure from organized interests in society. Business groups have been the principal source of these pressures. As the cases in chapters 3–7 detail, two considerations have figured prominently in the calculus of organized groups seeking trading blocs.

One factor is the growing scale of manufacturing, which dates from the inception of the moving assembly line and techniques for high-pressure chemical synthesis in the early twentieth century to modern innovations in development, design, and "learning by doing" in microelectronics and IT. Scale economies are prevalent in a range of industries, including integrated circuits, consumer electronics, automobiles, and industrial and synthetic chemicals. This technological development makes enlarged markets and common standards attractive to firms facing competitive pressure to produce on a large scale.

Economic studies, government reports, and press accounts routinely tout scale effects as potential benefits of regional integration. A few scholars have incorporated scale considerations in studies of trading blocs (e.g., Chase 2003; Milner 1997; Busch and Milner 1994; Froot and Yoffie 1993). Yet empirical work to date has not examined these variables in a systematic fashion on a large number of cases. This book, by demonstrating the importance of scale economies in the political activities of business groups seeking regional arrangements, fills that gap.

A second, more recent trend is the growth of production sharing—the practice of dispersing production across borders to locate different stages where they can be most efficiently performed. In products ranging from microchips to televisions, automobiles, computers, and cell phones, the manufacturing process involves multiple countries. Often production sharing is regionally oriented, so multinational companies have incentives to seek special arrangements to liberalize trade and safeguard investment across the borders that link geographically separated production facilities.

As production sharing has expanded with technological changes and advances in IT, differences in national standards and regulatory practices have emerged as prominent concerns for firms doing business across borders. In particular, TRIMs are a significant policy issue for multinational companies that have developed or that seek to establish regional procurement networks. Yet the political economy of trade remains rooted in the study of barriers to trade at national borders; regulatory rules inside national boundaries have received little analytical attention. The argument in this book illuminates why regional arrangements have become attractive to multinational firms as a framework to promote liberalization and deregulation in FDI.

Following these premises, the book shows that the formation of trading blocs in the interwar period responded to domestic pressure for larger markets so producers could gain scale economies. Recently, the need for integrated regional markets to allow firms to concentrate production, increase scale, and split up the production process has been central to the single market program in the EC, free trade in North America, and tentative steps toward regionalism in East Asia.

These findings challenge work in the field that explains trading blocs in terms of alliances and power politics (Gruber 2000; Gowa 1994), transaction costs in multilateral negotiations (Haggard 1997), and intergovernmental bargains among nations (Moravcsik 1998). Regional arrangements, the book maintains, cannot be understood without analyzing how market competition and technological change affect group interests and how shifting preferences and domestic coalitions shape policy responses. To illuminate these factors, the book incorporates scale economies and production sharing into a domestic approach to the political economy of trade.

Implications for the Trading System

Analysts who welcome the trend toward trading blocs contend that it accelerates progress toward global free trade by breaking negotiations into small groups of states with similar interests. As multilateral discussions have moved from tariffs to nontariff barriers and "inside the border" regulatory measures, this view proposes, regional groupings of interlocking free trade areas can more effectively promote the multilateral integration of the world economy. Critics of trading blocs counter that these arrangements are designed to fortify protectionist barriers and divert trade. From this perspective, regional blocs are likely to raise new trade barriers against outsiders, hindering progress toward global free trade. Moreover, these analysts argue, discriminatory arrangements undermine the WTO and weaken the MFN norm at its core. The result is a "patchwork quilt" of competing regional, bilateral, and multilateral agreements. In the worst case scenario, some even suggest that recent trends threaten to unleash protectionist pressures reminiscent of the 1930s, presaging a return to the mercantilist conflict of the interwar period.

In this book's explanatory framework, either result is possible. The analytical approach suggests that regionalism promotes global trade liberalization when it creates opportunities for producers to restructure manufacturing facilities. Specifically, when companies expand output to serve a larger regional market or deepen production-sharing networks, manufacturing costs decline, and the need for trade protection against outsiders diminishes. Alternatively, protectionism is more likely to take root when firms cannot effectively capture scale economies or engage in production sharing.

The Interwar Collapse

Chapters 3 and 4 provide a new interpretation of protectionism and trading blocs in the 1930s. These case studies argue that domestic pressure for trade protection and the formation of imperial blocs responded to technological changes that increased the optimal scale of manufacturing. Because the United States controlled a market of continental proportions, it alone among the major powers had no need for a larger economic area. Elsewhere, the rise of heavy industry coincided with efforts to obtain foreign markets to compensate for the small size of the nation state. This reaction was most intense in Japan, Britain, and Germany—countries big enough to support industries with large returns to scale, but too small to permit many factories to operate close to MES. Because national boundaries severely constrained producers in these countries, firms and industry groups sought protectionist policies and the creation of imperial blocs. Britain already had an empire, so it needed only to negotiate commonwealth preferences at the Ottawa Conference. In Japan and Germany, however, captive markets had to be acquired rather than brokered, and so conquest became a tool of foreign economic policy.

The key factor was the asymmetry between the United States and other countries in the scale of production and the size of national markets. Producers from the United States were so far ahead in the use of mass production techniques that their presence in foreign markets threatened to stunt the growth of the same industries in the rest of the world. Because producers in lagging nations could not compete on an equal basis, they embraced protectionism. Yet they could not flourish inside national markets that were small compared to the optimal scale of production. Only through captive export outlets sheltered from U.S. competition could firms in these industries increase market shares enough to reach internationally viable scales of production.

Contemporary Trading Blocs: Beachheads, Not Fortresses

In contrast to the interwar period, recent regional arrangements have joined countries that already imposed few, if any, border controls on the movement of one another's goods and services. When the EC moved to complete the single market, its customs union was two decades old, and no formal trade barriers (other than Article 115 restraints) existed across European borders. Before the CUSFTA treaty, more than three-quarters of Canada-U.S. trade was duty free. Though trade barriers in Mexico were more significant at the start of the NAFTA negotiations, the country had slashed tariffs, eliminated import licensing, and removed most quotas. Border measures simply were not significant impediments to trade when these agreements were formulated.

In addition to removing the surviving border barriers to trade, contemporary regional arrangements have extended inside national borders to harmonize regulatory practices, create institutional frameworks to settle disputes, and establish codes related to services, intellectual property, government procurement, foreign investment, and TRIMs. The single-market program targeted a series of trade impediments rooted in incompatible product standards, technical requirements, and administrative and customs procedures in EC countries. The CUSFTA and NAFTA treaties incorporated unprecedented provisions to strengthen intellectual property rights, open public procurement, liberalize FDI, and eliminate TRIMs. Japan's economic partnership with Singapore (JSEPA) included innovative measures such as the creation of an electronic network to ease customs administration.

The formation of these regional arrangements validates the continued importance of scale economies. When manufacturing had been fragmented due to regional barriers to producing and marketing goods on a wider scale, industries with large returns to scale sought trade liberalization and harmonized policy regimes. In the EC, companies had to operate on a national basis because different technical and product standards, preferential practices in government procurement, and other nontariff barriers survived the customs union's formation. In response, large firms lobbied individually and through the ERT for the 1992 program so they could standardize product runs for a Europe-wide market. In North America, "miniature replica" plants, vestiges of import substitution in Canada and Mexico, could not survive once protectionist policies were liberalized, but they also could not be integrated with U.S. production as long as trade barriers and TRIMs remained in place. To rationalize and streamline these operations, U.S. multinationals sought free trade agreements with Canada and Mexico to eliminate trade barriers and regulatory rules on foreign investment. In all of these cases, the desire to gain scale economies was a strong motive for regional trade liberalization.

In addition to large returns to scale, production-sharing networks have been a second crucial factor in the formation of regional arrangements. With more opportunities to locate stages of manufacturing across borders, many firms have established regional production strategies that rely on intrafirm trade in technology, parts, and components. Firms from the United States introduced this practice by outsourcing labor-intensive tasks to Mexico and Canada. Companies involved in intrafirm and OAP trade were energetic advocates of CUSFTA and NAFTA. Many firms in the EC also spread manufacturing across borders, though data limitations made it difficult for me to systematically establish a correlation with pressure to complete the single market. In Asia, Japanese multinationals have developed offshore procurement bases in ASEAN countries and China, and reverse imports into Japan are growing. Preliminary evidence suggests that production sharing in the Asian region helped to build support for free trade with Singapore.

Compared to the 1930s, trade diversion has been less of a priority in modern trading blocs. Firms in Japan, Britain, and continental Europe surmounted their great size disadvantages during postwar reconstruction, so international differences in scales of production at the plant level narrowed considerably. Rising incomes produced larger national markets, which helped to loosen the geographic constraints on industries with large returns to scale. And today the power of exclusion is more limited than in the past: foreign companies can invest inside trading blocs to share in the benefits of regional integration. These factors have promoted external trade liberalization or limited the imposition of new trade barriers, in striking contrast to interwar imperial protection.

Thus, the forces driving today's regionalism differ from those that led to the collapse of the trading system in the 1930s. Contemporary trading blocs have not been protectionist instruments. External trade barriers have declined of late in U.S. industries with large returns to scale; though it is difficult to establish this with the same certainty for the EU, there is evidence that protectionist lobbying has declined in these industries. These findings support a central implication of the book: regional arrangements can help to prepare companies—and countries—to more vigorously pursue multilateral trade liberalization by creating opportunities for firms to restructure. Popular prophecies about the fragmentation of the world economy into self-contained regional groupings are simply misguided; extant trading blocs do not pose a threat to the multilateral trading system.

To be sure, modern trading blocs contain discriminatory and exclusive elements. *Discrimination* exists when exports from outside the region face external barriers that do not apply to products traded within the region. *Exclusion* occurs through efforts to prevent outsiders from investing around external barriers to reap benefits from regional trade liberalization. Both discrimination and exclusion are important features of recent regional arrangements. It is important therefore to evaluate the effects of these measures on outsiders.

Discrimination and Exclusion

In the EU and NAFTA, the common external tariff (in the EU), staging periods for free trade (in NAFTA), antidumping actions, and rules of origin favor companies located inside these trading blocs, at the expense of outsiders. The USITC (1993, ix) explains, "NAFTA rules of origin are intended to ensure that the benefits of tariff reductions will accrue principally to the NAFTA parties." Willy de Clercq, the former EC commissioner for external relations, made the point in plainer language: "We are not building a single market in order to turn it over to hungry foreigners" (Winters 1993, 207). The objective is simply to assist indigenous industries. However, the effects on outsiders vary.

The EU: Discriminating against Outsiders

European integration had very different implications for companies based in the United States and those based in Japan. Since the Treaty of Rome, U.S. multinationals have maintained a strong commercial presence in Europe. Historically, the European sales of U.S. affiliates have surpassed exports from the United States by a factor of at least five. Because U.S. affiliates in the EC were created as autonomous units independent of their parent companies, they could easily increase output and local content in response to external trade barriers. As a result, U.S. multinationals have been well positioned to benefit from European integration. Back in 1958, Ford told the U.S. House of Representatives (1958a, 238–44) that while "the United States w[ould] find the European market virtually closed to its manufactured goods," the EC's formation was a favorable development because "existing plants will be expanded and in some instances relocated" in response to the opening of regional trade. Deere welcomed the opportunity to centralize assembly and manufacturing at different locations

(Broehl 1984, 663–64), while ITT could benefit through its "forward commercial bases in Europe" (U.S. House of Representatives 1962, 2:1256). Discrimination and trade diversion were no concern for these companies.

The single market program also offered large benefits for U.S. multinationals. Once divergent national regulations for food and beverages, chemicals, pharmaceuticals, automobiles, and telecommunication equipment were phased out, affiliates in different EC countries could be closely integrated with one another. For U.S. multinationals in these industries, regulatory harmonization was more important than export freedom from the outside. Writing before the single market's completion, Hufbauer (1990, 24–25) noted: "EC-1992 . . . holds great promise for General Motors, International Business Machines, Merck, American Telephone and Telegraph, and a long list of other U.S. firms with a strong presence in Europe." As a result, industry groups representing large U.S. companies strongly supported the 1992 program.

For export-dependent firms, however, European integration caused more harm than help. Origin rules, procurement practices, antidumping measures, and the common external tariff strongly favored companies located inside the EC over those exporting to it. Semiconductor rules of origin requiring wafer fabrication in Europe caused Intel, Motorola, and Texas Instruments to expand local capacity or make new investments. Directives stipulating 50 percent EC content for procurement contracts in heavy electric machinery and telecommunication gear likewise led multinationals to bolster their local presence. Smaller firms that did not manufacture in Europe, or that operated EC plants with low local content, had to export over the tariff wall (USITC 1990c, chap. 6, 30–31, 44–45). Thus, the single market was good news for U.S. multinationals but "bad news for exporters, especially small ones without the scale of operations to justify locating in Europe" (U.S. Congress 1991, 199).

Because U.S. multinationals had been "Europeanized" long before the single-market program, they could not be excluded from reaping the same restructuring gains as European-owned firms. By 1989, more than 2 million Europeans worked in affiliates of U.S. companies. IBM-Europe employed 109,000. Moreover, IBM, Ford, AT&T, and other firms maintained lobbying offices in Brussels and, in some cases, devoted more resources to their political efforts than their European competitors, so "their well-being [was] as important to the Community as the well-being of strictly European firms" (Bowen 1991a, 267–68).

For Japan, however, European integration was a negative development. Japanese multinationals were latecomers to the EC. In 1989, Japan's European affiliates employed only sixty thousand workers; mostly these subsidiaries acted as distributors for exports rather than stand-alone production plants. At the launch of the single-market program, Japanese industry manufactured less than 20 percent of its European sales locally; by comparison, 80 percent of U.S. sales in the EC were produced there.

Because of concerns that fortress Europe would block exports, the 1992 program unleashed a flood of Japanese FDI, particularly in consumer electronics and automobiles. Japanese affiliates accounted for 40 percent of European VCR capacity and 25 percent of color TVs by 1990. Automakers Toyota, Honda, and Nissan surpassed one million vehicles, more than 10 percent of the EU market, by the mid-1990s. But Japanese transplants came onstream at lower volumes than factories at home, so initially they could not exploit scale economies.[1] Japan's EC affiliates also relied on technology and components imported from corporate parents in Japan.

In response, Brussels wielded powers of exclusion against Japanese companies that could not have been effectively applied to U.S. multinationals. Japanese VCRs, photocopiers, desktop printers, and other electronics faced 45 percent origin rules. To enforce antidumping orders, the European Commission levied anticircumvention duties on products with less than 40 percent EC content.[2] France pushed (unsuccessfully) for 80 percent EC content rules in the Nissan Bluebird dispute, and subsequently the British government secured commitments from Nissan, Toyota, and Honda for 85 percent EC content within three years of operations.[3]

As long as Japanese companies depended on exports for their European sales, they were easy targets first for quantitative restraints and antidumping measures to discriminate against their products, then later content rules and anticircumvention orders to deny their affiliates EC treatment. But transplants enabled Japanese firms to gain a foothold in the EC to support expansion to larger production volumes. Components suppliers soon followed original equipment manufacturers, and Japanese multinationals reconstituted their

1. A Philips executive predicted, "Japanese factories in Europe are going to suffer in the future, because they are all very small. . . . Some of these factories are only producing 100–200,000 television sets per year" (Dai 1996, 143). The largest TV plant, a Hitachi factory in Britain, produced 320,000 units, one-fourth of the volume in Japan; VCR plants manufactured 150,000–200,000 units, compared to 1 million or more in Japan (Cawson et al. 1990, 325–26).

2. After a series of disputes over photocopiers, printers, electronic typewriters, electronic weighing scales, and hydraulic excavators, Japan successfully challenged "screwdriver assembly" rules in dispute settlement. The EC subsequently modified the rule, ostensibly to ensure WTO consistency, but in the process the measure was broadened to cover false origin declarations, altered products, and assembly kits due to circumvention complaints involving cameras, bicycles, and compact disks (WTO 2001 1:67–68).

3. These figures were higher than local content in Japan's North American plants, and satisfying them required the local manufacture of both engines and transmissions (U.S. Congress 1991, 207).

Japan-based procurement networks in the EC. Once European electronics companies began to outsource production to Asia, Japanese transplants generally maintained higher EC content. Thereafter, powers of exclusion could be wielded only by targeting foreign affiliates directly—which Brussels did not do, despite ambiguous language in the auto VER that limited Japanese transplants to 1.2 million EU sales.

Thus, the single-market program Europeanized Japanese multinationals. In fact, several U.S. and Japanese multinationals have gained admission into European industry groups. Some even joined protectionist lobbies after they had achieved fully integrated production in the EC: Ford and GM consistently backed restraints on Japanese autos; U.S. multinationals with EC affiliates, except for Intel, supported tougher origin rules for semiconductors (Flamm 1990, 272). Japanese transplants even backed tariff increases on VCRs to blunt import competition from South Korea and smaller Japanese firms (Cawson et al. 1990, 327–28).

To conclude, the single-market program harmed exporters through discrimination, but foreign companies invested around external barriers and established local production to mitigate export dependence. Despite the EC's use of content rules and other TRIMs, limited powers of exclusion allowed multinationals to share in the benefits of the single-market program. In a few cases, foreign companies were an additional constituency for external trade protection in the EC.

NAFTA: Excluding Outsiders

In North America as in the EC, Japan was slow to establish a local presence. While European firms had developed manufacturing capabilities in the United States, Japanese firms depended on exports to the U.S. market at the time of NAFTA. However, Japan was better positioned in North America than in the EC. Trade restraints on automobiles, consumer electronics, semiconductors, and steel forced Japanese firms to begin investing early in the 1980s. In the ensuing years, Japanese companies acquired or forced out of business most U.S. consumer electronics producers and made major inroads in the beleaguered steel industry. Under the automobile VER, production in Japan's U.S. affiliates reached 2 million as exports from Japan declined to 2.3 million in 1992 from 3.6 million in 1986.[4] Japanese companies also built substantial capacity in

4. "The Enemy Within" 1993, 68.

Canada and Mexico for television and automotive assembly, picture tubes, and automotive engines.

Free trade offered large benefits to multinational companies that had established regional procurement networks with high North American content. For example, Nissan and Volkswagen owned engine and automotive assembly plants in Mexico with volumes comparable to those of U.S. rivals. In some cases, foreign multinationals could capture larger gains than North American firms. Free trade, U.S. electronics suppliers and labor unions complained, "would also allow Japanese-owned television manufacturers on both sides of the border to rationalize their production and gain market share at the expense of the integrated television manufacturers in the United States" (U.S. Senate 1986, 185).

To limit the benefits for Asian and European companies, particularly new entrants that had not established fully integrated production in the region, free trade agreements included rules of origin. Notably, the NAFTA treaty strengthened CUSFTA rules of origin for automobiles, computers, electronics, home appliances, industrial machinery, ball bearings, steel, textiles, and apparel—all major Japanese exports, fueling suspicion that the arrangement had been crafted to obstruct Japan. These measures pressured Asian electronics and telecommunications producers to relocate to North America to compete with companies receiving NAFTA treatment. In automobiles, NAFTA delayed duty-free status for firms that had not initiated production under Mexico's Automotive Decrees. Mexican TRIMs continued to apply to these companies, but not the Big Three, Volkswagen, or Nissan. Toyota, Honda, and Hyundai pushed for NAFTA origin rules of 50 percent or less; Volkswagen and Nissan initially backed this figure, but both firms later concluded that a higher origin rule afforded additional protection against these late entrants (Hufbauer and Schott 1992, 226; Cameron and Tomlin 2000, 134–35).

Other exclusive measures in NAFTA have received less attention. Foreign multinationals that do not qualify for NAFTA treatment lost three significant benefits they had previously enjoyed. First, Mexico eliminated maquiladora privileges for goods exported to the United States and Canada. In place of duty-free trade, there are 5 percent tariffs for twenty product categories; other items must pay the difference between Mexican and U.S. (or Canadian) tariffs to enter these markets. For Matsushita and other Japanese electronics firms, which source parts and components in Asia, the new policy is less favorable than the one in place at the time they invested.[5] Second, exports from Mexico to the

---

5. "Japanese Fall Foul of Rise in Mexico Costs," *Financial Times*, December 21, 2000, 12.

United States no longer receive tariff preferences under GSP and OAP provisions. The loss of preferential status primarily harms Asian affiliates producing automotive products, consumer electronics, office machines, and electrical machinery because these goods tend to have low North American content, which makes it difficult to satisfy NAFTA origin rules. Third, the CUSFTA treaty terminated APTA privileges for foreign automakers in Canada. In 1996, export-based and production-based duty remissions, incentives that motivated Toyota, Honda, and Nissan to invest in Canada, were fully phased out. Thus, firms that do not qualify for NAFTA treatment are worse off under the new trade regime.

These measures were major factors pushing the EC to negotiate free trade with Mexico to achieve NAFTA parity.[6] At this writing, Japan has just completed a similar arrangement as a drawbridge for its automakers and consumer electronics companies over the protectionist moats in the NAFTA treaty.[7]

Liberalization and Discrimination

Why have recent regional arrangements involved discrimination and exclusion? Some of these measures are plain concessions to protectionist groups to blunt the negative impact of trade liberalization. But in many cases, they are necessary to persuade companies to restructure. Without such provisions, eliminating past biases would threaten producers that have labored under policy distortions and discourage them from making risky investments to reorient unproductive operations.

In the EC before 1992, nontariff barriers encouraged inefficient behavior: consumer electronics firms manufactured in multiple plants instead of centralizing production, steel companies left outmoded capacity in operation rather than retiring it, and automakers vertically integrated production in national markets when specialization across borders would have been cheaper. Similar actions occurred in North America: U.S. multinationals established miniature replicas in all three markets, even when concentration at one location would have been economically optimal; Mexican and Canadian affiliates manufactured high-cost local inputs and sold unprofitable exports to corporate parents; and small-scale plants oriented to host markets coexisted with large, export-oriented factories, particularly in Mexico. In both Europe and

---

6. Under the EU-Mexico Free Trade Agreement, completed in 2000, trade barriers will be eliminated by 2007, two years before NAFTA tariff schedules are fully phased in. Significantly, Mexico's 20 percent tariff on EU automobiles immediately dropped to 3.3 percent, and this duty was eliminated in 2003 (WTO 2001 1:102 n. 40).

7. "Mexico and Japan Expect to Sign Trade Agreement," *New York Times*, September 17, 2004, 1.

North America, excess duplication, short product runs, and insufficient specialization plagued established companies. Yet these practices responded rationally to the policies in place at the time capital was sunk in manufacturing structures.

If new entrants could freely invest in an open trading climate without having to satisfy the same regulations, competitive pressure would discourage incumbents from making costly investments to reorganize. The European Commission, for example, lamented that Japanese automotive affiliates "work with the most up-to-date facilities right from the start." Its study concluded: "the Japanese are being favored to the disadvantage of established European manufacturers who cannot abandon existing plants . . . because of problems associated with the closure of facilities" (Commission of the European Communities 1990, 46). Similarly, U.S. automobile and computer companies told the USITC that they would not be able to compete on equal terms with foreign producers once trade barriers and TRIMs were phased out.

As a result, established companies locked in to preexisting trade and regulatory regimes tend to demand two sets of safeguards to proceed with restructuring. First, they want governments to issue irrevocable commitments to liberalize trade and industrial practices to guard against the risk of policy reversals. Second, they need governments to guarantee that they will be protected against new entrants while they adjust to a new policy climate. To satisfy these demands, regional trade agreements enumerate explicit obligations, establish rules that discriminate between incumbents and new entrants, and provide transitional protection.

The prototype was the APTA, which amounted to a regulatory contract between Canada and the Big Three. The CUSFTA treaty later extended mutual free trade to all products and eliminated most TRIMs. In effect, U.S. multinationals agreed to rationalize North American manufacturing, provided that Canada codified its pledge to undertake trade and regulatory liberalization in a formal treaty with provisions to shelter incumbents from newly established competitors. The NAFTA treaty likewise was designed to ensure that Mexico's unilateral reforms were durable so that trade barriers could not be restored and state control over foreign investors reinstated *ex post*. In short, today's trading blocs have been commitment devices for states and firms, not tools to divert foreign trade and investment.

Regional Arrangements and the WTO

GATT Article XXIV governs the formation of trading blocs under multilateral rules. This provision exempts customs unions, free trade areas, and "interim agreements" from the discipline of MFN obligations. It further stipulates that parties to such arrangements liberalize "substantially all the trade" between them and set tariffs that (individually or collectively) "shall not be higher or more restrictive" than before. To ensure that interim agreements lead to free trade areas of customs unions in a "reasonable amount of time," members must submit a "plan and schedule."[8]

Economists have long complained that Article XXIV is so fraught with undefined terms, ambiguities, and loopholes that the GATT secretariat has no legal discipline over regional arrangements. Bhagwati (1991, 58) laments, "regional blocs are indeed GATT-consistent, even if they may be considered threatening to GATT's basic conception of the world trading system." Since the creation of the GATT, 121 working parties have found only one case of full compliance with Article XXIV, yet no regional arrangement has been judged to be nonconforming.[9] This record prompted a former deputy director-general to complain (WTO 1995a, 70–71):

> of all the GATT articles, this is one of the most abused, and those abuses are among the least noted. Unfortunately, therefore, those framing any new [regional arrangement] need have little fear that they will be embarrassed by some GATT body finding them in violation of their international obligations and commitments and recommending that they abandon or alter what they are about to do.

With the formation of the WTO, members approved a "Memorandum of Understanding on Article XXIV" and created a Committee on Regional Trade Agreements to conduct future reviews. Since then, free trade areas and customs unions have flourished, but the WTO has yet to adopt a single report on Article XXIV compliance.

Many analysts maintain that the MFN rule is sacred; all liberalization must be nondiscriminatory to avert the recrudescence of 1930s-style protectionism. Yet it is not clear that the present flexibility is worse than dogmatic adherence to MFN. The case studies in this book strongly suggest that U.S. and European companies favorable to regional free trade would not have accepted the same liberalization on MFN terms. Discriminatory provisions in these arrangements illustrate the practical difficulty of eliminating behind-the-border regulatory measures multilaterally. Comparable measures to liberalize trade and indus-

8. "Regional Trade Agreements: Goods Rules," WTO, http://www.wto.org/english/tratop_e/region_e/regatt_e.htm#gatt.

9. This was the 1993 customs union between the Czech and Slovak republics, two countries that had been joined together as an independent state for the previous seventy-five years.

trial policy worldwide would have required too many special undertakings to negotiate among a large number of actors. Moreover, MFN rules prevent states from cushioning the blow of trade and regulatory liberalization to compensate firms for the costs imposed on them by past policies.[10] Simply, discrimination is the price of liberalization designed to encourage firms to organize resources more efficiently.

Particularly in the area of FDI, the absence of multilateral rules has encouraged regional initiatives. The TRIMs Agreement, which failed to institute comprehensive rules like those for intellectual property, services, and national standards, "is frequently interpreted to represent a failure of the Uruguay Round to make significant progress on investment issues" (Brewer and Young 1998, 458). Though WTO members have faced pressure to eliminate local content, trade balancing, and foreign exchange-balancing requirements, most developing nations missed the January 2000 deadline for implementing their commitments, and nine countries received extensions of up to seven years.[11] In several cases, multinational firms joined host governments in seeking delays. Meanwhile, "the use of investment-diverting and investment-distorting measures not covered in the current agreement has vastly increased" (Moran 2000, 223). This has made TRIMs an important feature of recent regional arrangements—which have, in turn, established detailed codes for FDI presently lacking at the multilateral level.

In sum, trading blocs can be springboards for freer trade worldwide, as long as they effectively promote industrial restructuring. Over time, companies that reorganize manufacturing facilities inside regional arrangements tend to become more favorable to multilateral liberalization. In the transition period while these adjustments are taking place, FDI by firms located outside the region mitigates the negative external effects of discrimination and exclusion. Finally, the healthy (albeit imperfect) multilateral structure in the WTO encourages further liberalization and discourages overt protectionism. Thus, the book concludes with a sanguine appraisal of the future of the global trading system in a world of regional arrangements.

10. It is worth noting, for example, that Nissan and Volkswagen received the same treatment under NAFTA as the Big Three.

11. "Nations Fail to Agree on Investment," *Financial Times*, January 25, 2000, 14.

Appendix
Measuring the Scale of Production

The static version of hypothesis 5, discussed in chapter 2, anticipates that industries with scale disadvantages compared to foreign competitors are likely to support external trade protection. To evaluate this hypothesis statistically, chapters 3 and 4 employ an index of unit costs (labeled *Scale*) derived from data on relative scales of production and engineering estimates of the returns to scale.

In general, unit costs with economies of scale are given by

Unit costs $= \beta x^n$,

where β is a constant, x is the position on the cost curve, and n is the slope of the cost curve. Following this rule, an index of relative costs can be computed as

Unit cost$_{i \cdot j} = \beta (x_i / x_j)^n$,

where x_i is the scale of output in country i and x_j the scale of output in country j.

As an example, consider the British and U.S. tire industries in 1930. On a per factory basis, Britain produced 347,514 tires (table 8) and the United States produced 860,858 tires (table 13). In engineering estimates, tire production at one-half of MES increases unit costs by 5 percent compared to MES levels; assuming a constant elasticity of unit cost with respect to scale, this implies a slope of -0.07. Thus, the cost indices are

Britain: $(347{,}514 / 860{,}858)^{-0.07} = 1.065$

United States: $(860{,}858 / 347{,}514)^{-0.07} = 0.938$

The cost index will converge toward 1 when scales are nearly equal or returns to scale are small. Figures greater than 1 indicate cost disadvantages, while figures less than 1 indicate cost advantages. *Scale* therefore should be positively correlated with measures of external trade protection, such as tariff rates.

References

Records of the U.S. National Archives

RG 20, Records of the Office of the Special Adviser to the President on Foreign Trade (SAFT), Records of the SAFT Trade Agreements Committee.

RG 59, General Records of the Department of State, Bureau of European Affairs, Country Director for Canada (EUR/CAN).

RG 81, Records of the U.S. International Trade Commission, Records of the U.S. Tariff Commission, 1917–71.

RG 151, Records of the Bureau of Foreign and Domestic Commerce, Office of International Trade—European Division.

RG 489, Records of the International Trade Administration, Domestic and International Business Administration, Bureau of International Economic Policy and Research, Office of International Trade Policy.

Secondary Sources and Government Publications

Abraham, David. 1981. *The Collapse of the Weimar Republic: Political Economy and Crisis.* Princeton: Princeton University Press.

Agnelli, Giovanni. 1989. The Europe of 1992. *Foreign Affairs* 68 (4): 61–70.

Agriculture and Protection. 1923. *Economist,* November 10.

Allen, G. C. 1933. *British Industries and Their Organization.* London: Longmans, Green.

———. 1940a. Japanese Industry: Its Organization and Development to 1937. In *The Industrialization of Japan and Manchukuo, 1930–1940: Population, Raw Materials and Industry,* edited by E. B. Schumpeter, 477–786. London: Macmillan.

———. 1940b. *Japanese Industry: Its Recent Development and Present Condition.* New York: Institute of Pacific Relations.

Alt, James E., and Michael Gilligan. 1994. The Political Economy of Trading States: Factor Specificity, Collective Action Problems and Domestic Political Institutions. *Journal of Political Philosophy* 2 (2): 165–92.

Alt, James E., Jeffry Frieden, Michael J. Gilligan, Dani Rodrik, and Ronald Rogowski. 1996. The Political Economy of International Trade: Enduring Puzzles and an Agenda for Inquiry. *Comparative Political Studies* 29 (6): 689–717.

Andersen, P. Nyboe. 1946. *Bilateral Exchange Clearing Policy.* London: Oxford University Press.

273

Backman, Jules. 1962. *The Economics of the Electrical Machinery Industry.* New York: New York University Press.

Bailey, Michael A., Judith Goldstein, and Barry R. Weingast. 1997. The Institutional Roots of American Trade Policy: Politics, Coalitions, and International Trade. *World Politics* 49 (3): 309–38.

Bain, Joe S. 1959. *Industrial Organization.* New York: John Wiley.

Balassa, Bela. 1961. *The Theory of Economic Integration.* Homewood: Richard D. Irwin.

Baldwin, Richard E., and Paul R. Krugman. 1988. Industrial Policy and International Competition in Wide-Bodied Jet Aircraft. In *Trade Policy Issues and Empirical Analysis,* edited by Robert E. Baldwin, 45–71. Chicago: University of Chicago Press.

———. 1992. Market Access and International Competition: A Simulation Study of 16K Random Access Memories. In *Imperfect Competition and International Trade,* edited by Gene M. Grossman, 179–200. Cambridge, MA: MIT Press.

Basch, Antonín. 1943. *The Danube Basin and the German Economic Sphere.* New York: Columbia University Press.

Bauer, Raymond, Ithiel de Sola Pool, and Lewis Anthony Dexter. 1963. *American Business and Public Policy: The Politics of Foreign Trade.* New York: Atherton Press.

Beasley, W. G. 1987. *Japanese Imperialism, 1894–1945.* Oxford: Clarendon Press.

Berghahn, Volker R. 1996. German Big Business and the Quest for a European Economic Empire in the Twentieth Century. In *Quest for Economic Empire: The European Strategies of German Big Business in the Twentieth Century,* edited by Volker R. Berghahn, 1–33. Providence: Berghahn Books.

Berglund, Abraham, and Philip G. Wright. 1929. *The Tariff on Iron and Steel.* Washington, DC: Brookings Institution.

Bergsten, C. Fred. 2001. America's Two-Front Economic Conflict. *Foreign Affairs* 80 (2): 16–27.

Bernard, Mitchell, and John Ravenhill. 1995. Beyond Product Cycles and Flying Geese: Regionalization, Hierarchy, and the Industrialization of East Asia. *World Politics* 47 (2): 171–209.

Bhagwati, Jagdish. 1991. *The World Trading System at Risk.* Cambridge, MA: MIT Press.

———. 1993. Regionalism and Multilateralism: An Overview. In *New Dimensions in Regional Integration,* edited by Jaime de Melo and Arvind Panagariya, 22–51. Cambridge: Cambridge University Press.

———. 1998. *A Stream of Windows: Unsettling Reflections on Trade, Immigration, and Democracy.* Cambridge, MA: MIT Press.

Bidwell, Percy. 1956. *What the Tariff Means to American Industries.* New York: Harper.

Board of Trade. 1918a. Committee on Commercial and Industrial Policy. *Final Report of the Committee on Commercial and Industrial Policy after the War.* London: H.M. Stationary Office (hereafter, HMSO).

———. 1918b. Departmental Committee on the Electrical Trades. *Report of the Departmental Committee on the Position of the Electrical Trades after the War.* London: HMSO.

———. 1918c. Departmental Committee on the Engineering Trades. *Report of the Departmental Committee on the Position of the Engineering Trades after the War.* London: HMSO.

———. 1918d. Departmental Committee on the Iron and Steel Trades. *Report of the*

Departmental Committee on the Position of the Iron and Steel Trades after the War. London: HMSO.

———. 1918e. Departmental Committee on the Textile Trades. *Report of the Departmental Committee on the Position of the Textile Trades after the War.* London: HMSO.

———. 1925–33. Department of Overseas Trade. *Economic Conditions in Germany.* London: HMSO.

———. 1928a. Committee on Industry and Trade. *Survey of Metal Industries.* London: HMSO.

———. 1928b. Committee on Industry and Trade. *Survey of Textile Industries.* London: HMSO.

———. 1928–33. Department of Overseas Trade. *Economic Conditions in Japan.* London: HMSO.

———. 1929. Committee on Industry and Trade. *Final Report of the Committee on Industry and Trade.* London: HMSO.

———. 1930. Customs and Excise Department. *Annual Statement of the Trade of the United Kingdom with Foreign Countries and British Countries.* London: HMSO.

———. 1934. *Final Report on the Fourth Census of Production.* London: HMSO.

———. 1963. *Report on the Census of Production, 1958.* London: HMSO.

Booth, Alan, and Melvyn Pack. 1985. *Employment, Capital, and Economic Policy: Great Britain, 1918–1939.* Oxford: Basil Blackwell.

Borkin, Joseph. 1978. *The Crime and Punishment of IG Farben.* New York: Free Press.

Borrus, Michael, Dieter Ernst, and Stephan Haggard. 2000. Introduction: Cross-Border Production Networks and the Industrial Integration of the Asia-Pacific Region. In *International Production Networks in Asia: Rivalry or Riches?* edited by Michael Borrus, Dieter Ernst, and Stephan Haggard, 1–30. London: Routledge.

Bosses Want the Common Market Brussels Never Built. 1984. *Economist,* May 26.

Bowden, Sue, and Avner Offer. 1994. Household Appliances and the Use of Time: The United States and Britain since the 1920s. *Economic History Review* 47 (4): 725–48.

Bowen, Harry P. 1991a. Consumer Electronics. In *The European Challenge: Industry's Response to the 1992 Program,* edited by David G. Mayes, 255–68. London: Harvester Wheatsheaf.

———. 1991b. Electronic Components and Semiconductors. In *The European Challenge: Industry's Response to the 1992 Program,* edited by David G. Mayes, 209–54. London: Harvester Wheatsheaf.

Boyce, Robert W. D. 1987. *British Capitalism at the Crossroads, 1919–1932: A Study in Politics, Economics, and International Relations.* Cambridge: Cambridge University Press.

Bradford and Protection. 1923. *Economist,* November 3.

Bradford's Cry for Protection. 1923. *Economist,* September 15.

Brady, Robert A. 1933. *The Rationalization Movement in German Industry: A Study in the Evolution of Economic Planning.* Berkeley: University of California Press.

Brander, James A. 1995. Strategic Trade Policy. NBER Working Paper 5020. National Bureau of Economic Research, Cambridge, MA.

Brander, James A., and Barbara J. Spencer. 1992. Tariff Protection and Imperfect Competition. In *Imperfect Competition and International Trade,* edited by Gene M. Grossman, 107–20. Cambridge, MA: MIT Press.

Brenton, Paul A. 2002. The Changing Nature and Determinants of EU Trade Policy. In *Globalizing Europe: Deepening Integration, Alliance Capitalism, and Structural Statecraft*, edited by Thomas L. Brewer, Paul A. Brenton, and Gavin Boyd, 205–41. Northampton: Edward Elgar.

Brewer, Thomas L., and Stephen Young. 1998. Investment Issues at the WTO: The Architecture of Rules and the Settlement of Disputes. *Journal of International Economic Law* 1 (3): 457–70.

Broadberry, S. N. 1997. *The Productivity Race: British Manufacturing in International Perspective, 1850–1990*. Cambridge: Cambridge University Press.

Broehl, Wayne G., Jr. 1984. *John Deere's Company: A History of Deere and Company and Its Times*. New York: Doubleday.

Brown, Benjamin H. 1943. *The Tariff Reform Movement in Great Britain, 1881–1895*. New York: Columbia University Press.

Buigues, Pierre, Fabienne Ilzkovitz, and Jean-François Lebrun. 1990. The Impact of the Internal Market by Industrial Sector: The Challenge for the Member States. *European Economy* 40 (special edition): 1–114.

Burn, Duncan. 1961. *The Economic History of Steelmaking, 1867–1939*. Cambridge: Cambridge University Press.

Busch, Marc L., and Helen V. Milner. 1994. The Future of the International Trading System: International Firms, Regionalism, and Domestic Politics. In *Political Economy and the Changing Global Order*, edited by Richard Stubbs and Geoffrey Underhill, 259–76. New York: St. Martin's Press.

Busch, Marc L., and Eric Reinhardt. 1999. Industrial Location and Protection: The Political and Economic Geography of U.S. Nontariff Barriers. *American Journal of Political Science* 43 (3): 1028–50.

Cadot, Olivier, Jaime de Melo, and Marcelo Olarreaga. 2001. Can Bilateralism Ease the Pains of Multilateral Trade Liberalization? *European Economic Review* 45 (1): 27–44.

Calingaert, Michael. 1994. Government-Business Relations. In *Europe and the United States: Competition and Cooperation in the 1990s*, edited by Glennon J. Harrison, 30–45. Armonk: M.E. Sharpe.

Cameron, Maxwell A., and Brian W. Tomlin. 2000. *The Making of NAFTA: How the Deal Was Done*. Ithaca: Cornell University Press.

Canadian Tariff Problems. 1933. *Economist*, December 16.

Capie, Forrest. 1983. *Depression and Protectionism: Britain between the Wars*. London: Allen and Unwin.

Carr, J. C., and W. Taplin. 1962. *History of the British Steel Industry*. Cambridge, MA: Harvard University Press.

Casella, Alessandra. 1996. Large Countries, Small Countries and the Enlargement of Trade Blocs. *European Economic Review* 40 (2): 389–415.

Caves, Richard E. 1996. *Multinational Enterprise and Economic Analysis*. 2nd ed. Cambridge: Cambridge University Press.

Caves, Richard E., and Michael E. Porter. 1976. Barriers to Exit. In *Essays on Industrial Organization in Honor of Joe S. Bain*, edited by Robert G. Masson and P. David Qualls, 36–69. Cambridge, MA: Ballinger Publishing.

Cawson, Alan, Kevin Morgan, Douglas Webber, Peter Holmes, and Anne Stevens. 1990.

Hostile Brothers: Competition and Closure in the European Electronics Industry. Oxford: Clarendon Press.

Cecchini, Paolo. 1988. *The European Challenge, 1992: The Benefits of a Single Market.* Aldershot: Gower.

Chandler, Alfred D., Jr. 1990. *Scale and Scope: The Dynamics of Industrial Capitalism.* Cambridge, MA: Belknap Press.

Chase, Kerry A. 2003. Economic Interests and Regional Trading Arrangements: The Case of NAFTA. *International Organization* 57 (1): 137–74.

———. 2005. Multilateralism Compromised: The Mysterious Origins of GATT Article XXIV. *World Trade Review* 4 (3), forthcoming.

Chin, Rockwood Q. P. 1937. Cotton Mills, Japan's Economic Spearhead in China. *Far Eastern Survey* 6 (23): 261–67.

Coal and Tariffs. 1923. *Economist,* December 1.

Coleman, D. C. 1969. *Rayon.* Vol. 2 of *Courtaulds: An Economic and Social History.* Oxford: Clarendon Press.

Commission of the European Communities. 1985. *The European Consumer Electronics Industry.* Luxembourg: Office for Official Publications of the European Communities.

———. 1988a. *The EC-92 Automobile Sector.* Vol. 11 of *Research on the 'Cost of Non-Europe.'* Luxembourg: Commission of the European Communities.

———. 1988b. *The 'Cost of Non-Europe' in the Foodstuffs Industry.* Vol. 12 of *Research on the 'Cost of Non-Europe.'* Luxembourg: Commission of the European Communities.

———. 1988c. *The 'Cost of Non-Europe' in the Textile-Clothing Industry.* Vol. 14 of *Research on the 'Cost of Non-Europe.'* Luxembourg: Commission of the European Communities.

———. 1988d. *The 'Cost of Non-Europe' in the Pharmaceutical Industry.* Vol. 15 of *Research on the 'Cost of Non-Europe.'* Luxembourg: Commission of the European Communities.

———. 1990. *The Effect of Different State Aid Measures on Intra-Community Competition: Exemplified by the Case of the Automotive Industry.* Luxembourg: Commission of the European Communities.

———. 1997. *Economies of Scale.* Single Market Review Series, subseries 5—Impact on Competition and Scale Effects, vol. 4. Luxembourg: Commission of the European Communities.

Conybeare, John A. C. 1987. *Trade Wars: The Theory and Practice of International Commercial Rivalry.* New York: Columbia University Press.

Cooper, Andrew Fenton. 1989. *British Agricultural Policy, 1912–1936: A Study in Conservative Politics.* Manchester: Manchester University Press.

Cooper, C. A., and B. F. Massell. 1965. Toward a General Theory of Customs Unions for Developing Countries. *Journal of Political Economy* 73 (5): 461–76.

Corden, W. M. 1972. Economies of Scale and Customs Union Theory. *Journal of Political Economy* 80 (3): 465–75.

Cortada, James W. 1993. *Before the Computer: IBM, NCR, Burroughs, and Remington Rand, and the Industry They Created, 1865–1956.* Princeton: Princeton University Press.

Costello, Declan, and Jacques Pelkmans. 1991. The Removal of National Quotas and "1992." In *The Annual Review of European Community Affairs, 1991*, edited by Peter Ludlow, Jørgen Mortensen, and Jacques Pelkmans, 75–85. London: Brassey's.

The Cotton Trade and Ottawa. 1932. *Economist*, May 14.

Cowles, Maria Green. 1995. Setting the Agenda for a New Europe: The ERT and EC 1992. *Journal of Common Market Studies* 33 (4): 501–26.

Cox, Ronald W. 1996. Explaining Business Support for Regional Trade Agreements. In *Business and the State in International Relations*, edited by Ronald W. Cox, 109–27. Boulder: Westview Press.

Cumings, Bruce. 1984. The Origins and Development of the Northeast Asian Political Economy: Industrial Sectors, Product Cycles, and Political Consequences. *International Organization* 38 (1): 1–40.

Dai, Xiudian. 1996. *Corporate Strategy, Public Policy and New Technologies: Philips and the European Consumer Electronics Industry*. Oxford: Pergamon.

Daly, D. J., and D. C. MacCharles. 1986. *Canadian Manufactured Exports: Constraints and Opportunities*. Montreal: Institute for Research on Public Policy.

Davenport-Hines, R. P. T. 1984. *Dudley Docker: The Life and Times of a Trade Warrior*. Cambridge: Cambridge University Press.

Davies, Robert Bruce. 1976. *Peacefully Working to Conquer the World: Singer Sewing Machines in World Markets, 1854–1920*. New York: Arno Press.

Davies, Stephen, and Bruce Lyons. 1996. *Industrial Organization in the European Union: Structure, Strategy, and the Competitive Mechanism*. Oxford: Clarendon Press.

Department of Commerce and Industry. Various years. Bureau of Statistics. *The Statistics of the Department of Commerce and Industry*. Tokyo: Department of Commerce and Industry.

Department of Finance. 1935. *The Import Tariff of Japan, 1934*. Tokyo: Herald Press.

Destler, I. M. 1995. *American Trade Politics*. 3rd ed. Washington, DC: Institute for International Economics.

Dick, Andrew R. 1994. Does Import Protection Act as Export Promotion? Evidence from the United States. *Oxford Economic Papers* 46 (1): 83–101.

Dixit, Avinash K. 1992. Optimal Trade and Industrial Policies for the U.S. Automobile Industry. In *Imperfect Competition and International Trade*, edited by Gene M. Grossman, 157–78. Cambridge, MA: MIT Press.

Doner, Richard F. 1993. Japanese Foreign Investment and the Creation of a Pacific Asian Region. In *Regionalism and Rivalry: Japan and the United States in Pacific Asia*, edited by Jeffrey A. Frankel and Miles Kahler, 159–214. Chicago: University of Chicago Press.

Dore, Ronald P. 1986. *Flexible Rigidities: Industrial Policy and Structural Adjustment in the Japanese Economy, 1970–1980*. Stanford: Stanford University Press.

Dornseifer, Bernd. 1995. Strategy, Technological Capability, and Innovation: German Enterprises in Comparative Perspective. In *Innovations in the European Economy between the Wars*, edited by François Caron, Paul Erker, and Wolfram Fischer, 197–226. Berlin: Walter de Gruyter.

Drummond, Ian M. 1974. *Imperial Economic Policy, 1917–1939: Studies in Expansion and Protection*. London: Allen and Unwin.

Dunlop, Kathleen Edith. 1949. The History of the Dunlop Rubber Co., Ltd., 1888–1939. Ph.D. dissertation, University of Illinois-Urbana.

Dunning, John H. 1956. The Growth of U.S. Investment in U.K. Manufacturing Industry, 1856–1940. *Manchester School of Economic and Social Studies* 24 (3): 245–69.

Duus, Peter. 1995. *The Abacus and the Sword: The Japanese Penetration of Korea, 1895–1910*. Berkeley: University of California Press.

Dykes, James G. 1982. *Background on the Automotive Products Trade Act.* Toronto: Motor Vehicle Manufacturers Association.

Eastman, H. C., and S. Stykolt. 1967. *The Tariff and Competition in Canada.* Toronto: Macmillan.

Eckes, Alfred E., Jr. 1995. *Opening America's Market: U.S. Foreign Trade Policy since 1776.* Chapel Hill: University of North Carolina Press.

Eichengreen, Barry. 1989. The Political Economy of the Smoot-Hawley Tariff. *Research in Economic History* 12: 1–43.

Eichengreen, Barry, and Douglas A. Irwin. 1995. Trade Blocs, Currency Blocs and the Reorientation of World Trade in the 1930s. *Journal of International Economics* 38 (1): 1–24.

Elbaum, Bernard. 1986. The Steel Industry before World War I. In *The Decline of the British Economy,* edited by Bernard Elbaum and William Lazonick, 51–81. Oxford: Clarendon Press.

Elbaum, Bernard, and William Lazonick. 1986. An Institutional Perspective on British Decline. In *The Decline of the British Economy,* edited by Bernard Elbaum and William Lazonick, 1–17. Oxford: Clarendon Press.

Ellis, Howard S. 1941. *Exchange Control in Central Europe.* Cambridge, MA: Harvard University Press.

Emerson, Michael, Michel Aujean, Michel Catinat, Philippe Goybet, and Alexis Jacquemin. 1988. *The Economics of 1992: The EC Commission's Assessment of the Economic Effects of Completing the Internal Market.* Oxford: Oxford University Press.

Encarnation, Dennis J. 1992. *Rivals beyond Trade: America versus Japan in Global Competition.* Ithaca: Cornell University Press.

The Enemy Within. 1933. *Economist,* June 12.

English, Maurice. 1984. The European Information Technology Industry. In *European Industry: Public Policy and Corporate Strategy,* edited by Alexis Jacquemin, 227–73. Oxford: Clarendon Press.

Ernst, Dieter. 2000. Evolutionary Aspects: The Asian Production Networks of Japanese Electronics Firms. In *International Production Networks in Asia: Rivalry or Riches?* edited by Michael Borrus, Dieter Ernst, and Stephan Haggard, 80–109. London: Routledge.

Eurostat. Various years. *Panorama of EU Industry.* Luxembourg: Office for Official Publications of the European Communities.

———. Various years. *Structure and Activity of Industry.* Luxembourg: Office for Official Publications of the European Communities.

Evans, John W. 1971. *The Kennedy Round in American Trade Policy: The Twilight of the GATT?* Cambridge, MA: Harvard University Press.

Fearon, Peter. 1978. The Vicissitudes of a British Aircraft Company: Handley Page Ltd. between the Wars. *Business History* 20: 63–86.

Federal Task Force on the Canadian Motor Vehicle and Automotive Parts Industries. 1983. *An Automotive Strategy for Canada: Report of the Federal Task Force on the*

Canadian Motor Vehicle and Automotive Parts Industries. Ottawa: Minister of Supply and Services Canada.

Feenstra, Robert C., Gordon H. Hanson, and Deborah L. Swenson. 2000. Offshore Assembly from the United States: Production Characteristics of the 9802 Program. In *The Impact of International Trade on Wages,* edited by Robert C. Feenstra, 85–122. Chicago: University of Chicago Press.

Feldenkirchen, Wilfried. 1999. *Siemens, 1918–1945.* Columbus: Ohio State University Press.

Fielder, Nicola. 2000. The Origins of the Single Market. In *State-Building in Europe: The Revitalization of Western European Integration,* edited by Volker Bornschier, 75–92. Cambridge: Cambridge University Press.

Fishlow, Albert, and Stephan Haggard. 1992. *The United States and the Regionalization of the World Economy.* Paris: OECD Development Center.

Flamm, Kenneth. 1987. *Targeting the Computer: Government Support and International Competition.* Washington, DC: Brookings Institution.

———. 1990. Semiconductors. In *Europe 1992: An American Perspective,* edited by Gary Clyde Hufbauer, 225–92. Washington, DC: Brookings Institution.

Fletcher, William Miles, III. 1989. *The Japanese Business Community and National Trade Policy, 1920–1942.* Chapel Hill: University of North Carolina Press.

Frankel, Jeffrey A. 1997. *Regional Trading Blocs in the World Economic System.* Washington, DC: Institute for International Economics.

Frankel, Jeffrey A., and Miles Kahler. 1993. Introduction. In *Regionalism and Rivalry: Japan and the United States in Pacific Asia,* edited by Jeffrey A. Frankel and Miles Kahler, 1–18. Chicago: University of Chicago Press.

Franko, Lawrence G. 1976. *The European Multinationals: A Renewed Challenge to American and British Big Business.* New York: Harper and Row.

Frieden, Jeffry A. 1991. *Debt, Development, and Democracy: Modern Political Economy and Latin America, 1965–1985.* Princeton: Princeton University Press.

———. 1999. Actors and Preferences in International Relations. In *Strategic Choice and International Relations,* edited by David A. Lake and Robert Powell, 39–76. Princeton: Princeton University Press.

Frieden, Jeffry A., and Ronald Rogowski. 1996. The Impact of the International Economy on National Policies: An Analytical Overview. In *Internationalization and Domestic Politics,* edited by Robert O. Keohane and Helen V. Milner, 25–47. Cambridge: Cambridge University Press.

Friedman, David. 1988. *The Misunderstood Miracle: Industrial Development and Political Change in Japan.* Ithaca: Cornell University Press.

Froot, Kenneth A., and David B. Yoffie. 1993. Trading Blocs and Incentives to Protect: Implications for Japan and East Asia. In *Regionalism and Rivalry: Japan and the United States in Pacific Asia,* edited by Jeffrey A. Frankel and Miles Kahler, 125–53. Chicago: University of Chicago Press.

Fuss, Melvyn, and Leonard Waverman. 1987. A Sectoral Perspective: Automobiles. In *Perspectives on a U.S.-Canadian Free Trade Agreement,* edited by Robert M. Stern, Philip H. Trezise, and John Whalley, 217–30. Washington, DC: Brookings Institution.

Gardner, Lloyd C. 1964. *Economic Aspects of New Deal Diplomacy.* Madison: University of Wisconsin Press.

Gardner, Richard N. 1969. *Sterling-Dollar Diplomacy: The Origins and the Prospects of Our International Economic Order.* 2nd ed. New York: McGraw-Hill.

Garside, W. R. 1998. Party Politics, Political Economy, and British Protectionism, 1919–1932. *History* 83 (269): 47–65.

Garten, Jeffrey E. 1993. *A Cold Peace: America, Japan, Germany, and the Struggle for Supremacy.* New York: Times Books.

Gaster, Robin. 1994. Redefining the Rules of the Game. In *Europe and the United States: Competition and Cooperation in the 1990s,* edited by Glennon J. Harrison, 257–70. Armonk: M.E. Sharpe.

GATT. 1992. *Trade Policy Review: United States.* Geneva: GATT.

———. 1993. *Trade Policy Review: European Communities.* Geneva: GATT.

Ghellinck, Elisabeth de. 1991. The Chemical and Pharmaceutical Industries. In *The European Challenge: Industry's Response to the 1992 Programme,* edited by David G. Mayes, 337–71. London: Harvester Wheatsheaf.

Gilligan, Michael J. 1997. Lobbying as a Private Good with Intra-Industry Trade. *International Studies Quarterly* 41 (3): 455–74.

Gilpin, Robert. 1971. The Politics of Transnational Economic Relations. *International Organization* 25 (3): 398–419.

———. 2000. *The Challenge of Global Capitalism: The World Economy in the 21st Century.* Princeton: Princeton University Press.

———. 2001. *Global Political Economy: Understanding the International Economic Order.* Princeton: Princeton University Press.

Goldstein, Judith. 1993. *Ideas, Interests, and American Trade Policy.* Ithaca: Cornell University Press.

Goodman, John B., Debora Spar, and David B. Yoffie. 1996. Foreign Direct Investment and the Demand for Protection in the United States. *International Organization* 50 (4): 565–91.

Gourevitch, Peter. 1986. *Politics in Hard Times: Comparative Responses to International Economic Crises.* Ithaca: Cornell University Press.

Gowa, Joanne. 1989. Rational Hegemons, Excludable Goods, and Small Groups: An Epitaph for Hegemonic Stability Theory? *World Politics* 41 (3): 307–24.

———. 1994. *Allies, Adversaries, and International Trade.* Ithaca: Cornell University Press.

Gowa, Joanne, and Edward D. Mansfield. 1993. Power Politics and International Trade. *American Political Science Review* 87 (2): 408–20.

Granatstein, J. L. 1985. Free Trade between Canada and the United States: The Issue That Will Not Go Away. In *The Politics of Canada's Economic Relationship with the United States,* edited by Denis Stairs and Gilbert R. Winham, 11–54. Toronto: University of Toronto Press.

Grant, Wyn. 1993. Pressure Groups and the European Community: An Overview. In *Lobbying in the European Community,* edited by Sonia Mazey and Jeremy Richardson, 27–46. Oxford: Oxford University Press.

Grant, Wyn, William Paterson, and Colin Whitston. 1988. *Government and the Chemical Industry: A Comparative Study of Britain and West Germany.* Oxford: Clarendon Press.

Grenzebach, William S., Jr. 1988. *Germany's Informal Empire in East-Central Europe:*

German Economic Policy toward Yugoslavia and Romania, 1933–1939. Stuttgart: Steiner Verlag.

Grilli, Enzo. 1992. Trade Policies in Italy. In *National Trade Policies,* edited by Dominick Salvatore, 173–96. Westport: Greenwood Press.

Grossman, Gene M. 1992. Introduction. In *Imperfect Competition and International Trade,* edited by Gene M. Grossman, 1–19. Cambridge, MA: MIT Press.

Grossman, Gene M., and Elhanan Helpman. 1996. Rent Dissipation, Free Riding, and Trade Policy. *European Economic Review* 40 (7): 795–803.

———. 2002. *Interest Groups and Trade Policy.* Princeton: Princeton University Press.

Gruber, Lloyd. 2000. *Ruling the World: Power Politics and the Rise of Supranational Institutions.* Princeton: Princeton University Press.

Grunwald, Joseph, and Kenneth Flamm. 1985. *The Global Factory: Foreign Assembly in International Trade.* Washington, DC: Brookings Institution.

Guerrieri, Paolo. 2000. International Competitiveness, Regional Integration, and Corporate Strategies in the East Asian Electronics Industry. In *International Production Networks in Asia: Rivalry or Riches?* edited by Michael Borrus, Dieter Ernst, and Stephan Haggard, 31–56. London: Routledge.

Guisinger, Stephen E. 1985. *Investment Incentives and Performance Requirements: Patterns of International Trade, Production, and Investment.* New York: Praeger Publishers.

Haas, Ernst B. 1958. *The Uniting of Europe.* Stanford: Stanford University Press.

Haber, L. F. 1971. *The Chemical Industry, 1900–1930: International Growth and Technological Change.* Oxford: Clarendon Press.

Hadley, Eleanor M. 1970. *Antitrust in Japan.* Princeton: Princeton University Press.

Haggard, Stephan. 1988. The Institutional Foundations of Hegemony: Explaining the Reciprocal Trade Agreements Act of 1934. *International Organization* 42 (1): 91–119.

———. 1997. The Political Economy of Regionalism in Asia and the Americas. In *The Political Economy of Regionalism,* edited by Edward D. Mansfield and Helen Milner, 20–49. New York: Columbia University Press.

Hallgarten, George W. F. 1952. Adolf Hitler and German Heavy Industry, 1931–1933. *Journal of Economic History* 12: 222–46.

Hannah, Leslie. 1976. *The Rise of the Corporate Economy.* London: Methuen.

Hanson, Brian T. 1998. What Happened to Fortress Europe? External Trade Policy Liberalization in the European Union. *International Organization* 52 (1): 55–85.

Hatch, Walter. 2002. Vertical Ties across Borders: Do Japanese Production Networks Jeopardize Competitive Markets in Southeast Asia? *Washington University Global Studies Law Review* 1 (1–2): 233–62.

———. 2004. When Strong Ties Fail: U.S.-Japanese Manufacturing Rivalry in Asia. In *Beyond Bilateralism: U.S.-Japan Relations in the New Asia-Pacific,* edited by Ellis S. Krauss and T. J. Pempel, 154–75. Stanford: Stanford University Press.

Hatch, Walter, and Kozo Yamamura. 1996. *Asia in Japan's Embrace: Building a Regional Production Alliance.* Cambridge: Cambridge University Press.

Hathaway, Oona A. 1998. Positive Feedback: The Impact of Trade Liberalization on Industry Demands for Protection. *International Organization* 52 (3): 575–612.

Hayes, J. P. 1993. *Making Trade Policy in the European Community.* New York: St. Martin's Press.

Hayes, Peter. 1987. *Industry and Ideology: IG Farben in the Nazi Era.* Cambridge: Cambridge University Press.

———. 1996. The European Strategies of IG Farben, 1925–1945. In *Quest for Economic Empire: The European Strategies of German Big Business in the Twentieth Century,* edited by Volker R. Berghahn, 55–64. Providence: Berghahn Books.

Haynes, William. 1945. *Background and Beginnings, 1609–1911.* Vol. 1 of *The American Chemical Industry.* New York: Van Nostrand.

———. 1954. *The Chemical Companies.* Vol. 6 of *The American Chemical Industry.* New York: Van Nostrand.

Helleiner, G. K. 1977. Transnational Enterprises and the New Political Economy of U.S. Trade Policy. *Oxford Economic Papers* 29 (1): 102–16.

Helpman, Elhanan, and Paul R. Krugman. 1985. *Market Structure and Foreign Trade: Increasing Returns, Imperfect Competition, and the International Economy.* Cambridge, MA: MIT Press.

———. 1989. *Trade Policy and Market Structure.* Cambridge, MA: MIT Press.

Heuss, Theodor. 1994. *Robert Bosch: His Life and Achievements.* New York: H. Holt.

Hindley, Brian, and Patrick A. Messerlin. 1993. Guarantees of Market Access and Regionalism. In *Regional Integration and the Global Trading System,* edited by Kym Anderson and Richard Blackhurst, 358–84. New York: St. Martin's Press.

Hine, Robert C., and Pier Carlo Padoan. 2001. External Trade Policy. In *Competitiveness and Cohesion in EU Policies,* edited by Ronald Hall, Alasdair Smith, and Loukas Tsoukalis, 61–107. Oxford: Oxford University Press.

Hirschman, Albert O. 1945. *National Power and the Structure of Foreign Trade.* Berkeley: University of California Press.

———. 1981. *Essays in Trespassing: Economics to Politics and Beyond.* Cambridge: Cambridge University Press.

Hiscox, Michael J. 1999. The Magic Bullet? The RTAA, Institutional Reform, and Trade Liberalization. *International Organization* 53 (4): 669–98.

———. 2002. *International Trade and Political Conflict: Commerce, Coalitions, and Factor Mobility.* Princeton: Princeton University Press.

Ho, Samuel Pao-San. 1984. Colonialism and Development: Korea, Taiwan, and Kwantung. In *The Japanese Colonial Empire, 1895–1945,* edited by Ramon H. Myers and Mark R. Peattie, 347–98. Princeton: Princeton University Press.

Hogan, William T. 1971. *Economic History of the Iron and Steel Industry in the United States.* Lexington: D.C. Heath.

Holmes, Peter, and Alasdair Smith. 1995. Automobile Industry. In *European Policies on Competition, Trade, and Industry: Conflict and Complementarities,* edited by Pierre Buigues, Alexis Jacquemin, and André Sapir, 125–59. Aldershot: Edward Elgar.

Homze, Edward L. 1976. *Arming the Luftwaffe: The Reich Air Ministry and the German Aircraft Industry, 1919–1939.* Lincoln: University of Nebraska Press.

Horstmann, Ignatius J., and James R. Markusen. 1986. Up the Average Cost Curve: Inefficient Entry and the New Protectionism. *Journal of International Economics* 20 (3–4): 225–47.

Howell, Thomas R., William A. Noellert, Jesse G. Kreier, and Alan Wm. Wolff. 1988. *Steel and the State: Government Intervention and Steel's Structural Crisis.* Boulder: Westview Press.

How Europe's Phone Monopolies Are Warding off the U.S. Giants. 1984. *Business Week,* August 20.

Hufbauer, Gary Clyde. 1990. An Overview. In *Europe 1992: An American Perspective,* edited by Gary Clyde Hufbauer, 1–64. Washington, DC: Brookings Institution.

Hufbauer, Gary Clyde, and Andrew James Samet. 1982. Investment Relations between Canada and the United States. In *Canada and the United States: Dependence and Divergence,* edited by Willis C. Armstrong, Louise S. Armstrong, and Francis O. Wilcox, 103–51. Cambridge, MA: Ballinger Publishing.

Hufbauer, Gary Clyde, and Jeffrey J. Schott. 1992. *North American Free Trade: Issues and Recommendations.* Washington, DC: Institute for International Economics.

Hutchinson, Sir Herbert. 1965. *Tariff Making and Industrial Reconstruction: An Account of the Work of the Import Duties Advisory Committee, 1932–1939.* London: George G. Harrap.

Iron and Steel Reorganization. 1932. *Economist,* January 16.

Irwin, Douglas A. 1994. The Political Economy of Free Trade: Voting in the British General Election of 1906. *Journal of Law and Economics* 37 (1): 75–108.

Ishida, Takeshi. 1968. The Development of Interest Groups and the Pattern of Political Modernization in Japan. In *Political Development in Modern Japan,* edited by Robert E. Ward, 293–336. Princeton: Princeton University Press.

Ishii, Osamu. 1981. *Cotton-Textile Diplomacy: Japan, Great Britain, and the United States, 1930–1936.* New York: Arno Press.

Islam, Shafiqul. 1993. Foreign Aid and Burdensharing: Is Japan Free Riding to a Co-prosperity Sphere in Pacific Asia? In *Regionalism and Rivalry: Japan and the United States in Pacific Asia,* edited by Jeffrey A. Frankel and Miles Kahler, 321–72. Chicago: University of Chicago Press.

Jackson, J. M. 1954. British Exports and the Scale of Production. *Manchester School of Economic and Social Studies* 22 (1): 90–112.

James, Harold. 1986. *The German Slump: Politics and Economics, 1924–1936.* Oxford: Clarendon Press.

Japan: The Rise of the Cotton Industry. 1927. *Board of Trade Journal,* January 20.

JETRO. 1995. *White Paper on Foreign Direct Investment.* Tokyo: JETRO.

———. 2000. *Report on Closer Economic Relations between Japan and Mexico.* http://www.jetro.go.jp/ec/e/report/fta_mexico/index.html.

———. 2001. *White Paper on International Trade.* http://www.jetro.go.jp/it/e/pub/whitepaper/trade2001.pdf.

———. 2002. *White Paper on International Trade and Investment.* http://www.jetro.go.jp/it/e/pub/whitepaper/2002.pdf.

———. 2003. *Prospects for Free Trade Agreements in East Asia.* http://www.jetro.go.jp/ec/e/stat/surveys/fta_eastasia.pdf.

Johnson, Chalmers. 1982. *MITI and the Japanese Miracle: The Growth of Industrial Policy, 1925–1975.* Stanford: Stanford University Press.

Johnson, Harry G. 1965. An Economic Theory of Protectionism, Tariff Bargaining, and the Formation of Customs Unions. *Journal of Political Economy* 73 (3): 256–83.

Joint Study Group. 2000. *Japan-Singapore Economic Agreement for a New Age Partnership.* http://www.meti.go.jp/english/report/data/gJ-SFTA1e.pdf.

Jones, F. C. 1949. *Manchuria since 1931.* London: Oxford University Press.

Kaiser, David E. 1980. *Economic Diplomacy and the Origins of the Second World War: Germany, Britain, France, and Eastern Europe, 1930–1939.* Princeton: Princeton University Press.

Kemp, M. C., and H. Y. Wan. 1976. An Elementary Proposition Concerning the Formation of Customs Unions. *Journal of International Economics* 6 (1): 95–97.

Keohane, Robert O. 1984. *After Hegemony: Cooperation and Discord in the World Economy.* Princeton: Princeton University Press.

Kindleberger, Charles P. 1973. *The World in Depression, 1929–1939.* Berkeley: University of California Press.

Krasner, Stephen D. 1976. State Power and the Structure of International Trade. *World Politics* 28 (3): 317–47.

Krishna, Pravin. 1998. Regionalism and Multilateralism: A Political Economy Approach. *Quarterly Journal of Economics* 113 (1): 227–51.

Krueger, Anne O. 1997. Problems with Overlapping Free Trade Areas. In *Regionalism versus Multilateral Trade Arrangements,* edited by Takatoshi Ito and Anne O. Krueger, 9–23. Chicago: University of Chicago Press.

———. 1999. Free Trade Agreements as Protectionist Devices: Rules of Origin. In *Trade, Theory and Econometrics: Essays in Honor of John S. Chipman,* edited by James R. Melvin, James C. Moore, and Raymond Riezman, 91–102. London: Routledge.

Krugman, Paul. 1981. Intra-Industry Specialization and the Gains from Trade. *Journal of Political Economy* 89 (5): 959–74.

———. 1991. Is Bilateralism Bad? In *International Trade and Trade Policy,* edited by Elhanan Helpman and Assaf Razin, 9–23. Cambridge, MA: MIT Press.

———. 1992. Import Protection as Export Promotion: International Competition in the Presence of Oligopoly and Economies of Scale. In *Imperfect Competition and International Trade,* edited by Gene M. Grossman, 75–86. Cambridge, MA: MIT Press.

———. 1993. Regionalism versus Multilateralism: Analytical Notes. In *New Dimensions in Regional Integration,* edited by Jaime de Melo and Arvind Panagariya, 58–79. Cambridge: Cambridge University Press.

Lake, David A. 1988. *Power, Protection, and Free Trade: International Sources of U.S. Commercial Strategy, 1887–1939.* Ithaca: Cornell University Press.

Lancashire and Ottawa. 1932. *Economist,* June 25, 1401.

Lavergne, Réal P. 1983. *The Political Economy of U.S. Tariffs: An Empirical Analysis.* Toronto: Academic Press.

Lawrence, Robert Z. 1996. *Regionalism, Multilateralism, and Deeper Integration.* Washington, DC: Brookings Institution.

Lazonick, William. 1986. The Cotton Industry. In *The Decline of the British Economy,* edited by Bernard Elbaum and William Lazonick, 18–50. Oxford: Clarendon Press.

League of Nations. 1935. Economic and Financial Section. *Considerations on the Present Evolution of Agricultural Protectionism.* Geneva: League of Nations.

———. 1938. Economic and Financial Section. *Report on Exchange Control.* Geneva: League of Nations.

———. Various years. Economic and Financial Section. *International Statistical Yearbook.* Geneva: League of Nations.

Legewie, Jochen. 2000. Production Strategies of Japanese Firms: Building up a Regional Production Network. In *Corporate Strategies for Southeast Asia after the Crisis: A*

Comparison of Multinational Firms from Japan and Europe, edited by Jochen Legewie and Hendrick Meyer-Ohle, 74–99. New York: Palgrave.

Levy, Philip I. 1997. A Political-Economic Analysis of Free-Trade Agreements. *American Economic Review* 87 (4): 506–19.

Levy, Philip I., and T. N. Srinivasan. 1996. Regionalism and the (Dis)advantage of Dispute-Settlement Access. *American Economic Review* 86 (2): 93–98.

Liepmann, H. 1938. *Tariff Levels and the Economic Unity of Europe: An Examination of Tariff Policy, Export Movements, and the Economic Integration of Europe, 1913–1931.* London: Allen and Unwin.

Lipson, Charles. 1982. The Transformation of Trade: The Sources and Effects of Regime Change. *International Organization* 36 (2): 417–55.

Lockwood, William W. 1955. *The Economic Development of Japan: Growth and Structural Change, 1868–1938.* Princeton: Princeton University Press.

Looking Askance at Ottawa. 1936. *Economist,* February 15.

Lorenz, Edward, and Frank Wilkinson. 1986. The Shipbuilding Industry, 1880–1965. In *The Decline of the British Economy,* edited by Bernard Elbaum and William Lazonick, 109–34. Oxford: Clarendon Press.

Lowe, Marvin E. 1942. *The British Tariff Movement.* Washington, DC: American Council on Public Affairs.

MacDougall, Donald, and Rosemary Hutt. 1954. Imperial Preference: A Quantitative Analysis. *Economic Journal* 64 (254): 233–57.

Machado, Kit G. 1994. PROTON and Malaysia's Motor Vehicle Industry: National Industrial Policies and Japanese Regional Production Strategies. In *Japan and Malaysian Development in the Shadow of the Rising Sun,* edited by Jomo K. S., 291–325. London: Routledge.

Mackintosh, Ian. 1986. *Sunrise Europe: The Dynamics of Information Technology.* Oxford: Basil Blackwell.

Magee, Stephen P., William A. Brock, and Leslie Young. 1989. *Black Hole Tariffs and Endogenous Policy Theory: Political Economy in General Equilibrium.* Cambridge: Cambridge University Press.

Maggi, Giovanni, and Andres Rodriguez-Clare. 1998. The Value of Trade Agreements in the Presence of Political Pressures. *Journal of Political Economy* 106 (3): 574–601.

Manchester and Protection. 1923. *Economist,* January 6.

Manchester and "Safeguarding of Industries." 1921. *Economist,* August 27.

Mansfield, Edward D. 1993. Effects of International Politics on Regionalism in International Trade. In *Regional Integration and the Global Trading System,* edited by Kym Anderson and Richard Blackhurst, 199–217. New York: St. Martin's Press.

Mansfield, Edward D., and Helen V. Milner. 1999. The New Wave of Regionalism. *International Organization* 53 (3): 589–627.

Mansfield, Edward D., and Jon C. Pevehouse. 2000. Trade Blocs, Trade Flows, and International Conflict. *International Organization* 54 (4): 775–808.

Mansfield, Edward D., and Eric Reinhardt. 2003. Multilateral Determinants of Regionalism: The Effects of GATT/WTO on the Formation of Preferential Trading Arrangements. *International Organization* 57 (4): 829–62.

Markham, Jesse W. 1952. *Competition in the Rayon Industry.* Cambridge, MA: Harvard University Press.

———. 1958. *The Fertilizer Industry: Study of an Imperfect Market.* Nashville: Vanderbilt University Press.

Marrison, Andrew. 1996. *British Business and Protection, 1903–1932.* Oxford: Clarendon Press.

Marshall, Herbert, Jr., Frank A. Southard, and Kenneth W. Taylor. 1936. *Canadian-American Industry: A Study in International Investment.* New Haven: Yale University Press.

Mason, Mark. 1992. *American Multinationals and Japan: The Political Economy of Japanese Capital Controls, 1899–1980.* Cambridge, MA: Harvard University Press.

———. 1994. Elements of Consensus: Europe's Response to the Japanese Automotive Challenge. *Journal of Common Market Studies* 32 (4): 433–53.

Mason, T. W. 1968. The Primacy of Politics: Politics and Economics in National Socialist Germany. In *The Nature of Fascism,* edited by S. J. Woolf, 165–95. London: Weidenfield and Nicolson.

Mattli, Walter. 1999. *The Logic of Regional Integration: Europe and Beyond.* Cambridge: Cambridge University Press.

Mazey, Sonia, and Jeremy Richardson. 1993. Introduction: Transference of Power, Decision Rules, and Rules of the Game. In *Lobbying in the European Community,* edited by Sonia Mazey and Jeremy Richardson, 3–26. Oxford: Oxford University Press.

McGee, John, and Susan Segal-Horn. 1992. Will There Be a European Food Processing Industry? In *Europe and the Multinationals: Issues and Responses for the 1990s,* edited by Stephen Young and James Hamill, 21–46. Aldershot: Edward Elgar.

McGillivray, Fiona. 1997. Party Discipline as a Determinant of the Endogenous Formation of Tariffs. *American Journal of Political Science* 41 (2): 584–607.

McGuire, Steven M. 1999. Trade Tools: Holding the Fort or Declaring Open House? In *European Industrial Policy and Competitiveness: Concepts and Instruments,* edited by Thomas C. Lawton, 72–92. New York: St. Martin's Press.

McLaughlin, Andrew, and Grant Jordan. 1993. The Rationality of Lobbying in Europe: Why Are Euro-Groups So Numerous and So Weak? Some Evidence from the Car Industry. In *Lobbying in the European Community,* edited by Sonia Mazey and Jeremy Richardson, 122–61. Oxford: Oxford University Press.

Memorandum on Coal in Japan and Manchuria. 1933. *Far Eastern Survey,* January 15.

Messerlin, Patrick A. 2001. *Measuring the Costs of Protection in Europe: European Commercial Policy in the 2000s.* Washington, DC: Institute for International Economics.

METI. 1988. Research and Statistics Department. *Census of Manufactures, 1986: Report by Industries.* Tokyo: METI.

———. 2002a. *Report on the WTO Consistency of Trade Policies by Major Trading Partners.* http://www.meti.go.jp/english/report/data/gCT002coe.html.

———. 2002b. *Summary of the 31st Survey of Overseas Business Activities.* http://www.meti.go.jp/english/statistics/downloadfiles/h2c400de.pdf.

———. 2003. *Quarterly Survey of Japanese Business Activities: Historical Data.* http://www.meti.go.jp/english/statistics/downloadfiles/h2c3c2ue.xls.

Milner, Helen V. 1988. *Resisting Protectionism: Global Industries and the Politics of International Trade.* Princeton: Princeton University Press.

———. 1997. Industries, Governments, and Regional Trade Blocs. In *The Political Economy of Regionalism,* edited by Edward D. Mansfield and Helen Milner, 77–106. New York: Columbia University Press.

Milner, Helen V., and David B. Yoffie. 1989. Between Free Trade and Protectionism: Strategic Trade Policy and a Theory of Corporate Trade Demands. *International Organization* 43 (2): 239–72.

Milward, Alan S. 1984. *The Reconstruction of Western Europe, 1945–51.* Berkeley: University of California Press.

Mitsubishi Economic Research Bureau. 1936. *Japanese Trade and Industry: Present and Future.* London: Macmillan.

Molle, Willem. 1993. Oil Refineries and Petrochemical Industries: Coping with the Mid-Life Crisis. In *The Structure of European Industry,* 3rd ed., edited by H. W. de Jong, 43–63. Dordrecht: Kluwer Publishers.

———. 1994. *The Economics of European Integration: Theory, Practice, Policy.* 2nd ed. Aldershot: Dartmouth.

Molony, Barbara. 1989. Noguchi Jun and Nitchitsu: Investment Strategy of a High-Technology Enterprise. In *Managing Industrial Enterprise: Cases from Japan's Prewar Experience,* edited by William D. Wray, 229–68. Cambridge. MA: Harvard University Press.

Moran, Theodore H. 2000. Investment Issues. In *The WTO after Seattle,* edited by Jeffrey J. Schott, 223–41. Washington, DC: Institute for International Economics.

Moravcsik, Andrew. 1998. *The Choice for Europe: Social Purpose and State Power from Messina to Maastricht.* Ithaca: Cornell University Press.

Morici, Peter, Arthur J. R. Smith, and Sperry Lea. 1982. *Canadian Industrial Policy.* Washington, DC: National Planning Association.

Müller, Jürgen, and Nicholas Owen. 1989. The Effect of Trade on Plant Size. In *The European Internal Market: Trade and Competition,* edited by Alexis Jacquemin and Andre Sapir, 173–84. Oxford: Oxford University Press.

Mundell, Robert A. 1957. International Trade and Factor Mobility. *American Economic Review* 47 (3): 321–35.

Myers, Ramon H. 1996. Creating a Modern Enclave Economy: The Economic Integration of Japan, Manchuria, and North China, 1932–1945. In *The Japanese Wartime Empire, 1931–1945,* edited by Peter Duus, Ramon H. Myers, and Mark R. Peattie, 136–70. Princeton: Princeton University Press.

National Industrial Conference Board. 1931. *Rationalization of German Industry.* New York: National Industrial Conference Board.

National Institute of Economic and Social Research. 1943. *Trade Regulations and Commercial Policy of the United Kingdom.* Cambridge: Cambridge University Press.

Notter, Harley A. 1949. *Postwar Foreign Policy Preparation, 1939–1945.* Washington, DC: U.S. Department of State.

OECD. 1994. *Trade and Investment: Transplants.* Paris: OECD.

O'Halloran, Sharyn. 1994. *Politics, Process, and American Trade Policy.* Ann Arbor: University of Michigan Press.

Okimoto, Daniel I. 1989. *Between MITI and the Market: Japanese Industrial Policy for High Technology.* Stanford: Stanford University Press.

Olson, Mancur. 1965. *The Logic of Collective Action: Public Goods and the Theory of Groups.* Cambridge, MA: Harvard University Press.

Orden, David. 1996. Agricultural Interest Groups and the North American Free Trade Agreement. In *The Political Economy of American Trade Policy,* edited by Anne O. Krueger, 335–82. Chicago: University of Chicago Press.

Oriental Economist. 1935. *Foreign Trade of Japan: A Statistical Survey.* Tokyo: Oriental Economist.

The Ottawa Conference. 1932. *Foreign Policy Reports,* December 21.

Overy, R. J. 1994. *War and Economy in the Third Reich.* Oxford: Clarendon Press.

Owen, Nicholas. 1983. *Economies of Scale, Competitiveness, and Trade Patterns within the European Community.* Oxford: Oxford University Press.

Oye, Kenneth A. 1992. *Economic Discrimination and Political Exchange: World Political Economy in the 1930s and the 1980s.* Princeton: Princeton University Press.

Parliament of Canada. 1982. Standing Senate Committee on Foreign Affairs. *Canada's Trade Relations with the United States.* Vol. 2 of *Canada-United States Relations.* Ottawa: Standing Senate Committee on Foreign Affairs.

Parrini, Carl P. 1969. *Heir to Empire: United States Economic Diplomacy, 1916–1923.* Pittsburgh: University of Pittsburgh Press.

Pastor, Robert A. 1980. *Congress and the Politics of U.S. Foreign Economic Policy.* Berkeley: University of California Press.

Pearce, Joan, and John Sutton. 1985. *Protection and Industrial Policy in Europe.* London: Royal Institute of International Affairs.

Peres, Wilson. 1990. *Foreign Direct Investment and Industrial Development in Mexico.* Paris: OECD Development Center.

Pomfret, Richard. 1997. *The Economics of Regional Trading Arrangements.* Oxford: Oxford University Press.

Porter, J. H. 1979. Cotton and Wool Textiles. In *British Industry between the Wars: Instability and Industrial Development, 1919–1939,* edited by Neil K. Buxton and Derek H. Aldcroft, 25–47. London: Scolar Press.

Pratten, C. F. 1971. *Economies of Scale in Manufacturing Industry.* Cambridge: Cambridge University Press.

———. 1988. A Survey of the 'Economies of Scale.' In *Studies on the Economics of Integration,* vol. 2 of *Research on the 'Cost of Non-Europe.'* Luxembourg: Commission of the European Communities.

Prime Minister's Office. 1962. Bureau of Statistics. *1960 Establishment Census of Japan.* Tokyo: Prime Minister's Office.

Radosh, Ronald. 1967. American Manufacturers, Canadian Reciprocity, and the Origins of the Branch Factory System. *CAAS Bulletin* 3 (1): 19–54.

Ramstetter, Eric D. 1996. Estimating Economic Activities by Japanese Transnational Corporations: How to Make Sense of the Data? *Transnational Corporations* 5 (2): 107–43.

Ránki, György. 1983. *Economy and Foreign Policy: The Struggle of the Great Powers for Hegemony in the Danube Valley, 1919–1939.* New York: Columbia University Press.

Ravenhill, John. 1995. Economic Cooperation in Southeast Asia: Changing Incentives. *Asian Survey* 35 (9): 850–66.

Reader, W. J. 1970. *The Forerunners, 1870–1926.* Vol. 1 of *Imperial Chemical Industries: A History.* London: Oxford University Press.

———. 1975. *The First Quarter-Century, 1926–1952.* Vol. 2 of *Imperial Chemical Industries: A History.* London: Oxford University Press.

Redford, Arthur. 1956. *Manchester Merchants and Foreign Trade, 1850–1939.* Manchester: Manchester University Press.

Reich, Simon. 1996. Fascism and the Structure of German Capitalism: The Case of the Automobile Industry. In *Quest for Economic Empire: The European Strategies of German Big Business in the Twentieth Century,* edited by Volker R. Berghahn, 65–94. Providence: Berghahn Books.

Richardson, H. W. 1967. *Economic Recovery in Britain, 1932–1939.* London: Weidenfeld and Nicolson.

———. 1968. Chemicals. In *The Development of British Industry and Foreign Competition, 1875–1914,* edited by Derek H. Aldcroft, 274–306. London: Allen and Unwin.

Richardson, Martin. 1993. Endogenous Protection and Trade Diversion. *Journal of International Economics* 34 (3–4): 309–24.

Rogowski, Ronald. 1987. Trade and the Variety of Democratic Institutions. *International Organization* 41 (2): 203–23.

———. 1989. *Commerce and Coalitions: How Trade Affects Political Cleavages.* Princeton: Princeton University Press.

Rooth, T. 1985. Trade Agreements and the Evolution of British Agricultural Policy in the 1930s. *Agricultural History Review* 33 (2): 173–90.

———. 1992. *British Protectionism and the International Economy: Overseas Commercial Policy in the 1930s.* Cambridge: Cambridge University Press.

Ropke, Wilhelm. 1934. *German Commercial Policy.* London: Longmans, Green.

Royal Commission on the Automotive Industry. 1961. *Report.* Ottawa: Queen's Printer.

Royal Commission on the Economic Union and Development Prospects for Canada. 1985. *Report.* Vol. 1. Ottawa: Minister of Supply and Services Canada.

Safarian, A. E. 1966. *Foreign Ownership of Canadian Industry.* Toronto: McGraw-Hill.

Sally, Razeen. 1995. *States and Firms: Multinational Enterprises in Institutional Competition.* London: Routledge.

Sandholtz, Wayne. 1992. *High-Tech Europe: The Politics of International Cooperation.* Berkeley: University of California Press.

Sandholtz, Wayne, and John Zysman. 1989. 1992: Recasting the European Bargain. *World Politics* 62 (1): 95–128.

Saul, S. B. 1977. The Mechanical Engineering Industries in Britain, 1860–1914. In *Essays in British Business History,* edited by Barry Supple, 31–48. Oxford: Clarendon Press.

Saxonhouse, Gary R. 1993. Pricing Strategies and Trading Blocs in East Asia. In *Regionalism and Rivalry: Japan and the United States in Pacific Asia,* edited by Jeffrey A. Frankel and Miles Kahler, 89–119. Chicago: University of Chicago Press.

Sazanami, Yoko, Shujiro Urata, and Hiroki Kawai. 1995. *Measuring the Costs of Protection in Japan.* Washington, DC: Institute for International Economics.

Schattschneider, E. E. 1935. *Politics, Pressure, and the Tariff: A Study of Free Private Enterprise in Pressure Politics, as Shown in the 1929–1930 Revision of the Tariff.* Englewood Cliffs: Prentice-Hall.

Scheinberg, Stephen. 1973. Invitation to Empire: Tariffs and American Economic Expansion in Canada. *Business History Review* 47 (2): 218–38.

Scherer, F. M. 1970. *Industrial Market Structure and Economic Performance.* Chicago: Rand McNally.

Scherer, F. M., Alan Beckenstein, Erich Kaufer, Dennis R. Murphy, and Francine Bougeon-Massen. 1975. *The Economics of Multi-Plant Operation: An International Comparisons Study.* Cambridge, MA: Harvard University Press.

Schran, Peter. 1994. Japan's East Asia Market, 1870–1940. In *Japanese Industrialization and the Asian Economy,* edited by A. J. H. Latham and Heita Kawakatsu, 201–38. London: Routledge.

Schröter, Harm G. 1996. Europe in the Strategies of Germany's Electrical Engineering and Chemicals Trusts, 1919–1939. In *Quest for Economic Empire: The European Strategies of German Big Business in the Twentieth Century,* edited by Volker R. Berghahn, 35–54. Providence: Berghahn Books.

Schröter, Verena. 1983. The IG Farbenindustrie AG in Central and Southeast Europe, 1926–38. In *International Business and Central Europe, 1918–1939,* edited by Alice Teichova and P. L. Cottrell, 139–72. New York: St. Martin's Press.

Schuknecht, Ludger. 1992. *Trade Protection in the European Community.* Chur: Harwood Academic Publishers.

Scollay, Robert, and John P. Gilbert. 2001. *New Regional Trading Arrangements in the Asia Pacific?* Washington, DC: Institute for International Economics.

Servan-Schreiber, J. J. 1968. *The American Challenge.* New York: Atheneum.

Sharp, Margaret. 1991. The Single Market and European Technology Policies. In *Technology and the Future of Europe: Global Competition and the Environment in the 1990s,* edited by Christopher Freeman, Margaret Sharp, and William Walker, 59–76. London: Pinter Publishers.

Silberston, A. 1972. Economies of Scale in Theory and Practice. *Economic Journal* 82 (325): 369–92.

The Silk Duties. 1932. *Economist,* May 14.

Sleuwaegen, Leo. 1991. The Truck Industry. In *The European Challenge: Industry's Response to the 1992 Program,* edited by David G. Mayes, 92–129. London: Harvester Wheatsheaf.

Smith, Alasdair, and Anthony J. Venables. 1988. Completing the Internal Market in the European Community: Some Industry Simulations. *European Economic Review* 32 (7): 1501–25.

Snyder, Rixford Kinney. 1944. *The Tariff Problem in Great Britain, 1918–1923.* Stanford: Stanford University Press.

Spaulding, Robert Mark, Jr. 1989. The Political Economy of German Foreign Trade Policy in Eastern Europe, 1890–1960. Ph.D. dissertation, Harvard University.

Srinivasan, T. N., John Whalley, and Ian Wooton. 1993. Measuring the Effects of Regionalism on Trade and Welfare. In *Regional Integration and the Global Trading System,* edited by Kym Anderson and Richard Blackhurst, 52–79. New York: St. Martin's Press.

Stanbrook, Clive, and Philip Bentley. 1996. *Dumping and Subsidies: The Law and Procedures Governing the Imposition of Antidumping and Countervailing Duties in the European Community.* 3rd ed. London: Kluwer Law International.

Statistisches Bundesamt. 1965. *Zensus im Produzierenden Gewerbe, 1962: Industrie und Handwerk.* Stuttgart: W. Kohlammer.

Statistisches Reichsamt. 1929. *Gewerbliche Betriebszählung: Die Gewerblichen Betriebe und Unternehmungen im Deutschen Reich.* Statistik des Deutschen Reichs, vol. 413. Berlin: Verlag von Reimar Hobbing.

Stein, Arthur A. 1984. The Hegemon's Dilemma: Great Britain, the United States, and International Economic Order. *International Organization* 38 (2): 355–86.

Stephen, Roland. 2000. *Vehicle of Influence: Building a European Car Market.* Ann Arbor: University of Michigan Press.

Stigler, George. 1968. *The Organization of Industry.* Homewood: Richard D. Irwin.

Strandmann, Hartmut Pogge von. 1986. Imperialism and Revisionism in Interwar Germany. In *Imperialism and After: Continuities and Discontinuities,* edited by Wolfgang J. Mommsen and Jürgen Osterhammel, 90–119. London: Allen and Unwin.

Supreme Commander for the Allied Powers. Various years. Economic and Scientific Section. *Japanese Economic Statistics.* Tokyo: Economic Planning Agency.

Svennilson, Ingvar. 1954. *Growth and Stagnation in the European Economy.* Geneva: United Nations.

Tarr, David G. 1988. The Steel Crisis in the United States and the European Community: Causes and Adjustments. In *Issues in US-EC Trade Relations,* edited by Robert E. Baldwin, Carl B. Hamilton, and André Sapir, 173–98. Chicago: University of Chicago Press.

Task Force on the Structure of Canadian Industry. 1968. *Foreign Ownership and the Structure of Canadian Industry.* Ottawa: Queen's Printer.

Taussig, F. W. 1931. *The Tariff History of the United States.* 8th ed. New York: G. P. Putnam's Sons.

Taylor, Mark Z. 1995. Dominance through Technology: Is Japan Creating a Yen Bloc in Southeast Asia? *Foreign Affairs* 74 (6): 14–20.

Tharakan, P. K. M., and J. Waelbroeck. 1994. Antidumping and Countervailing Duty Decisions in the E.C. and in the U.S.: An Experiment in Comparative Political Economy. *European Economic Review* 38 (1): 171–93.

Thurow, Lester C. 1992. *Head to Head: The Coming Economic Battles among Japan, Europe, and America.* New York: William Morrow.

Tiedemann, Arthur E. 1971. Big Business and Politics in Prewar Japan. In *Dilemmas of Growth in Prewar Japan,* edited by James William Morley, 267–316. Princeton: Princeton University Press.

Tilton, Mark. 1996. *Restrained Trade: Cartels in Japan's Basic Materials Industries.* Ithaca: Cornell University Press.

Tolliday, Steven. 1984. Tariffs and Steel, 1916–1934: The Politics of Industrial Decline. In *Businessmen and Politics: Studies of Business Activity in British Politics, 1900–1945,* edited by John Turner, 50–75. London: Heinemann.

———. 1987. *Business, Banking, and Politics: The Case of British Steel, 1918–1939.* Cambridge, MA: Harvard University Press.

Tornell, Aaron, and Gerardo Esquivel. 1997. The Political Economy of Mexico's Entry into NAFTA. In *Regionalism versus Multilateral Trade Arrangements,* edited by Takatoshi Ito and Anne O. Krueger, 25–55. Chicago: University of Chicago Press.

Toshiyuki, Mizoguchi. 1989. The Changing Pattern of Sino-Japanese Trade, 1884–1937. In *The Japanese Informal Empire in China, 1895–1937,* edited by Peter Duus, Ramon H. Myers, and Mark R. Peattie, 10–30. Princeton: Princeton University Press.

Traves, Tom. 1984. The Political Economy of the Automobile Tariff, 1926–31. In *Essays in Canadian Business History,* edited by Tom Traves, 134–50. Toronto: McClelland and Stewart.

Turner, Henry Ashby, Jr. 1985. *German Big Business and the Rise of Hitler.* Oxford: Oxford University Press.

Tyson, Laura D'Andrea. 1992. *Who's Bashing Whom? Trade Conflict in High-Technology Industries*. Washington, DC: Institute for International Economics.

Udagawa, Masaru. 1990a. Business Management and Foreign-Affiliated Companies in Japan before World War II. In *Foreign Business in Japan before World War II*, edited by Takeshi Yuzawa and Masaru Udagawa, 1–30, vol. 16 of *The International Conference on Business History*. Tokyo: University of Tokyo Press.

———. 1990b. The Move into Manchuria of the Nissan Combine. *Japanese Yearbook on Business History* 7: 3–29.

UNCTAD. 2001. *World Investment Report, 2001: Promoting Linkages*. http://www.unctad.org/en/docs//wir01full.en.pdf.

———. 2002. *World Investment Report, 2002: Transnational Corporations and Export Competitiveness*. http://www.unctad.org/en/docs//wir2002_en.pdf.

UNCTC. 1988. *Transnational Corporations in World Development: Trends and Prospects*. New York: UNCTC.

———. 1990. *Regional Economic Integration and Transnational Corporations in the 1990s: Europe 1992, North America, and Developing Countries*. Current Studies Series A, no. 15. New York: UNCTC.

———. 1991. *World Investment Report, 1991: The Triad in Foreign Direct Investment*. http://www.unctad.org/en/docs//wir91ove.en.pdf.

United Nations 1993. Department of Economic and Social Affairs. *Industrial Commodity Statistics Yearbook*. New York: United Nations.

Urata, Shujiro. 1993. Japanese Foreign Direct Investment and Its Effect on Foreign Trade in Asia. In *Trade and Protectionism*, edited by Takatoshi Ito and Anne O. Krueger, 273–99. Chicago: University of Chicago Press.

Uriu, Robert M. 1996. *Troubled Industries: Confronting Economic Change in Japan*. Ithaca: Cornell University Press.

U.S. Bureau of Economic Analysis. 1992. *U.S. Direct Investment Abroad: 1989 Benchmark Survey*. Washington, DC: U.S. GPO.

U.S. Bureau of Foreign and Domestic Commerce. 1924. *The German Dyestuffs Industry*. Washington, DC: U.S. GPO.

———. 1930. *Foreign Commerce and Navigation of the United States*. Washington, DC: U.S. GPO.

———. 1931. *American Branch Factories Abroad*. Washington, DC: U.S. GPO.

———. Various years. *Commerce Reports*. Washington, DC: U.S. GPO.

U.S. Bureau of the Census. 1918. *Census of Manufactures, 1914*. Washington, DC: U.S. GPO.

———. 1930. *Fifteenth Census of the United States: Manufactures, 1929*. Washington, DC: U.S. GPO.

———. 1961. *United States Census of Manufactures, 1958*. Washington, DC: U.S. GPO.

———. 1997. *1992 Economic Census*. Report Series, CD-ROM Disc 1J. Washington, DC: U.S. GPO.

U.S. Congress. 1983. Office of Technology Assessment. *International Competitiveness in Electronics*. OTA-ISC-200. http://www.wws.princeton.edu/cgi-bin/byteserv.prl/~ota/disk3/1983/8314_n.html.

———. 1987. Office of Technology Assessment. *The U.S. Textile and Apparel Industry: A Revolution in Progress*. OTA-TET-332. http://www.wws.princeton.edu/cgi-bin/byteserv.prl/~ota/disk2/1987/8733_n.html.

———. 1991. Office of Technology Assessment. *Competing Economies: America, Europe, and the Pacific Rim.* OTA-ITE-498. http://www.wws.princeton.edu/cgi-bin/byteserv.prl/~ota/disk1/1991/9112_n.html.

———. 1992. Office of Technology Assessment. *U.S.-Mexico Trade: Pulling Together or Pulling Apart?* OTA-ITE-545. http://www.wws.princeton.edu/cgi-bin/byteserv.prl/~ota/disk1/1992/9241_n.html.

U.S. Department of Commerce. 1993. International Trade Administration. *North American Free Trade Agreement: Opportunities for U.S. Industries.* Washington, DC: U.S. GPO.

U.S. Department of State. 2001. *Western Europe.* Vol. 12 of *Foreign Relations of the United States, 1964–68.* Washington, DC: U.S. GPO.

U.S. General Accounting Office. 1992. *North American Free Trade Agreement: U.S.-Mexican Trade and Investment Data.* GAO/GGD-92-131. Gaithersburg, MD: General Accounting Office.

U.S. House of Representatives. 1929. Committee on Ways and Means. *Tariff Readjustment, 1929.* 70th Congress, 2nd session.

———. 1940. Committee on Ways and Means. *Extension of Reciprocal Trade Agreements Act.* 76th Congress, 3rd session.

———. 1943. Committee on Ways and Means. *Extension of Reciprocal Trade Agreements Act.* 78th Congress, 1st session.

———. 1945. Committee on Ways and Means. *1945 Extension of Reciprocal Trade Agreements Act.* 79th Congress, 1st session.

———. 1947. Committee on Ways and Means. *Reciprocal Trade Agreements Program.* 80th Congress, 1st session.

———. 1949. Committee on Ways and Means. *1949 Extension of the Reciprocal Trade Agreements Act.* 81st Congress, 1st session.

———. 1953. Committee on Ways and Means. *Trade Agreements Extension Act of 1953.* 83rd Congress, 1st session.

———. 1955. Committee on Ways and Means. *Trade Agreements Extension.* 84th Congress, 1st session.

———. 1956a. Committee on Ways and Means. *Administration and Operation of Customs and Tariff Laws and the Trade Agreements Program.* 84th Congress, 2nd session.

———. 1956b. Committee on Ways and Means. *Organization for Trade Cooperation.* 84th Congress, 2nd session.

———. 1958a. Committee on Ways and Means. *Foreign Trade Policy.* 85th Congress, 1st session.

———. 1958b. Committee on Ways and Means. *Renewal of Trade Agreements Act.* 85th Congress, 2nd session.

———. 1962. Committee on Ways and Means. *Trade Expansion Act of 1962.* 87th Congress, 2nd session.

———. 1965. Committee on Ways and Means. *United States-Canada Automotive Products Agreement.* 89th Congress, 1st session.

———. 1986. Committee on Banking, Finance and Urban Affairs. *United States-Canada Economic Relations.* 99th Congress, 2nd session, serial 99-97.

———. 1988. Committee on Ways and Means. *United States-Canada Free Trade Agreement.* 100th Congress, 2nd session, serial 100-59.

————. 1990. Committee on Ways and Means. *United States-Mexico Economic Relations.* 101st Congress, 2nd session, serial 101-108.

————. 1991. Committee on Ways and Means. *Proposed Negotiation of a Free Trade Agreement with Mexico.* 102nd Congress, 1st session, serial 102-19.

————. 1992a. Committee on Ways and Means. *Draft Final Text of the Results of the Uruguay Round of Multilateral Trade Negotiations.* 102nd Congress, 2nd session, serial 102-81.

————. 1992b. Committee on Ways and Means. *North American Free Trade Agreement.* 102nd Congress, 2nd session, serial 102-135.

————. 1993a. Committee on Government Operations. *The North American Free Trade Agreement and Its Impact on the Textile/Apparel/Fiber and Auto and Auto Parts Industries.* 103rd Congress, 1st session, serial 103-1.

————. 1993b. Committee on Ways and Means. *North American Free-Trade Agreement (NAFTA) and Supplemental Agreements to the NAFTA.* 103rd Congress, 1st session, serial 103-48.

————. 1994a. Committee on Ways and Means. *Trade Agreements Resulting from the Uruguay Round of Multilateral Trade Negotiations.* 103rd Congress, 2nd session, serial 103-73.

————. 1994b. Committee on Ways and Means. *Uruguay Round of Multilateral Trade Negotiations.* 103rd Congress, 1st session, serial 103-47.

USITC. 1990a. *Review of Trade and Investment Liberalization Measures by Mexico and Prospects for Future United States-Mexican Relations, Phase I: Recent Trade and Investment Reforms Undertaken by Mexico and Implications for the United States.* USITC Publication 2275. Washington, DC: USITC.

————. 1990b. *Review of Trade and Investment Liberalization Measures by Mexico and Prospects for Future United States-Mexican Relations, Phase II: Summary of Views on Prospects for Future United States-Mexican Relations.* USITC Publication 2275. Washington, DC: USITC.

————. 1990c. *The Effects of Greater Economic Integration within the European Community on the United States: First Follow-Up Report.* USITC Publication 2268. Washington, DC: USITC.

————. 1993. *Potential Impact on the U.S. Economy and Selected Industries of the North American Free-Trade Agreement.* USITC Publication 2596. Washington, DC: USITC.

U.S. Senate. 1929. Committee on Finance. *Tariff Act of 1929.* 71st Congress, 1st session.

————. 1951. Committee on Finance. *Trade Agreements Extension Act of 1951.* 82nd Congress, 1st session.

————. 1955. Committee on Finance. *Trade Agreements Extension.* 84th Congress, 1st session.

————. 1958. Committee on Finance. *Trade Agreements Act Extension.* 85th Congress, 2nd session.

————. 1962. Committee on Finance. *Trade Expansion Act of 1962.* 87th Congress, 2nd session.

————. 1986. Committee on Finance. *Negotiation of United States-Canada Free Trade Agreement.* 99th Congress, 2nd session, S. Hrg. 99-743.

————. 1987. Committee on Finance. *United States-Canada Free Trade Negotiations.* 100th Congress, 1st session, S. Rpt. 100-49.

———. 1989a. Committee on Finance. *United States-Canada Free Trade Agreement, 1988.* 100th Congress, 2nd session, S. Hrg. 100-1007.

———. 1989b. Committee on the Judiciary. *The Potential Impact of the United States-Canada Free Trade Agreement on the American Steel Industry.* 100th Congress, 2nd session, S. Hrg. 100-1055.

———. 1991. Committee on Finance. *United States-Mexico Free Trade Agreement.* 102nd Congress, 1st session, S. Hrg. 102-75.

———. 1992. Committee on Finance. *North American Free Trade Agreement.* 102nd Congress, 2nd session, S. Hrg. 102-1032.

———. 1994. Committee on Finance. *Uruguay Round of Multilateral Trade Negotiations.* 103rd Congress, 1st session, S. Hrg. 103-479.

USTC. 1920. *Reciprocity with Canada: A Study of the Arrangement of 1911.* Washington, DC: USTC.

———. 1922. *Digest of Tariff Hearings before the Committee on Finance, United States Senate, on the Bill H.R. 7456.* Washington, DC: USTC.

———. 1936. *Recent Developments in the Foreign Trade of Japan, Particularly in Relation to the Trade of the United States.* Report no. 105, 2nd series. Washington, DC: USTC.

———. 1937. *Chemical Nitrogen: A Survey of Processes, Organization, and International Trade.* Report no. 114, 2nd series. Washington, DC: USTC.

———. 1943. *Foreign-Trade and Exchange Controls in Germany: A Report on the Methods and Policies of German Foreign-Trade Control, with Special Reference to the Period 1931 to 1939.* Report no. 150, 2nd series. Washington, DC: USTC.

———. 1945a. *Annotated Tabular Survey of the Trade of Japan Proper (Including That with Korea and Formosa).* Washington, DC: USTC.

———. 1945b. *Japanese Trade Studies: Special Industry Analysis No. 1–37.* Washington, DC: USTC.

———. 1953. *Motorcycles and Parts: Report on the Escape-Clause Investigation.* Report no. 180, 2nd series. Washington, DC: USTC.

———. 1960. *Typewriters: Report on Escape-Clause Investigation No. 7-84.* Washington, DC: USTC.

———. 1961. *Rayon Staple Fiber: Report on Escape-Clause Investigation No. 7-95.* TC Publication 12. Washington, DC: USTC.

USTR. 1994. *The Uruguay Round of Multilateral Trade Negotiations: Report of the Industry Sector and Functional Advisory Committees (ISAC/IFAC).* Washington, DC: USTR.

Uyeda, Teijiro. 1933. *Recent Changes in the Japanese Tariffs.* Tokyo: Nippon Press.

Viner, Jacob. 1950. *The Customs Union Issue.* New York: Carnegie Endowment for International Peace.

———. 1951. *International Economics.* Glencoe: Free Press.

Volkmann, Hans-Erich. 1990. The National Socialist Economy in Preparation for War. In *The Buildup of German Aggression,* edited by Wilhelm Deist, Manfred Messerschmidt, Hans-Erich Volkmann, and Wolfram Wette, 159–372, vol. 1 of *Germany and the Second World War.* Oxford: Clarendon Press.

Wei, Shang-Jin, and Jeffrey A. Frankel. 1996. Can Regional Blocs Be a Stepping Stone to Global Free Trade? *International Review of Economics and Finance* 5 (4): 339–47.

Wells, Louis T., Jr. 1992. *Conflict or Indifference? U.S. Multinationals in a World of Regional Trading Blocs.* Paris: OECD Development Center.

Wilkins, Mira, and Frank Ernest Hill. 1964. *American Business Abroad: Ford on Six Continents*. Detroit: Wayne State University Press.

Williams, Glen. 1986. *Not for Export: The International Competitiveness of Canadian Manufacturing*. Toronto: McClelland and Stewart.

Wilson, Joan Hoff. 1971. *American Business and Foreign Policy, 1920–1933*. Lexington: University Press of Kentucky.

Winters, L. Alan. 1993. The European Community: A Case of Successful Integration? In *New Dimensions in Regional Integration*, edited by Jaime de Melo and Arvind Panagariya, 202–28. Cambridge: Cambridge University Press.

Wolff, Alan W. 1990. U.S.-Japan Relations and the Rule of Law: The Nature of the Trade Conflict and the American Response. In *Japan's Economic Structure: Should It Change?* edited by Kozo Yamamura, 137–65. Seattle: Society for Japanese Studies.

Wolman, Paul. 1992. *Most Favored Nation: The Republican Revisionists and U.S. Tariff Policy, 1897–1912*. Chapel Hill: University of North Carolina Press.

Wonnacott, Paul. 1988. The Auto Sector. In *The Canada-United States Free Trade Agreement*, edited by Jeffrey J. Schott and Murray G. Smith, 101–9. Washington, DC: Institute for International Economics.

Wright, Philip G. 1935. *Trade and Trade Barriers in the Pacific*. Stanford: Stanford University Press.

WTO. 1995a. *Regionalism and the World Trading System*. Geneva: WTO.

———. 1995b, 2001. *Trade Policy Review: European Union*. Geneva: WTO.

———. 1995c, 1999. *Trade Policy Review: Thailand*. Geneva: WTO.

———. 1996, 2000a. *Trade Policy Review: Singapore*. Geneva: WTO.

———. 1997. *Trade Policy Review: Malaysia*. Geneva: WTO.

———. 1998a. *Trade Policy Review: Indonesia*. Geneva: WTO.

———. 1998b, 2000b. *Trade Policy Review: Japan*. Geneva: WTO.

Wurm, Clemens. 1993. *Business, Politics, and International Relations: Steel, Cotton, and International Cartels in British Politics, 1924–1939*. Cambridge: Cambridge University Press.

Yamamura, Kozo. 1994. The Deliberate Emergence of a Free Trader: The Japanese Political Economy in Transition. In *Japan: A New Kind of Superpower?* edited by Craig Garby and Mary Brown Bullock, 35–52. Washington, DC: Woodrow Wilson Center Press.

Yamazawa, I. 1975. Industrial Growth and Trade Policy in Prewar Japan. *Developing Economies* 13 (1): 38–65.

———. 1990. *Economic Development and International Trade: The Japanese Model*. Honolulu: East-West Center.

Yarbrough, Beth V., and Robert M. Yarbrough. 1992. *Cooperation and Governance in International Trade*. Princeton: Princeton University Press.

The Yen Block: A New Balance in Asia? 1989. *Economist*, July 15.

Yonekura, Seiichiro. 1994. *The Japanese Iron and Steel Industry, 1850–1990: Continuity and Discontinuity*. New York: St. Martin's Press.

Yoshimatsu, Hidetaka. 1998. Japan's Keidanren and Political Influence on Market Liberalization. *Asian Survey* 38 (3): 328–45.

———. 2000. *Internationalization, Corporate Preferences, and Commercial Policy in Japan*. New York: St. Martin's Press.

————. 2002. Preferences, Interests, and Regional Integration: The Development of the ASEAN Industrial Cooperation Arrangement. *Review of International Political Economy* 9 (1): 123–49.

Young, Louise. 1998. *Japan's Total Empire: Manchuria and the Culture of Wartime Imperialism.* Berkeley: University of California Press.

Young, Stephen, Neil Hood, and James Hamill. 1988. *Foreign Multinationals and the British Economy: Impact and Policy.* London: Croom Helm.

Zavatta, Roberto. 1993. The Pulp and Paper Industry. In *The Structure of European Industry,* 3rd ed., edited by H. W. de Jong, 91–120. Dordrecht: Kluwer Publishers.

Zeile, William J. 2003. Trade in Goods within Multinational Companies: Survey-Based Data and Findings for the United States of America. BEA Papers, U.S. Bureau of Economic Analysis. http://www.bea.doc.gov/bea/papers/IFT_OECD_Zeile.pdf.

Zeiler, Thomas W. 1992. *American Trade and Power in the 1960s.* New York: Columbia University Press.

————. 1999. *Free Trade, Free World: The Advent of GATT.* Chapel Hill: University of North Carolina Press.

Index

Note: Page references to tables and figures are indicated by italic.